PERSONS, PARTS AND PROPERTY

The debate over whether human bodies and their parts should be governed by the laws of property has accelerated with the pace of technological change. Having long held that a corpse could not be property, the common law first recognised that there could be a property interest in human tissue in some circumstances in the early 1900s, but it was not until a string of judicial decisions and statutory regulation in the 1990s and early 2000s that the place of this 'exception' was cemented. The 2009 decision of the Court of Appeal of England and Wales in *Yearworth & Ors v North Bristol NHS Trust* added a new dimension to the debate by supporting a move towards a broader, more principled basis for finding (or rejecting) property rights in human tissue. However, the law relating to property rights in human bodies and their parts remains highly contested. The contributions in this volume represent a collation of the broad spectrum of analyses on offer, and provide a detailed exploration of the salient legal and theoretical puzzles arising out of the body-as-property question.

Persons, Parts and Property

How Should We Regulate Human Tissue in the 21st Century?

Edited by

Imogen Goold,
Kate Greasley,
Jonathan Herring
and
Loane Skene

• HART •
PUBLISHING
OXFORD AND PORTLAND, OREGON
2016

Published in the United Kingdom by Hart Publishing Ltd
16C Worcester Place, Oxford, OX1 2JW
Telephone: +44 (0)1865 517530
Fax: +44 (0)1865 510710
E-mail: mail@hartpub.co.uk
Website: http://www.hartpub.co.uk

Published in North America (US and Canada) by
Hart Publishing
c/o International Specialized Book Services
920 NE 58th Avenue, Suite 300
Portland, OR 97213-3786
USA
Tel: +1 503 287 3093 or toll-free: (1) 800 944 6190
Fax: +1 503 280 8832
E-mail: orders@isbs.com
Website: http://www.isbs.com

First published in hardback 2014
Paperback edition, 2016

Hart Publishing is an imprint of Bloomsbury Publishing plc.

British Library Cataloguing in Publication Data
Data Available

ISBN: HB: 978-1-84946-546-5
PB: 978-1-50990-989-6

Typeset by Hope Services, Abingdon
Printed and bound in Great Britain by
Lightning Source UK Ltd

ACKNOWLEDGEMENTS

Compiling this collection has been a wonderful experience. We have had the opportunity to work with some fantastic people, and held some very stimulating workshops in the UK and Australia. We were very fortunate to be supported in this endeavour by an Oxford Melbourne Law School Research Partnership grant, kindly awarded from a generous gift by Allan Myers QC. We are very grateful for this support, which enabled us to bring together colleagues from many institutions to debate the issues, making this a truly collaborative piece of work.

We would like to thank Natasha Simonsen, Lorren Eldridge and Lomin Saayman for their excellent research assistance.

We are also indebted to Richard, Rachel, Mel and all at Hart Publishing for their support throughout the project.

TABLE OF CONTENTS

Acknowledgements v
Editors and Contributors ix
Table of Cases xi
Table of Statutes xix

1. **Introduction** 1
Imogen Goold, Kate Greasley, Jonathan Herring and Loane Skene

2. **Impressions on the Body, Property and Research** 9
Dianne Nicol, Don Chalmers, Rebekah McWhirter and Joanne Dickinson

3. **The Problems of Biobanking and the Law of Gifts** 25
Cameron Stewart, Wendy Lipworth, Lorena Aparicio, Jennifer Fleming and Ian Kerridge

4. **Unintended Side Effects of the National Health Service** 39
Thomas Krebs

5. **Public Umbilical Cord Blood Banking and Charitable Trusts** 53
Cameron Stewart, Lorena Aparicio, Wendy Lipworth and Ian Kerridge

6. **Property Rights in the Human Body: Commodification and Objectification** 67
Kate Greasley

7. **Property Rights in Human Biological Material** 89
Simon Douglas

8. **The Boundaries of Property Law** 109
Jesse Wall

9. **Abandonment and Human Tissue** 125
Imogen Goold

10. **Cadavers, Body Parts and the Remedial Problem** 157
Remigius N Nwabueze

11. **Alternatives to a Corporate Commons: Biobanking, Genetics and Property in the Body** 177
Donna Dickenson

12. The Problem with Alternatives: The Importance of Property Law in Regulating Excised Human Tissue and *In Vitro* Human Embryos 197
Lyria Bennett Moses

13. Why We Need a Statute Regime to Regulate Bodily Material 215
Jonathan Herring

14. Human Biomaterials: The Case for a Property Approach 231
Imogen Goold and Muireann Quigley

15. Raising Issues With a Property Law Approach 263
Loane Skene

16. Conclusion 281

Index 301

EDITORS AND CONTRIBUTORS

Editors

Dr Imogen Goold is Associate Professor of Law at the University of Oxford, and a Fellow and Tutor of St Anne's College

Ms Kate Greasley is Junior Research Fellow in law at University College, Oxford

Prof Jonathan Herring is Professor of Law at the University of Oxford, and a Fellow and Tutor of Exeter College

Prof Loane Skene is a Professor at the Melbourne Law School and an Adjunct Professor in the Faculty of Medicine, Dentistry and Health Sciences at the University of Melbourne

Contributors

Ms Lorena Aparicio is the Strategic Project Manager at the Australian Bone Marrow Donor Registry and a doctoral scholar at the Centre for Values, Ethics and the Law in Medicine, School of Public Health, University of Sydney

Dr Lyria Bennett Moses is Senior Lecturer in Law at the University of New South Wales

Prof Don Chalmers is Distinguished Professor and Director of the Centre for Law and Genetics at the University of Tasmania

Prof Donna Dickenson is Emeritus Professor of Medical Ethics and Humanities at the University of London, a Research Associate at the HeLEX Centre at the University of Oxford, and an Honorary Senior Research Fellow at the University of Bristol

Prof Joanne Dickinson is a cancer geneticist and leader of Cancer, Genetics and Immunology at the Menzies Research Institute, University of Tasmania

Dr Simon Douglas is Associate Professor of Law at the University of Oxford, and a Fellow and Tutor of Jesus College

Dr Jennifer Fleming is a Postdoctoral Research Associate at the Centre of Values Ethics and the Law in Medicine, University of Sydney

Prof Ian Kerridge is Director of the Centre for Values, Ethics and the Law in Medicine at the Sydney Medical School, University of Sydney and Haematologist/ BMT Physician at Royal North Shore Hospital, Sydney

Dr Thomas Krebs is Associate Professor of Commercial Law at the University of Oxford, and a Fellow of Brasenose College

Dr Wendy Lipworth is a Postdoctoral Research Fellow at the Australian Institute of Health Innovation, University of New South Wales and the Centre for Values, Ethics and the Law in Medicine, University of Sydney

Dr Rebekah McWhirter is a Postdoctoral Research Fellow at the Menzies Research Institute, University of Tasmania and the Menzies School of Health Research, Darwin

Prof Dianne Nicol is Deputy Director of the Centre for Law and Genetics and Chair of Academic Senate at the University of Tasmania

Dr Remigius N Nwabueze is a Senior Lecturer in Law at the University of Southampton

Dr Muireann Quigley is Senior Lecturer in Biomedical Ethics and Law, Centre for Ethics in Medicine, University of Bristol

Prof Cameron Stewart is a Professor at the Centre for Health Governance, Law and Ethics at the University of Sydney Law School and an associate of the Centre for Values, Ethics and the Law in Medicine at the Sydney Medical School

Dr Jesse Wall is a Junior Research Fellow and Stipendiary Lecturer in Law at Merton College, Oxford

TABLE OF CASES

Australia

Attorney-General (NSW) v Perpetual Trustee Co Ltd (1940) 63 CLR 209 ....60, 63
Attorney-General for New South Wales v Fulham [2002] NSWSC 629 63
Australian Incentive Plan Pty Ltd v Babcock & Brown International Pty Ltd (No 2) [2011] VSC 43 62
Bazley v Wesley Monash IVF [2010] QSC 118 ....2, 4, 15, 25, 54, 75–76, 120, 203, 206, 211, 236, 265
Costin v Costin (1997) NSW Conv R 55..32
E Inman (dec'd) [1965] VR 238 63
Estate of Schultz [1961] SASR 377 64
Eurella Community Services Inc v Attorney-General for the State of New South Wales [2010] NSWSC 566...63
FAI Insurances Ltd v Custom Credit Corp Ltd (1980) 29 ALR 505 272
Gilchrist Watt & Sanderson Pty Ltd v York Products Pty Ltd [1970] 1 WLR 1262 (PC).....127
Gill v Gill (1921) 21 SR (NSW) 400 35
Halwood Corporation Ltd v Chief Commissioner of Stamp Duties (1994) 33 NSWLR 395..207
Hammond v Hammond [2007] NSWSC 106 35
HAX v TV [2009] QCA 401 34
Hunter Region SLSA Helicopter Rescue Service Ltd v Attorney-General (NSW) [2000] NSWSC 456...62
Ikeuchi v Liu [2001] QSC 54...34
In the Matter of Creditors' Trust of Jackgreen (International) Pty Ltd [2011] NSWSC 748...62
In the Matter of the Daquino Family Trust [2009] NSWSC 429...62
Jocelyn Edwards; Re the estate of the late Mark Edwards [2011] NSWSC 478..............2, 4, 15, 25, 54, 120, 122, 203, 206, 211, 232, 236, 265
Johnstone & Wilmot v Kaine (1923) 23 Tas LR 43..136
Kauter v Kauter [2003] NSWSC 741 35
Keane v Carter [1994] 12 WAR 20..136
Keays v Carter [2003] WASC 23 34
Milirrpum v Nabalco Pty Ltd (1971) 17 FLR 141...207
Moorhouse v Angus & Robertson [1981] 1 NSWLR 700 136
Munday v Australian Capital Territory [2000] FCA 653 ....136, 137
Num-Hoi, Pon Yu, Soon-Duc Society Inc v Num Pon Soon Inc (2001) 4 VR 527 62
O'Sullivan Partners (Advisory) Pty Ltd v Foggo [2012] NSWCA 40....................................35
Papathanasopoulos v Vacopoulos [2007] NSWSC 502 34
*Penfolds Wines Pty Ltd v Ellio*t (1946) 74 CLR 204...257
Perpetual Trustee Co Ltd v St Luke's Hospital (1939) 39 SR (NSW) 408..............................64
PQ v Australian Red Cross Society [1992] 1 VR 19...268
R v Phuc & Van [2000] VSC 242 276

Re H, AE (No 2) [2012] SASC 177 .... 4, 25, 54, 203, 206, 265
Re Jigrose Pty Ltd [1994] 1 Qd R 382 .... 136, 137
Re Permanent Trustee Australia Ltd (1994) 33 NSWLR 547 62
Re Saunders Nominees Ptd Ltd; ex parte Saunders Nominees Pty Ltd [2007] WASC 152 62
Re Section 22 of the Human Tissue and Transplant Act 1982; ex parte C [2013] WASC 3 .... 4, 25, 54, 203, 206, 265
Re Simpson (dec'd) [1961] QWN 50 64
Roche v Douglas as Administrator of the Estate of Edward Rowan (dec'd) [2000] WASC 146 .... 203, 236, 242, 248, 269
Rogers v Whitaker (1992) 175 CLR 479 59
Royal National Agricultural and Industrial Association v Chester (1974) 3 ALR 486 61
Smith v Tamworth City Council (1997) 41 NSWLR 680 202
Stone v Registrar of Titles [2012] WASC 21 32
Taylor v Taylor (1910) 10 CLR 218 64
The Cram Foundation v Corbett-Jones [2006] NSWSC 495 63
The Incorporated Council of Law Reporting of the State of Queensland v FCT (1971) 125 CLR 659 63
The Kean Memorial Trust Inc v AG for SA (No 2) [2007] SASC 133 62
Tomasevic v Jovetic [2011] VSC 131 62
*Victoria Park Racing and Recreation Grounds Co Ltd v Taylo*r (1937) 58 CLR 479 207
Yanner v Eaton (1999) 201 CLR 351 .... 206, 209, 264

Canada

Stewart v Gustafson [1999] 4 WWR 695 .... 136, 137

European Court of Human Rights

Jones v United Kingdom [2005] ECtHR 42639/04 166

Iceland

Ragnhilder Gudmundsdóttir v The State of Iceland 151/2003 (Sup Ct 2003) 167

New Zealand

Greenpeace of New Zealand Incorporated [2012] NZCA 533 61
YMCA New Zealand Soldiers Great War Memorial Trust [2013] NZHC 2516 61

United Kingdom

A-G v Guardian Newspapers (No 2) [1988] UKHL 6 123
AB and others v Leeds Teaching Hospital NHS Trust [2004] EWHC 644 (QB) 3, 119, 158, 203, 232, 240–241, 248, 257, 288,
Addis v Gramophone Co Ltd [1909] AC 488 (HL) 47
Alcock v Chief Constable of South Yorkshire Police [1992] 1 AC 310 (HL) 43, 48, 163, 243
Allen v Flood [1898] AC 1 (HL) 106
Anning v Anning [1907] HCA 13; (1907) 4 CLR 1049 32
Archer v Williams [2003] EWHC 1670 (QB) 123
Armory v Delamirie (1722) 1 Strange 505, 93 ER 664 (KB) 94, 97, 100, 127
Arthur v Anker [1997] QB 564 (CA) 257
Attia v British Gas [1988] QB 304 (CA) 49, 119, 243, 244

Barbara v Home Office [1884] 134 NLJ 888....................48
Barber v Somerset County Council [2004] UKHL 13....................243
Barnes v Hampshire CC [1969] 3 All ER 746;[1969] 1 WLR 1563 (HL)....................44
Barnett v Chelsea Hospital [1969] 1 QBD 428; [1968] 1 All ER 1068 (QB)....................44
Bentinck Ltd v Cromwell Engineering Co [1971] 1 QB 324, [1970] 3 WLR 1113, [1971] 1 All ER 33 (CA)....................134, 135
Blades v Higgs (1865) 11 HL Case 621; 11 ER 1474....................213
Bluck v Information Commissioner (2007) 98 BMLR 1....................123
Boardman v Phipps [1967] 2 AC 46 (HL)....................160
Boardman v Sanderson [1961] EWCA Civ 6; [1964] 1 WLR 1317 (CA)....................45
Broad v Bevan (1823) 38 ER 198....................35
Burrows v HM Coroner for Preston [2008] EWHC 1387 (QB)....................166
Campbell v MGN [2004] UKHL 22....................113, 123, 166
Caparo Industries plc v Dickman [1990] UKHL 2; [1990] 2 AC 605....................42, 43, 50, 161
Chester v Ashfar [2005] 1 AC 134 (HL)....................160
Cochrane v Moore (1870) 25 QBD 57 (CA)....................94, 97
Coco v AN Clark (Engineers) Ltd [1969] RPC 41....................166
Cohen v Sellar [1926] 1 KB 536....................34
Commissioner for Customs & Excise v Barclays Bank plc [2006] UKHL 28....................43, 44
Commissioner for Special Purposes of Income Tax v Pemsel [1891] AC 531 (HL).....61, 62, 63
Commissioners of Taxation v Word Investments (2008) 236 CLR 204....................63
Corin v Patton [1990] HCA 12; (1990) 169 CLR 540....................32
Cornelius v de Taranto [2001] EMLR 12....................123
Costello v Chief Constable of Derbyshire Constabulary [2001] EWCA Civ 381....................101
Crystal Palace Trustees v Minister of Town and Country Planning [1951] 2 Ch 132 (Ch)....................63
D Pride & Partners (a firm) v Institute for Animal Health [2009] EWHC 685 (QB)....................105
Davidson v Garrett [1899] CCC 200....................158
Dobson and another v North Tyneside Health Authority and another [1996] EWCA Civ 1301; [1996] 4 All ER 474 (CA)....................3, 25, 54, 74, 184, 189, 202, 240–241, 247–248
Doodeward v Spence [1908] HCA 45; (1908) 6 CLR 406....................1, 3, 14, 25, 54, 74–75, 150, 202–203, 206, 232, 240, 241, 243–244, 264–265, 268–270
Drane v Evangelou [1978] 1 WLR 455 (CA)....................48
Egerton v Earl Brownlow (1853) 10 ER 359 (HL)....................32
Ellerman's Wilson Line Ltd v Webster [1952] 1 Lloyd's Rep 179 (KB)....................132, 134
Elwes v Brigg Gas Co (1886) 33 Ch D 562....................35
Errington v Errington and Wood [1951 EWCA Civ 2; [1952] 1 KB 290....................32
Esso v Mardon [1976] EWCA Civ 4; [1976] QB 801 (CA)....................44
Evans v UK (2006) 43 EHRR 21....................225
Farley v Skinner [2001] UKHL 49....................48, 119, 244
Fouldes v Willoughby (1841) 8 M & W 540, 151 ER 1153 (Exch)....................94
Fowler v Lanning [1959] 1 QB 426; [1959] 1 All ER 290 (QB)....................257
Gilmour v Coates [1949] AC 426 (HL)....................61
Gregg v Coates (1856) 53 ER 13....................35
Gregg v Scott [2005] UKHL 2; [2005] 2 AC 176....................41
Hamilton Jones v David & Snape [2003] EWHC 3147 (Ch)....................50
Hartley v Moxham (1842) 114 ER 675 (QB)....................257
Haynes v James & Charles Dodd [1990] 2 All ER 815 (CA)....................47

Haynes's Case (1614) 77 ER 1389 .... 13, 202, 237–239
Hedley Byrne v Heller & Partners Ltd [1964] AC 465 (HL) 43, 44, 45
Helena Partnerships Ltd v Commissioner for Her Majesty's Revenue and Customs [2012] EWCA Civ 569 62
Henderson v Merrett Syndicates [1994] UKHL 5; [1995] 2 AC 145 (HL) 44
Heywood v Wellers [1976] QB 446 (CA) 47
Hibbert v McKiernan [1948] 2 KB 142 133
Hicks v Chief Constable of the South Yorkshire Police [1992] All ER 65; [1992] PIQR 433 (HL) 48
Hood v Oglander (1865) 55 ER 733 33
Hunt v Hourmount [1983] CLY 983 47
Hunter v British Coal Corporation [1998] 2 All ER 97 (CA) 243
Jackson v Horizon Holidays [1974] EWCA Civ 12; [1975] 1 WLR 1468 (CA) 47
Jacobs v Davis [1917] 2 KB 532 34
Jarvis v Swans' Tours [1972] EWCA Civ 8; [1973] QB 233 (CA) 47, 244, 270
Jarvis v Williams [1955] 1 WLR 71 (CA) 97
Jeffries v Great Western Railway (1856) 5 Ell & Bl 802; 119 ER 680 .... 100, 101
Johnson v Unisys Limited [2001] UKHL 13 244
Kais v Turvey (1994) 17 Fam LR 498 34
Kearry v Pattinson [1939] 1 KB 471; 1 All ER 65 (CA) 213, 264
Kekewich v Manning (1851) 1 DGM & G 176; (1851) 42 ER 519 32
Kuwait Airways Corp v Iraqi Airways Co and another (nos 4 & 5) [2002] UKHL 19, [2002] 2 AC 886 (HL) 115, 257, 267
Leigh and Sillavan v Aliakmon Shipping Co Ltd (Aliakmon) [1985] UKHL 10; [1986] AC 785 (HL) 42
Letang v Cooper [1965] 1 QB 232; [1964] 2 All ER 929n (CA) 257
Macaura v Northern Assurance Co Ltd [1925] AC 619 (HL) 272
McDonald v Coys of Kensington [2004] EWCA Civ 47; [2004] 1 WLR 2775 (CA) 168
McLoughlin v O'Brian [1983] 1 AC 410 (HL) 45, 48, 118, 119, 243
Messenger v Andrews (1828) 38 ER 885 35
Milroy v Lord [1862] EWHC Ch J78; (1862) 45 ER 1185 32
Moffatt v Kazana [1969] 2 QB 152 (Ass) 127, 129, 134
Murphy v Brentwood [1991] 1 AC 398 (HL) 43
National Anti-Vivisection Society v Inland Revenue Commissioners [1948] AC 31 (HL) 61, 62
National Coal Board v JE Evans & Co (Cardiff) Ltd [1951] 2 KB 861 (CA) 257
National Provincial Bank v Ainsworth [1965] AC 1175 (HL) 171, 207, 208
Norman v Federal Commissioner of Taxation [1963] HCA 21; (1963) 109 CLR 9 .... 31, 32
OBG Ltd v Allan [2007] UKHL 21; [2008] 1 AC 1 (HL) 93, 116
Oppenheim v Tobacco Securities Co Ltd [1951] AC 297 (HL) 61
Page v Smith [1995] UKHL 7; [1996] AC 155 (HL) 48, 163
Parker v British Airways Board [1982] QB 1004 (CA) 94, 127, 128
Phelps v Hillingdon LBC [2001] 2 AC 619 (HL) 44
Pierce v Bemis (The Lusitania) [1986] 1 All ER 1011 (QB) 131
Pilcher v Rawlins (1872) LR 7 Ch 259 38
Potter v Commissioners of Inland Revenue (1854) 156 ER 392 207
R (Ghai) v Newcastle City Council [2010] EWCA Civ 59; [2010] 3 WLR 737 (CA) 166
R (Nicklinson) v Ministry of Justice [2014] UKSC 38; [2013] EWCA Crim 961 286

R (on the application of Quintavalle) v Secretary of State for Health [2003] UKHL 13; [2003] 2 WLR 692 (HL) 200
R (Rickets) v Basildon Magistrates' Court [2011] 1 Cr App R 15, [2010] EWHC 2358 (Admin) 127, 133
R v Bentham [2005] UKHL 18; [2005] 1 WLR 1057 (HL) 95, 209, 250
R v Edwards and Stacey (1877) Cox CC 384 .... 132, 135, 136
R v Gibson [1990] 2 QB 619; [1991] 1 All ER 439 (CA) 211, 296
R v Herbert [1961] JPLGR 12 .... 205, 232
R v Kelly [1998] 3 All ER 741; (1999) QB 621 (CA) 3, 14, 25, 54, 74–75, 133, 170, 184, 189, 202–203, 232, 239, 240–244, 265, 268
R v Lynn (1788) 2 T R 732, 2 Term Rep 733 .... 238, 239, 240
R v Peters (1843) 1 Car & K 245 135
R v Price (1884) 12 QBD 247 239
R v Rostron [2003] EWCA Crim 2206; [2003] All ER 269 (CA) 133
R v Rothery [1976] Crim LR 691 (CA) 74, 205, 232, 268
R v Sharpe (1857) 169 ER 959 .... 202, 239
R v Small [1987] Crim LR 777 (CA) 132
R v Welsh [1974] RTR 478 .... 74, 205, 232, 268
R v William White (1912) 7 Cr App R 266 (CA) 132
Re Bateman [1925] 94 LJKB 791 39
Re Compton [1945] Ch 123 (CA) 61
Re Hodge [1940] Ch 260 35
Re Moore (1886) 55 LJ Ch 418 .... 35c
Re Reed (1842) Car & M 307 131
Re Resch's Will Trusts; Le Cras v Perpetual Trustee Co Ltd [1969] 1 AC 514 (PC) 63
Re Ridgway (1885) 15 QBD 447 252
Re Scientific Investment Pension Plan Trusts [1999] Ch 53 33
Re Williams; Williams v Williams [1897] 2 Ch 12 35
Rees v Engelbach (1871) LR 12 Eq 225 35
Reeves v Commissioner of Police of the Metropolis [2000] 1 AC 360 (HL) 44
Robot Arenas v Waterfield [2010] EWHC 115 (QB) 129, 130, 134
Rowe v Vale of White Horse DC [2003] EWHC 388 (QB) 168
Ruxley Electronics v Forsyth [1995] UKHL 8; [1996] AC 344 (HL) 47
Savile v Roberts (1698) a91 Eng Rep 1147; [1696] 1 Ld Raym 274 (KB) 48
Scottish Burial Reform and Cremation Society v Glasgow Corp [1967] UKHL 3; [1968] AC 138 (HL) 61
Sidaway v Governors of Bethlem Royal Hospital [1985] AC 871 (HL) 59
Smith v Bush [1990] UKHL 1; [1990] 1 AC 831 (HL) 44
Spartan Steel and Alloys Ltd v Martin [1973] QB 27 (CA) 43
Spring v Guardian Assurance [1995] 2 AC 296 (HL) 44
Summers v Salford Corporation [1943] AC 283 (HL) 47
The Case of Swans (1592) 7 Co Rep 15b; 77 ER 435 .... 213, 264
The Egypt (1932) 44 Ll LR 21 135
Verderame v Commercial Union Assurance Co plc [1992] BCLC 793 50
Vigers v Cook [1919] 2 KB 475 (CA) 169
Vine v Waltham Forest Council [2000] 1 WLR 2383 (CA) 91, 94, 257
W v Essex [2001] 2 AC 592; [2000] 2 All ER 237 (HL) 243
Wainwright v Home Office [2004] 2 AC 406 (HL) 164

Walter v Alltools Ltd (1944) 171 LT 371; [1944] 61 TLR 39 48
Watts v Morrow [1991] 4 All ER 937 (CA) 244
White v Chief Constable of South Yorkshire [1999] 2 AC 455 (HL) 43, 48
Wilkinson v Downton [1897] 2 QB 57 (QB) 164
Williams v Natural Life Health Foods [1998] UKHL 17; [1998] 1 WLR 830 (HL) 44
Williams v Phillips (1957) 41 Cr App Rep 5 ....132, 135
Williams v Williams (1882) 20 Ch D 659 (Ch) 74, 239, 265
Wilson v Lombank Ltd (1963) 1 All ER 740 (Ass) 257
Wynne v Fletcher (1857) 53 ER 423 32
Yearworth and others v North Bristol NHS Trust [2009] EWCA Civ 37; [2010] QB 1 ....1, 2, 4–5, 14–15, 25, 39, 40–54, 75–77, 85, 107, 115–116, 119–120, 149, 153, 164, 185, 198, 202–203, 205, 209, 211, 225, 227, 232, 236, 243–244, 253–256, 265–268, 270–273, 287–288, 290, 297

United States of America

All Cargo Transport, Inc v Florida East Coast Railway Co 355 So 2d 178 (Fla 3d DCA 1987) 170
Armstrong v H&C Communications 575 So 2d 280 (Dist Ct App 1991) 166
Association for Molecular Pathology et al v Myriad Genetics et al (2013) 569 US 12 ....179, 192, 195
AZ v BZ 725 NE 2d 1051 (Mass 2000) 204
Brotherton v Cleveland 923 F 2d 477 (6th Cir 1991) 204
Casey et all v 23andMe, Inc and Does 1-100 Case No 13-CV-2847 S D CA 180
Christensen v Superior Court 54 Cal 3d 868 (Su Ct Cal 1992) 158, 161, 162, 165, 168
Cobbs v Grant 8 Cal 3d 229 (1972) 163
Dahl v Angle 222 Ore App 572 (Or Ct App 2008) 205
Davidson v City of Westminster 32 Cal 3d 197 (1982) 165
Davis v Davis 842 SW 2d 588 (Tenn Sup Ct 1992) 204
Dilger et al v 23andMe, Inc Case No 14-CV-00296 SD CA 180
Doe v Dyer-Goode 389 Pa Super 151 (Pennsylvania Sup Ct 1989) 166
Doe v High-Tech Institute, Inc 972 P 2d 1060 (1998) 167
Eads v Brazelton (1861) 22 Ark 499 137
Ex parte Szyzcgiel 51 NYS 2d 699 (Sup Ct 1944) 137
Exelby v Handyside (1749) 2 East PC 652 97
FAI Insurances Ltd v Custom Credit Corp Ltd (1980) 29 ALR 505 272
Greenberg v Miami Children's Hospital Research Institue 264 F Supp 2d 1064 (SD Fla 2003) 16, 22, 113, 158, 163, 168, 188, 193–194, 232
Grimes v Kennedy Krieger Institute 782 A2d 807 (Md Ct App 2001) 169
Guthrie et al v 23andMe, Inc Case No 14-CV-01258 WD PA 180
Havasupai Tribe v Arizona Board of Regents (consolidated suit numbers 1 CA-CV 07-0454 and 1 CA-CV 07-0801) (CA App Ariz 2008) 158
Hecht v Kaplan 221 Ad 2d 100 (Sup Ct New York 1996) 166
Hecht v Superior Court (Kane) [1993] 16 Cal App 4th 836; (1993) 20 Cal Rptr 775 ....14, 75, 76, 77, 120, 205
Hubenschmidt v Shears 270 NW 2d 2 (Sup Ct Mich 1978) 166
Janicki v Hospital of St Raphael 46 Conn Supp 204 (Conn Superior Court 1999) 204
Jeter v Mayo Clinic Arizona 121 P 3d 1256 (Ariz Ct App 2005) 205

Kass v Kass 696 NE 2d 174 (NY Ct App 1998)....................204
Kurchner v State Farm Firm Arm and Casualty Co 858 So 2d 1220 (Fla Ct App 2003).....205
Lamm v Shingleton 55 SE 2d 810 (1949)....................169
Martin et al v 23andMe, Inc Case No 14-CV-00429 ND CA....................180
Mayo v Prometheus 132 S Ct 1289 (US 2012)....................182
Moore v Regents of University of California (1990) 51 Cal 3d 120 (Sup Ct Cal); 793 P 2d 479.................... 9–10, 15–16, 20–22, 78–82, 101–106, 113, 138, 141, 152, 158, 160–163, 167–175, 194, 198, 203–204, 207–208, 232, 258–259, 269, 276, 298
Norman-Bloodsaw v Lawrence Berkeley Laboratory 135 F 3d 1260 (9th Cir 1998)....158, 167
Pierce v Proprietors of Swan Point Cemetery (1872) 10 RI 227, 14 Am Rep 667....................104
Reber v Reiss 42 A 3d 1131 (Pa Superior Court 2012)....................204
Ritter v Couch 76 SE 428 (Sup Ct App 1912)....................159
Silkwood v Kerr-McGee Corporation 637 F 2d 743 (1980)....................166
Spreter et al v 23andMe, Inc Case No 14-CV-0487 SD CA....................180
Stanton et al v 23andMe, Inc Case No 14-CV-00294 ND CA....................180
State v Walker 119 Ariz 121, 579 P2d 1091 (1978)....................137
Stefani et al v 23andMe, Inc Case 1:13-CV-13206 GAO....................180
Szafranski v Dunston (2013) 993 NE 2d 502 (Ill App)....................204
Tarasoff v Regents of University of California 17 Cal 3d 425 (1976)....................161
US v Arora 860 F Supp 1091 (1994)....................116, 203, 205
US v Comprehensive Drug Testing, Inc 513 F 3d 1085 (9th Cir 2008)....................167
US v Veatch 674 F2d 1217, 1220 (9th Cir 1981)....................137
US v Wiederkehr 33 MJ 539 (AFCMR 1991)....................137
Venner v State of Maryland 30 Md App 599 (1976), 354 A2d 483 Md App (1976)....................137, 140, 142, 143, 150, 155, 204, 223
Washington University v Catalona 437 F Supp 2d 985 (US District Court Missouri Eastern Division, 2006); 490 F 3d 667 (2007)....................16, 22, 36, 37, 97, 103, 183, 189, 203, 204, 205, 232, 236, 248, 249, 250, 252, 253, 258
Waters v Fleetwood 212 Ga 161 (1956)....................166
York v Jones 717 F Supp 421 (ED Va 1989)....................205

TABLE OF STATUTES

Australia

Assisted Reproductive Technology Act 1997 (Qld)
s21 122

Charitable Trusts Act 1962 (WA)
s21(1) 62

Charitable Trusts Act 1993 (NSW)
s6 62

Charities Act 2013 (Cth)
s7 62
s12(1) 61
s12(1)(a) 63
s12(1)(b) 64

Charities Procedure Act 1812 62

Civil Law (Property) Act 2006 (ACT)
s201 32
s205 31

Conveyancing Act 1919 (NSW)
s12 31
s23(b)(1) 31
s23(c) 32

Conveyancing and Law of Property Act 1884 (Tas)
s60(1) 31
s60(2) 32
s86 31

Explosives Act 2003 (NSW) 205

Firearms Act 1996 (NSW)
Pt 6 210

Human Tissue Act 1983 (NSW)
s32 211

Imperial Acts Application Act 1969 (NSW)
s9(2) 61

Land Titles Act 1925 (ACT)
s57(1) 31

Land Title Act 1994 (Qld)
s181 31

Land Titles Act 1980 (Tas)
s39(1) 31

Land Title Act 2000 (NT)
s184 31

Law of Property Act 1936 (SA)
s15 31
s28(1) 31
s29 32

Law of Property Act 2000 (NT)
s9(1) 31
s10 32
s182 31

Poisons and Therapeutic Goods Act 1966 (NSW) 205, 210

Privacy Act 1988 20
s95A 37

Property Law Act 1958 (Vic)
s52(1) 31
s53 32
s134 31

Property Law Act 1969 (WA)
s33(1) 31
s34 32

Property Law Act 1974 (Qld)
s10(1) 31
s11 32
s199 31

Protection of the Environment Operations Act 1997 (NSW)
s144A 211

Real Property Act 1886 (SA)
s67 31

Real Property Act 1900 (NSW)
s41(1) 31

Religious Successory and Charitable Trusts Act 1958 (Vic)
s61 62

Transfer of Land Act 1893 (WA)
s58(1) 31

Transfer of Land Act 1958 (Vic)
s40(1) 31

Trustee Act 1925 (ACT)
s94A 62
s104 61
sch 1 61

Trustee Act 1936 (SA)
s60(2) 62
s66 62

Trusts Act 1973 (Qld)
s103(1) 61
s106(2) 62

New Zealand

Charity Act 2006
s5 61

United Kingdom

Anatomy Act 1832 14

Charities Act 2011
s3 61

Consumer Protection Act 1987 276

Coroners and Justice Act 2009
s71 231

Criminal Damage Act 1971
s5 292

Data Protection Act 1998 165

Environmental Protection Act 1990
s87(4a)(a) 274

Family Law Act 1996 289
s1 229

Firearms Act 1968
s17(2) ... 95

Human Fertilisation and Embryology Act 1990 ... 76, 122, 204, 228, 244, 245, 246, 267, 270, 284, 289
s12(1) ... 121
s41 ... 121
sch 3 ... 121

Human Fertilisation and Embryology Act 2008 ... 76, 228, 245, 284
sch 3 ... 207

Human Rights Act 1998 ... 231

Human Tissue Act (Scotland) 2006 ... 231

Human Tissue Act 1961 ... 3, 245

Human Tissue Act 2004 ... 82, 103, 105, 122, 150, 151, 154, 159, 160, 175, 184, 225, 228, 231, 247, 249, 259, 261, 279, 284, 289, 293
s1(7) ... 245
s1(8) ... 245
s1(9) ... 245
s4(1)(a) ... 107
s5 ... 245
s5(1) ... 121
s8(1) ... 121
s25 ... 245
s32 ... 245, 294
s32(7) ... 121
s32(9) ... 5, 184
s32(9)(c) ... 1, 203, 235
s33 ... 245
s34 ... 211
s44 ... 145
s45 ... 148, 153, 165, 245
s53(1) ... 287
s54(7) ... 235
sch 1 ... 245
sch 3 ... 246

Judicature Act 1873
s25(6) ... 31

Law of Property Act 1925
s52 ... 31
s53 ... 32

Limitation Act 1980
s3(1) 128

Sale of Goods Act 1979 .... 251, 276

Slave Trade Acts 1824, 1843, 1873 231

Slavery Abolition Act 1833 231

Statute Law (Repeals) Act 1998 231

Statute of Charitable Uses 1601 60

Statute of Frauds 1677 .... 31, 32

Supply of Goods and Services Act 1982
s13 39

Theft Act 1968
s1 131
s2 132
s2(1)(c) 128
s4 240
s5 131
s5(1) 133

Torts (Interference with Goods) Act 1977
s1 256
s1(d) 114
s3 258
s11(1) 257

Town and Country Planning Act 1990
s57 107

United States of America

18 Vermont State Acts 9330 188

California Penal Code § 367g (2008) 207

National Research Act 1974 (US) 18

Instruments

Australia

Rules of the Supreme Court 1971 (WA)
Order 52 rule 3(1) 242–243

United States of America

California Health and Safety Code (USA)
s 7054.4 103

Conventions

Additional Protocol of the Convention on Human Rights and Biomedicine Concerning Transplantation of Organs and Tissues of Human Origin, ETS 2002, no 168
Art 21 211
Art 22 211

Council of Europe's Convention for the Protection of Human Rights and Dignity of the Human Being With Regard to the Application of Biology and Medicine ETS 1997, no 164
Art 21 211

European Convention of Human Rights
Art 4 231

UNESCO Universal Declaration on the Human Genome and Human Rights (1997)
Art 1 178

1

Introduction

IMOGEN GOOLD, KATE GREASLEY, JONATHAN HERRING and LOANE SKENE

Over the last four decades, the question of whether property rights ought to be exercisable in relation to human body parts has been a matter of ongoing debate in both the Anglo-Australian courts and the academic literature, with legal academics, philosophers, ethicists and sociologists, among others, weighing in on a wide range of questions raised in the debate. A series of decisions in the UK and Australian courts have fuelled this debate, evidencing a movement towards some acceptance of limited property rights in some kinds of tissue. The Australian High Court decision in *Doodeward v Spence* (1908) saw the common law recognise that at least a possessory interest in human tissue could arise following the lawful application of work and skill to preserve it. A string of cases in the 1990s and early 2000s cemented the place of this 'exception', while parallel statutory regulation came in the form of the new Human Tissue Act (UK), enacted in 2004 as a result of extensive organ-retention inquiries, most notably at the Alder Hey and Bristol hospitals. The new Act included a provision to mirror the *Doodeward* exception, lending it legislative force.[1]

The law's position, therefore, seemed fairly certain but remained highly contested, with many criticisms raised by commentators on all sides of the body-ownership debate. In 2009, the decision by the UK Court of Appeal in *Yearworth and others v North Bristol NHS Trust* (2009) brought a new dimension to the debate by supporting a move towards a broader, more principled basis for finding (or rejecting) property rights in tissue. Consequently, the debate over whether human bodies and their parts should be governed by the laws of property has accelerated.[2] In the light of the *Yearworth* decision and a number of Australian

[1] Human Tissue Act 2004, s 32(9)(c). Shaun Pattinson has argued that, in fact, the whole of the Act takes a property approach, while Jonathan Herring and P-L Chau argue that the provision reflects an assumption that biomaterials are not generally property. J Herring and P-L Chau, 'My Body, Your Body, Our Bodies' 15 *Medical Law Review* 34; SD Pattinson, 'Directed Donation and Ownership of Human Organs' (2011) 31(3) *Legal Studies* 392–410.

[2] See, eg S Harmon and G Laurie, '*Yearworth v North Bristol NHS Trust*: Property, Principles, Precedents and Paradigms' (2010) 69(3) *Cambridge Law Journal* 476–93; N Priaulx, 'Managing Novel Reproductive Injuries in the Law of Tort: The Curious Case of Destroyed Sperm' (2010) 17(1) *European Journal of Health Law*, 81–95; SHE Harmon, '*Yearworth v North Bristol NHS Trust*: A Property Case of Uncertain Significance?' (2010) 13(4) *Medicine, Health Care and Philosophy* 343–50; C Hawes, 'Property

decisions that arguably follow a similar approach, a collection of chapters on the many issues raised within this debate seemed timely.[3] This was particularly the case given the increasingly broad range of ways in which human biomaterials are used, and the new values they have acquired, as many of the chapters in this collection evidence.[4]

In this collection, we bring together legal academics, philosophers and sociologists from both the UK and Australia to delve into the detail of the merits or otherwise of a property approach to the regulation of human biomaterials. The collection comprises an assortment of contributions that address the broad doctrinal and theoretical questions, and also drill down into some of the highly specific legal issues implicated in the body-ownership debate. However, we wanted to do more than merely present a collection of views on the question of whether property law is the right mechanism for regulating human biomaterials. From the start, we committed ourselves to a collaborative process in which all authors would be invited to review one another's work with a view to promoting cross-fertilisation of ideas across the chapters. Authors were also encouraged to reference one another's work, and respond to arguments put forward by other contributors to the collection. Our goal, through this collaborative process, was to produce a collection that encapsulates the body–property debate and allowed contributors both to present their views, and address those with whom they both agreed and disagreed.

Why Property?

We have called our collection *Persons, Parts and Property: How Should We Regulate Human Tissue in the Twenty-First Century*, putting the property question front and centre. Many of the chapters in this collection, however, eschew what we call a 'property approach' to the regulation of biomaterials, preferring the law of consent, or a new legislative scheme.[5] Why, then, did we make the application of

Interests in Body Parts: *Yearworth v North Bristol NHS Trust*' (2010) 73(1) *MLR* 130–40; L Skene, 'Proprietary Interests in Human Bodily Material: *Yearworth*, Recent Australian Cases on Stored Semen and Their Implications' (2012) 20(2) *Medical Law Review* 227–45; J Wall, 'The Legal Status of Body Parts: A Framework' (2011) 31(4) *Oxford Journal of Legal Studies* 783–804; M Pawlowski, 'Property in Body Parts and Products of the Human Body' (2009) 30 *Liverpool Law Journal* 35. See also R Hardcastle, *Law and the Human Body: Property Rights, Ownership and Control* (Oxford, Hart Publishing, 2007); RN Nwabueze, 'Donated Organs, Property Rights and the Remedial Quagmire' (2008) 16 *Medical Law Review* 201; C Fabre, *Whose Body is it Anyway? Justice and the Integrity of the Person* (Oxford, Oxford University Press, 2008); AV Campbell, *The Body in Bioethics* (Oxford, Routledge-Cavendish, 2009); D Dickenson, *Body Shopping: Converting Body Parts to Profit* (London, Oneworld Publications, 2009).

[3] *Bazley v Wesley Monash IVF* [2010] QSC 118; *Jocelyn Edwards; Re the estate of the late Mark Edwards* [2011] NSWSC 478.

[4] See also I Goold, 'Why Does It Matter How We Regulate the Use of Human Body Parts?' (2014) 40 *Journal of Medical Ethics* 3.

[5] By 'property approach' we mean recognising that biomaterials can constitute items of property at law, and hence individuals can exercise property rights in relation to them.

property concepts the focus of our collection? The reasons are in part historical. The roots of Anglo-Australian case law lie in string of cases beginning (some argue) in the seventeenth century. Goold and Quigley trace this line of cases in their chapter. By the nineteenth century an entrenched prohibition on regarding the human corpse as an item of property had emerged, often referred to the 'no property in a corpse' rule. However, in the early twentieth century the High Court of Australia took the first step away from this approach when faced with the question of how to deal with a claim in detinue for the return of a two-headed foetus preserved in a jar that had been used as an exhibit for some decades. In a landmark decision that has attracted a great deal of attention (and criticism), the court held that the showman who exhibited it had sufficient possessory rights to maintain his claim, and that a corpse of this kind could be subject to such rights if the application of lawful work and skill had transformed it into something other than a corpse awaiting burial.[6] This approach would later become known as the 'work and skill exception' to the prohibition on the ownership of a corpse.

There was little development in the Anglo-Australian jurisprudence until a series of challenging situations came before the UK courts from the mid 1990s onwards. Over the course of these decisions, detailed in Goold and Quigley's chapter, the 'work and skill' exception was cemented as good law in the UK.[7] These cases attracted considerable academic attention, not least because of the unclear ambit and jurisprudential foundations of the exception. During this period it became increasingly apparent that the regulatory frameworks in both countries were insufficiently broad to effectively manage the expanding uses of human tissue, and the reactive approach of the courts in the cases that came before them was creating as many problems as it was solving. By gradually introducing a partial property approach, the UK courts were being swayed by the appeal of dealing with biomaterials as property without (understandably) accounting for the wider context in which their decisions were operating. These problems were exacerbated by the burgeoning use of biomaterials in research, the new challenges raised by markets in those materials, and the increasing privacy concerns created by more widely and cheaply available genetic testing. New uses for biomaterials in the fields of stem cell research, the growing culture of biobanking and the emergence of commercial ventures offering direct-to-consumer testing and storage of umbilical cord blood fostered an ever more complex matrix of issues. In Australia, the Human Tissue Acts that had been passed in the early 1980s to manage organ transplantation were becoming dated. Similarly, following the organ retention revelations of the early 2000s, the UK's 1961 Human Tissue Act was clearly in need of overhaul to bring it into line with modern views on the appropriate way to regulate biomaterials. Like the Australian legislation, it was drafted to cover a particular context (the research context) and as a reaction to a

[6] *Doodeward v Spence* (1908) 6 CLR 406.

[7] *Dobson and another v North Tyneside Health Authority and another* [1996] 4 All ER 474; *R v Kelly* [1998] 3 All ER 741; *AB and others v Leeds Teaching Hospital NHS Trust* [2004] EWHC 644 (QB).

newly recognised concern (the retention of organs). In both jurisdictions, an effective, comprehensive regulatory scheme was sorely lacking.

This lacuna was tested when, in 2008, six men sought compensation for the psychological harm they suffered upon learning that the semen they had had stored to preserve their fertility before undergoing radiation treatment had been negligently destroyed. The facts of *Yearworth* are explored in detail in (among others) Skene's chapter in this collection, and they will not be rehearsed here. The case drew attention from the academic community for two main reasons. First, as already noted, it arguably represented a step towards a more broad-based property approach.[8] Secondly, it brought the limitations of the current framework to the fore, as the Court of Appeal found itself faced with the lacunae many commentators had been highlighting in the preceding years. Unable to accommodate the men's claim within damages for personal injury or breach of contract, it dealt with the problem by finding that the men could be considered to have property rights in their semen, and hence could bring a claim in bailment. It explicitly moved away from the 'work and skill exception' and adopted what some consider a more principled approach to determining when property rights over biomaterials might be found.

The *Yearworth* decision influenced the Australian courts in a number of other cases concerning the use of semen, holding in each that the widow of a deceased man could be entitled to possession of the man's stored semen for use in reproductive treatment.[9] As Skene points out in this collection, 'in both of those cases, as in *Yearworth*, the judges discussed the application of principles of bailment, which in turn involved a finding that bodily material can be property and that people may sometimes have property rights in their own bodily material'.[10]

In contrast to the judicial approach in these cases, the legislative frameworks in both Australia and the UK are arranged around the principle of consent to use of biomaterials, providing direction on what kinds of uses of biomaterials are permitted and when the consent of the person from whom they were taken will be required for that use. As the case law continues to develop alongside these legislative instruments, a growing tension has emerged. As they continue to diverge in their approach, the law has become less coherent in its attempts to manage all the many and varied ways in which biomaterials are used, and the numerous conflicts that arise over that use. It is for this reason that this collection focuses on the notion of property, because we are coming increasingly closer to a situation in which these tandem approaches cannot work together effectively. If the courts continue down the path they appear to have chosen, the case law will diverge still further from the legislative frameworks in place, and conflicts between the two are

[8] See Goold and Quigley, ch 14 in this volume, but also *cf* L Rostill, 'The Ownership That Wasn't Meant To Be: *Yearworth* and Property Rights in Human Tissue' (2014) 40 *Journal of Medical Ethics* 14.

[9] *Bazley v Wesley Monash IVF Pty Ltd* [2010] QSC 118; *Jocelyn Edwards; Re the estate of the late Mark Edwards* [2011] NSWSC 478; see also, *Re H, AE (No 2)* [2012] SASC 177; *Re Section 22 of the Human Tissue and Transplant Act 1982; ex parte C* [2013] WASC 3.

[10] Skene, ch 15 in this volume.

inevitable. For example, we can already see how this divergence may have implications. The Human Tissue Act in the UK recognises the work and skill exception, but is silent on the potentially wider basis for finding that human biomaterials are property developed in *Yearworth*. It is, therefore, not clear whether biomaterials found to be property in accordance with the decision in *Yearworth* will fall within section 36(9) of the Act. We may well see further conflicts if the courts' approach to the rights of individuals over their tissue do not reflect the provisions of the legislation, such as those uses for which consent is (and is not) required. It is also untenable to develop two regulatory approaches that are meant to work together, but increasingly divergent on the essential question of the legal status of biomaterials.

A question one might ask at this point is why the courts have chosen to go down the path of a property approach. Some of the chapters in this collection explore this point, outlining some of the appeal of property law as a means of regulating biomaterials. Douglas, Goold and Quigley, and to some extent Stewart et al, present a case for a property approach, arguing variously for the applicability of property as means of regulating dealings over a thing. Conversely, Skene, Wall and Herring draw out some of the problems with a property approach.

Themes

With these concerns in mind, the chapters in this collection work through the issues currently facing us in this area. The body as property debate ranges over numerous areas of concern: property rights in gametes, organ shortages, donations, sale of body parts and black markets, and technological advancements with the use of cell lines and patenting problems. The debate is also engaged with philosophical questions about the nature of the self and personal identity, and how these affect how we should deal with biomaterials. The chapters in this collection cover many of these issues, including research use of human tissue, organ markets, patent issues, moral rights and the law relating to tissue, banking of tissue and umbilical cord blood, and biobanking.

Questions about how to appropriately regulate human tissue often centre around its use in the medical research context. Three chapters in this collection provide valuable discussions of this aspect of the debate. Nicol et al provide an overview of the ethical and legal issues raised by the use of human tissue in the research context, and consider how the property law model might apply there. They examine the various ways that human tissue is used in research, with particular focus on newly emerging technologies. Following a description of the existing ethical and legal frameworks for regulating the use of human tissue in research, they provide an introductory critical analysis of the pros and cons of the current regulation, followed by an exploration of the extent to which property law would provide a more or less suitable framework for regulating research uses of human tissue.

Stewart et al build on this background by introducing a particular area of growing concern: biobanking. As they note, in the twentieth century the practice of biobanking grew to become a major component of education and research in the healthcare sector. However, the practice raises a number of ethical and legal concerns including issues of consent, problems of unanticipated findings, and issues of control and access. They argue that applying the law of gifts is essential to unpacking the problems of biobanking. Stewart et al outline another area of key, current interest: umbilical cord blood (UCB) banking. Such banking raises particularly vexed issues because of the interplay of public and private interests. While both public and private researchers have interests in the access to UCB, so too do individuals who may want to store UCB for their own benefit. They consider the question of how we should balance these various demands on UCB, arguing that the best model to draw upon is to treat the public UCB bank as a form of public property similar to Crown land, mineral resources, timber or native fauna. Dickenson picks up on the possibility of a commons approach to biomaterials when she examines the aim of the online genetic testing service 23andMe to create a research biobank from the tissue samples sent in by its customers and from the subsequent epidemiological and lifestyle questionnaires that customers are also asked to complete. She argues that the notion of the commons, and of the 'corporate commons' in particular, could be seen as a powerful and practical tool for ensuring that restrictive genetic patenting does not impede rather than assist clinical biomedicine.

These chapters begin to demonstrate how the debate around regulation of human biomaterials is interwoven with multiple, complex themes. The first is the importance of consent and the autonomy of the person who is the source of the biomaterials. The second is the tension between these concepts and the demands of the community, which has an interest in the benefits of research. We can also include the research community and various kinds of commercial ventures in this area of tension. Concerns about commercialisation and commodification are also important themes that cut across much of the debate in this area. For some, property is synonymous with commodification, and hence worries about treating parts of people as commodities are also criticisms of taking a property approach. Worry about the harm that will result from allowing financial exchanges for human materials are a key issue in the debate over regulation. The ethics of commercial markets in biomaterials is explored in Greasley's chapter.

We might wonder why the body–property debate has continued so long without resolution. Why is there such a divergence of views? It is important to note is that while there is disagreement about the *way* to regulate, for the most part there is not a great deal of disagreement about the *goals* of regulating. Most commentators agree that there is a need protect and promote individual autonomy in relation to human biomaterials, although they disagree on the extent of such protection. It is also widely agreed that supporting medical research is important.

Such research requires access to biomaterials, and few in the debate would argue that we should prevent access entirely. It is when these demands conflict that some explanation of the divergence can be seen. A strong commitment to individual autonomy in this context can lead to a desire for legal controls that ensure individual, rather than community needs, determine when access to biomaterials can be obtained. It is on this basis that some, such as Herring, resist a property approach on the ground that it may (depending on the incarnation) place individual control over tissue above other demands. It is concerns of this kind that lead some, such as Dickenson, to argue for conceptualising biomaterials as a community resource in some contexts.

However, the main reason for the divergence within the debate rests on differences of opinion about which is the best legal mechanism to balance these competing demands; and there is no easy answer to this, as the chapters in this collection demonstrate. For example, while some, such as Herring, argue that a legislative framework might be the most effective solution given that it can be shaped to accommodate the particular issues raised by human biomaterials, Bennett Moses rightly flags some of the problems that beset the creation of new regulatory schemes. Conversely, Douglas and others in this collection point to the logic of including biomaterials in the scheme of legal protections that manage our dealings with things. While this point stands, it is rightly open to the concerns raised elsewhere in this collection about the problematic implications of so doing of the kind explored by Skene and Wall. Bennett Moses addresses some of the concerns about imposing a property framework on biomaterials, arguing that the application of property law will not necessarily lead to the kind of dire outcomes, such as markets in organs, that some suggest.

There is also the question of what should be driving our approach to the issues in this area. Should it be pragmatism? Should we take an instrumental approach that promotes the best outcomes for research or for the community? Or is it more important to produce a framework that is underpinned by coherent jurisprudence? What is the relevance of the ethical debate around issues such as the harms of commodification, or the value of altruism? There are many ways of framing the questions in this debate, and many ways of approaching them.

Perspectives

The issues arising can (and should) be considered from a range of perspectives. From a legal perspective, we can consider the regulatory questions at the macro-level, thinking about the extant legal frameworks that could accommodate rights in human bodily material, and the obstacles that might be encountered when employing them for this purpose. To this end, some in this collection, such as Skene, consider the application of existing frameworks based on consent and privacy, while others, such as Goold and Quigley, Douglas and Stewart et al, approach the question from the other side, analysing the potential application of property principles. Herring proposes deploying a specifically targeted legislative framework. In addition to such overarching explorations, some chapters in this collection also focus on the fine-grained detail of some of the legal questions. For example, Nwabueze directs his attention to the question of remedies, while Goold provides a detailed analysis of the application of the concept of divesting abandonment and Stewart et al consider the application of the law of gifts.

Approaching the regulatory question purely from a legal perspective will be insufficient in the context of human biomaterials. Tissue removed from the human body is, for many reasons, not like anything else. It has symbolic significance. It has psychological significance, as the experience of the aftermath of Alder Hey made abundantly clear. It carries personal information about the individual from whom it was taken, and about their family members. How we treat that tissue arguably has implications for how we think about and treat people. Therefore, it is important to take account of the ethics of how we deal with biomaterials, and our regulatory approach should be reflective of the many values inherent in those materials, as well as our own values as a community. Herring and Dickenson both touch on these aspects of community value in their chapters, with Herring also arguing that only legislation can really provide a sufficiently nuanced approach to adequately reflect and protect the complex personal and social interests in body parts. In opposition, Goold and Quigley argue that property can capture such interests, and in some instances provide better protection.

It was never our intention to produce a collection that came to a single, agreed conclusion. But we also wanted to do more than simply present a range of views and leave it to the reader to choose from among them. We hoped to explore our areas of disagreement, but also to discover points on which we concurred, or might be able to come to some consensus. In the conclusion, we draw together the perspectives in this collection and distil these areas of agreement and otherwise to present a number of potential approaches to the question of how to regulate biomaterials. We hope that in doing so, we have taken a step closer to resolving this debate, and so come nearer to finding a means for the law to manage the many interests in, and uses of, biomaterials in a manner that best captures all of our concerns and goals.

2

Impressions on the Body, Property and Research

DIANNE NICOL, DON CHALMERS, REBEKAH McWHIRTER and JOANNE DICKINSON

Introduction

The late twentieth and early twenty-first centuries have seen remarkable developments in biomedical research, ignited by the sequencing of the human genome and the derivation of embryonic stem cells from human embryos.[1] These developments in cell and genetic technologies have been accompanied by continuing debates about whether or not individuals can assert property rights once their tissue has been donated for research purposes. Individuals who make their tissue available for research purposes may wish to assert such rights for a number of reasons, including to secure the return or destruction of their tissue, to assert control over how and for what purpose their tissue is used, and even to assert control over the downstream process of commercialising technological advances arising from research use of their tissue, including profit-sharing. Until recently, these debates have remained focused on 'Victorian precedents on body stealing and such arcana'.[2] Today, it would seem that we are no further advanced in resolving these debates than we were more than 20 years ago, when the US Supreme Court was first given the opportunity to rule on the status of human tissue donated for research purposes in the infamous case of *Moore v Regents of University of California* (the *Moore* case).[3] At that stage, the Court seemed reluctant to impose strictures on scientific research through property law, as illustrated by the following quote:

> In effect, what Moore is asking us to do is to impose a tort duty on scientists to investigate the consensual pedigree of each human cell sample used in research. To impose

[1] See, eg International Human Genome Sequencing Consortium, 'Initial Sequencing and Analysis of the Human Genome' (2001) 409 *Nature* 860; JA Thomson et al, 'Embryonic Stem Cell Lines Derived from Human Blastocysts' (1988) 282 *Science* 1145.

[2] O Dyer, 'Working Party Speaks Out on Use of Human Tissue' (1995) 310 *British Medical Journal* 31159, quoting Professor Ian Kennedy.

[3] *Moore v Regents of University of California* 51 Cal 3d 120 (Supreme Court of California, 1990).

> such a duty, which would affect medical research of importance to all of society, implicates policy concerns far removed from the traditional, two-party ownership disputes in which the law of conversion arose. Invoking a tort theory originally used to determine whether the loser or the finder of a horse had the better title, Moore claims ownership of the results of socially important medical research, including the genetic code for chemicals that regulate the functions of every human being's immune system.[4]

This chapter explores how shifts in judicial attitudes towards property in human tissue since the *Moore* case might play out in the research context, and whether there is a need for this form of judicial intervention in the already complex regulatory environment. The focus of the chapter is on the post-donation status of human tissue.

Allusions to painters and paintings have been made from time to time in the context of debates around the nature of property law. In positing his creation-without-wrong thesis, the late JW Harris argued eloquently that painters who own their canvas and their paints can justly claim to be the owners of the pictures they painted.[5] Extending JW Harris' painting thesis into the modern research context, had Monet borrowed canvas, or paint, or even a paint brush from his friend Renoir to create one of his series of pictures of water lilies in his garden at Giverny, no-one would claim that Renoir owned all or part of the pictures, would they? This suggests that it would be difficult for donors of tissue used for research to claim property rights in the end products of that research, whether tangible (for example, stem cell lines) or intangible (for example, patents), even though their tissue is the canvas upon which the research was undertaken.[6] However, this does not end the argument as to whether donors might have control over how their tissue is used, through residual property rights associated with the tissue itself or through other regulatory requirements imposed on researchers. Here, we take Harris' allusions to painting and painters one step further, from realism to abstraction. First, the historical context of use of human tissue for research is considered. The chapter then traces the outline to the unfinished portrait of property law, with a focus on the uncertain legal status of human tissue for donors and their descendants. The ethical and legal landscape for research use of human tissue and the obligations it entails are then sketched. The question that is posed is whether these two drawings can be brought together as a single integrated picture.

[4] ibid, 155.

[5] See JW Harris, *Property and Justice* (Oxford, Clarendon Press, 1996) 204. See also the commentary by M Quigley, 'Property in Human Biomaterials – Separating Persons and Things?' (2012) 32 *Oxford Journal of Legal Studies* 659.

[6] D Nicol, 'Property in Human Tissue and the Right of Commercialisation: The Interface between Tangible and Intellectual Property' (2004) 30 *Monash University Law Review* 139.

Historical Context

Human tissue has held a central place in the history of medicine and medical research. It also evokes strong but diverse emotional and spiritual responses; the great monotheistic religions of Judaism, Christianity and Islam hold different views about the nature of the human body and human tissue.[7] The twentieth century saw remarkable advances in medical science in relation to the clinical and transplantation uses of human tissue: blood transfusions were perfected and became commonplace; blood itself could be fractionated into various medicines and therapeutic products; transplantation of regenerative and non-regenerative tissue achieved high rates of success; and embryos were transferred to address infertility through *in vitro* fertilisation.

By the close of the twentieth century, human tissue had become a major source material for the knowledge-based genomics revolution. Now, in the twenty-first century, stem-cell technology is claimed to be 'the greatest and most exciting medical breakthrough', promising 'very great potential benefits' in regenerative medicine.[8] Whole genome sequencing is also rapidly becoming a practical reality.[9] The detailed genomic data being collected by research laboratories around the world will provide an invaluable resource for studying human disease, particularly when data sets from different populations are linked and analysed together.[10] These are complex technological advances, requiring a highly skilled workforce, state of the art laboratories and large tranches of research funding from both the public and the private sector. Although human tissue is an essential raw material, its core value is as the canvas upon which genetic scientists and technologists undertake their artistry.

In parallel, there has been ongoing debate surrounding the complex ethical, social and legal issues that are raised by advances in cell and genetic technologies. From the 1970s and 80s, the new, American-inspired discipline of 'bioethics'[11] has begun to look into issues associated with the allocation of medical resources in light of new developments in medical technology, including *in vitro* fertilisation, cloning and genetic testing.[12] Since that time, there have been a plethora of national and international statements on ethical conduct of research, all of which recognise the importance of human rights and the ethical principle of respect for

[7] P Komesaroff, *Troubled Bodies: Critical Perspectives on Postmodernism, Medical Ethics and the Body* (Melbourne, Melbourne University Press, 1995).

[8] See, generally, House of Representatives Standing Committee on Legal and Constitutional Affairs, 'Human Cloning: Scientific, Ethical and Regulatory Aspects of Human Cloning and Stem Cell Research' (AGPS, 2001) 3.23–3.34.

[9] D Chalmers, D Nicol, M Otlowski and C Critchley, 'Personalised Medicine in the Genome Era' (2013) 20 *Journal of Law and Medicine* 577.

[10] M Bobrow, 'Balancing Privacy with Public Benefit' (2013) 500 *Nature* 123.

[11] H Tristram, *The Foundations of Bioethics* (New York, Oxford University Press, 1986) 9.

[12] G Annas, 'American Bioethics and Human Rights: The End of all our Exploring' (2004) 32 *Journal of Law, Medicine & Ethics* 659.

research participants. These statements generally require that research risks and benefits are disclosed to research participants, that participants give their voluntary consent, and that researchers are held accountable, not only to participants, but also to their peers and to human research ethics committees. They also recognise that one of the greatest challenges for research ethics 'is to balance that right to privacy against the legitimate interests that society has in enjoying the benefits of scientific advances'.[13] Privacy laws add legislative teeth to these statements on research ethics in many jurisdictions.

These debates are as lively now as they have ever been. The release of DNA sequence information from an identified cell line in early 2013 highlighted cracks in the ethical framework for research use of human tissue, particularly for tissue samples collected prior to the institution of modern consent requirements.[14] This release of sequence information prompts a reconsideration of the role of property law in resolving disputes about use of human tissue for research purposes. It leads us to question whether human tissue really is a blank canvas on which to apply the artistry of modern genetic and cell technologies.

In the mid twentieth century, cells taken from a young African-American woman, Henrietta Lacks, were immortalised without her consent into what was to become known as the HeLa cell line.[15] The unique attributes of the HeLa cell line have made it highly valuable in the medical research context, from its use by Jonas Salk in the development of the polio vaccine in the early 1950s onwards.[16] Ongoing concerns from descendants of Henrietta Lacks about failure to respect the family's right to privacy and autonomy came to a head in early 2013. DNA sequence information from a HeLa cell line was made publicly available by the highly regarded European Molecular Biology Laboratory and the equally highly respected science journal *Nature* prepared to publish a paper by a different research group that included more detailed sequence information. It was argued by the family that this represented a breach of their privacy as a result of the detailed genetic information being made public. It appears that these justifiable privacy concerns of the descendants of Henrietta Lacks were not considered until the family themselves raised them.[17] The lack of consideration of these concerns was surprising given that issues around making detailed genetic information from individuals publicly available had come to the fore several years earlier with the advent of genome wide association studies, and had largely been dealt with through the generation of data access agreements and restricted access portals.

[13] Submission from the Federal Privacy Commissioner March 2002 to the ALRC/AHEC Report 96, *Essentially Yours: The Protection of Human Genetic Information in Australia* (Australian Government, 2003).

[14] R Skloot, 'The Immortal Life of Henrietta Lacks: The Sequel', *New York Times* (New York, 12 March 2013).

[15] R Skloot, *The Immortal Life of Henrietta Lacks* (Waterville, ME, Gale Cengage Learning, 2011).

[16] ibid. Skloot documents in some detail the contribution that the HeLa cell line has made to medical research.

[17] E Callaway, 'Deal Done over HeLa Cell Line' (2013) 500 *Nature* 132.

In August 2013 it was announced that an agreement had been reached between the director of the National Institutes of Health (NIH) and the Lacks family that sequence information will henceforth only be made available to medical researchers through a controlled-access system. Researchers will be required to submit applications to a new HeLa Genome Data Access working group, which will be based at the NIH and will include within its membership two members of the Lacks family.[18] Meanwhile, these events have, in part, been the trigger for a review of the whole US regulatory regime for the protection of human subjects in research, with particular focus on the nature of the relationship between researchers and participants.[19] It is timely, then, to reflect on the following question: would recognition of the property rights in the HeLa cell line by the Lacks family have made a difference to them in their quest to limit open access to familial genetic information?

Property in Human Tissue

The foundational bioethical principle of autonomy allows individuals to exercise control over their own bodies. Despite this, it has long been thought that there is no property in human bodies as such. This stems from a line of early case law suggesting that there is no property in a buried corpse.[20] Here, key events are highlighted to explain how we reach the conclusion at the end of this section that the courts may struggle to articulate a sound legal rationale for holding that individuals who donate tissue for research purposes have ongoing ownership rights in the donated tissue for the purpose of pursing an action for conversion[21] or other similar property-related actions.

The widely accepted starting point in this story is *Haynes's Case*.[22] Haynes dug up the bodies of three men and one woman, removed the winding sheets in which they were wrapped and then reburied the bodies. The issue was who owned the winding sheets. The court held that the dead body is not capable of possession, that is, a dead body cannot *hold* property. However, this case has been taken as authority for the proposition that a dead body cannot *be* property.[23] The courts later found it necessary to craft a legal mechanism for dealing with unburied corpses and they did this by providing a limited right for executors to exercise

[18] KL Hudson and FS Collins, 'Family Matters' (2013) 500 *Nature* 141.

[19] ibid.

[20] See, eg I Goold, *Flesh and Blood: Owning Our Bodies' and Their Parts* (Oxford, Hart Publishing, forthcoming). See also P Matthews, 'Whose Body? People as Property' (1983) 36 *Current Legal Problems* 193; RS Magnusson, 'Proprietary Rights in Human Tissue' in N Palmer and E McKendrick (eds), *Interests in Goods*, 2nd edn (Routledge, 1998).

[21] Conversion is an action attached to personal property, arising when one person converts another's property for their own use.

[22] *Haynes's Case* (1614) 77 ER 1389.

[23] Goold, *Flesh and Blood: Owning Our Bodies' Parts*, above n 20.

possession over a corpse up to the time of burial.[24] The use of human bodies in the medical context also has a long history, extending back to the nineteenth century, when disinterred corpses were vital resources in the development of the discipline of anatomy.[25] The English Anatomy Act 1832 and the licensing of anatomy instructors and students redressed the improper supply of dead bodies for use in medical schools.

The line of case law continues with judicial recognition of an exception to the no property rule for dead bodies, as illustrated by the early Australian case of *Doodeward v Spence*.[26] In this case, the Australian High Court had to decide whether there was property in the corpse of a two-headed baby that had been stored in a jar and exhibited by the plaintiff, a showman. Although the three judges on the bench gave somewhat different reasons for their decisions, the case has come to be authority for the proposition that a distinction can be drawn between a mere corpse awaiting burial and a body or part of a body that had, through work and skill, acquired some attributes differentiating it from the corpse.[27] More recently, the UK case of *R v Kelly*[28] followed the line of argument in *Doodeward*, that material subjected to processing acquired the attributes of property. Body parts stored in jars at the Royal College of Surgeons were held to be the property of the College and hence it could bring an action for theft.

Other, more complicated issues arise when considering body parts taken from living bodies. There are no clear precedents directly on point from the old case law, although it was generally assumed that the legal position was that there was no property in body parts either. One possible reason for the lack of opportunity for judicial consideration in the past was that there was little or no commercial value in excised body parts. The assumption was either that there was no property in the body part at the time of removal (it was *res nullius*) or, if there was some sort of property right, consent to removal entailed abandonment or gifting of any property claims to the surgeon or hospital removing the tissue.[29]

A series of cases relating to sperm deposits have challenged the 'no property' notion. Some of these have focused on removal of sperm post-mortem. There has been some equivocation in these cases as to whether the *Doodeward* work and skill exception applies.[30] The sperm donation cases *ante morte* are of more interest for present purposes. Particular attention is focused on three of the key cases here. The US case of *Hecht v Superior Court (Kane)*[31] focused on whether vials of sperm

[24] ibid.

[25] O Dyer, 'Working Party Speaks Out on Use of Human Tissue' (1995) 310 *British Medical Journal* 31159, quoting Professor Ian Kennedy; R Scott, *The Body as Property* (London, Allen Lane, 1981) ch 1; M Sappol, *A Traffic in Dead Bodies: Anatomy and Embodied Social Identity in Nineteenth-Century America* (Princeton, NJ, Princeton University Press, 2002).

[26] *Doodeward v Spence* (1908) 6 CLR 406.

[27] See, eg, *Doodeward v Spence* (1908) 6 CLR 406, 414 per Griffith CJ.

[28] *R v Kelly* [1998] 3 All ER 741.

[29] M Quigley, 'Property in Human Biomaterials – Separating Persons and Things?', above n 5, 659.

[30] Reviewed in L Skene, 'Proprietary Interests in Human Bodily Material: *Yearworth*, Recent Australian Cases on Stored Semen and their Implications' (2012) 20 *Medical Law Review* 227.

[31] *Hecht v Superior Court (Kane)* [1993] 16 Cal App 4th 836.

collected prior to death could be bequeathed by will. The court concluded that, at the time of his death, the donor had an ownership interest in his ejaculated sperm that was sufficient to give the probate court jurisdiction. Some 16 years later, the UK decision of *Yearworth v North Bristol NHS Trust*[32] focused on the destruction of sperm specimens from six men who claimed they had suffered mental harm as a result of this destruction. The court held that this was compensable through gratuitous bailment on the basis that the donors retained ownership rights because the sperm was being held for future use by them. The Australian case of *Bazley v Wesley Monash IVF*[33] related to sperm taken prior to death but not mentioned in the donor's will. The court held that property continued to subsist in the sperm and that ownership resided in the donor's personal representative following his death.[34]

These cases mark a significant development in the law relating to property rights in human tissue, in that they reflect judicial recognition that individuals can legally claim to have property rights in tissue removed from their bodies. However, the jurisprudential rationale to explain how and when these property rights crystallise remains obscure. Attempts to use separation, or even separation with intention to use, as a suitable rationale have been emphatically debunked by Muireann Quigley, and other more compelling explanations remain to be elucidated.[35] As the focus of this chapter is on the status of human tissue once it has been donated for research, it is not on point to delve further into these complex jurisprudential questions.

In these cases the courts seemed willing to recognise ongoing property rights because the sperm had been taken for storage and future use *by the donor*. The situation is different when tissue is provided for research purposes, because there is no intention of return to the donor.[36] In the *Moore* case this issue was squarely raised. The question was whether John Moore retained any property right in his spleen cells, such that he could sue his treating physician for converting them to his own use for profit. The case arose because Moore was a sufferer of hairy cell leukaemia and had his spleen removed as part of his treatment. The Mo cell line, derived from Moore's spleen cells, was subsequently patented and proved to be a commercial success. Moore sued for conversion and for breach of fiduciary duty or lack of informed consent. The majority decision of the Californian Supreme

[32] *Yearworth v North Bristol NHS Trust* [2010] QB 1.

[33] *Bazley v Wesley Monash IVF* [2010] QSC 118. It should be noted that the case of *Jocelyn Edwards; Re the estate of the late Mark Edwards* [2011] NSWSC 478, though also relating to stored sperm, raises somewhat different considerations as the sperm in this case was collected post mortem.

[34] See Skene, 'Proprietary Interests in Human Bodily Material: *Yearworth*, Recent Australian Cases on Stored Semen and their Implications', above n 30 and references to other academic commentary therein.

[35] Quigley, 'Property in Human Biomaterials – Separating Persons and Things?', above n 5.

[36] For reviews of recent case law, see R Hakimian and D Korn, 'Ownership and Use of Tissue Specimens for Research' (2004) 292 *Journal of American Medical Association* 2500; MJ Allen, MLE Powers, KS Gronowski and AM Gronowski, 'Human Tissue Ownership and Use in Research: What Laboratorians and Researchers Should Know' (2010) 56 *Clinical Chemistry* 1675.

Court emphatically rejected the notion that Moore could sue in conversion, but accepted that the other grounds were available.

Since *Moore* there have been two other notable decisions in the US which together provide some hints as to the subsistence and scope of property rights in human tissue. The first was *Greenberg v Miami Children's Hospital*.[37] In this case the plaintiffs and others were involved as research participants in a study being conducted by researchers at the Miami Children's Hospital into Canavan's disease. This is a genetic disorder afflicting children of Eastern European Jewish descent, causing stunted development, lack of muscle tone, blinding and ultimately death. In 1994 the gene causing Canavan's disease was isolated and a test was developed. Unknown to the plaintiffs, a patent application was also filed and issued in 1997.

The Greenbergs and others brought an action against the hospital on a number of grounds, including conversion. The dispute was settled out of court, although one opportunity was provided for judicial consideration of the plaintiffs' case when the defendants filed a motion to dismiss. The court decided that the motion should be upheld in part, holding that the 'plaintiffs have no cognizable property interest in body tissue and genetic matter donated for research under a theory of conversion'. The court interpreted *Moore* to hold that 'the use of the results of medical research inconsistent with the wishes of the donor was not conversion, because the donor had no property interest at stake after the donation was made'.[38] This is important because it indicates that the predicament for the plaintiffs was not so much that they never had property rights in their tissue but that by the act of donation they had relinquished all such rights.

In *Catalona* the dispute was between the researcher, Catalona and the university with regard to ownership of prostate cancer tissue samples. Donors had sought to transfer ownership to Catalona after he left the university. The court held that there was no bailment relationship between the donors and the university as ownership of the tissue had been transferred as *inter vivos* gifts under the law of Missouri, stating that

> [the bailment] argument fails for the simple reason that when a 'gift' is made, the giftor/donor has no expectation of getting the 'gift' back; however, when a 'bailment' is made, the bailor has every expectation of receiving back the subject of the bailment.[39]

If these cases accurately reflect law in the US and in other common law jurisdictions, donations of tissue for research purposes amount to absolute *inter vivos* gifts. On this basis, property law will not come to the aid of donors even when they raise legitimate concerns as to the conduct of researchers using their stored tissue or using cell lines derived from their tissue. This would seem to be the case

[37] *Greenberg v Miami Children's Hospital Research Institute* 264 F Supp 2d (US District Court Florida Miami Division, 2003) 1063.

[38] ibid, 1074.

[39] *Washington University v Catalona* 437 F Supp 2d 985 (US District Court Missouri Eastern Division, 2006) 1001.

irrespective of whether or not donors have cognate property rights in their tissue prior to donation. Given the evolving nature of the jurisprudence in this area, any predictions as to how the courts might approach this question are speculative at best. However, based on the rationales articulated in the most recent sperm donation cases, there seems to be little room for the courts to manoeuvre in crafting residual property rights for donors of tissue provided for research purposes, in the absence of express contractual provisions.

Despite this, some organisations involved in long-term storage of human tissue for research purposes in both the public and private sector require donors to disavow any possible 'property rights' in their tissue, suggesting that they see the law as unsettled on this question. UK Biobank, one of the largest public sector organisations involved in long-term storage of tissue and genetic date for research, states in section IIA of its Ethics and Governance Framework that 'Participants will not have property rights in the samples'.[40] Similarly, 23andme, one of the largest companies involved in direct to consumer genetic testing and storage of genetic data for future research, includes the following term in its consent form:

> Waiver of Property Rights: You understand that by providing any sample, having your Genetic Information processed, accessing your Genetic Information, or providing Self-Reported Information, you acquire no rights in any research or commercial products that may be developed by 23andMe or its collaborating partners. You specifically understand that you will not receive compensation for any research or commercial products that include or result from your Genetic Information or Self-Reported Information.[41]

Thus, it would seem that, for these organisations at least, the paintbrushes are still being applied to the unfinished property portrait.

Ethical and Legal Governance of Research Involving Human Tissue

Alongside this property portrait, brushstrokes have gradually been applied to the ethical and legal landscape for research use of human tissue. There are two major themes in this developing landscape: the consent of the participant, and the privacy and confidentiality of their personal information.

The Nuremberg Code was the watershed in the development of modern research ethics.[42] The Code was a direct response to the inhumane and cruel

[40] UK Biobank Ethics and Governance Framework, available at: www.ukbiobank.ac.uk/wp-content/uploads/2011/05/EGF20082.pdf?phpMyAdmin=trmKQlYdjjnQIgJ%2CfAzikMhEnx6.

[41] 23andme Terms of Service, cl 6(k), available at: www.23andme.com/about/tos/.

[42] D Chalmers, 'International Medical Research Regulation: From Ethics to Law' in S McLean (ed), *First Do No Harm* (Aldershot, Ashgate Publishing, 2006) 81–100.

experimentation conducted in Nazi concentration camps.[43] Similar revelations were later to emerge about Japanese atrocities in biological and chemical 'experiments' conducted on prisoners in Unit 731 in China between 1932 and 1945.[44] The Nuremberg Code laid down 10 principles for ethical and voluntary participation in research and represents a significant landmark in the progress towards the regulation of human experimentation. These 10 principles were developed and amplified in the seminal Declaration of Helsinki, formally developed and adopted by the 18th World Medical Assembly in Helsinki in June 1964. The Declaration has been amended on many occasions and established the key pillar of voluntary consent of all research participants in medical research. The other key pillars are: independent review of the project by an ethics committee, proper assessment of the risk, competent researchers and research merit.

Events in the US also had a significant impact in the international development of medical research ethics. The Tuskegee Syphilis Study[45] was one of a number of publicised and egregious failures of proper human research standards. In response, the National Research Act 1974 established the National Commission for the Protection of Human Subjects of Biomedical and Behavioral Research and, importantly, required each institution conducting federally supported research involving human subjects to establish an institutional review board. The formalisation of the US review board system has been influential in the development of research ethics committees around the world.

While variations exist between national ethics frameworks, there is a remarkably consistent foundation which emphasises respect for individual autonomy, beneficence (or non-maleficence) and justice, and these values are reiterated in bioethical commentary.[46] In Australia, for example, research is expected to be conducted according to the principles and values outlined in the National Statement on Ethical Conduct in Human Research, Values and Ethics: Guidelines for Ethical Conduct in Aboriginal and Torres Strait Islander Health Research, and the Australian Code for the Responsible Conduct of Research.[47] Although these

[43] See G Annas and M Grodin (eds), *The Nazi Doctors and the Nuremberg Code: Human Rights in Human Experimentation* (New York, Oxford University Press, 1992); D Winkler and J Barondess, 'Bioethics and Anti-Bioethics in Light of Nazi Medicine: What We Must Remember?' (1993) *Kennedy Institute of Ethics Journal* 39.

[44] JB Nie, NY Guo, M Selden and A Kleinman (eds), *Japan's Wartime Medical Atrocities: Comparative Inquiries in Science, History, and Ethics* (London and New York, Routledge, 2010). Unlike the German Nuremberg trials, many of the scientists in Unit 731 were not prosecuted or evidence was suppressed by the US forces.

[45] B Furrow, T Greaney, S Johnson, T Jost and R Schwartz, *Health Law*, 2nd edn (St Paul, MN, West Group, 2000) 979.

[46] TL Beauchamp and JF Childress, *Principles of Biomedical Ethics* (Oxford, Oxford University Press, 1979); RM Veatch, *A Theory of Medical Ethics* (New York, Basic Books, 1981); TH Engelhardt, *The Foundations of Bioethics* (New York, Oxford University Press, 1986).

[47] National Health and Medical Research Council, *National Statement on Ethical Conduct in Human Research* (Canberra, Australian Government, 2007); National Health and Medical Research Council, *Values and Ethics: Guidelines for Ethical Conduct in Aboriginal and Torres Strait Islander Health Research* (Canberra, Australian Government, 2003); Australian Research Council and National Health and Medical Research Council, *Australian Code for the Responsible Conduct of Research* (Canberra, Australian Government, 2007).

guidelines are not legally binding, they are enforced through a complex system of self-regulation. Institutions, academic journals and funding bodies require that studies are approved and monitored by accredited human research ethics committees (HRECs), and ethical review is conducted with explicit reference to these guidelines, law and normative ethics. The consequences for transgression of these guidelines can include withdrawal of ethical approval, cessation of research activity, revocation of funding, and non-publication or retraction of academic papers. Part of the reason for the success of the self-regulation of research ethics is the centrality of public trust to the ongoing success of health and medical research. Trust in the entire research enterprise is damaged by unethical practices, providing substantial incentive for researchers and institutions to contribute to creating a culture of ethical research.

Aside from formal recognition that research involving human tissue is a required area for ethics review, there has also been a raft of official reports on this topic, which have contributed to the positive changes in attitudes and practices. The Nuffield Council in the UK published their report, *Human Tissue: Ethical and Legal Issues*, in 1995 on the ethical and legal framework for medical and scientific uses of human tissue in organ transplantation, pharmaceutical testing and genetic research.[48] This was followed the National Bioethics Advisory Commission report *Research Involving Human Biological Materials: Ethical Issues and Policy Guidance* in 1998, that recognised the importance of human biological materials continuing for biomedical research and that it was 'crucial that the more than 282 million specimens already in storage remain accessible under appropriate conditions and with appropriate protections for the individuals who supplied this material'.[49] In the same year, the European Group on Ethics in Science and New Technologies published their *Opinion on Human Tissue Banking* recommending, inter alia, that standards be developed for the quality and safety of human tissues and surveys undertaken in member states on the procurement, storage and distribution of human tissues and imports. Subsequently, the Colleges of Pathology in the US and the UK developed a consensus statement in 1999 that set a new direction for human tissue research considering the ethical issues of genetic testing and the use of stored archives in research, education, audit and quality control.[50]

Research utilising the data and tissue provided by human participants is governed by privacy laws as well as ethics frameworks. Legal obligations relating to privacy can be divided into three main forms in the common law world. First, the equitable duty of confidentiality obliges researchers not to use or disclose participant information for any reason other than that for which it was provided, although it includes exceptions to use or disclose information in cases where

[48] www.nuffieldbioethics.org/human-tissue/human-tissue-human-tissue-uk-developments.

[49] National Bioethics Advisory Commission, *Research Involving Human Biological Materials: Ethical Issues and Policy Guidance* (1998).

[50] Royal College of Pathologists, *Consensus Statement of Recommended Policies for Uses of Human Tissue in Research Education and Quality Control* (London, Royal College of Pathologists, 1999) 15. See also, R Ashcroft, 'The Ethics of Re-using Archived Tissue for Research' (2000) 26 *Neuropathy and Applied Neurobiology* 408.

consent has been provided, where it is in the public interest, or where it is authorised by a statutory authority. Secondly, privacy legislation regulates the use and disclosure of personal information, which includes any data from which an individual's identity could reasonably be ascertained.[51] This definition represents a shifting baseline, in that technical and computational advances allow for the identification of data and samples that once would have reasonably been considered deidentified.[52] Finally, researchers may also be bound to contractual obligations relating to privacy and ethical conduct under funding and data access agreements.

Given the speed with which research capabilities are expanding, based largely on technological developments, regulatory approaches that employ prescriptive methods – either in the form of legislation or guidelines – are unable adequately to address the range of issues that these new capabilities introduce. As a result, HRECs increasingly require evidence of extensive community consultation as part of new research projects, particularly in potentially controversial or emergent fields, such as biobanking, genetic research in indigenous populations, or unspecified future use of samples collected in clinical trials.[53] Involving participants as partners in the research process, rather than passive subjects, is known as participatory governance and is recognised as an effective mechanism for engaging with challenging ethical issues, for greater recognition of the role of social determinants of health, and for contributing to promoting scientific literacy and public trust in health research.[54] Participatory approaches extend traditional methods in two important ways: respect and autonomy can be extended to groups as well as individuals; and informed consent becomes an ongoing process of dialogue between researchers and participants rather than a single, focused exchange of (often limited) information for agreement to use samples and data.

Just as the property model remains an unfinished canvas, so too, the research governance landscape could benefit from some further application of Renoir's brushes. At present, there are widespread community expectations that all research involving humans, including research involving human tissue, will be conducted ethically, professionally and equitably with the prior knowledge and voluntary consent of participants. However, the Lacks and Moore case studies illustrate that it was not that long ago that tissue was routinely used for research purposes without the consent of the donor. More recently, on the other side of the

[51] In Australia, for example, The Privacy Act 1988 (Aus) specifies a set of Australian privacy principles that federal government organisations and private entities collecting personal information must comply with.

[52] This includes advances in data linkage and use of genomic identification methods: M Gymrek et al, 'Identifying Personal Genomes by Surname Inference' (2013) 339 *Science* 321.

[53] H Gottweis and G Lauss, 'Biobank Governance in the Post-genomic Age' (2010) 7 *Personalised Medicine* 187; M Brant Castellano, 'Ethics of Aboriginal Research' (2004) 1 *Journal of Aboriginal Health* 98; MW Foster et al, 'The Role of Community Review in Evaluating the Risks of Human Genetic Variation Research' (1999) 64 *American Journal of Human Genetics* 1719.

[54] M Yarborough, K Fryer-Edwards, G Geller and RR Sharp, 'Transforming the Culture of Biomedical Research from Compliance to Trustworthiness: Insights from Nonmedical Sectors' (2009) 84 *Academic Medicine* 472; RE McWhirter, D Nicol, D Chalmers and JL Dickinson, 'Body Ownership and Research' (2013) 21(2) *Journal of Law and Medicine* 323.

Atlantic, wide critical coverage was given to the UK inquiries into hospitals in Bristol and Liverpool concerning the improper and non-consensual storage of human organs and tissue samples.[55]

If we look, with the wisdom of hindsight, to the HeLa cell line case, would the modern brushes have painted a different and more satisfactory picture? Under the present system, an HREC reviewing this project would require those involved in collecting, cultivating and disseminating Lacks' cells to change a number of critical actions. First, Lacks' treating clinicians would need to obtain her informed consent prior to taking a tissue sample, including providing her with information about the potential risks involved, what the sample would be used for, who would have access to the sample, any commercialisation potential and benefit sharing plans. Secondly, the researchers would need to have a clear plan in place to protect Lacks' privacy, including – but not limited to – a better coding system than using the first two letters of her name, and not disclosing her identity to the press or other team members beyond her treating clinician. Thirdly, there would need to be a clear plan for recontacting family members, taking into account their right to refuse, but not overburdening them with constant requests for consent to minor changes in research protocols. It would be a fair summary to say that very little of the way this case was handled would meet with the approval of modern HRECs.

The four major issues at the centre of the controversy surrounding HeLa cells are: consent; privacy, both for Lacks and for her family; commercialisation; and mistrust. Had the laws and guidelines now established been in force in the 1950s, Henrietta Lacks would have given her informed consent (or the sample would not have been taken); she would have been informed about the potential for commercialisation if her cells were able to be kept alive; and her identity – and that of her family – would have remained confidential. But what of the arguable breach of privacy for her family members entailed by the 2013 public release of the HeLa sequence data?[56] Although current laws and guidelines do not explicitly address this situation, had the researchers involved engaged best practice and involved Lacks' family members in some form of participatory governance process,[57] the subsequent furore may well have been avoided. Indeed, the NIH were ultimately forced to engage in precisely this sort of process, working closely with the family

[55] Department of Health UK, *Human Bodies, Human Choices: The Law on Human Organs and Tissue in England and Wales – A Consultation Report* (2002).

[56] It could be argued that the HeLa cell line contains so many genetic mutations stemming from its source as a tumour sample and from having been grown in culture for more than 60 years that it would be difficult to infer much about heritable variants with any accuracy, that the cell line is almost ubiquitous and could therefore be sequenced by any researcher with access to the appropriate equipment, and that it is difficult to make conclusions about relatives' health from genomic data alone. However, these points remain contentious, and fail to acknowledge the likely development of more advanced technological or computational methods that may negate these points or the difficulty of recalling data once publicly released.

[57] The right of family members to control the use or disclosure of genetic data remains unclear. However, this instance is further complicated by the fact that consent was not originally obtained, and that the identity of Henrietta Lacks, and that of her family, is so widely known.

to establish a plan that balanced the family's concerns with the needs of the scientific community.[58] The family have stated that they are not interested in hindering biomedical research – in fact, they have expressed pride in the fact that their relative's cells have helped so many people – but their experience with scientists over the past six decades has been confusing, upsetting and has contributed to a mistrust of scientific intentions.[59] Involving the family in the research process as equal partners would help to address these issues, perhaps more effectively than the potential divisiveness of relying on a property claim.

In conclusion, an application of modern research governance requirements would provide a better, but not necessarily perfect, picture. It will only be perfect if all of the constituent artists behave according to the highest ethical standards of the time in the research studio.

Do We Need Property?

This chapter illustrates the point that to date there has been no support from the courts for the recognition of ongoing donor property rights in tissue donated for research purposes. One major problem is a lack of relevant cases coming to the courts; another is the reluctance of those judges who are given the opportunity to consider this issue to shackle research to the monolith of property law. Rather, the courts in *Moore*, *Greenberg* and *Catalona* were more comfortable with recognising the role played by voluntary consent of the tissue donor.

In the context of the HeLa case study, it would be unthinkable that a cell line of this nature could be created *de novo* at this point in time without full engagement with the research ethics framework. There may have been times during the past 60 years when clear recognition of ongoing donor property rights in tissue might have assisted Henrietta Lacks' descendants in being involved in the governance of research utilising the HeLa cell line. Practically, given the circumstances of the time, it must be seen as unlikely that a court hearing the case would have taken such a step.

The power of publicity and the increasing recognition on the part of science policy makers of the importance of community trust have coalesced in 2013 to provide a solution to the HeLa cell predicament which is respectful to the descendants of Henrietta Lacks and guarantees ongoing research access to this important resource. In this context, then, it could be argued that a property regime for dealing with human tissue samples donated for research purposes is otiose. But what if the NIH had not taken the concerns expressed by the descendants of Henrietta Lacks seriously? Could a case be made for asserting that they have ongo-

[58] R Skloot, 'The Immortal Life of Henrietta Lacks: the Sequel', *New York Times*, above n 14; KL Hudson and FS Collins, 'Family Matters' (2013) 500 *Nature* 141.

[59] R Skloot, *The Immortal Life of Henrietta Lacks*, above n 15.

ing property rights? Could property law be used as a weapon against the researchers involved in sequencing the HeLa cell line? Aside from the obvious problem of lack of precedent, questions would need to be asked about whether there is a sufficient link to the original cells taken from Lacks' body. Arguably, there was sufficient exercise of skill involved in isolating and maintaining the cell line over successive generations to break the chain of ownership.[60] It is difficult to know whether the courts would see Henrietta Lacks' cells as a blank canvas or a fully formed masterpiece.

While Renoir could not have claimed ownership if Monet used his canvas and materials to paint *Water Lilies*, he deserved some acknowledgement. So too should we distinguish between ownership of the research endeavours resulting from the use of human tissue and the right to proper attribution, recognition and respect (within the broader context of protection of privacy). In the modern research context there is probably now a need to revise the current rather limp consequences of research impropriety. There is a need for wider responsibility from all actors in the research endeavour. The modern movement towards participatory governance, embracing the direct and future interests of the participants is an important step in the right direction. This is classically illustrated by the governance mechanisms being introduced by large-scale population biobanks. This would resonate with JW Harris' view that property rights should be based on fundamental minimalist conceptions of justice including natural equality, autonomous choice and bodily integrity.[61]

There may be cases that come to the courts in the future which raise questions around whether donors have residual property rights in tissue donated for research purposes, but such cases are only likely to arise where there have been egregious abuses of research protocols. In such instances, property law remains a useful weapon of last resort, particularly if the judiciary embraces arguments relating, for example, to conditional gifting.[62] As such, it is not denied that property law remains an integral part of the broad regulatory canvas for research use of human tissue. However, it is only ever likely to provide a minor brushstroke in this context.

[60] Recognised by the US Office of Technology Assessment as 'difficult, often an art'. See D Nicol 'Property in Human Tissue and the Right of Commercialisation: the Interface Between Tangible and Intellectual Property' (2004) 30 *Monash University Law Review* 139 at 151.

[61] JW Harris, *Property and Justice* (Oxford, Clarendon Press, 1996) 171–76.

[62] See, eg C Stewart, J Fleming and I Kerridge, 'The Law of Gifts, Conditional Donation and Biobanking' (2013) 21(2) *Journal of Law and Medicine* 351.

3

The Problems of Biobanking and the Law of Gifts

CAMERON STEWART, WENDY LIPWORTH, LORENA APARICIO, JENNIFER FLEMING and IAN KERRIDGE

Introduction

The practice of biobanking is of major importance to biomedical research in modern western economies. However, biobanking is beset by a number of ethical and legal concerns including issues of consent, control and privacy. Recent developments in the networking of biobanks and the sharing of samples and data have exacerbated these issues. This paper outlines these problems and then examines how they can be understood through the law of gifts.

Much of the debate on how tissue is donated to biobanks has occurred without reference to the law of gifts. This is most probably due to the *res nullius* rule, which, until recently, has prevented unprocessed human tissue from being considered an object of property.[1] However, recent changes to the common law's approach to human tissue invite a reconsideration of the role that gifts law can play in tissue banking (and tissue donation more generally).[2] This paper assumes that tissue which has not been subject to work and skill may nevertheless be held as property and that the decision to donate to a tissue bank can be treated as an example of a legally recognised gift.

The paper begins with an example of tissue banking and the legal and ethical issues which it raises. Most prominent among these difficulties is the focus in tissue banking on informed consent, a doctrine originally designed to deal with negligence advice and bodily interferences in medical treatment and research. While understandable, the focus on informed consent has created a number of problems particularly in areas of unspecified research, unanticipated findings and privacy.

[1] *Doodeward v Spence* (1908) 6 CLR 406; *Dobson v North Tyneside Health Authority* [1997] 1 WLR 596; *R v Kelly and Lindsay* [1999] QB 621.

[2] *Yearworth v North Bristol NHS Trust* [2010] QB 1; *Bazley v Wesley Monash IVF Pty Ltd* [2011] 2 Qd R 207; *Re Edwards* (2011) 81 NSWLR 198; *Re H (No 2)* [2012] SASC 177; *Re Section 22 of the Human Tissue and Transplant Act 1982; ex parte C* [2013] WASC 3.

The chapter then moves to review the basic law of gifts by examining the elements of gifts in both law and equity and the requirements for conveying them. The chapter also explains the law's capacity to creates the possibility of conditional dispositions which allow donors to maintain some rights over the tissue, with the possibility of a form of interest which would enable the donor to regain possession and control of their tissue in the case of a breach. This paper argues that an application of the law of gifts is a flexible and useful way of reconceptualising the ethical and legal difficulties of biobanking.

Biobanks and Biobank Networks

What Are Biobanks and What Do They Do?

Biobanks (also known as tissue banks, biorepositories and tissue repositories) are collections of human body materials that can be used in medical treatments (for example, blood banks or cornea banks), research, teaching, law enforcement (for example, DNA collections) and museums. The body tissues that make up biobanks may have been removed from healthy donors, from patients in the course of medical diagnosis or therapy, or from bodies post-mortem.

By collecting and storing large numbers of tissue samples from healthy populations and/or patients with a particular disease, researchers are able to correlate characteristics of the tissue with the aetiology, prognosis or treatment responsiveness of a disease. Advances in science and laboratory technology such as tissue immortalisation, rapid genome sequencing, genome-wide association studies, mass spectrometry and tissue microarrays, together with a deeper understanding of systems biology and advances in information technology enable researchers to extract enormous amounts of genetic or other molecular data from tissue samples, and to find clinically significant patterns in these data.[3]

Biobanks facilitate 'translational' research because they enable researchers to identify 'biomarkers' that tell them which patients are most likely to develop a disease and/or respond to a particular treatment. In this way, prevention and therapy can be 'targeted' or 'personalised' to those who express a particular biomarker. Many cancer cells, for example, express particular genes or proteins that contribute to the aetiology, prognosis or treatment responsiveness of the tumour. Once these markers are discovered, pharmaceutical companies can develop 'targeted' therapies, such as 'Herceptin' for breast cancer and 'Gleevec' for chronic

[3] PH Watson et al, 'Evolutionary Concepts in Biobanking – The BC BioLibrary' (2009) *Journal of Translational Medicine* 7; RWG Watson, EW Kay and D Smith, 'Integrating Biobanks: Addressing the Practical and Ethical Issues to Deliver a Valuable Tool for Cancer Research' (2010) 10 *Nature Reviews Cancer* 646; BM Knoppers et al, 'From Genomic Databases to Translation: A Call to Action' (2011) 37 *Journal of Medical Ethics* 515.

myeloid leukaemia, and those funding medicines can limit access to those who are most likely to respond to these (often very expensive) treatments.[4]

The globalisation of research and the increasing involvement of the pharmaceutical and biotechnology industry in research have also provided a major impetus for the development and expansion of biobanks. To support the discovery of biomarkers, most clinical trials now include the collection and storage of tissue as part of their standard protocol.[5] However, while the biomedical and commercial value of biobanks have been widely recognised by industry, government and philanthropic bodies it has also become clear that the storage and use of biobanked materials in research continues to stimulate numerous unresolved and emerging ethical and legal tensions.

Emerging Problems in Biobanking Practice

Key among the problems of biobanking is the issue of consent. While it used to be the norm for residual tissue removed in the course of diagnosis or therapy to be used for research without consent,[6] it is now widely accepted that donors need to be asked for permission to store and use their samples.[7] Ethical disagreements about consent frequently centre on the tension between individual autonomy, or respect for persons, and the 'common good' – a tension that is seen to be particularly significant in the context of biobanking research because this often depends upon the participation of large numbers of people (including healthy populations), many of whom are unlikely to benefit from the results of the research. This tension is increased by the fact that pharmaceutical and biotechnology companies are increasingly creating their own biobanks as part of their basic research and clinical trial activities, with the intention of benefiting shareholders rather than tissue donors.[8] In this context, it is arguably important to ensure that donors are fully informed of the potential risks and benefits of their donation.[9]

Informed consent is a legal and ethical doctrine concerned with ensuring that medical practitioners inform patients about the material risks of treatment and research interventions. It is primarily focused on providing a patient with enough information for them to be able to decide whether or not to become involved in a

[4] Watson et al, 'Evolutionary Concepts in Biobanking', above n 3, 7; Watson, Kay and Smith, 'Integrating Biobanks' above n 3, 646.

[5] BM Knoppers, MnH Zawati et al, 'Sampling Populations of Humans Across the World: ELSI Issues' (2012) 13 *Annual Review of Genomics and Human Genetics* 395.

[6] B Morrell et al, 'Cancer as Rubbish: Donation of Tumour Tissue for Research' (2011) 21 *Qualitative Health Research* 75–81.

[7] EW Clayton et al, 'Informed Consent for Genetic Research on Stored Tissue Samples' (1995) 22 *Journal of the American Medical Association* 1786; L Trommelmans, J Selling and K Dierickx, 'The Importance of the Values Attached to Cells for a Good Informed Consent Procedure in Cell Donation for Tissue Engineering Purposes' (2009) 10 *Cell and Tissue Banking* 293.

[8] Knoppers, Zawati et al, above n 5.

[9] S Cervo et al, 'An Effective Multisource Informed Consent Procedure for Research and Clinical Practice: An Observational Study of Patient Understanding and Awareness of Their Roles as Research Stakeholders in a Cancer Biobank' (2013) *BMC Medical Ethics* doi: 10.1186/1472-6939-14-30.

course of treatment or research. Given that most tissue is collected during a medical or research intervention, on one hand, it makes sense that the same model of consent as for tissue banking be employed. However, on the other hand, it can also be argued that informed consent is an inappropriate model to adopt for biobanking because donors will be asked to consent to having their tissue used in unspecified future research where the risks are completely unknown.[10] Moreover, the tissue is no longer part of the donor's body so concepts of the harm and benefit of research necessary take on quite different forms. Given the lack of knowledge about what will happen to the tissue in the future consent processes must be very broad, so broad that they arguably bear little resemblance to an 'informed' consent process.[11]

A number of other ethical issues arise in the context of biobanking research. First, because even a single cell contains a donor's entire genome, steps need to be taken by researchers to ensure that information derived from donated tissue does not find its way into the hands of, for example, employers or insurance companies.[12] Second, there is the issue of whether and how research findings should be reported to tissue donors.[13] While it is standard for consent forms to state that donors will not benefit personally from donating their tissue to biobanks, it is unclear when information becomes clinically significant and thus when researchers have an obligation to return information to tissue donors and/or their healthcare professionals.[14] Third, some cultural groups see human tissue as having particular moral or religious significance. For these groups, even a tumour removed in the course of diagnosis or treatment might need to be stored or discarded according to particular rules or rituals.[15]

[10] C Stewart, J Fleming and I Kerridge, 'The Law of Gifts, Conditional Donation and Biobanking' (2013) 21(2) *Journal of Law and Medicine* 351; T Caulfield, R Brown and E Meslin, 'Challenging a Well Established Consent Norm? One Time Consent for Biobank Research' (2007) 4 *Journal of International Biotechnology Law* 69; T Caulfield, 'Biobanks and Blanket Consent: The Proper Place of the Public Good and Public Perception Rationales' (2007) 18 *Kings Law Journal* 209; M Otlowski, 'Developing an Appropriate Consent Model for Biobanks: In Defence of "Broad" Consent' in J Kaye and M Stranger (eds), *Principles and Practice of Biobank Governance* (Ashgate, Aldershot, 2009); and National Health and Medical Research Council of Australia, *Biobanks Information Paper* (2010) 23–25.

[11] CJ Allen, M Yann and P Granados, 'Data Sharing, Biobanks and Informed Consent: A Research Paradox' (2013) 7 *McGill Journal of Law and Health* 85.

[12] B Elger, 'Ethics and Privacy of Biobanks' (2013) 35 *Clinical Therapeutics* e116; G Lauss et al, 'Towards Biobank Privacy Regimes in Responsible Innovation Societies: ESBB Conference in Granada 2012' (2013) 11 *Biopreservation and Biobanking* 319; S Burningham, 'Cell Therapy Research and Innovation: Identifying the Emerging Privacy Challenges' (2012) 12 *Medical Law International* 204; J Sándor, 'From Private to Public? Legal Concepts of the Right to Privacy and Ownership in the Regulation of Biobanks' in K Dierickx and P Borry (eds), *New Challenges for Biobanks: Ethics, Law and Governance* (Antwerp, Intersentia, 2009) 123–36; LO Ursin, 'Biobank Research and the Right to Privacy' (2008) 29 *Theoretical Medicine and Bioethics* 267.

[13] SA Alessi, 'The Return of Results in Genetic Testing: Who Owes What to Whom, When, and Why?' (2013) 64 *Hastings Law Journal* 1697.

[14] EW Clayton, 'Incidental Findings in Genetics Research Using Archived DNA' (2008) 36 *Journal of Law and Medical Ethics* 286, 212; SM Wolf, BN Crock et al, 'Managing Incidental Findings and Research Results in Genomic Research Involving Biobanks and Archived Data Sets' (2012) 14 *Genetic Medicine* 361; L Black et al, 'Funding Considerations for the Disclosure of Genetic Incidental Findings in Biobank Research' (2013) 84 *Clinical Genetics* 397.

[15] RE Axler et al, 'Why Might People Donate Tissue for Cancer Research? Insights From Organ/Tissue/Blood Donation and Clinical Research' (2008) 75 *Pathobiology* 323.

From Biobanks to Biobanking Networks

Another recent ethical problem for biobanking relates to networking. While biobanks have historically been defined in terms of their institutional or geographical location, increasingly human specimens are becoming part of national and international networks of biobanks. This has been made possible by new scientific and computer technologies which have increased our ability to categorise, organise and share samples and data, and it is now broadly accepted that biobanks have the greatest potential as resources for translational research if they are networked, nationally and internationally.[16] This is simply because the larger and more integrated a biobank, the greater the power of the research that can be conducted.

As part of a global project (see www.genebanc.eu) funded by the European Commission's 6th Framework Programme, Shickle and colleagues identified six types of non-mutually exclusive or exhaustive categories of biobanking networks which include:

- 'storage' networks, where storage facilities are shared among biobanks to reduce cost and raise quality;
- 'bring-and-share storage' networks, which offer lower fee structures for researchers to encourage sharing of resources with other researchers;
- 'catalogue' networks, which maintain a database that is searchable by external researchers seeking samples for their research;
- 'partnership' networks, which attempt to share costs and effort in recruitment;
- 'contribution' networks, where people contribute relevant specimens to disease specific biobank(s); and
- 'expertise' networks, which share expertise rather than samples.[17]

There are many types of research which can only be conducted if biobanks are networked. For some research questions, enormous numbers of samples are needed. For example, in the case of tissue collected from healthy populations for longitudinal analyses (observing a population for the occurrence of a disease and attempting to isolate relevant aetiological biomarkers), it is estimated that the DNA of about 10,000 diseased individuals needs to be analysed in order to identify a relevant genetic variant.[18] Biobank networks are also crucial in the study of rare diseases, where a single researcher cannot possibly collect enough

[16] J Kaye, 'From Single Biobanks to International Networks: Developing e-Governance' (2011) 130 *Human Genetics* 377; J Kaye, 'Building a Foundation for Biobanking: The 2009 OECD Guidelines on Human Biobanks and Genetic Research Databases' (2010) 17 *European Journal of Health Law* 187; J Kaye et al, 'Data Sharing in Genomics – Re-Shaping Scientific Practice' (2009) 10 *Nature Reviews Genetics* 331.

[17] D Shickle et al, 'Inter- and Intra-Biobank Networks: Classification of Biobanks' (2010) 77 *Pathobiology* 181.

[18] M Asslaber and K Zatloukal, 'Biobanks: Transnational, European and Global Networks' (2007) 6 *Briefings in Functional Genomics and Proteomics* 193.

samples,[19] and even common diseases such as cancer and heart disease are increasingly seen to comprise a number of rare disease subsets characterised by, for example, specific genetic polymorphisms.[20] Networks are also essential in cases where it is socially and logistically difficult to obtain tissue – for example collecting post-mortem brain tissue in the face of a decline in the number of autopsies conducted and more stringent consent requirements for tissue retention.[21] Pharmaceutical companies also need large networks of biobanks in order to meet the regulatory requirement that they study samples and data from populations of different ethnic origins in the course of their clinical trials.[22] Finally, it has become increasingly clear that single biobanks, particularly those maintained by single institutions, are rarely sustainable and are inefficient, duplicating the resources and activities of other similar biobanks.[23]

While the networking of biobanks undoubtedly holds major scientific, commercial and social promise, networking raises similar ethical and legal concerns to the practice of individual biobanks. However, these issues become far more complex when research is globalised and tissues are shared across borders.[24] The primary concern, as described by Hoeyer, is that:

> The move towards large-scale population-based biobanks and huge international collaborations might very well . . . cut the ties between the individual patient and the research community in ways that make researchers less accountable to donor interests.[25]

[19] YR Rubinstein et al, 'Creating a Global Rare Disease Patient Registry Linked to a Rare Diseases Biorepository Database: Rare Disease-HUB (RD-HUB)' (2010) 31 *Contemporary Clinical Trials* 394; ML Oster-Granite et al, 'Down Syndrome: National Conference on Patient Registries, Research Databases, and Biobanks' (2010) 104 *Molecular Genetics and Metabolism* 13.

[20] Asslaber and Zatloukal, 'Biobanks', above n 18; Watson, Kay and Smith, 'Integrating Biobanks', above n 3, 646.

[21] JE Bell et al, 'Management of a Twenty-First Century Brain Bank: Experience in the BrainNet Europe Consortium' (2008) 115 *Acta Neuropathologica* 497.

[22] Asslaber and Zatloukal, above n 18.

[23] D Catchpoole et al, 'The Importance of Biorepository Networks. The Australasian Biospecimens Network-Oncology' (2007) 28 *Australasian Journal of Medical Science* 16–20. A number of networks have been established. Such initiatives to date include (among many others) the promotion of the pan-European Biobanking and Biomolecular Resources Research Infrastructure (BBMRI) (cordis.europa.eu/esfri/roadmap.htm). This resource offers a 'distributive hub structure' and includes 261 biobanks over 23 countries with a total of more than 16 million samples: D Chalmers, 'Genetic Research and Biobanks' (2011) 675 *Methods in Molecular Biology* 1. Other networks include the Organisation for Economic Co-operation and Development (OECD) global Biological Resources Centres network (http://wdcm.nig.ac.jp/brc.pdf), the cancer Biomedical Informatics Grid (CaBIG) (cabig.nci.nih.gov), the International Cancer Genome Consortium (www.icgc.org), the Public Population Project in Genomics (P3G) (www.p3gconsortium.org), EuroBioBank (www.eurobiobank.org), EPIC, GenomEUtwin, TuBaFrost (www.tubafrost.org), and BrainNet Europe II (BNE) (www.brainnet-europe.org/).

[24] CI Emerson et al, 'Access and Use of Human Tissues from the Developing World: Ethical Challenges and a Way Forward Using a Tissue Trust' (2011) 12 *BMC Medical Ethics*; E Smith, 'The Limits of Sharing: An Ethical Analysis of the Arguments For and Against the Sharing of Databases and Material Banks' (2011) 18 *Accountability in Research-Policies and Quality Assurance* 357.

[25] KL Hoeyer, 'Size Matters: The Ethical, Legal, and Social Issues Surrounding Large-Scale Genetic Biobank Initiatives' (2012) 21 *Norsk Epidemiologi* 211, 213.

Therefore, the key problem raised by networking is how to maintain a relationship between donors and wider members of the network who have had no previous relationship with the donor.

The Law of Gifts

A gift is a voluntary transfer of property where one person, the 'donor', transfers property to another person, the 'donee' or 'volunteer'. A voluntary transfer is one that is not supported by consideration, which means that nothing of value is given in exchange for the donated property. Commonly, most people would associate money with being valuable consideration but common law and equity recognise a wide variety of behaviours which constitute consideration, including promises (such as to perform a task, to marry or to forebear from suing), labour or a reciprocal transfer of property rights.

Conveying Gifts

The method of conveying a gift will depend on the nature of the property which is being donated, and whether the transaction is being done legally or equitably. Since the Statute of Frauds 1677 (UK), gifts of legal interests in land need to be made by deed.[26] A gift of an interest in land may also need to be registered to pass the legal title to the done, particularly in jurisdictions which have the Torrens system of title.[27]

For personal property, gifts of choses in action (incorporeal personal property) must be in writing, and the chose must be given absolutely (which effectively precludes part ownership of a chose in action being gifted at law, that is, it is not possible to give 50 per cent of your right to royalties at law).[28] In contrast, a gift of goods does not require writing to be effective. All that is required is an intention to pass ownership of the goods and delivery of the goods (either physically or constructively).[29]

[26] Law of Property Act 1925 (UK), s 52; Conveyancing Act 1919 (NSW), s 23B(1); Law of Property Act 2000 (NT), s 9(1); Law of Property Act 1936 (SA), s 28(1); Conveyancing and Law of Property Act 1884 (Tas), s 60(1); Property Law Act 1958 (Vic), s 52(1); Property Law Act 1969 (WA), s 33(1). In Queensland the requirement is for writing: Property Law Act 1974 (Qld), s 10(1).

[27] Land Titles Act 1925 (ACT), s 57(1); Real Property Act 1900 (NSW), s 41(1); Land Title Act 2000 (NT), s 184; Land Title Act 1994 (Qld), s 181; Real Property Act 1886 (SA), s 67(1); Land Titles Act 1980 (Tas), s 39(1); Transfer of Land Act 1958 (Vic), s 40(1); Transfer of Land Act 1893 (WA), s 58(1).

[28] The original provision was Judicature Act 1873 (UK), s 25(6). In Australia the relevant sections are Civil Law (Property) Act 2006 (ACT), s 205; Conveyancing Act 1919 (NSW), s 12; Law of Property Act 2000 (NT), s 182; Property Law Act 1974 (Qld), s 199; Law of Property Act 1936 (SA), s 15; Conveyancing and Law of Property Act 1884 (Tas), s 86; Property Law Act 1958 (Vic), s 134; Property Law Act 1969 (WA), s 20. It is possible to give a part interest in equity: *Norman v Federal Commissioner of Taxation* (1963) 109 CLR 9.

[29] S Fisher, *Commercial and Personal Property Law* (Sydney, Butterworths, 1997) 446–47.

Property can also be donated in equity. However, equity took a negative attitude to the enforcement of incomplete gifts of legal property that could have been given at law, but where the donor failed to comply with the legal requirements. Equity adopted the maxims that 'equity does not perfect an imperfect gift' and 'equity would not assist a volunteer'.[30] However, there are circumstances in which equity will allow equitable title to pass to a donor, namely, where the donor has both done everything necessary to effect the transaction and has put the property beyond his/her recall.[31] In such cases equity will treat the gift as having been completed and such equitable gifts grant the donee an equitable title which can be enforced against the donor and third parties.

Equity allows gifts of property which were not assignable at law to be completed as long as the donor manifested a complete and irrevocable intention to give the property.[32] The classic example of such a transaction is the trust, where the legal owner either declares that they hold the property for the benefit of another, or where they transfer the property to a trustee to hold the legal title for the benefit of another. The trust was not recognised by common law courts but was enforced in equity, hence the title of the beneficiaries being classified as an equitable interest. However, the Statute of Frauds provisions require some of these gifts, namely trusts of land (but not personalty) and gifts of subsisting equitable interests (in both land and personalty), to be in writing.[33]

Conditional Gifts

Gifts can be given with or without conditions. If conditions are stipulated it is important to distinguish between those conditions that must be satisfied prior to the gift taking effect (*conditions precedent*)[34] and those conditions that must be satisfied after the gift has passed (*conditions subsequent*).[35] A condition precedent will be recognisable because it must logically be satisfied before the gift can take effect (for example, 'I give my house to A if A reaches the age of 25 years'). A condition subsequent will be recognisable because the gift is given but is able to be defeated if there is a breach (for example, 'I give the house to A as long as he continues to use it as his common residence').[36]

[30] RP Meagher, JD Heydon and MJ Leeming, *Meagher, Gummow and Lehane's Equity: Doctrines and Remedies*, 4th edn (Sydney, LexisNexis Butterworths, 2002) 227.

[31] *Milroy v Lord* (1862) 45 ER 1185; *Anning v Anning* (1907) 4 CLR 1049; *Corin v Patton* (1990) 169 CLR 540 at 580; *Costin v Costin* (1997) NSW Conv R 55–811; *Stone v Registrar of Titles* [2012] WASC 21.

[32] *Kekewich v Manning* (1851) 42 ER 519 at 524; *Norman v Federal Commissioner of Taxation* (1963) 109 CLR 9.

[33] Law of Property Act 1925 (UK), s 53; Civil Law (Property) Act 2006 (ACT), s 201; Conveyancing Act 1919 (NSW), s 23C; Law of Property Act 2000 (NT), s 10; Property Law Act 1974 (Qld), s 11; Law of Property Act 1936 (SA), s 29; Conveyancing and Law of Property Act 1884 (Tas), s 60(2); Property Law Act 1958 (Vic), s 53; Property Law Act 1969 (WA), s 34.

[34] *Errington v Errington and Wood* [1952] 1 KB 290.

[35] *Egerton v Earl Brownlow* (1853) 10 ER 359.

[36] *Wynne v Fletcher* (1857) 53 ER 423.

In gifts subject to a condition precedent, the donor retains title to the property until the condition is satisfied. In gifts subject to conditions subsequent, the property passes to the donee, but the donor retains a right to resume the title if there is a breach, the nature of which depends on whether the condition subsequent creates a determinable interest.[37]

Conditions Subsequent and Determinable Interests

What is a determinable interest? A distinction can be drawn between an absolute gift that is subject to a condition subsequent and gift which grants a determinable interest that automatically ends on the breach of a condition. The absolute gift which is subject to a condition subsequent, in effect, grants a complete interest, that is then divested on the breach of the condition. In contrast, a determinable interest is one granted with the condition built into it so that the interest is itself defined by the breach of the condition. Such a determinable interest is viewed as naturally coming to an end when the condition is breached.[38]

The differences between these two types of condition relate purely to the form and wording of the disposition.[39] For example, a trust 'to A for life, but if A ceases to use the property as a hotel, then to B' is considered to create an interest which is subject to a condition subsequent.[40] The life interest is granted to A but can be artificially cut short by the event of A no longer using the property as a hotel. However, if the trust was worded 'to B for life until B ceases to use the property as a hotel', B's life interest is always limited in time to the event of the property no longer being used as a hotel. If and when the property is no longer used as a hotel, B's estate comes naturally to an end.

While these semantic distinctions are unlikely to approved by anyone other than property lawyers, they have practical effects. First, in the case of a determinable interest in land the donor always retains an interest in the property (a 'possibility of reverter' or 'reverter' interest) which continues even though the property has been given and which returns to full ownership automatically on breach. In contrast, a breach of a condition subsequent gives the donor a right to resume title ('a right of re-entry') but only if it is exercised. The donor's interest is therefore notionally stronger in cases of determinable interests than in cases of conditions subsequent.

Secondly, there are a number of other public policy rules which might strike down a condition.[41] If the condition is part of a determinable interest it is not

[37] N Cox, 'Conditional Gifts and Freedom of Testation: Time for Review?' (2001) 9 *Waikato Law Review* 24.

[38] *Hood v Oglander* (1865) 55 ER 733 at 737.

[39] *Re Scientific Investment Pension Plan Trusts* [1999] ch 53.

[40] See P Radan and C Stewart, *Principles of Australian Equity and Trusts* 2nd edn (Sydney, LexisNexis, 2013) ch 17.

[41] These will not be discussed here but include the rule against restraints on alienation, the rule against perpetuities, the rule against illegal gifts, and public policies against certain conditions such as

possible to separate the condition from the gifts and the entire gift will fail, causing it to revert back to the donor. If, however, the gift is not subject to a conditional limitation but merely a condition subsequent, the condition is severable and the striking down of the condition will leave the gift to stand, free of the offending condition.

Conditional Gifts and Goods

The examples of conditional gifts given above have been those involving gifts of land. Can gifts of personal property be subject to conditions which create rights similar to reverters or rights of re-entry? Holdsworth says that the common law never recognised that a donor of a conditional gift of goods retained a property interest in them (like a possibility of reverter).[42] A gift of goods for a limited time (such as a life estate) was said to be a gift forever and the donee was free to do with the property as he or she pleased.

However, there are exceptions to this general rule. For example, common law enforced conditions subsequent for gifts of goods in contemplation of marriage. Such gifts are said to be made on the condition that if the marriage does not proceed the goods (such as the engagement ring) will be returned.[43] It is not clear whether the common law recognised any estate in the donor prior to the failure of the couple to marry but, in any event, equity will ordinarily step in and hold the property on a resulting or constructive trust. This indicates that the donor, at the very least, retains an equitable interest (probably because the donee is bound by conscience to give back the gift).[44]

Equity also provided a number of other mechanisms for granting a proprietary interest to the donor in a conditional gift. The simplest way was for the gift to take the form of a trust. Trusts of goods can be subject to conditions on how the beneficial interest is to be enjoyed (for example, 'I give the car to A on trust for B until B marries'). Once B marries the trust would end and the property would revert on a resulting trust back to the donor.

those which forbid marriage, encourage divorce, the separation of parent and child, and conditions which encourage immoral meretricious sexual relations: Stewart, Fleming and Kerridge, 'The Law of Gifts' above n 10.

[42] WS Holdsworth, *A History of English Law*, 4th edn (London, Methuen, 1936) vol VII, 470. This limit applies to gifts *inter vivos* but not gifts made in a will: N Crago, 'Bequests of Tangible Chattels in Succession' (1999) 28 *Western Australian Law Review* 199, 201. Blackstone disagreed with this and felt a conditional gift made *inter vivos* could create future interests at law, if contained in a deed: W Blackstone, *Commentaries on the Laws of England* (Oxford, Oxford University Press, 1765–69) vol 2, 398. This position was adopted in America, arguably because of the slave trade where there was pressure to recognise future interests in slaves (which were, in most states, classed as goods): JC Gray, 'Future Interests in Personal Property' (1901) 14 *Harvard Law Review* 397; LM Simes, 'Future Interests in Chattels Personal' (1930) 39 *Yale Law Journal*; P Bordwell, 'Interests in Chattels Real and Personal' (1936) 1 *Missouri Law Review* 119.

[43] *HAX v TV* [2009] QCA 401; *Papathanasopoulos v Vacopoulos* [2007] NSWSC 502; *Keays v Carter* [2003] WASC 23; *Cohen v Sellar* [1926] 1 KB 536; *Jacobs v Davis* [1917] 2 KB 532.

[44] *Ikeuchi v Liu* [2001] QSC 054; *Kais v Turvey* (1994) 17 Fam LR 498.

Equity would also recognise a condition which created a personal equitable obligation on the part of the donee to perform some act if they have been given property. In some circumstances the courts will interpret a conditional disposition as imposing a personal equitable obligation on the donee, such as the payment of an amount of money – for example, an annuity – to a third party.[45] Sometimes the obligation to the third party will be less definite, such as an obligation to 'support' or 'take care' of a third party, or make sure they 'want for nothing'.[46] The donee in such gifts is subject to a personal equitable obligation which is enforceable but which does not create a property right in the donor or a third-party beneficiary.[47] Nor does a breach of the obligation give rise to a forfeiture of the gift, unless the donor takes action for specific performance of the condition.[48]

Applying Gifts Law to Biobanking

How then might gifts law be applied to donations of human tissue for biobanking? The starting point is to determine the proprietary nature of human tissue – is it real property, a chose in action or a good? Clearly, human tissue is not real property, except, possibly, in those rare cases where it has been buried or frozen in the ground.[49] Apart from those rare occasions, human tissue is a physical thing which can be possessed and which is not attached to land. The most natural property category would therefore be goods, which in terms means that a gift can be made of tissue according to the general law of goods (subject to the requirements of applicable human tissue legislation).

However, a single focus on goods may be misleading because biobanking not only includes a gift of the tissue but permission to derive products such as immortal cell lines and genetic sequences from the tissue. Donors may also give access to their health records with permission for those records to be used in data linkage. On that basis, it is possible to conceive that a tissue donor may not only be donating the tissue as a good, but also giving a number of related choses in action.

The next step would be to determine the nature of any conditions attached to the gift. It is in this area that property law has a great advantage over the law of informed consent. Informed consent is *positively permissive* (for example, 'I consent to research protocol X, which carries a risk of Y'). The duty of informed

[45] *O'Sullivan Partners (Advisory) Pty Ltd v Foggo* [2012] NSWCA 40 at [93]–[99]; *Re Hodge* [1940] Ch 260; *Re Williams; Williams v Williams* [1897] 2 ch 12 at 19; *Rees v Engelbach* (1871) LR 12 Eq 225.

[46] *Re Moore* (1886) 55 LJ Ch 418; *Broad v Bevan* (1823) 38 ER 198; *Hammond v Hammond* [2007] NSWSC 106.

[47] *Gill v Gill* (1921) 21 SR (NSW) 400.

[48] *Kauter v Kauter* [2003] NSWSC 741; *Messenger v Andrews* (1828) 38 ER 885; *Gregg v Coates* (1856) 53 ER 13.

[49] Buried items are considered fixtures and therefore part of the land: *Elwes v Brigg Gas Co* (1886) 33 Ch D 562.

consent requires that the researcher provide information on what may happen to the tissue and the attendant risks involved, even though this is extremely difficult or impossible to know in tissue banking because very little or nothing is known about the risks of unspecified research. In contrast, the law of conditional gifts is *negatively permissive*. It focuses on the expressed and implied limits of what is permitted by the donor (for example, 'I donate my tissue to A so long as it is not used for human cloning'). Such limits have the advantage of being capable of expression when the gift is given, unlike a statement by a donor about material risk for research which hasn't been invented yet. By focusing on what the donor does not want there is a better chance of the donee behaving in a way that respects the donor's autonomy.

If the participant is unconcerned about future research and does not seek to limit it, there needs to be very few conditions laid out in the gift. Conversely, if the donor has very specific concerns about the types of research the tissue will be used to perform (such as cultural or religious concerns) these can be set out in the donation (for example, 'I give my tissue to A on the condition that the tissue and its derivative products will not be used for research involving embryonic stem cells'). Similarly, if the donor has concerns about being contacted if there are unanticipated findings these again can be set out as a condition. The flexibility of gifts law allows for these different concerns to be accommodated.

Are there some conditions which should always be implied in a gift to a biobank? As with the example of gifts in contemplation of marriage, it might be argued that there are conditions which should always be implied in any gift to a biobank because of the inherent nature of what is being given. At the very least, gifts of human tissue would arguably be made on the condition that the donor will be able in most cases to remove the tissue from biobank, or have it destroyed, should they change their mind, at least before the tissue has itself been consumed by the research. Another obvious condition would be that the donor's health information be keep confidential to the researchers accessing the tissue bank. Another condition may be the requirement that any research that is conducted on the tissue must be approved by a human research ethics committee.[50]

The only reported case of a court considering a conditional gift of human tissue is *Washington University v Catalona*.[51] In this case a researcher recruited several thousand participants to provide tissue for a study into the genetic causes of prostate cancer. When the researcher decided to relocate to another institution he wanted to take the tissue bank with him. However, Washington University claimed that the tissue bank had been created by its employee and, as such, the bank belonged to Washington University. The participants argued that they had donated their tissue on the condition that it be used for research only by that particular researcher. Washington University disputed that, saying that the tissue had been donated to the institution and not to an individual.

[50] Stewart, Fleming and Kerridge, above n 10.
[51] *Washington University v Catalona* 490 F 3d 667 (2007).

Both at trial and on appeal it was found that the tissue had been donated to the university as valid and binding gifts. The court relied on both the consent form and the surrounding circumstances of the research project, such as the practices of the researcher (particularly how he would often destroy samples in his research), as further evidence that the donors had intended to give the university property rights equating to ownership. The court was prepared to find that there was an implied condition that the donors could withdraw their tissue from the study (and, in some cases, demand that it be destroyed). However, the court refused to find that there was any condition (express or implied) which allowed the donors to control the identity of who performed research on the tissue.

Catalona illustrates the importance of both express and implied conditions in the donation of human tissue. While the court was prepared to find for an implied term of a right to have the property removed from the research protocol, the lack of express terms relating to who could use the tissue was fatal to the donors' claims that they could control who had access to the tissue. This certainly puts the onus on tissue donors to be consciously aware of what limitations they wish to place on their donations and creates concerns about the ability of donors to do so (which will be discussed below).

A final illustration of why a conditional gift model is more useful than an informed consent model comes when one reflects on the biobanking network problem which was discussed above. In biobank networks third parties have access to tissue and may borrow or take tissue samples, even though they do not have direct consent to do so from the donors. In informed consent terms there is no duty to provide information about material risks because there is no relationship with the donor. Requiring the third party to seek direct consent from the donor is impractical and defeats the purpose of the network. However, by not having direct consent there is a risk that the interests of donors are even further removed from the researcher's behaviour. Sometimes regulation may try to enforce such an obligation, for example by requiring the research to be approved by a human research ethics committee. However, research ethics committees may try to impose a 're-consent' process, which (as we have said) may be impractical. Alternatively, in the Australian context, the committee may approve the research without consent (if the committee believes the research to be in the public interest) but this further reduces the ability of the donor to maintain some interest in the tissue.[52]

If one adopts a conditional gift approach, these problems may be avoided because the donor arguably continues to have an interest in the property which should be effective against third parties in the network. If we adopt the position stated above that a gift of human tissue is a gift of goods (with some related choses in action), the conditions of the gift should be enforceable in common law, like gifts in contemplation of marriage. Equity would go on to recognise that the

[52] The relevant Australian law is Privacy Act 1988 (Cth), s 95A. See also National Health and Medical Research Council, *Guidelines Approved Under Section 95A of the Privacy Act 1988* (2001).

donors retain an equitable interest in the tissue (as it does in gifts in contemplation of marriage, or in personal equitable obligations) because it would be unconscionable for the biobank network members to take the tissue subject to conditions and then ignore them. If the conditions are breached equity could order specific performance of the obligation, equitable compensation or a constructive trust over the tissue to protect it against further interference. The only situation in which a third party may have a defence is if the third party is a bona fide purchaser for value, without notice of the conditions.[53] However, in a biobank network that will be highly unlikely as the original conditions of the gift will ordinarily be known, or should be known, by the third parties. As such they will have notice and be bound to respect the equity of the donor. Alternatively, third parties in networks may themselves be volunteers, receiving the tissue as a gift, again with the result that they are subject to the earlier equity of the donors because they are not purchasers for value.

There remain some practical concerns. The first is the assumption that donors are in a position to bargain for conditions being imposed. Biobanks may be tempted to create standard agreements which will be unconditional, leaving them with the greatest amount of freedom and donors with no remaining interest. One way to counterbalance this problem would be to introduce implied terms, as discussed above. These could either be introduced through the common law method (as they were in gifts in contemplation of marriage) or through statute (as they are in socially important contracts such as leases and sale of land). Implied terms would create a minimum standard of behavioural expectation.

Conclusion

The law of gifts provides a new way of considering gifts of human tissue to biobanks. It is by no means a panacea for all of the ethical and legal problems of biobanking. However, the advantage of a gift approach is that it respects the fact that donors wish to maintain some modicum of control over what happens to their tissue after it has been given, by recognising a continuing proprietary interest. The rules are flexible and allow for degrees of control. This gives donors some choice in how to donate their tissues and for what purposes. On the other hand, the rules are complicated and may not be easily understood by donors who may not think to express their desires in binding ways when donating. This problem raises the further issue of what terms the courts should imply into gifts of tissue that would provide basic protection for donors of human tissue. Thankfully, the law of gifts already has an arsenal of different approaches (including implied terms and statutory protections) that might mitigate these concerns.

[53] This is known as the rule in *Pilcher v Rawlins* (1872) LR 7 ch 259.

4

Unintended Side Effects of the National Health Service

THOMAS KREBS

Introduction

In the UK's National Health Service (NHS) medical care is provided free at the point of delivery. In lawyers' language, medical services are supplied for no consideration. Sometimes these medical services are defective. In contrast to patients in most other countries, the law of contract will not assist those who suffer harm as a result: they have no contractual relationship with the NHS. The law of tort usually steps in. It is well established that a provider of medical services owes a duty to the recipient of such services 'to use diligence, care, knowledge, skill and caution in administering the treatment. No contractual relation is necessary, nor is it necessary that the service be rendered for reward.'[1] The duty obliges the provider of medical services to exercise this care to improve the patient's physical and mental health in respect of which he or she was consulted.[2] Normally, therefore, not having a contractual relationship with the medical practitioner will not matter, particularly since his or her duty in contract would be pretty much the same as the duty of care in tort: to use reasonable care and skill.[3]

In *Yearworth v North Bristol NHS Trust* the absence of a contract almost made a difference.[4] Diagnosed with cancer and about to undergo chemotherapy, the claimants sought to preserve their chances of procreation by depositing samples of semen in the hospital's fertility storage unit, where they would be kept in liquid nitrogen at a very low temperature. Through the Trust's (admitted) want of care, the storage unit malfunctioned and the claimant's semen and with it, it appeared, their chances of ever becoming fathers, perished irretrievably. As a result, the claimants suffered considerable distress which, for some of them, led to actual

[1] *R v Bateman* [1925] 94 LJKB 791, 794, per Lord Hewart CJ.
[2] C Walton, S Wood, R Cooper and S Todd, *Charlesworth & Percy on Negligence*, 12th edn (London, Sweet & Maxwell, 2010) 9-110.
[3] Supply of Goods and Services Act 1982, s 13.
[4] *Yearworth v North Bristol Trust* [2009] EWCA Civ 37.

psychiatric illnesses. They sought to recover damages in the Exeter County Court.[5] The defendants admitted a breach of duty but argued that no damages were recoverable because the claimants had not suffered damage that was actionable. District Judge Daniels therefore ordered four preliminary issues to be decided, three of which are of relevance to this short paper, namely: (1) whether the destruction of the sperm could be classified as 'personal injury'; (2) whether, failing that, its destruction constituted loss of property; and (3) if so, (i) how such loss was to be valued, and (ii) whether psychiatric injury flowing from such loss of property could in principle give rise to a claim for damages. Judge Griggs in the Exeter County Court decided all these issues against the claimants, putting an end to their claims. The claimants successfully appealed to the Court of Appeal. While the Court agreed that damage to sperm outside the claimants' bodies could not constitute personal injury, it held that such sperm could very well constitute 'property', with the result that damage to it constituted actionable loss in the law of tort. The Court further decided that the claimants were able to pursue actions in bailment, making remedies available that were closer to contractual than tortious remedies.

The Court of Appeal's attempts to classify the ruined sperm as 'property' or to recharacterise the relationship between the claimants and the Trust as bailment may be symptomatic of a more fundamental problem with negligence law generally. In the words of Nicky Priaulx, 'negligence illustrates a continued preference for physical bodily harm in determinations of actionability'.[6] She regards the decision in *Yearworth* as predominately result-driven: while the damage suffered by the claimants is not readily classified as physical injury, 'to suggest that these individuals are *not* harmed, or that their suffering is less than that which would be sustained by virtue of a physical bodily injury seems absurd'.[7] She argues that the losses suffered by the *Yearworth* claimants look and feel like personal injury, while they are in fact a species of psycho-social harm not readily recoverable in the tort of negligence, and that in trying to accommodate such (intuitively meritorious) claims, the courts are increasingly lacking the necessary normative compass.

The problem for the law, as she acknowledges, is that it needs to identify criteria by which meritorious claimants receive compensation while keeping the floodgates firmly shut. The focus of the Court of Appeal on whether property rights could be said to exist in bodily fluids is an example of what she calls 'hair-splitting' in 'hybrid' cases.[8] In this paper, I will suggest that this 'hair-splitting' exercise was quite unnecessary. The law is now sufficiently well developed to award compensation in cases such as *Yearworth* without having to bend over backwards to identify emasculated property rights (emasculated because, as explained by the Court of Appeal, they lack many of the qualities that are nor-

[5] *Yearworth v North Bristol NHS Trust*, 2008 WL 5044430, [2008] LS Law Medical 535.

[6] N Priaulx, 'Humanising Negligence: Damaged Bodies, Biographical Lives and the Limits of Law' (2012) 33 *Adelaide Law Review* 177, 178.

[7] ibid, 188.

[8] ibid, 177.

mally understood to be characteristic if not determinative of property rights). It will be suggested that, outside certain well- and not-so-well-defined areas in which the law imposes duties of care (or, looking at the issue from the claimant's perspective, in which the law grants universally protected rights such as property rights), duties of care can arise in appropriate cases where the defendant can be shown to have assumed responsibility for the claimant's welfare, and this can extend beyond the typical example of purely economic interests.

This paper will first consider two competing models of tort liability: the 'loss' model and the 'rights' model. It is suggested that under either model the concept of assumption of responsibility could have produced the same outcome as that achieved, by a more circuitous route, by the Court of Appeal. The paper then considers the remedies that would be available for a negligence claim based on voluntary assumption of responsibility as opposed to a contract claim.

Duty of Care, Assumption of Responsibility and Actionable Damage

Professor Robert Stevens has pointed out that there are two incompatible conceptions of the law of torts that are discernable within the common law. He refers to these as the 'loss model' and the 'rights model'.[9] Under the loss model, Stevens explains, 'the defendant should be liable where he is at fault for causing the claimant loss unless there is a good reason why not'. Under this model, 'damage is the gist',[10] and a claimant will have to show that the loss he has suffered is of a kind that is actionable as 'not all kinds of damage can give rise to a successful action in negligence'.[11] It is possible to argue that, under this model, the concept of the duty of care is redundant,[12] and this is borne out by the decision of the Exeter County Court in *Yearworth*: although the defendants admitted that they were under a duty to the claimants to take reasonable care of the sperm, this duty was entirely unenforceable if its breach did not and could not result in actionable loss; thus, it was entirely meaningless for the defendants to concede a breach of duty. The competing 'rights model', on the other hand, first asks whether the claimant had a right against the defendant, the law of torts being concerned 'with the secondary obligations generated by the infringement of primary rights'.[13] I shall examine the questions which arose in *Yearworth* under both of these models without expressing a preference for either model. It will become apparent that, whichever model one chooses, the

[9] R Stevens, *Torts and Rights* (Oxford, Oxford University Press, 2007) 2.

[10] J Stapleton, 'The Gist of Negligence' (1988) 104 *Law Quarterly Review* 213, 213; *Gregg v Scott* [2005] UKHL 2, [2005] 2 AC 176 [99] (Baroness Hale), cited by Stevens, above n 9 at 2.

[11] Walton, Wood, Cooper and Todd, *Charlesworth & Percy on Negligence*, above n 2 at 9-110.

[12] Stevens, *Torts and Rights*, above n 9 at 1, citing OW Holmes, 'The Path of the Law' (1897) 10 *Harvard Law Review* 457 at 471–72 and several others.

[13] Stevens, above n 9 at 2.

claimants should have been able to recover substantial damages without necessarily having to establish either personal injury or property rights over the sperm.

Yearworth under the 'loss model' of torts law

Counsel for the claimants had conceded that, if the destruction of the sperm could not be regarded as personal injury, following *Leigh and Sillavan v Aliakmon Shipping Co Ltd (Aliakmon)*,[14] no claim in tort could lie unless the claimants could show that they had property rights in the sperm. Following this concession, the claimants could only prevail if they could show that they had suffered personal – physical – injury or damage to property. Lord Brandon of Oakbrook had said in *Aliakmon* that

> [i]n order to enable a person to claim in negligence for loss caused to him by reason of loss of or damage to property, he must have had either the legal ownership of or a possessory title to the property concerned at the time when the loss or damage occurred.

This dictum caused the Court of Appeal in *Yearworth* to set out to answer the difficult, controversial and emotive question of whether sperm could constitute 'property' for these purposes. However, on a careful reading of the dictum it becomes clear that this was hardly necessary. The ratio of *Aliakmon* only applies where (1) property is lost or damaged, and (2) a person seeks to recover loss, typically economic loss, sustained as a result. If it is accepted that counsel for the defendants was right in arguing that sperm cannot constitute 'property', the question never arises, for the loss sustained was not consequential upon the loss of or damage to 'property' in the first place. While it is true that, 'in cases where personal injury of a physical nature has been sustained or where actual damage to or loss of a person's property has been suffered, a duty to take care has readily been imposed',[15] the common law has imposed duties of care in respect of purely economic and purely psychiatric losses as well, although it is no doubt true that the law 'has struggled to find a consistent approach' to when such duties should be found.[16] The best starting point under the 'loss model' is Lord Bridge's speech in *Caparo Industries plc v Dickman*,[17] in which he identified three criteria by which, in novel cases, the imposition of a duty of care could be justified. They are: (1) foreseeability of damage; (2) proximity; and (3) 'fairness, justice and reasonableness'. These criteria are, obviously, fairly open-ended. What this 'test' amounts to is that where a claimant has suffered loss as a result of a defendant's negligence this loss should be compensated unless there are good reasons why the defendant should be immune from liability.[18] One such reason is of particular relevance here, namely the danger that the defendant might be made subject to liability of

[14] *Leigh and Sillavan v Aliakmon Shipping Co Ltd (Aliakmon)* [1986] AC 785.
[15] Walton, Wood, Cooper and Todd, above n 2 at 9-110.
[16] ibid.
[17] *Caparo Industries plc v Dickman* [1990] 2 AC 605, 617–18.
[18] Stevens, above n 9 at 2.

indeterminate scope and amount (sometimes referred to as the 'floodgates' argument). Because of this danger, the courts have placed considerable obstacles in the path of those seeking to recover compensation for losses that are purely economic[19] or psychiatric.[20] The consequences of a person's negligence can have far-reaching consequences that are nevertheless foreseeable (and thus not too remote): if I hit a person with my car, rendering him unfit for work, this will cause economic and, possibly, psychiatric losses to people connected to him: he will no longer generate profits for his employer, for example, and may no longer be spending money himself, thus causing losses to those who would otherwise have sold him goods and services. In addition, his injury or death will cause distress and possibly psychiatric harm to those near and dear to him.[21] Recovery for purely economic or psychiatric harm is thus generally only allowed subject to limiting devices of greater or lesser sophistication, subsumed under the 'proximity' stage of the *Caparo* 'test'. In the context of pure economic loss, the limiting device of choice has been the idea of 'voluntary assumption of responsibility',[22] while a claimant who suffers psychiatric injury as a result of somebody else's physical injury must satisfy three – rather arbitrary – requirements: close ties of love and affection with the 'primary' victim, proximity in time and space, and a direct visual or aural impact of the event or its immediate aftermath.[23]

In *Hedley Byrne v Heller* the claimants were a firm of advertising agents. They had been concerned about the financial stability of one of their clients (for whose forward orders they had assumed personal liability as *del credere* agents) and made inquiries of their clients' bankers, the defendants. On the strength of the information received, they continued placing orders on behalf of their clients, who later became insolvent, causing significant losses to the claimants. The action against the defendants was unsuccessful (because, on the facts, the defendants had given the information 'without prejudice' and had, arguably, not been negligent in any event), but the House of Lords still considered whether, on such a fact scenario, a duty of care could ever be established. Lord Devlin strongly suggested that, where one person, possessed of a special skill, had undertaken responsibility for the affairs of another, a duty of care could arise in tort notwithstanding the absence of consideration and thus contractual duties. It is true that assumption of responsibility has been predominantly relied on in the context of pure economic loss caused by negligent misstatements. However, while the incidence of duties of care has generally been severely curtailed in recent years,[24] there has been a significant expansion of liability where the defendant can be said to have voluntarily assumed

[19] *Spartan Steel and Alloys Ltd v Martin* [1973] QB 27; *Caparo Industries plc v Dickman* [1990] 2 AC 605.

[20] *Alcock v Chief Constable of South Yorkshire Police* [1992] 1 AC 310.

[21] An additional problem with psychiatric harm is that lawyers still treat diagnoses of psychiatric illness with some suspicion.

[22] *Hedley Byrne v Heller & Partners Ltd* [1964] AC 465.

[23] *White v Chief Constable of South Yorkshire* [1999] 2 AC 455, 502 (Lord Hoffmann).

[24] Most importantly in *Caparo Industries plc v Dickman* [1990] 2 AC 605; *Murphy v Brentwood* [1991] 1 AC 398; *Commissioner for Customs & Excise v Barclays Bank plc* [2006] UKHL 28.

a duty. Although the law of tort does not generally impose a duty of care in respect of pure omissions, a duty of care will arise where it has been voluntarily accepted; thus, a prison authority must take care of inmates,[25] a school authority of pupils[26] and a doctor of patients[27] notwithstanding the absence of a contract between them. This expansion has been referred to as paradoxical,[28] but is in fact readily explicable: the nexus 'voluntary assumption of responsibility' negates the danger of floodgates and renders the parties sufficiently proximate for a duty of care to be imposed even in respect of purely economic losses, and, in that context, the idea has been applied and developed in a large number of important cases.[29]

According to Lord Devlin in *Hedley Byrne*, the fact that there would have been a contract but for the absence of consideration is significant: rather than 'inventing' consideration, the courts should openly find that there has been a voluntary assumption of responsibility in such cases. It might be suggested that, in *Yearworth*, where it was impossible to find a contract, the Court of Appeal fell into the related trap of trying to find a property right which liability in the tort of negligence could then 'latch onto'. Given that there can be no doubt that a psychiatrist, or even a general practitioner, prescribing drugs or providing counselling to treat a patient complaining of mental health issues will be liable if, through his negligence, the patient's mental health further deteriorates (or if he fails to treat such a patient because of a negligent misdiagnosis), it seems entirely uncontroversial that the defendants in *Yearworth* were in precisely that position: they generated three documents in respect of each man by which they set out what they were going to do with the sperms and in fact stipulated that they undertook 'to look after them with all possible care'. Can there be a clearer example of voluntary assumption of responsibility? However, given the (unfortunate) concession by their counsel that there could be no recovery unless the loss complained of could be described as personal injury or property loss, the Court of Appeal never considered this possibility. It thus becomes clear that, on the loss-based model which is probably dominant in England, it was entirely unnecessary to discuss the emotive and controversial issue of whether it is possible to have property rights over sperm, other bodily fluids or, indeed, body parts.

Yearworth under the 'rights model' of torts law

The rights model of torts law, advocated by Stevens, does not look at the claimant's loss but asks whether any of the claimant's primary rights have been infringed

[25] *Reeves v Commissioner of Police of the Metropolis* [2000] 1 AC 360.

[26] *Barnes v Hampshire CC* [1969] 1 WLR 1563; *Phelps v Hillingdon LBC* [2001] 2 AC 619.

[27] *Barnett v Chelsea Hospital* [1969] 1 QBD 428.

[28] V Harpwood, *Modern Tort Law*, 7th edn (London, Cavendish, 2009) 80.

[29] For example, *Esso v Mardon* [1976] QB 801; *Smith v Bush* [1990] 1 AC 831; *Spring v Guardian Assurance* [1995] 2 AC 296; *Henderson v Merrett Syndicates* [1995] 2 AC 145; *Williams v Natural Life Health Foods* [1998] 1 WLR 830; *Commissioner for Customs & Excise v Barclays Bank plc* [2006] UKHL 28, [2006] 3 WLR 1.

by the defendant's negligence. This begs the question, of course, what primary rights a person possesses. As a starting point, we can take those rights that are conferred on persons by birth: the right to life, freedom and bodily integrity. These are rights that are exigible against the whole world.[30] Some such rights are acquired not by birth but by a different process. Thus, property rights, exigible against the whole world (except against a person with a better title), may be acquired by sale, gift, inheritance or original manufacture. Then there are rights that are not exigible against the whole world but only against individual persons – contract rights are the primary example. The rights model of the law of torts asks whether any such primary rights have been violated by the alleged tortfeasor. If the answer to this question is 'yes', then all foreseeable (that is, non-remote) losses consequential upon the infringement should likewise be recoverable: the claimant is to be put in as good a position as if the wrong (that is, the tortious infringement of the primary right) had not been committed.

This analysis works well for straightforward personal injury cases and cases involving interference with property rights. It also convincingly explains why pure economic losses, as opposed to economic losses consequent upon physical damage to property or personal injury, are not generally recoverable: there simply is no 'general right to wealth', while there are, of course, rights of property. The analysis is not very good at explaining, however, why those who suffer psychiatric harm cannot, without more, recover damages from those who have negligently caused that harm in circumstances in which the harm being suffered was foreseeable.[31] The law does recognise a freestanding right to mental health,[32] and it is difficult to see why, where that right is infringed, there should be no general recoverability of damages. In *Yearworth* itself, the Court of Appeal seems to follow the rights model in that it assumes that, absent the three factors which entitle a victim to recover as a 'secondary' victim following the witnessing of a traumatic event, there could only be recovery if the claimants' claim could 'piggy-back' on the breach of a primary right, namely either bodily integrity (hence the inquiry whether damage to the sperm could in any way be characterised as personal injury) or property (hence the, controversial, inquiry into whether the sperm could be subject to property rights). However, the Court of Appeal seemed to think that the only primary rights the infringement of which could give rise to such secondary claims to damages were rights that are good against all the world. As Stevens points out, under the rights model this is not the case, contractual rights being the prime example. However, even without a contract, rights can be conferred on individuals. It is interesting that, like Lord Devlin in *Hedley Byrne* he uses the gratuitous bailment as a clear example of the creation of such rights in the

[30] Stevens, above n 9 at 2.

[31] Stevens recognises this and argues that the arbitrary requirements described above should be abolished and replaced by a general foreseeability test. See Stevens, above n 9 at 56.

[32] *Boardman v Sanderson* [1964] 1 WLR 1317; *McLoughlin v O'Brian* [1983] 1 AC 410; both cited by Stevens, above n 9 at 55.

absence of contract.[33] However, the rights of the bailor against the gratuitous bailee clearly do not exhaust the examples of voluntarily created rights recognised by English law. Thus, it was more than arguable in *Yearworth* that the Trust had voluntarily assumed responsibility for the safety of the defendants' sperm in its facility, thus creating primary rights that the claimants possessed against it. Again, because of counsel's unfortunate concession, the Court of Appeal did not consider this question. It is interesting however, that, having determined that the claimants could be said to possess property rights over the sperm, this made them bailors, and the defendants bailees, of them. Was it really necessary, given that, according to Lord Devlin, bailment is a prime example of voluntary assumption of responsibility, to take the preliminary step of finding that the claimants were owners of the sperm?

In discussing bailment, the Court of Appeal expressed the (controversial) view that liability in bailment was *sui generis* and that it arose neither in contract nor in tort. However, the discussion of bailment was clearly intended to enable an award of damages which was closer to contract than to tort. This takes us to the second part of this paper, namely to the question of whether there are any remedial consequences which flow from the characterisation of the claims as tortious, contractual or based on bailment.

Remedies

Contract

Had the claimants in *Yearworth* been privately insured, or had they chosen to pay for the storage of their sperm, they would have had contractual rights against the storage facility. What difference would this have made? In practice, the Court of Appeal would clearly not have considered the controversial question of whether sperm is capable of being 'owned', and the case would have been of much less interest for this volume. It was argued above that the tort of negligence should have been able to furnish the result the Court of Appeal eventually reached without considering that question. Still, a claim for breach of contract would have been much more unequivocally based on the defendants' undertaking than a claim in negligence.

One of the chief differences between claims in negligence and contract is that breach of contract is actionable per se, without having to prove loss. Often, of course, such a claim will prove a *brutum fulmen* in that, without loss, the only damages available are likely to be nominal damages, and a victory in such a claim may well turn out to be pyrrhic in that the claimant runs the risk of being penalised in costs. The starting point of the common law, in assessing loss, is rather

[33] Stevens, above n 9 at 2.

materialistic: it asks what the claimant's balance sheet position after the breach is as compared to what it would have been had the contract been kept. The leading case was *Addis v Gramophone Co Ltd*, a case of wrongful dismissal.[34] The claimant sought to recover damages not just for his lost wages and commissions, but also for his feelings which had been hurt by the particularly unkind manner of his dismissal. This latter part of his claim was dismissed by the House of Lords. Lord Gorrell made it clear that, in wrongful dismissal claims as in breach of contract claims generally, only 'money losses' were recoverable. However, the law of contract has always allowed for compensation for some 'non-money' losses – damages for pain and suffering following personal injuries, for example, though in most cases based on tort, damages can also be awarded for breach of contract,[35] and this is entirely uncontroversial. Damages can also be recovered for recognised psychiatric illnesses where these were caused by a breach of contract,[36] so that the claims of the claimants in *Yearworth* in respect of this head of loss would have been very strong indeed had they been able to point to a contract with the storage facility.[37]

The law of contract has, however, been reluctant to award damages in respect of mental distress or disappointment. The reason for this is no doubt a fear that *all* contract claimants would add a head of damages in respect of loss of peace of mind, worry, or mental distress, even where the contracts breached were entirely commercial.[38] However, in recent years the law has recognised that not all contracts are entered into with a view to monetary gain; on the contrary, some contracts are meant to provide pleasure, enjoyment, peace of mind or relief from distress. The first cases in which this was recognised involved ruined holidays,[39] but there have since been cases involving solicitors failing to take out a non-molestation injunction,[40] the mental satisfaction foregone by having a shallower pool constructed than contractually agreed,[41] and the upset and aggravation

[34] *Addis v Gramophone Co Ltd* [1909] AC 488.

[35] *Summers v Salford Corporation* [1943] AC 283.

[36] A Burrows, *Damages for Torts and Breach of Contract*, 3rd edn (Oxford, Oxford University Press, 2004) 324.

[37] Causation would, whether the claim is brought in tort or for breach of contract, always be slightly problematic, given the uncertainty surrounding IVF treatment. The claimants would have had to show, on a balance of probabilities, that they would not have developed their psychiatric illnesses had the sperm not been destroyed. The defendant would no doubt have strongly argued that it was more likely than not that any IVF treatment would have failed and that this would have had the exact same consequences as being told about the loss of the sperm. The claimants would then have countered that the effects of a failed course of IVF treatment would not have had the same traumatic effect as being told, out of the blue, that they would never be fathers because their deposited sperm had been allowed to thaw.

[38] In *Hayes v James & Charles Dodd* [1990] 2 All ER 815 Staughton LJ famously observed: 'I would not view with enthusiasm the prospect that every shipowner in the Commercial Court, having successfully claimed for unpaid freight or demurrage, would be able to add a claim for mental distress while he was waiting for his money' (at 823).

[39] *Jarvis v Swans' Tours* [1973] QB 233; *Jackson v Horizon Holidays* [1975] 1 WLR 1468; *Hunt v Hourmount* [1983] CLY 983.

[40] *Heywood v Wellers* [1976] QB 446.

[41] *Ruxley Electronics v Forsyth* [1996] AC 344.

caused by a survey that failed to warn of aircraft noise after a specific request to look into it.[42] It is thus reasonably certain that the claimants in *Yearworth* would have been able to recover in respect of their mental distress (and their disappointment at not being able to procreate): this was precisely the object of the arrangement they entered into with the storage facility. The Court of Appeal characterised the case in terms of bailment precisely because they thought that, in bailment, damages were assessed according to contractual, rather than tortious, principles. There is thus a reasonably detailed discussion of the principles by which contract damages for disappointment and mental distress are awarded, before the Court then reaches the conclusion that, as such damages would have been recoverable in contract, they should be recoverable in bailment, too.

Tort

The judgment of the Court of Appeal in *Yearworth* is clearly drafted on the assumption that, in the tort of negligence, there can be no recovery in respect of mental distress or, indeed, psychiatric harm outside the rules on primary and secondary victims set out in cases such as *Page v Smith*[43] and *Alcock*.[44] It is certainly true that, while the law of torts is, in fact, generally more willing to allow recovery in respect of mental distress,[45] this is not the case when it comes to negligence. Thus, in *Hicks v Chief Constable of the South Yorkshire Police*[46] Lord Bridge said:

> It is perfectly clear law that fear by itself, of whatever degree, is a normal human emotion for which no damages can be awarded. Those trapped in the crush at Hillsborough who were fortunate enough to escape without injury have no claim in respect of the distress they suffered in what must have been a truly terrifying experience.

The first hurdle for a claimant to overcome will usually be to show a recognised psychiatric illness,[47] and even then, he will only be able to recover if he was 'within the zone of danger', and thus a primary victim, or if he can prove a sufficiently proximate relationship with the primary victim to qualify as a secondary victim.

There is a strong argument that the courts' reluctance to allow damages to be recovered in respect of mental distress is misguided in circumstances in which liability in the tort of negligence has already been established (subject, of course, to remoteness).[48] The argument is particularly strong if one adopts the 'rights

[42] *Farley v Skinner* [2001] UKHL 49, [2002] AC 732.

[43] *Page v Smith* [1996] AC 155.

[44] *Alcock v Chief Constable of South Yorkshire Police* [1992] 1 AC 310.

[45] Burrows, *Damages for Torts and Breach of Contract*, above n 36 at 334; *Walter v Alltools Ltd* [1944] 61 TLR 39 (false imprisonment); *Savile v Roberts* [1696] 1 Ld Raym 274 (malicious prosecution); *Barbara v Home Office* [1884] 134 NLJ 888 (assault and battery); *Drane v Evangelou* [1978] 1 WLR 455 (trespass to land – wrongful eviction by landlord).

[46] *Hicks v Chief Constable of the South Yorkshire Police* [1992] PIQR 433, 436.

[47] *McLoughlin v O'Brian* [1983] 1 AC 410, 431 (Lord Bridge); *White v Chief Constable of the South Yorkshire Police* [1999] 2 AC 455, 501 (Lord Hoffmann).

[48] See, to the same effect, Burrows, above n 36 at 336; Stevens, above n 9 at 56.

model' of tort law. An example is the well-known case of *Attia v British Gas*.[49] The claimant came home one day to find that an engineer who was supposed to fix her heating system had in fact set her home on fire. She watched it burn for some considerable time. This, unsurprisingly, caused her considerable distress, and, she alleged, an actual psychiatric illness. The defendant argued that she would have to establish that she fell within one of the recognised categories of 'secondary victim' in order to succeed, but the Court of Appeal disagreed. Dillon LJ said, in an illuminating passage:

> How far is it right that the law should allow a claim for damages against a wrongdoer, where the wrong done by the wrongdoer was primarily a wrong done to someone other than the claimant, and the claimant is a person of whom, at the relevant time, the wrongdoer had no knowledge and who may then have been far away from the scene of the wrongdoer's act? This difficulty is particularly concerned with whether the wrongdoer owed any duty of care to the claimant. But that difficulty does not arise in the present case because in the present case there is no problem of proximity. The defendants knew about the plaintiff and unquestionably owed a duty of care to her not to start a fire in her house. If her claims for damage to the house and contents had not been settled, she would have brought the one action against the defendants in which she would have pleaded the negligence of the defendants in starting the fire and would have gone on to assert that, by reason thereof, she had suffered and was suffering damage and loss, which would be put under two headings, viz. (1) damage to the house and contents; and (2) damage for nervous shock. The issues at the trial, assuming the facts pleaded, including the psychiatric illness, were proved, would have been (a) causation and (b) foreseeability of the damage as a question of remoteness. I can see no good reason why, in such a context, the law should have refused to allow her damages for 'nervous shock' if she could get over the hurdles of causation and foreseeability as an aspect of remoteness.

In the language of rights, Dillon LJ is saying that, once the claimant has shown that her property rights have been infringed, she can recover all non-remote losses flowing from that infringement – he is expressly refusing to ask himself whether psychiatric harm is a loss in respect of which damages are recoverable. *Yearworth* can, of course, be analysed in the same way. The whole inquiry into whether or not the claimants had property in the sperm was necessary because it was only once a property or other protected right had been infringed that damages consequential upon the destruction of the sperm became recoverable. However, as pointed out above, it would have been open to the claimants to argue that the defendant storage unit had accepted responsibility for the sperm by accepting it for storage. If this had been done by way of contract, it seems beyond doubt that substantial damages in respect of psychiatric illnesses, mental distress and disappointment would have been recoverable. The same should be true if the cause of action is in the tort of negligence, in respect of the breach of a duty voluntarily assumed. Thus, Professor Burrows argues that

[49] *Attia v British Gas* [1988] QB 304.

> the extension of tortious negligence to the negligent performance of services causing pure economic loss, and the acceptance of concurrent liability, presumably means that mental distress damages are recoverable in the tort action provided they would be recoverable in that situation for breach of contract. In other words, mental distress damages will be recoverable provided one can show that an important object of the services was to provide mental satisfaction or freedom from distress.[50]

In *Verderame v Commercial Union Assurance Co plc*[51] this parallel between available remedies in tort and contract was drawn, although, on the facts, it meant that no remedy was available in either. The defendant insurance brokers had made the unfortunate mistake of arranging insurance cover in respect of goods owned by the claimant's company in the claimant's own name and not the name of the company. When the company's entire stock was stolen, the insurer denied liability on the grounds that the claimant had no insurable interest. The Court of Appeal held, in respect of the claimant's claim for damages for 'anxiety, depression and inconvenience' that such losses could not be recovered in contract (this being a contract of insurance rather than one for the provision of enjoyment or mental satisfaction) and this also precluded recovery in the tort of negligence. Balcombe LJ said:

> I, of course, accept that for some kinds of tort – for example, assault or defamation – damages for mental distress may be recoverable without the necessity of showing physical damage. But the tort here relied on is that of negligence, and one is back again to the principles stated in *Caparo v Dickman*: as a matter of policy can you claim damages for distress said to result from negligence of the type which is alleged in this particular pleading? That must be a matter of policy, and I agree . . . that there is no reason why the policy should be different from that which applies where there is the breach of a contractual duty.

In *Hamilton Jones v David & Snape*[52] a solicitor's negligence had allegedly led to the claimant's child being abducted to Tunisia. The claim was framed concurrently in contract and tort. The defendant's argument, relying on *Verderame*, was that, since there could be no recovery of damages in respect of mental distress in the tort of negligence, there should be no such recovery in contract, either. Dillon LJ disagreed, arguing that

> if a head of claim . . . is recoverable in contract, the fact that it may not normally be recoverable in tort should not prevent it being recoverable in contract. The logic of the reasoning in *Verderame* suggests, if anything, that the approach to damages in tort in a case such as this is governed by the approach to damages in contract.

There is thus strong academic and some judicial authority for the proposition that, where a defendant gives an undertaking which would, but for the lack of consideration, amount to a contract, that defendant's liability in negligence will be controlled by the same factors as it would be in contract, namely, whether the

[50] Burrows, above n 36 at 324.
[51] *Verderame v Commercial Union Assurance Co plc* [1992] BCLC 793, cited by Burrows, ibid.
[52] *Hamilton Jones v David & Snape* [2003] EWHC 3147, [51].

undertaking is one which was meant to safeguard the claimant's mental wellbeing in that it would provide him with freedom from distress, worry or aggravation. This chapter has argued at length that this is precisely what the undertaking given in *Yearworth* was meant to do.

Conclusion

Yearworth is an important case in that it carefully considers the question whether and in what circumstances there can be ownership of body parts and bodily fluids and substances so as to trigger liability in the law of tort and bailment. This paper sought to show that this discussion, interesting though it may be, was unnecessary. The tort of negligence would have been able to protect the claimants and award them damages in respect of their mental distress and, *a fortiori*, their psychiatric injuries suffered as a result of the defendant's negligence. Unfortunately, counsel for the claimants appears to have overlooked the possibility of establishing a duty of care through voluntary assumption of responsibility. Had he framed the claimants' case in these terms, this would, it is argued here, have opened up all remedies which would have been available to the claimants had they paid for the defendant's services. The conclusion that the claimants had property rights in their sperm is likely to have far-reaching consequences in other areas of the law, and it is unfortunate that it was reached in a case that was quite as results-driven as *Yearworth*.

5

Public Umbilical Cord Blood Banking and Charitable Trusts

CAMERON STEWART, LORENA APARICIO,
WENDY LIPWORTH and IAN KERRIDGE

Introduction

Umbilical cord blood (UCB) is the blood from foetal and maternal circulation in the placenta and umbilical cord. This blood is rich in haematopoietic stem cells. These cells have the capacity for self-renewal, proliferation and differentiation – developing into all of the mature blood cells and maintaining bone marrow function throughout life.[1]

Since the late 1980s, haematopoietic stem cells collected from UCB have been successfully used in haematopoietic stem cell transplantation (HSCT) to treat leukaemia or bone marrow failure syndromes, as an alternative source of stem cells to those obtained from bone marrow or peripheral blood. As a result, many societies have heavily invested in public banking of cord blood units to provide them as a resource for treatment and research.

This chapter examines the nature of public cord blood banking (with a particular focus on the Australian experience) and the notions of 'stewardship' and 'custodianship' that have been a feature of other accounts of biobanking.[2] Since 2009 a number of common law decisions have recognised the possibility that the *res nullius* rule (which prevents unprocessed human tissue from being considered an object of property) may be relaxed. Some scholars have begun to examine how notions of stewardship and custodianship might work within a property law

[1] KK Ballen, E Gluckman and HE Broxmeyer, 'Umbilical Cord Blood Transplantation: The First 25 Years and Beyond' (2013) 122 *Blood* 491; JE Wagner and E Gluckman, 'Umbilical Cord Blood Transplantation: The First 20 Years' (2010) 47 *Seminars in Hematology* 3; E Gluckman, 'Umbilical Cord Blood Transplant in Human' (1996) *Hematology and Cell Therapy* 38.

[2] BR Jeffers, 'Human Biological Materials in Research: Ethical Issues and the Role of Stewardship in Minimizing Research Risks' (2001) 24 *Advances in Nursing Science* 32; PH Williams, K Schepp, B McGrath and P Mitchell, 'The Stewardship Model Current Viability for Genetic Biobank Practice Development' (2010) 33 *Advances in Nursing Science* E41.

framework.[3] Following the work of Winickoff and Winickoff, this chapter will argue that donations of UCB (and tissue more generally) are best regarded as charitable gifts and that public UCB banks might be reimagined as charitable trusts.[4]

The chapter begins by reviewing the history of UCB banking (with a focus on the Australian experience) and the concepts of tissue stewardship and custodianship that are a feature of public biobanking. It then reviews the law of charity and sets out its basic elements. The final part of the chapter applies charity law to public UCB banks, arguing that charity law provides a legal framework for understanding the nature of the steward/custodian relationship in the context of UCB donation.

Umbilical Cord Blood and the Emergence of Public Banking in Australia and Internationally

Since the late 1980s, haematopoietic stem cells collected from UCB have been successfully used in HSCT for leukaemia or bone marrow failure syndromes, as an alternative source of stem cells to those obtained from bone marrow or peripheral blood.[5] There are a number of advantages of using UCB for HSCT. The first is that the collection of UCB, which occurs at the time of delivery, does not require a surgical procedure (as is needed for bone marrow collection) or administration of drugs (which is needed for collecting stem cells from peripheral blood). The second advantage of UCB is that, because of the relative 'immaturity' of the neonatal immune system, there is less necessity for complete immunological (HLA) matching between the donor and recipient. Thirdly, because UCB is taken from a

[3] The traditional rule prevented tissue from being the subject of property rights, unless it had been transformed by work and skill: *Doodeward v Spence* (1908) 6 CLR 406; *Dobson v North Tyneside Health Authority* [1997] 1 WLR 596; *R v Kelly and Lindsay* [1999] QB 621. Recent cases have opened up the possibility of having property rights in tissue which are not based on the work and skill exception: *Yearworth v North Bristol NHS Trust* [2010] QB 1; *Bazley v Wesley Monash IVF Pty Ltd* [2011] 2 Qd R 207; *Re Edwards* (2011) 81 NSWLR 198; *Re H (No 2)* [2012] SASC 177; *Re Section 22 of the Human Tissue and Transplant Act 1982; ex parte C* [2013] WASC 3.

[4] DE Winickoff and RN Winickoff, 'The Charitable Trust as a Model for Genomic Biobanks' (2003) 349 *New England Journal of Medicine* 1180.

[5] United States National Marrow Donor Program, *Disease-Specific HCT Indications and Outcomes Data*, available at: https://bethematchclinical.org/transplant-indications-and-outcomes/disease-specific-indications-and-outcomes/. Bone marrow transplant is an established treatment modality for many patients with acute or chronic leukaemias, lymphomas, or bone marrow failure syndromes. Haematopoietic progenitor (or stem) cells for transplantation may be sourced from umbilical cord blood or from adult donors. In adults, there are two types of haematopoietic progenitor cell donation: bone marrow and peripheral blood stem cell. Bone marrow donation involves a surgical procedure in which liquid marrow is extracted from the back of the pelvic bone. Peripheral blood stem cell donation is a non-surgical procedure in which haematopoietic progenitor cells are removed from the blood using a procedure similar to donating plasma. In each case, the cells are infused into bone marrow recipients following the administration of high doses of chemo/radiotherapy.

newborn, the donor blood is less likely to carry infection risks to the recipient. UCB also has the advantage of being immediately available because it is stored in umbilical cord banks.

Outcomes following UCB transplantation in adults and children are generally equivalent to outcomes of bone marrow or peripheral blood stem cell transplants. There are some limitations with using UCB for transplantation, particularly those related to the lower quantity of cells and prolonged time for engraftment (the length of time from transplantation before mature cells are seen in the recipient's blood). Questions are emerging about potential risks to the 'donor' related to early cord clamping and possible effects on haemoglobin and iron stores, but overall UCB transplantation is considered highly efficacious.[6]

As the advantages of cord blood transplantation have come to be recognised, and the number of cord blood transplants performed (particularly in children) has increased, an international network of 54 public cord blood banks have been established to support transplantation. Cord blood stored in publicly funded banks is generally available to anyone in the world for whom the blood is an immunological 'match', meaning that cord blood collected in one country might be used elsewhere. In the last 20 years an estimated 600,000 UCB units have been banked worldwide, and 20,000 have been used in the treatment of adults and children with life-threatening malignant and non-malignant diseases.[7]

In Australia, the first public cord blood bank opened in New South Wales in 1995, followed by one in Victoria in 1996, in Queensland in 1998 and in Western Australia in 2011. There are now a number of public cord blood banks, which are all affiliated to the Australian Bone Marrow Donor Registry (ABMDR). These include the Sydney Cord Blood Bank, Melbourne's BMDI Cord Blood Bank, the Queensland Cord Blood Bank in Brisbane and the Cord Blood Bank at Perth's King Edward Memorial Hospital. The Australian National Network of Umbilical Cord Blood Banks and Cord Blood Collection Centres (Auscord) provides national coordination of these banks. The Network includes 11 collection centres, the majority located at public hospitals in large metropolitan areas. There are participating hospitals in Sydney, Melbourne, Brisbane and Darwin. (The hospital in Darwin only accepts donations from indigenous Australians.) Auscord stores approximately 25,000 cord blood units, and around 100 of those are released for transplant each year.[8]

While the focus of UCB banking has traditionally been to provide UCB for transplant, UCB units have also become a useful resource for research.[9] This research explores the biological properties and potential therapeutic uses of

[6] SJ McDonald, P Middleton, T Dowswell and PS Morris, 'Effect of Timing of Umbilical Cord Clamping of Term Infants on Maternal and Neonatal Outcomes (Review)' (2013) 7 *Cochrane Database of Systematic Reviews* CD0047074.

[7] Wagner and Gluckman, 'Umbilical Cord Blood Transplantation: The First 20 Years', above n 1.

[8] Australian Bone Marrow Donor Registry, *Frequently Asked Questions* available at: www.abmdr.org.au/abmdr2/page/frequently-asked-questions

[9] W Fodor, 'Tissue Engineering and Cell Based Therapies, From the Bench to the Clinic: The Potential to Replace, Repair and Regenerate' (2003) 1 *Reproductive Biology and Endocrinology* 102.

haematopoetic stem cells, other stem cells present in cord blood (particularly mesenchymal stem cells), and the cord tissue. Animal and human pre-clinical and clinical studies are investigating the use of UCB in a range of diseases where the capacity for cellular regeneration and immunomodulation may be beneficial, including diabetes, arthritis, brain and spinal cord injury, and cerebral palsy.[10]

In Australia, the dual possibilities of therapeutic use and research use for UCB are acknowledged in the consent process. The Auscord consent form states:

> After quality control testing requirements are met, the banked cord blood will be available anonymously to patients needing treatment for blood disorders such as leukaemias and some types of cancer. If the cord blood is not suitable for banking, it may be disposed of appropriately, or used for quality control purposes or for research into stem cells or treatment of relevant diseases using protocols approved by an appropriate Human Research Ethics Committee.[11]

The use of UCB for therapy and research is an excellent example of the way in which advances in technology can transform our perception of human tissue as waste material into recognition of it as something highly valuable in both clinical and monetary terms. As Waldby observes, 'for hospitals and clinics that have the right of disposal, waste tissue has considerable commercial and epistemological value'.[12] This change of status has been viewed sociologically as 'a critical site for social change', modifying associations, relationships and institutions.[13] However, this means that UCB is now a commodity over which particular groups vie for control. As a consequence, cord blood stem cells have become a focus of public, medical and scientific debate, and issues of ownership and control frequently arise.

There are many ways in which this contest has become evident. The most obvious is the threat that private banking poses to the very viability of public cord blood banks, as UCB transplantation relies upon having sufficient numbers of cord blood units donated by people of diverse immuno-genetic heritage. The more cords that go to the private banks, the fewer cords there are available for the public banks. Controversy arises when people want access to their child's publicly banked UCB for use in experimental therapies, either for the child or for another family member. Controversy also surrounds the use of both publicly and privately stored UCB units for research that precludes their subsequent therapeutic use. Disputes of this kind mean that greater clarity is needed about the legal nature of stored UCB and the responsibilities of public banks in using these resources.

[10] H Zhou, S Chang and M Rao, 'Human Cord Blood Applications in Cell Therapy: Looking Back and Look Ahead' (2012) 12 *Expert Opinion on Biological Therapy* 1059.

[11] Auscord, 'Cord Blood Donation to Public Cord Blood Bank Informed Consent Form'.

[12] C Waldby and R Mitchell, *Tissue Economies: Blood, Organs and Cell Lines in Late Capitalism* (Durham, Duke University Press, 2006) 115.

[13] P Santoro, 'Liminal Biopolitics: Towards a Political Anthropology of the Umbilical Cord and the Placenta' (2011) 17 *Body & Society* 73–93, 76.

Concepts of Stewardship and Custodianship

One way in which commentators have tried to negotiate competing claims to banked human tissue is via the concept of stewardship. Stewardship is characterised by

> [t]he responsible use of resources, accountability for the well-being of another, and service to others. The steward acts to benefit others with an awareness that what is stewarded is something of value. (footnote omitted)[14]

According to Jeffers, in the tissue-banking context:

> Using a model of stewardship to guide the ethical conduct of research using human biological materials obligates the researcher to conserve the donor's values, traditions, and culture in ethical decision-making. Stewardship recognizes the importance of not only preserving the human dignity of individual research participants, but also changing what is stewarded to benefit the community of the participant. The change that occurs within a stewardship model increases the value of what is stewarded in order to achieve the outcomes of preservation of human dignity and benefit for the common good. It does not rule out possible benefits to the individual donating the material or the steward; however, the primary obligation of the steward is to improve what is given for the common good. The emphasis is protection of entrusted resources to serve common humanity. (footnotes omitted)[15]

Importantly, as the practice of biobanking grows from single purpose and isolated repositories to multinational networks of biobanked tissue, the concept of stewardship must also change. Fullerton et al make the point that:

> In most first generation biorepository research, the burden of stewardship fell to the originating investigator or institution and was achieved by faithfulness to the terms of informed consent and the adoption of data protections like anonymization. However, with the retention of identifying information, an expectation of ongoing oversight coordinated across independent institutions, and the need to maintain communication with participants in light of the openended nature of the research commitment, next-generation biorepository research entails far greater demands for stewardship and researcher accountability. These responsibilities may include taking due care with the analysis and sharing of confidential genetic and linked health information, the adoption of research goals consistent with the intentions of participants, and the avoidance of forms of dissemination (publications and similar) that promote harmful or derogatory conclusions about certain populations or groups.[16]

However, some authors characterise this way of holding tissue as 'custodianship'. Concepts of custodianship also emphasise the duty of the tissue bank to protect

[14] Jeffers, 'Human Biological Materials in Research: Ethical Issues and the Role of Stewardship in Minimizing Research Risks', above n 2 at 40.

[15] ibid.

[16] SM Fullerton et al, 'Meeting the Governance Challenges of Next-Generation Biorepository Research' (2010) 2 *Science Translational Medicine* 1.

and preserve the tissue, to protect the privacy of the donors, and to promote observance of and compliance with the donor's consent.[17] The Office of Biorepositories and Biospecimen Research, the US Department of Health and Human Services, National Institutes of Health and the National Cancer Institute have said, in a joint statement:

> Custodianship is the caretaking responsibility for biospecimens that extends from collection through research use. Responsible custodianship requires careful planning and transparent policies to ensure the long-term physical quality of the biospecimens, the privacy of human research participants, the confidentiality of associated data, and the appropriate use of biospecimens and data. In the interest of transparency, biospecimen resource policies should be made available to the public either electronically or for onsite inspection.[18]

As the discussion above indicated, the practice of public UCB banking is made difficult by the competing claims of therapeutic uses and research needs of society. Incorporating concepts of stewardship and custodianship into the regulatory frameworks of UCB biobanking would help to provide a framework which both reflects how public UCB banks see themselves and can be used to mediate disputes over access to these tissues. The challenge from a legal perspective is to choose a regulatory mechanism which respects the power of the public bank to control the resource of the biobanked tissue but in such a way that the bank fully adopts, and is regulated by, concepts of custodianship and stewardship.

One method might be to employ the doctrine of informed consent, which would focus on the act of donation and require that banks fully inform the donor of how the tissue is going to be taken, stored and used.[19] In ethics, informed consent is concerned with respecting patients' autonomy over their bodies and preventing bodily interference which has not been agreed to. When applied to tissue donation there is an assumption that this concept of bodily integrity can be extended to tissues which have been excised from the body. Applied in this way, the patient should be informed not only about the process of extracting the tissue but also about any future processes to which the excised tissue will be subjected.

In law, the doctrine of informed consent is a doctrine of negligence which is concerned with the duty to inform patients about the risks of medical treat-

[17] K Melham, G Marsden, J Wiles and D Jatavallabhula, 'Enacting Regulation: Tissue in Practice' (2013) 19 *Diagnostic Histopathology* 9; B Godard, J Schmidtke, JJ Cassiman and S Ayme, 'Data Storage and DNA Banking for Biomedical Research: Informed Consent, Confidentiality, Quality Issues, Ownership, Return of Benefits. A Professional Perspective' (2003) 11(2) *European Journal of Human Genetics* S88; G Hallmans and JB Vaught, 'Best Practices for Establishing a Biobank' in J Dillner (ed), *Methods in Biobanking* (New York, Springer, 2010).

[18] Office of Biorepositories and Biospecimen Research, US Department of Health and Human Services, National Institutes of Health and the National Cancer Institute, *NCI Best Practices for Biospecimen Resources 2011*, available at: biospecimens.cancer.gov/bestpractices.

[19] EW Clayton et al, 'Informed Consent for Genetic Research on Stored Tissue Samples' (1995) 22 *The Journal of the American Medical Association* 1786; L Trommelmans, J Selling and K Dierickx, 'The Importance of the Values Attached to Cells for a Good Informed Consent Procedure in Cell Donation for Tissue Engineering Purposes' (2009) 10 *Cell and Tissue Banking* 293.

ment.[20] Ordinarily, those risks are risks which may impact on the person's health, but in tissue donation the risks would relate to how the tissue would be used in research or treatment.

The main problem with informed consent in the tissue-banking context is that it is impossible to gain informed consent when a person is donating tissue for future unspecified uses. The whole benefit of tissue banking lies its potential to provide resources for unknown research and yet-to-be-discovered treatments.[21] Using the informed consent doctrine in tissue banking requires researchers to either 're-approach donors for informed consent to every new study or they have to apply a concept of "broad" consent at the time of collection which is so far removed from the informed consent doctrine that it becomes fictional'.[22]

Another option would be to employ contract law as a mechanism for regulating tissue use in UCB banking. While the primary mechanism in donation is the gifting of tissue it is possible to envisage the UCB bank providing promises to the donor about how the tissue will be used. The exchange of tissue for promises about future behaviour would, arguably, be valuable consideration that would support a legally binding contract. This would enable the donor to enforce the promises concerning future use, whether through specific performance or damages.

However, contract law suffers from a major shortcoming. The contract is only enforceable between the parties due to the doctrine of privity of contract. If the tissue passes out of the hands of the original bank and into the hands of other members of a biobank network, for example, contract law can no longer apply and the donor no longer has any direct control over the use of the tissue.

A third option is to apply a property-based approach. Unlike contract, where the rights exist only between the parties (*in personam*), property rights create rights that are enforceable against the world (*in rem*).[23] Those rights flow with the property and can control how third parties can have access to and use the

[20] In some jurisdictions (eg England and Wales) the medical profession can determine what types of risk should be communicated to patients (a doctor-based standard): *Sidaway v Governors of Bethlem Royal Hospital* [1985] AC 871. In other jurisdictions (eg Australia) a patient's own subjective desire for information may set the standard for information (a patient-based standard): *Rogers v Whitaker* (1992) 175 CLR 479.

[21] T Caulfield, R Brown and E Meslin, 'Challenging a Well Established Consent Norm? One Time Consent for Biobank Research' (2007) 4 *Journal of International Biotechnology Law* 69; T Caulfield, 'Biobanks and Blanket Consent: The Proper Place of the Public Good and Public Perception Rationales' (2007) 18 *Kings Law Journal* 209. But for a defence of broad consent, see M Otlowski, 'Developing an Appropriate Consent Model for Biobanks: In Defence of "Broad" Consent' in J Kaye and M Stranger (eds), *Principles and Practice of Biobank Governance* (Ashgate, Aldershot, 2009) and National Health Medical Research Council, *Biobanks Information Paper* (2010) 23–25.

[22] C Stewart, J Fleming and I Kerridge, 'The Law of Gifts, Conditional Donation and Biobanking' (2013) 21(2) *Journal of Law and Medicine* 351, 353. See also, B Hoffmann, 'Broadening Consent – And Diluting Ethics?' (2013) 35 *Journal of Medical Ethics* 125; LA Siminoff and HM Traino, 'Consenting to Donation: An Examination of Current Practices in Informed Consent for Tissue Donation in the US' (2013) 14 *Cell and Tissue Banking* 85.

[23] For a discussion of the costs and benefits of property rights, see S Douglas, 'The Argument for Property Rights in Body Parts: Scarcity of Resources' (2014) 40 *Journal of Medical Ethics* 23; J Wall, 'The Legal Status of Body Parts: A Framework' (2013) 31 *Oxford Journal of Legal Studies* 783.

property. Rights *in rem* have the potential to avoid the limitations of both the informed consent doctrine and contract law because of their ability to control behaviours of people accessing and using the property into the future. However, if a property approach were adopted it would need to be one which balanced out the interests of UCB banks as the holder of property and also protected and enforced concepts of stewardship and custodianship. In our view, the best legal relationship for that purpose is the charitable trust.

The Law of Charitable Trusts

Trusts are property relationships that originated in the equitable jurisdiction of Chancery during the Middle Ages. They remain incredibly useful and popular today. In an ordinary express trust, a person (the *trustee*) ordinarily holds the legal title to property on behalf of a third party (the *beneficiary*). The trustee is the legal owner but the beneficiaries have an equitable interest in the property. The trustee is a fiduciary, meaning that the trustee is obliged to refrain from acting in ways which cause conflict between his or her own interests and that of the beneficiaries. Trustees must also comply with the instructions contained in the trust instrument and comply with the intention of the creator of the trust (the *settlor*).

Charitable trusts are a species of express trust, but they are distinct because they exist for a purpose rather than for identifiable beneficiaries.[24] In a charitable trust, the legal title to property is transferred to the trustee with instructions on how the property may be employed towards the charitable purpose that serves the public interest. The charitable trust therefore employs private property rights but in such a way that they must both be used in accordance with the instructions of the settlor and in the service of the public interest.

There are two main requirements for a charitable trust to be valid. First, the trust must be created for a charitable purpose. Secondly, the trust must benefit the public.

What types of purpose are considered charitable? There is no exhaustive definition of the term 'charitable purpose'. Instead, the courts have traditionally begun with the *Statute of Charitable Uses 1601*,[25] which is sometimes referred to as the *Statute of Elizabeth*. The preamble to this statute contained a statement as to the types of charitable purpose that would be recognised at law. They included, in rough translation: the relief of poverty; the care of aged persons and the sick; the care of soldiers and mariners; the advancement of education through building universities and schools; the repair of bridges, havens, ports, churches and highways; the care of orphans; the maintenance of prisons; the marriage of poor maids; support for young tradesmen and persons decayed; the relief or redemp-

[24] *Attorney-General (NSW) v Perpetual Trustee Co Ltd* (1940) 63 CLR 209 at 222.

[25] *Statute of Charitable Uses 1601*, 43 Eliz I c 4.

tion of prisoners or captives; and relief for poor persons concerning the payment of taxes.

In the nineteenth century in *Commissioner for Special Purposes of Income Tax v Pemsel*,[26] Lord Macnaughten simplified the process further by dividing up the purposes in the preamble into four main groupings, namely, trusts for the relief of poverty; trusts for the advancement of education; trusts for the advancement of religion; and trusts for other purposes beneficial to the community not falling under the preceding heads.[27]

Until recently, the preamble was still employed by judges as a tool for determining whether or not a purpose was charitable.[28] The judges would begin with the preamble and would then test whether the proposed use of trust property falls within or is analogous to the traditional categories. Traditionally, this test was framed as whether the purpose was 'within its spirit and intendment' of the preamble.[29] Lord Reid discussed this process in *Scottish Burial Reform and Cremation Society v Glasgow Corp* and said that the courts should look for an analogy between the intended purpose and one that is either in the preamble or has already been recognised as charitable by the courts.[30]

Over the last 10 years, the UK, New Zealand and Australia have all adopted statutory tests for charitable purpose which have essentially preserved and codified the existing law, while trimming away some of the infelicities. In the UK the preamble has been replaced by a lengthy definition.[31] In New Zealand the statutory definition is based on the four *Pemsel* categories (meaning that the older preamble-style approach survives).[32] In Australia the codification is similar to the UK definition but this definition only applies at the federal level.[33] The Australian states are still bound by the older definitions and the test for whether the proposed purpose meets the spirit and intendment of the preamble.

As stated above, charitable trusts are often referred to as 'public' trusts because of the requirement that they confer a benefit on the general public.[34] The benefit must be for the entire public or for a significant proportion of it.[35]

Equity adopted a rebuttable presumption that trusts for the relief of poverty, trusts for education and trusts for the advancement of religion would be for the

[26] *Commissioner for Special Purposes of Income Tax v Pemsel* [1891] AC 531.

[27] ibid at 583.

[28] *Royal National Agricultural and Industrial Association v Chester* (1974) 3 ALR 486 at 487. In some jurisdictions the use of the preamble is recognised in legislation even though the Act has been repealed: *Trustee Act 1925* (ACT), s 104, sch 1; *Imperial Acts Application Act 1969* (NSW), s 9(2); *Trusts Act 1973* (Qld), s 103(1).

[29] *Gilmour v Coates* [1949] AC 426 at 442–43.

[30] *Scottish Burial Reform and Cremation Society v Glasgow Corp* [1968] AC 138 at 147.

[31] Charities Act 2011 (UK), s 3.

[32] Charity Act 2006 (NZ), s 5. See *YMCA New Zealand Soldiers Great War Memorial Trust* [2013] NZHC 2516; *Greenpeace of New Zealand Incorporated* [2012] NZCA 533 (leave to appeal granted in *Re Greenpeace of New Zealand Inc* [2013] NZSC 12).

[33] Charities Act 2013 (Cth), s 12(1).

[34] GE Dal Pont, *Equity and Trusts in Australia*, 5th edn (Sydney, Lawbook Co, 2011) 841.

[35] *National Anti-Vivisection Society v Inland Revenue Commissioners* [1948] AC 31; *Gilmour v Coats* [1949] AC 426; *Re Compton* [1945] ch 123; *Oppenheim v Tobacco Securities Co Ltd* [1951] AC 297.

benefit of the public. In contrast, trusts in the fourth *Pemsel* category would have to be proven to be beneficial.[36] This is also reflected in the Australian legislation.[37]

The public nature of charitable trusts also means that Crown has power to supervise their operation.[38] The Crown, usually acting through an Attorney-General or through courts of superior jurisdiction, is the only competent authority to protect and enforce charitable trusts.[39] The Attorneys-General of each jurisdiction represent the Crown's interests in matters of charitable trusts and have standing to appear in proceedings concerning charities. Indeed, the Attorney-General is a necessary party to any proceedings regarding a gift to charity that is made generally or for undefined charitable purposes, or for any proceedings concerning the alteration of a charity's rules.[40] The representatives of charitable institutions can also appear when they are involved in the administration of the trust. A statutory right to appear has been granted in some jurisdictions to persons who have an interest in the charitable trust.[41] Trustees also have a right to seek advice and get directions from the court.[42] Advice may be sought in relation to issues concerning the management or administration of the trust property.[43]

[36] *National Anti-Vivisection Society v Inland Revenue Commissioners* [1948] AC 31 at 42. But see *Helena Partnerships Ltd v Commissioner for Her Majesty's Revenue and Customs* [2012] EWCA Civ 569, where this approach was doubted.

[37] Charities Act 2013 (Cth), s 7. Section 7 stipulates that there is a rebuttable presumption that the requirement of public benefit set out in s 6(1) if the entity's purpose is any of the following:

(a) the purpose of preventing and relieving sickness, disease or human suffering;
(b) the purpose of advancing education;
(c) the purpose of relieving the poverty, distress or disadvantage of individuals or families;
(d) the purpose of caring for and supporting:
  (i) the aged; or
  (ii) individuals with disabilities;
(e) the purpose of advancing religion.

Special provisions also apply to trusts for indigenous Australians: s 9.

[38] *Num-Hoi, Pon Yu, Soon-Duc Society Inc v Num Pon Soon Inc* (2001) 4 VR 527; *Tomasevic v Jovetic* [2011] VSC 131.

[39] The jurisdiction originates from the ancient *parens patriae* jurisdiction, which gives the Crown and the courts the power to care for infants and the mentally disabled (who were traditionally classed 'idiots' and 'natural fools', or 'lunatics'): *Hunter Region SLSA Helicopter Rescue Service Ltd v Attorney-General (NSW)* [2000] NSWSC 456; *Australian Incentive Plan Pty Ltd v Babcock & Brown International Pty Ltd (No 2)* [2011] VSC 43 at [7].

[40] P Radan and C Stewart, *Principles of Australian Equity and Trusts*, 2nd edn (Sydney, LexisNexis, 2013) ch 18.

[41] See *Charities Procedure Act 1812*, 52 Geo III c 101, which appears to still apply in the Northern Territory; *Trustee Act 1925* (ACT), s 94A; *Charitable Trusts Act 1993* (NSW), s 6 (proceedings to be brought with the Attorney-General's permission or with the leave of the court); *Trusts Act 1973* (Qld), s 106(2), *Trustee Act 1936* (SA), ss 60(2), 66; *Religious Successory and Charitable Trusts Act 1958* (Vic), s 61 (two or more persons with the consent of a law officer); *Charitable Trusts Act 1962* (WA), s 21(1).

[42] *Re Permanent Trustee Australia Ltd* (1994) 33 NSWLR 547.

[43] *In the Matter of Creditors' Trust of Jackgreen (International) Pty Ltd* [2011] NSWSC 748; *In the Matter of the Daquino Family Trust* [2009] NSWSC 429; *Re Saunders Nominees Pty Ltd; ex parte Saunders Nominees Pty Ltd* [2007] WASC 152; *The Kean Memorial Trust Inc v AG for SA (No 2)* [2007] SASC 133.

Charitable trusts can charge for their services and may make a profit, as long as that profit is reinvested in the charitable purpose.[44] Charities may even own other businesses not otherwise associated with the charity and run them at a profit and still claim the benefit of charitable status.[45] This gives the charity the benefit of running their properties like a private property owner, while at the same time recognising that the profits must be reinvested in the charitable purposes.

Finally, an interesting feature of charitable trusts is that they can be varied when circumstances change and it is impossible or impractical to carry out the charitable objects of the trust in the way the creator of the trust originally intended. Such changes to charitable trusts are known as cy près schemes. As long as the creator of the trust has expressed a general charitable intention, the court will be able to reformulate the trust so that it will be able to continue serving its underlying charitable purpose. Cy près schemes can be applied in cases where the original terms of the trust have ceased to provide a suitable and effective method of using the trust property and more appropriate uses are available which accord with current policy or knowledge.[46]

Applying a Charitable Trust Framework to Public Umbilical Cord Blood Banks

Would public UCB banks be understood as having a charitable purpose? There are three bases on which it could be argued that they do.

First, given the focus of public UCB banks on providing therapeutic products, it could be argued that public banks are trusts for the relief of poverty. The poverty category includes trusts for the 'impotent', namely vulnerable people who may suffer from an illness or disability.[47] Gifts to hospitals and similar institutions also fall within the poverty category.[48]

[44] *The Incorporated Council of Law Reporting of the State of Queensland v FCT* (1971) 125 CLR 659 at 669–70; *Crystal Palace Trustees v Minister of Town and Country Planning* [1951] 2 Ch 132; *Re Resch's Will Trusts; Le Cras v Perpetual Trustee Co Ltd* [1969] 1 AC 514.

[45] *Commissioner of Taxation v Word Investments* (2008) 236 CLR 204.

[46] *Attorney-General for New South Wales v Fulham* [2002] NSWSC 629 at [12]–[17]. In *The Cram Foundation v Corbett-Jones* [2006] NSWSC 495, a cy près scheme was ordered for the use of a home which had been originally intended for the care of 'crippled' children. Changes in government policy to shift towards de-institutionalisation meant that the original terms were no longer a suitable and effective means of carrying out the donor's intention. The court agreed with a plan to use the property as a conference centre where the funds would go towards the care of children with disabilities.

[47] Examples of such trusts include: trusts for orphans (*Attorney-General (NSW) v Perpetual Trustee Co Ltd* (1940) 63 CLR 209); trusts for 'crippled children' (*The Cram Foundation v Corbett-Jones* [2006] NSWSC 495); trusts for 'retarded' or 'sub-normal' children (*Eurella Community Services Inc v Attorney General for the State of NSW* [2010] NSWSC 566); and trusts for the blind *Re Inman (dec'd)* [1965] VR 238. See also the Charities Act 2013 (Cth), s 12(1)(a) which includes 'advancing health' as a charitable purpose. Section 14 states that 'advancing health' includes the purpose of preventing and relieving sickness, disease or human suffering.

[48] *Re Resch's Will Trusts; Le Cras v Perpetual Trustee Co Ltd* [1969] 1 AC 514.

Secondly, the fact that public UCB banks provide material for research means that they are trusts for education.[49] The term 'education' includes research.[50] A number of research trusts have been found to be charitable, such as trusts for research into disease and trusts for cancer research.[51]

Thirdly, gifts for public health infrastructure can also fall within the fourth *Pemsel* category because they are trusts that are otherwise beneficial to the community.[52]

The combination of these three grounds means that there are very strong reasons for concluding that public UCB banks have a charitable purpose. There are equally strong grounds for saying that the public benefit test would also be satisfied. First, as public UCB banks appear to be trusts for poverty and education, there would be a presumption of public benefit. Even if there were not a presumption, the fact that public UCB banks provide therapies to a large number of patients from diverse backgrounds would mean that the public benefit test could easily be satisfied. The fact that UCB is also provided as a research resource for the community adds to this conclusion.

The Benefits and Costs of a Charitable Trust Approach

The most obvious benefit to employing a charitable trust approach is that it provides a legal mechanism for the regulation and enforcement of concepts of custodianship and stewardship in biobanking. The charitable trust model upgrades these ethical standards into legal ones with teeth.

First, this is achieved by giving donors and members of the general public an interest in the management of the trust and the ability to approach the court if they are concerned about breaches. Secondly, the Attorney-General and the Supreme Court both have the power to supervise and manage the trust, as a way of protecting the interests of the public. The charitable trust model does both of these things while still recognising the biobank's legal ownership of the tissue and its capacity to use the tissue commercially (in accordance with the terms of the trust). The combination of private rights and public interest is part of a robust regulatory model that has been tested for 800 years.

Donors to a biobank run as a charitable trust may also receive the benefit of greater involvement. It would be open to the biobank to adopt charitable trust forms, such as a board of governors, and donors and other members of the public would have an opportunity to be involved in the running of the bank.[53] A contin-

[49] See Charities Act 2013 (Cth), s 12(1)(b).

[50] *Taylor v Taylor* (1910) 10 CLR 218.

[51] *Estate of Schultz* [1961] SASR 377; *Re Simpson (dec'd)* [1961] QWN 50.

[52] *Perpetual Trustee Co Ltd v St Luke's Hospital* (1939) 39 SR (NSW) 408.

[53] Winickoff and Winickoff, 'The Charitable Trust as a Model for Genomic Biobanks', above n 4 at 1182.

ued and involved relationship may reduce the ethical dilemmas of consent to future research, incidental findings and unanticipated results, because the donors will be encouraged to stay in contact with the biobank.

The charitable trust model is also of benefit to the biobank. Under the charitable model the biobank can seek the help and advice of the courts about difficult issues of management. The biobank can also operate at a profit and maintain its charitable status. If circumstances change, and new opportunities for use and research arise that were not originally conceived by trust, the biobank can approach the court and seek to amend its terms of operation via the cy près doctrine. The charitable trust model therefore provides biobanks with support and flexibility. The underlying value of altruism, which is a feature of charitable trusts, may also encourage greater feelings of trust and community support for the biobank and higher rates of donation.

The cost of adopting this model is that there will be greater oversight and accountability and this may add to the running expenses of the organisation. Charitable trusts are subject to reporting and accounting requirements, but arguably these would be not much greater that the reporting requirements that biobanks already face.

Conclusion: Biobanks would Benefit from a Charitable Trust Model

This chapter has argued that current biobanking practices need to incorporate ethical values of custodianship and stewardship into their frameworks. Using the example of public cord blood banking, we have argued that the charitable trust model is a good model to adopt for this purpose. The charity model has the ability to balance out the private and public aspects of biobanking and incorporate a continuing concern for the interests of donors. The requirement that charitable trusts are run in the public interest is also fully compatible with the notion that biobanking occurs in a framework of community expectations and interests. A charitable trust model allows a biobank to balance out the different claims that are made to access and use tissue. While it does not resolve all the ethical concerns of biobanking, a charitable trust does provide a mechanism for donors to continue to have a relationship with their donated tissue, which is monitored and controlled by the Attorneys-General and courts of higher jurisdiction. Charitable trusts law is, therefore, a very suitable mechanism for introducing and enforcing obligations of stewardship and custodianship.

6

Property Rights in the Human Body: Commodification and Objectification

KATE GREASLEY

Introduction

Objection to the development of legal property rights in human body parts and material can come in a number of forms, but one of the more prevalent moral objections attacks such rights on the grounds that they improperly *commodify* that which ought to remain non-commodified, that is, the deeply personal. Commodification paradigmatically entails the fungibility or marketability of an object; an object is commodified when it is made reducible to a cash equivalent and the possible object of commercial transaction. Most commodities are, of course, entirely unproblematic. Clothes, furniture and electrical devices are all non-contentious examples. Commodification of an item is seen as crass or ideally avoided only in relation to particular things, things that are deemed in one way or another special or, perhaps, especially personal. The inappropriateness of commodifying particularly personal things is often thought to derive from certain collateral harms, such as subordination, social oppression or injustice. These harms target the social groups typically providing the commodified items – for example, prostitutes, paid kidney donors, or surrogates for pregnancy. Where the human body itself is the commodity in question, as in these examples, a significant part of the supposed wrong of commodification is what seems (at first) to be a more intrinsic kind of wrong: that of *objectification.*

Objectification is, in short, the treating as a mere thing something that is in fact more than that. Objectification can come about in a variety of ways, only one of which is commodification, and objectification is only one part of what *can* be wrong with commodification (many people object to the commodification of natural resources such as water, not because the resource is thereby objectified, but because, being so essential for all human life, it ought not to be monopolised). Why I say objectification only seems *at first* to be more of an intrinsic kind of wrong than the other harms associated with inapposite commodification will hopefully become clear as the discussion progresses. However, the notion that commodification of the human body and its parts amounts to the objectification of human beings is a serious source of objection to legal property rights in the human body. Importantly, the objection might well be directed not only at rights of outright sale, but at other, more limited rights of property in the human body that some common law jurisdictions have granted or have considered granting – rights to possess, control or profit from bodily material. These rights may not commodify absolutely; they do not turn body parts into items of simple trade. But as we shall see, commodification can be a matter of degree, and insofar as any of the disputed property rights partially treat the human body as an item of trade, one can also ask whether they objectify humans.

My aim in what follows here is first to give an account of why the commodification of the personal, and the human body in particular, is often considered objectionable, and the specific role that objectification plays in such thinking. Using what is gleaned from that part of the discussion, I will then briefly consider some of the main existing or potential legal property rights in the human body, and offer an analysis of how much the commodification and objectification concerns militate against the existence of the right in each case. The point of the exercise is not to derive concrete conclusions about every proposed right (for this, far more detail would need to be considered) but merely to demonstrate how the salient considerations ought to be accounted for in our reasoning process. *How* should one argue about the possible commodification of the human body through legal property rights?

Commodification and Objectification

The suggestion that legal property rights in the human body or body parts will improperly commodify those things is one that is generally levelled at the marketisation (legal or illegal) of all things deemed inappropriate objects of trade, other notable examples being sex, babies and human slaves. Naturally, not all property rights amount to commodification within the meaning of *marketability*; they do not all make the object in question *saleable*. The menu of possible property rights in the human body is more varied than that, as other contributors to this volume point out. But we might also recognise the wider sense in which the human body and its parts might be in some measure commodified whenever it is treated as property for any legal purposes. Recognising the proprietary nature of human tissue is to recognise that part of it which can be and is a desirable commodity, its severability from the progenitor, and its value independent from them. There are other ways the law can give credence to the proprietary conception of the human body further to permitting its marketisation.

But what is the harm in doing so? That is, what is the harm of commodifying that which ought not to be commodified? One part of the problem is that commodification can be a route to *objectification*. Martha Nussbaum defines objectification as 'treating *as an object* what is not really an object, what is in fact, a human being'.[1] In objectifying a person, one is thus 'making into a thing, treating as a thing, something that is really not a thing'.[2] This certainly does not mean that using other people as instruments, even partially, is always morally prohibited. As Leslie Green reminds us, Kant's imperative is to refrain from treating people *merely* as means, when they are also ends in themselves; it is not prohibited to treat them as a means *at all*.[3] For we *are* all objects as well as subjects; we are flesh and blood and bones and beating hearts, and recognising one another's objectivity cannot altogether be avoided. We *do* need other people instrumentally, right down to (perhaps, particularly) needing their bodies. What is more, Green argues that *being needed* instrumentally can even be an important part of human fulfilment; we desire to feel useful as means as well as valuable as ends in ourselves. Hence those who feel they are no longer able to fulfil any purpose as an instrument, whether it be through work or otherwise, can lack an important source of satisfaction. We do not wrongly objectify, then, whenever we acknowledge or rely on one another's instrumentality, but only when in doing so we suppress or disregard their nature as subjects. In Green's words:[4]

> Objectification is not reification. It is a matter of treating as a mere object something that is also more than an object; it is a matter of denying or devaluing their subjectivity, as failing to recognize them as 'ends in themselves'.

Hence, as regards *sexual* objectification:

> To be treated as a sex object is, in part, for one's own desires, hungers and needs in sex to be removed from view and to be seen solely as a means to the fulfilment of the desires, hungers and needs of another.

When used in its pejorative sense, objectification connotes something in excess; we might say it is the excessive amplifying of a person's 'thing-ness', and a correlative muting or drowning out of her *personhood*. The women who feature in pornography are people *as well* as objects of sexual desire; they are mothers, daughters and friends, with aspirations, proclivities, opinions and emotions. But all of these dimensions of their being are pushed out of the frame when mainstream (and I stress, *mainstream*) pornography reduces them to raw meat.[5]

[1] M Nussbaum, 'Objectification' (1995) 24 *Philosophy and Public Affairs* 249–91.

[2] ibid, 257.

[3] L Green, 'Pornographies' (2000) 8 *Journal of Political Philosophy* 27.

[4] ibid.

[5] Importantly, Green does not argue that all pornography is for this reason inherently wrong, for it is not his view that sexual objectification is wrong by definition. Rather, his central insight is that the harmfulness of sexual objectification in pornography is not an essential harm, but depends to a significant extent on other facts concerning the class of objectified persons and the intended audience of the pornographic material. The objectification of women in heterosexual, misogynistic pornography is harmful (if it is) because it objectifies a class of persons, women, who are, in the surrounding culture (and particularly for the target audience) already overly identified as sex objects, to the suppression of their subjectivity. It thus exacerbates and cultivates the existing sexual oppression of women. Conversely, the sexual objectification of performers in gay male pornography might just be an important *affirmation* of the objectivity of a different class of persons, whose identity as objects of desire is sidelined in mainstream culture.

When it comes to dealing with the human body and its parts more literally as 'things' – things which can be severed, moved around, controlled, bought and sold, sued over, and profited from – one initial point to make is that objectifying the body or the part through marketisation or some other kind of property right is not always tantamount to unduly objectifying the *person* from whence the part came. As we shall see, this depends entirely on whether the commodification of the part *reduces* the person *to* that part symbolically, in common thinking, rhetoric, or in the person's own sense of self-worth or identity. As with sexual objectification, there is not an inherent problem in recognising one another's 'thing-ness' in this sense – the sense in which we are literally *made* of useful and desirable bits and pieces. The objectification which is inherent in that recognition is problematic only insofar as it drowns out the subjective worth of some human beings. And crucially, whether this by-product obtains, and in what measure, is largely a function of the surrounding context – of whether, in particular, that context can accommodate the conception of those bits and pieces as things capable of being property while avoiding undue damage to the common conception of their progenitors as *persons*.

Some further elaboration is required here. Why and how can the commodification of certain things inflict harm by means of objectification? This question is the central concern of Margaret Radin's investigation in *Contested Commodities*.[6] At its core, Radin's thesis is that the commodification by saleability of certain items that ought to remain non-commodified – which are, in her terminology, *market-inalienable* – can do violence to forms of human flourishing by diminishing aspects of personhood such as freedom and identity. Where certain conditions are needed to foster self and social development, commodification of some personal things may undermine them by encouraging people to conceive of 'personal attributes, relationships and philosophical and moral commitments as monetizable and alienable from the self'. As Radin explains, a better view of personhood, and, for her, a view which is essential to human flourishing, understands many kinds of particulars – work, family, sexuality, altruism, personal attributes – as integral to the self, and not detachable from it.

But how is anyone's sense of personhood undermined when certain items are improperly made severable from human beings – if they are, in Radin's terms, market-*alienable*? Sometimes, Radin argues, the commodified version of an item is undesirable because the use of market rhetoric in respect of that thing might create and foster an inferior conception of human flourishing. If we take the example of transactional sex, the idea would be that the act is itself degrading or diminishing of personhood – that *this* thing, one's sexuality, cannot be severed from oneself through commodification without chipping away at a healthy conception of the self and self-worth. This is the more 'intrinsic' end of the market-inalienability argument, often bound up with dignitarian concerns that it is

[6] MJ Radin, *Contested Commodities* (Cambridge, MA, Harvard University Press, 1996). See also, M Radin, 'Market-Inalienability' (1987) 100 *Harvard Law Review* 1849–937.

simply degrading to alienate certain things from oneself.[7] On a closer look, however, the objection is rarely *purely* intrinsic, being at root concerned with existing conditions of social oppression which market-alienability might exacerbate. One example is the possible further entrenchment of patriarchy that might be encouraged when women alienate their reproductive labour through contract pregnancy, or their sexuality through prostitution, thereby reinforcing their social roles as breeders and sex objects, or so the argument goes.[8] Objectification is most troubling where it is linked with social disadvantage and oppression. In a world where it rarely presented such a danger, it is hard to imagine what 'free-floating' evil would be left in treating people merely as means.

In a different vein, Radin also argues that commodified versions of certain items can damage human flourishing by tainting or suppressing the value of the *non-commodified* version of that same thing. Radin calls this the 'domino theory'. The domino theory recognises that the commodified and non-commodified versions of some interactions or transfers do not easily co-exist, in which case, a choice might have to be made about which version to keep. This is because the market rhetoric that attaches to the commodified version cannot always be prevented from changing attitudes toward the non-commodified one. Taking again the example of paid sexual interactions, the concern would be that if the commodified version (bought sex) becomes prolific enough, it will be difficult to keep all sexual relationships, and sexuality in general, entirely free from transactional thinking. Against a background context in which there is often a going rate, '*free* love' will not be entirely uncontaminated. The cross-contamination might manifest in all sorts of ways: by parading a sense of sexual partners' 'market value', or by subtly introducing the notion that the interaction is always a transaction of sorts. As Radin summarises, 'to commodify some things is simply to preclude their non-commodified analogies from existing'. Michael Sandel expresses the same idea in saying that monetary values often 'crowd out' non-monetary ones.[9]

Another way in which Radin believes that commodification can harm non-monetary values, pursuant to the domino theory, is by precluding the expressive significance of altruism. Once market rhetoric enters a realm of transfers, she suggests, free transfers might no longer be so easily construed as such, or be able to completely maintain their altruistic value, given that they now have a definite monetary equivalent (something the market facilitates).[10] If blood can be bought

[7] For elaboration on this point, see C McLeod, 'For Dignity or Money: Feminists and the Commodification of Women's Reproductive Labour' in B Steinbock (ed), *Oxford Handbook of Bioethics* (Oxford, Oxford University Press, 2007) 258–81.

[8] ibid. McLeod provides a good explanation of the structure of this argument, as well as the antithetical view that paid reproductive labour can instead empower women and challenge their social designation as carers and breeders by redefining that labour as remunerated trade, rather than a normal part of feminine life.

[9] M Sandel, *What Money Can't Buy: The Moral Limits of Markets* (London, Allen Lane, 2012).

[10] As an example of this phenomenon, Michael Sandel cites the well-known case of an Israeli nursery whose organisers began to fine parents that were late picking up their children in an attempt to deter tardiness (ibid). Interestingly, rather than reduce the incidences of lateness, the fine only increased

in the marketplace, then I do not confer on anyone any special benefit by giving blood that I could not equally confer by giving a patient or hospital its cash value.

Significantly, Radin does not present us with a stark choice between absolute and zero commodification in any of her exemplar contexts, but lays out the third option of partial or incomplete alienability as a possible middle way – legally regulated surrogacy arrangements being one example. Though Radin's topic throughout is commodification of items through sale, her analysis of the market rhetoric and domino effect problems could pertain in part to the general proprietary conception of the human body and its parts. Treating the human body as property will always alienate and objectify it a little; it reminds us of, and is responsive to, its 'thing-ness'. The difficult challenge is that of ascertaining if and when such treatment bears out enough of the typical concerns about commodification and objectification to be unacceptable.

The Human Body as Legal Property

So what of the law? First, not every legal recognition of property rights in the human body or its parts will come with a meaningful objectifying excess. And even where it does, it still might not follow automatically that the property right ought therefore to be refused. Perhaps the excess is a trade-off the law should be willing to make. For instance, where the domino theory is the main countervailing reason against the recognition of property in a body part, it may transpire that the non-commodified form is simply not valuable enough to forgo the benefits of commodification; if we have to choose between them, perhaps we would rather keep the commodified version after all, all things considered. Such might be true of paid blood donations, legally permitted in the US. The non-commodified version of the same transfer is, of course, altruistic donation. However, maintaining the altruistic meaning of blood donation may simply be less important than ensuring that the maximum number of transfers takes place. One might think that the only truly concerning effect of weakening the association with altruism is a reduction in the *overall* number of transfers, altruistic or not.[11]

Historically, there might seem to be a certain amount of correlation between the legal recognition of property (or something like it) in bodies and body parts, and tyrannous forms of objectification. That correlation alone might provide reason to tread carefully when recognising new rights of this kind. Consider, for instance, the old laws of husbandry and the impossibility of marital rape, built on the idea that wives' bodies were at least in some ways possessed by their husbands

them as the parents began to think of it as a 'fee' for leaving their child longer, and were consequently less motivated to arrive on time out of consideration for the nursery workers.

[11] See R Titmuss, *The Gift Relationship: From Human Blood to Social Policy* (Allen & Unwin, London, 1970) for an interesting exploration of this possibility.

(albeit under the aegis of presumed consent), or the historical use of property law to facilitate slavery. To be sure, these examples are objectionable particularly because so far as people's bodies and their parts were being treated as property, the right to that property was vesting in *someone else*. But why should the law not just grant us all manner of property rights in our *own* bodies and parts? Conceiving of the body as property capable of being legally owned, controlled, or directed is no sinister idea where the owner or trustee is the person whose body it *is*.

Of course, we already *do* each own our own bodies, as much as anyone can own them, in the extra-legal realm. We control what happens to them, put them to use and move them from one place to another in ways that nobody else does. One immediate question arising, then, is what owning our own bodies as pieces of legal property would possibly mean, over and above all this. The law clearly has a role to play in protecting our liberty rights to control our own bodies, especially in protecting them from unwanted and harmful interference. These protections do not take the form of property rights, but of legal constraints on the actions (often, the harmful actions) of others – constraints found in criminal law, tort and public law (consider, particularly, the law of consent in criminal and medical law). Property rights, on the other hand, have never been the legal mechanism for protecting bodily integrity. Where legal property rights arise in anything, they are there chiefly to facilitate the possibility of *transferring* the possession, control or use of the object of property from one party to another – to make it *possible* that the object can be treated as a 'thing' in some fundamental ways.

Consequently, one might think that the main interests we have in controlling our own bodies are protected by legal mechanisms outside of property law, and that property law itself – and indeed, the whole proprietary conception of the human body – might instead be seen to constitute the main threat of losing that control through the *transfer* of property rights (think of our historical examples). The right to be free from non-consensual bodily interference is almost a categorical imperative in English common law. But if my body is my legal property, can I not transfer the ownership right to someone else? Could someone not win it from me, barter with me for it, make me bargain with them to get it back, or bestow it on someone else? The upshot of this thought is not that the suggestion of property rights in the human body or human tissue is unthinkable, but that there is reason to scrutinise such rights carefully, and to regard the property conception of the human body as incorporating a certain threat to personal autonomy, as well as the potential for its enhancement.

All this said, it is apparent that people sometimes want, and often have reason to want, more than mere liberty (freedom from interference) rights in their own bodies and body parts. They desire further kinds of controls and legally recognised interests in both their own human tissue, and tissue belonging to, or formerly part of, others. Just as much as individuals, various institutions may claim a moral right to possess and control body parts that come into their custody in particular ways, and, at times, those rights have been granted legal recognition. In what follows, I will briefly survey a few notable exceptions to the general 'no property in the human body' rule, the status quo in the common law jurisdictions of England and Wales, Australia and the US,[12] as well as some proposed expansions of property rights in human tissue which the courts have declined to support. My concern with each example is limited to considering what potential for harm to human flourishing attaches to the property right, and, if such potential exists, how the benefits of the right stack up against those possible harms.

The 'Work and Skill' Exception

The 'work and skill' doctrine is probably the most notable exception to the default rule in English common law that the human body and its separated parts lack proprietary status.[13] The earliest judicial recognition of the exception came in the 1908 Australian High Court decision *Doodeward v Spence* where the court held that the lawful preservation of a foetus cadaver gave the preserver a right to its possession. Subsequent to *Doodeward*, English law incorporated the 'application of skill' doctrine, upholding possessory rights in excised body parts where they had acquired different attributes by virtue of the right-holder's skill, usually by way of dissection or preservation. The practical significance of the exception, where it has been recognised, is to confer on the right-holder the simple right to continue possessing the body part, making it possible for the state to prosecute for its theft (*R v Kelly*), but not necessarily the right to sell, transfer or profit from it.

The question pertinent to this discussion is how or why the 'work and skill' doctrine could unduly objectify human beings by conceptualising preserved, excised body parts as property for the purposes of rightful possession. It is true that the legal framework to some extent objectifies the body parts *themselves* by assigning them a legal owner, and conceiving of them as property for the purposes of theft. The decisions certainly adumbrated one fundamental way in which the excised parts were 'things': they legally *belonged* to someone or some institution. The same was seen to be true of bodily material considered in the cases *R v Rothery* and *R v Welsh*, where blood and urine samples were respectively found to be property capable of being stolen from officials.[14] However, a number of considerations go against the idea that recognition of property rights in body parts through the 'work and skill' doctrine entails the objectification of *people.* One question to ask of the *Doodeward* and *Kelly* cases is whom the property right would objectify. The progenitors in both cases were deceased, making it difficult to argue that the property rights objectified *them* by giving their parts – or, in the case of *Doodeward*, the entire corpse – proprietary status. Merely treating the bodily material itself as an object (in at least one way) does not seem to be an instance of harmful objectification if there is no-one whose sense of personhood is thereby suppressed.

[12] *cf Doodeward v Spence* (1908) 6 CLR 406; *Williams v Williams* (1882) 20 Ch D 659.

[13] The exception was articulated in *Doodeward v Spence* (ibid); *R v Kelly* [1998] 3 All ER 741; *Dobson v North Tyneside Health Authority* (1997) 1 WLR. 596.

[14] *R v Rothery* [1976] Crim LR 691; *R v Welsh* [1974] RTR 478.

However, it might be argued that the 'work and skill' exception tends towards the objectification of human beings in general, simply by finding that human body parts are, in principle, capable of being turned into property. Perhaps, that is, the doctrine objectifies human beings as a class, by impressing (partly through facilitating) their reducibility to bits and pieces capable of being owned. This, too, I think, would be a mistaken analysis. One important reason for my saying so is that it is a central tenet of the work and skill exception that body parts in and of themselves are *not* pieces of property. As Griffiths CJ elaborated in *Doodeward*, something had to have been *done* to the cadaver that caused it to acquire 'some attributes differentiating it from a mere corpse awaiting burial'. In *Kelly*, the thing which needed to be done was the preservation of the body parts by a college which intended to use them as research specimens, and which Rose LJ believed gave them a 'use and significance beyond their mere existence'. It is widely understood that the Lockean notion of acquiring a right to something with which one 'mixes' one's labour is the underlying rationale of the work and skill exception. The implication is that it is not raw bodily material but the combined product of that material and the application of skill that is the object of the possessory right. As the judicial reasoning emphasised, only with the additional ingredient of skill can human tissue be turned into an altogether different order of thing – something capable of being possessed to the exclusion of others. One might even think that the requirement that tissue must first become something different before it can be possessed might even be regarded as an *affirmation* of the view that the human body in its natural state is not properly conceived of as a commodity. The insistence on labour, whether that be preservation, display or something else, arguably precludes the notion that the property right objectifies human beings per se, by implying that apart from a substantial change in nature, human tissue is not capable of being owned.

Control and Possession of Gametes

Next, we turn to the body of law that has generated limited property rights in gametes, most notably in stored semen, on behalf of those for whose benefit they were stored. A constrained right of ownership of the semen was found to arise in this situation in the UK case *Yearworth v North Bristol NHS Trust*, (the details of which can be found in many of the papers in this volume, especially Chapter 15) and in its American and Australian counterparts, *Hecht v Superior Court of Los Angeles County* and *Bazley v Wesley Monash*.[15] In all three cases, the courts recognised that where a progenitor or testator arranged to have his semen stored in a particular state so that it would be suitable for future use in fertility treatment, the stored semen belonged to the progenitor, or, upon his death, to his personal representatives, and could be treated as property for the purposes of upholding

[15] *Yearworth v North Bristol NHS Trust* [2009] EWCA Civ 37; *Hecht v Superior Court of Los Angeles County* (1993) 20 Cal Rptr 775; *Bazley v Wesley Monash IVF Pty Ltd* [2010] QSC 118.

negligence claims when the semen was destroyed (*Yearworth*), or to continue to enforce the terms of the storage agreement and *prevent* the storage facilities from destroying the samples (*Bazley*; *Hecht*).

It is worth highlighting that legal property rights in stored gametes were only ever called for in this context, over and above the statutory provisions for the storage and use of gametes in fertility treatment (in the UK, see the Human Fertilisation and Embryology Acts 1990 and 2008), because of certain disputes which arose after a progenitor died, or when negligent mistakes were made by the storing contractor, resulting in the gametes' destruction. Only by bringing the stored material within a property framework could the court in *Yearworth* infer a bailment agreement between the storage company and the testator, and hence award damages to his estate for the negligent breach of the bailment obligations. Similarly, the Australian court in *Bazley* had to conceive of the testator's semen as the property of his estate so as to hold that the respondent *in vitro* fertilisation unit held the straws of semen as bailees for his personal representative (his wife) which would be breached if they were destroyed without consent.

The question I am concerned with here is whether the conception of gametes as capable of being owned by the progenitor or his representatives in such circumstances threatens to bring in tow any of the quintessential harms of commodification or objectification. Do the successful bailment and damages claims in any way objectify the progenitors of the semen, living or dead, or the gametes themselves? Do they present an unacceptably objectified view of human beings in general, overly emphasising their instrumental worth as producers of gametic material, or new human life? Is there a valuable, *extra*-legal counterpart to the legal ownership of stored gametes, which might in some way be compromised by the proprietary right?

There is little reason for thinking that any such harm is threatened by the *Yearworth*-type right. It is true, I think, that gametes are more deeply personal examples of human tissue than, say, blood, hair or urine, owing to their crucial role in reproduction, their life-giving potential, and the meaningfulness of genetic offspring to the social and personal identity of progenitors. One might expect, then, that rendering gametes wholly alienable by making them the object of free market transactions may threaten more damage to human flourishing of the kind Radin describes than a parallel market in blood or hair (although it probably threatens far less damage to personhood, as well as social injustice, than the alienability of organs or sexuality). However, the effect of *Yearworth* and its ilk was not to treat human gametes as *fungible* – as something with a cash value and exchangeable on the free market. The decisions did treat the semen samples as commodities to the limited extent that they were regarded as usable material, severable from the men, capable of being transferred, stored and of being the subject of a bailment agreement. Most of all, they were capable of being legally *owned* by the men and of forming part of their estate. But ownership is just one hallmark of objectification, as Nussbaum explains. It does not necessarily imply any of the others: instrumentality, denial of subjectivity, fungibility, and so on. Nussbaum illustrates the point with an example of a Monet painting. Although the painting may be owned by a museum, it is not regarded as an object the same way as is a ballpoint pen. The Monet is still acknowledged to have value that transcends its instrumentality (indeed, it is not taken to be instrumentally valuable at all).

Further to this, anyone wishing to make the case that the *Yearworth*-type right harbours a commodification problem would need to show not that the decisions objectify gametes – gametes are not subjects, so treating them as property cannot be wrong to *them* – but that the effect of the ownership rights *in* gametes is to objectify *people*, to paint *them* as instrumental, to deny their subjectivity, to treat them as violable, fungible and so forth. How could the sort of property right recognised in *Yearworth* yield these kinds of conceptions of human beings themselves? The only argument that could be made is that by emphasising the partial severability and usefulness of the gametes, the ownership right symbolically *reduces* the progenitor to the material, emphasising the objective, 'thing-ness' of some personal part of him at the cost of diminishing the conception of him as an intrinsically valuable person.

This is surely too far a stretch. Although gametes are a more personal kind of bodily material than blood or urine, it is hard to believe that regarding them as capable of being owned for restricted purposes will do violence to our conception of personhood by promoting an instrumental view of human beings. In the cases themselves, the emphases of the judgments was not on the general usefulness or proprietary nature of this kind of human bodily material, but on the progenitors' special, individual, interests in what happened to it and the interests of their partners. In *Yearworth* it was of prime importance that although the men did not have exclusive power to direct the use of the sperm for *in vitro* fertilisation, they did have absolute 'negative control' over it, meaning the right to refuse its use or request its destruction. It was also seen as crucial that the sperm was generated by them, and that any rights in its future use were fundamentally theirs. The *Hecht* court similarly stressed the special nature of the testator's interest in his left-behind gametic material, particularly because of its life-giving potential, which made it 'unlike other human tissue'. Thus, although the decisions reached a determination that the sperm was in one way alienable from the progenitors, and properly treated as something which could be owned, the reasoning itself centred on the *personal* value of the material to the men who stored it, and all the reasons for which it was *not* simply alienable from the rest of them, and from their personal fulfilment or wishes. The material was quite emphatically *not* regarded as impersonally valuable 'stuff', disposable, or useable, upon expedience. In other words, it was the progenitors' *subjectivity* (*their* interests, *their* wishes, and *their* meaningful relationships) and the unique importance of the separated material to them and their loved ones that formed the basis of the proprietary right. To the extent that these decisions did treat the men's bodily material as a chattel, this was clearly not at the expense of denying or devaluing their subjective nature – their unique characteristics, their desires and aspirations. Quite the contrary: these were the motivating factors for declaring the semen capable of being owned.

Equity Rights in Converted Bodily Material (Cell Lines)

In *Moore v Regents of the University of California*, the Supreme Court of California was asked to consider whether to grant a claim in conversion from a claimant whose spleen cells had been used in a research project resulting in a lucrative, patented cell line.[16] John Moore was suffering from hairy cell leukaemia when, as part of his treatment, he underwent an operation to have his spleen removed. The two doctors treating him became aware that the cells from his spleen had rare qualities which would make them suitable for use in a separate research project and, without his knowledge, kept some of the tissue taken from his spleen to develop a cell line. The cell line was patented and sold for $15 million, with eventual profits said to exceed $3 billion. Among other actions, Moore claimed that he was entitled to a percentage of the profits generated by the cell line that was developed from his cells.

The majority of the court rejected this conversion claim, holding that the claimant needed to have continuing possession of the property that was converted for his claim to be successful. In this case, that meant continued ownership of the removed cells, which the court ruled Moore lacked, since once the cells were taken from his body, they were simply disposable human material (which usually would have been disposed of), not his personal property. This was the central legal point, but the judges were also minded to consider the relevance of questions about commodification of the human body. Allowing the claim would arguably have commodified Moore's cells (retrospectively) in one salient respect: it would have recognised them as personal property and as a source of profit. The question that the court had to consider, and the question I am concerned with here, is whether such a right would cultivate the kind of harms which justify market-inalienability.

It is worth saying, first, that no exploitation or oppression concern would appear to attach to the removal of Moore's cells in the first place. His spleen needed to be removed for therapeutic reasons, and there was nothing whatsoever disadvantaging that Moore was required to do, or was done to him, in order to obtain the cells. The facts of *Moore* might be contrasted with counterfactuals in which Moore had a rare blood marrow type wanted by doctors for use in transfusions, who bartered with him for increasing numbers of donations that were detrimental to his health, or in which the spleen removal operation was performed on him against his will in order to obtain the cells. Whereas the hypotheticals clearly entail harm to Moore in the pursuit of the market value of his cells, the facts of the case involved no such harm. Obtaining the potentially lucrative cells was a by-product of an operation necessary to preserve Moore's life. Though Moore did not consent to the later use of cells, there was no question of his not consenting to their removal, or of that removal not being in his best interests.

[16] *Moore v Regents of the University of California* (1990) 51 Cal 3d 120.

The moral question for the court was whether, once the cells had been consensually removed, and later converted into profit, it would entail too much by way of commodification of the human body to declare Moore entitled to some of those profits. Were any of the harms of commodification looming? It at least seems clear that the domino theory concern was not in play – that there was not any danger of damage to the non-commodified version of the same transaction. In *Moore*, the non-commodified version would presumably be his altruistic donation of the cells to the researchers, with no demand for compensation or a share of any profits. Yet to make the domino theory argument here one would first need to show that there is a special value and meaning in donations of this kind, before showing that the commodifying effect of the conversion right (Moore's right to some of the profits) would somehow have tainted the altruistic version by muddying the clarity of its expression. Finally, one would need to show that if a choice must be made, the altruistic version is to be preferred. To my mind, even the first condition is not clearly met in the *Moore* case. Moreover, though, it is doubtful whether the gratuitous transfer of rare cells for profit-oriented research is a valuable form of altruism, the expressive significance of which needs to be protected. The *Moore* example can be contrasted with blood and organ donation, where transfers of the kind are common, and where their association with altruism might be integral in encouraging more donations. Conversely, there was no concern at all in *Moore* that awarding the claimant some of the profits made from his cells would diminish the symbolic significance of altruistic transfers of any kind.

The next question then, is whether granting Moore's claim would involve the improper objectification of the human body through commodification – whether, that is, excised cells for use in cell lines are just the sorts of commodities which deny the subjective value of human beings and their status as persons and ends in themselves. At least one of the justices sitting on the California Supreme Court saw things exactly that way. In his concurring judgment, Justice Arabian voiced his concern over what he considered to be the moral impropriety of treating the human body as a commodity, something he regarded as a consequence of upholding Moore's claim:

> The plaintiff has asked us to recognise and enforce a right to sell one's own body tissue *for profit*. He entreats us to regard the human vessel, the single most venerated and protected subject in any civilized society, as equal with the basest commercial commodity. He urges us to commingle the sacred with the profane. He asks much.[17]

Curiously, however, another of the justices who also considered the commodification issue saw the matter precisely the other way round. Justice Mosk, in his dissenting opinion, judged that *refusing* to recognise the equity claim would engender the wrongful objectification of the human vessel. For him, it did not objectify the human body for Moore to be able to sell his cells for profit; it objectified his body that his cells were taken from him *for free*:

[17] ibid, 148.

> Research with human cells that results in significant economic gain for the researcher and no gain for the patient offends the traditional mores of our society in a manner impossible to quantify. Such research tends to treat the human body as a commodity a means to a profitable end. The dignity and sanctity with which we regard the human whole, body as well as mind and soul, are absent when we allow researchers to further their own interests without the patient's participation by using the patient's cells as the basis for a marketable product.[18]

Justice Broussard, also partially dissenting, followed Justice Mosk's remarks in refuting the notion that to deny Moore's claim would mean preserving the sanctity of the human body and distancing it from commodification:

> Far from elevating these biological materials above the marketplace, the majority's holding simply bars the plaintiff, the source of the cells, from obtaining the benefit of the cells' value, but permits the defendants, who allegedly obtained the cells from the plaintiff by improper means, to retain and exploit the full economic value of their ill-gotten gains free of their ordinary common law liability for conversion.[19]

In Justice Broussard's view, turning Moore's cells into a commodity was not necessarily improper, but the effect of the majority's decision was not, in any case, to preserve the sanctity of the human body and its separateness from the market realm, but rather to allow the doctors alone to reap all the benefits of commodification, an inequitable result.

The disagreement between Justices Arabian and Mosk hits upon an interesting tension within the commodification of intrinsically valuable things. When the Hope Diamond is described as 'priceless' the intended meaning is not that it is non-fungible – that it does not *have* a price. It does have a price, just an extortionate one. When desirable objects and interactions are described as 'priceless' in the famous Mastercard advert, that too is not meant to imply that they do not *have* a price, but quite the opposite: the subliminal message is that they *do*, and that the necessary price is always worth paying (so better have a Mastercard). The advertisement reminds viewers of two things at once: that some things are above money, but that money is nevertheless needed to acquire them. These two examples illustrate the point that placing a price tag on a thing doesn't always undermine its non-monetary value; in some ways it confirms it. At the same time, affixing a market price to certain 'contested commodities' *can* have a cheapening effect (for example, commodified sex, or baby-selling). These two contrasting implications of commodification sit alongside each other, and it not always very clear which of them holds most true. Consider the now somewhat antiquated social more according to which women expect new romantic partners to spend money on them, at the risk of otherwise feeling cheapened; is the romantic meaning of the interaction threatened by that standard, or enhanced by it?

In *Moore*, Justice Arabian and Justice Mosk took different views as to which side of the line the case fell. But there was, of course, a third possibility, more con-

[18] ibid, 174.
[19] ibid, 160.

sistent with Justice Broussard's opinion, that neither decision, for or against the claimant, would have had the effect of profoundly objectifying the human body. Justice Broussard denied that the majority decision in any way 'elevated' Moore's biological materials above the marketplace; it allowed other individuals, not just Moore himself, to benefit from them economically. Importantly, Broussard did not voice dissent about the use of Moore's cells for economic gain; he did not regard the commodification of the cells as necessarily improper, but only thought that denying Moore any of the benefits was inequitable. Underlying his reasoning then, rests the claim that profiting from the cells did not pose a serious moral problem. Turning again to Radin's framework for thinking through the appropriateness of commodification, there is much to support his judgment about this.

Converting Moore's cells into something profitable did, no doubt, commodify them to a certain degree. Yet it is difficult to see that this instance of commodification would seriously undermine Moore's own sense of personhood or subjectivity, whether or not Moore himself was given a cut. *He* was not in any way being equated to the commercial value of his cells, or in danger of being thus reduced by market rhetoric. This was particularly so given that, although the cell line was valuable, his cells were worthless in their original form. Only when teamed with advanced scientific research could they be *converted* into something potentially worth $3 billion. Similarly to the 'work and skill' exception, the effect is to direct much of the commercial emphasis away from Moore's body onto the technology and expertise needed to develop the cell line. The conversion process did not turn Moore into a walking gold mine, even retrospectively, or represent his body to others as a mere instrument for money-making, in large part because his cells were always worthless to everyone but a few researchers who could do something lucrative with them. Added to this is the equally important consideration that there was no background context against which the court's acknowledgement of property in Moore's converted cells would perpetuate an existing condition of subordination – one of the most problematic factors in objectification. Sufferers of hairy cell leukaemia were not already overly identified as sources of pharmaceutical profit in the way that women have been identified as instruments for reproduction and sex.

Had the Californian court thought it fit to award Moore a share of the profits from the cell line, his subjective worth would not, in my view, have been any the more compromised. It cannot be that just by awarding the *progenitor* a stake in the commercial value of his cells the court would have changed an otherwise benign instance of commodification into something harmful and personhood-denying. The sanctity of the human vessel cannot have been violated simply through the recognition of Moore's right to the profits already being made from his cells. At the same time, to deny him a cut, as the court did, did not treat him as a mere thing either. It did not proclaim him or represent him as merely a means to an end or a source of revenue because, contrary to Justice Broussard's intimation, the researchers did not 'exploit' him for material gain. Though the cells were retained and used non-consensually, they were not *extracted* from Moore using coercion, but as part of a consensual therapeutic operation. As Justice Panelli noted in his majority judgment, there was no concern about non-consensual intervention or assault to Moore's bodily integrity. Had Moore known the potential value of his spleen cells, he no doubt would have tried to obtain compensation for their extraction and use ahead of the operation. That he was denied the opportunity of doing so did not mean that he was made into an instrument, since treating his illness was still the primary reason for the splenectomy. All in all, the objectification worry did not bear out meaningfully on either alternative.

Commercial Transfer of Bodily Material and Commercial Use of the Body (Surrogacy)

Lastly we come to the paradigmatic form of commodification: sale. A great deal can be said about sale of body parts and bodily material as a topic in its own right, but I shall try to keep my remarks here brief and simply give an indication of how the pertinent considerations manifest in some different contexts.

Sale is the central focus of Radin's own discussion of 'contested commodities'. It is apparent that one of Radin's core justifications for market-inalienability applies to the marketisation of the human body and bodily material in a way it does not apply to other examples of property rights in the human body discussed so far. This is what Radin calls the prophylactic argument, or the problem of 'desperate exchanges'. A free market in human body parts has the propensity to stifle human flourishing specifically by providing a platform on which exploitative transactions take place and moreover, transactions that are damaging or undignified for the vending party. Especially when an item of property is very personal, Radin argues, there can be good reason to suspect that the circumstances under which the holder places it on the market amount to economic duress – and that suspicion might justify banning sales.

A good case study for the prophylactic argument in the human body context is the buying and selling of organs from live donors, most commonly, kidneys. In the UK, the Human Tissue Act 2004 bans commercial dealings in human organs and other bodily material for the purposes of transplantation (section 32) but thriving black markets in kidneys exist in many areas of the world, most notably certain regions of India, and some academics have even called for a more lenient legal approach to kidney-brokering with live donors as an answer to the dearth of kidneys for transplantation. As it applies to the organ-selling context, the prophylactic argument expresses concern that most (maybe all) transactions would be 'desperate' ones, and that the market would be an exploitative enterprise, playing on the limited choices of the poor. Part of the objection is that desperate exchanges are not truly consensual, which is a reason against facilitating them, but it also seems to claim that there are some things, including organs, which it is always damaging to alienate from oneself for money, and that a market improperly makes this option irresistible to the badly off.

In the realm of organ sales, the 'desperate exchanges' problem probably captures the greatest potential harm to human flourishing bound up with commodification, and is somewhat different from the 'pure' objectification, market rhetoric and domino effect problems. Where the commercial dealings are seriously detrimental to the vendors, it might be viewed as the more direct route to the social oppression of certain groups. The worry is not primarily that such dealings will foster an inferior conception of classes of human beings (one which views them more as organ production lines than as persons), but that it directly harms and exploits *particular* human beings. The measure of this harm and exploitation will no doubt vary with the importance of the bodily material sold. While the 'desperate exchanges' problem looms large in kidney-brokering, it may be thought less of a countervailing concern where the object of sale is regenerative or surplus material such as blood or hair or gametes, if only because their severance does not inflict a permanent, serious loss on the vendor.

However, Radin's sophisticated account acknowledges an added complication for the prophylactic argument. As she explains, when applied to coercion through poverty, the argument might be deeply troubling. We may feel that it only adds insult to injury to refuse the would-be seller the money she would gain from selling a personal item where desperate circumstances render the money more valuable to her than the item (the body part) that she is losing, and represents the only way to better her situation. Radin expresses it this way:

> If we think respect for persons warrants prohibiting a mother from selling something personal to obtain food for her starving children, we do not respect her personhood more by forcing her to let them starve instead.[20]

This is what Radin calls the 'problem of transition' or the 'double bind'. Granted, it would be far better if no-one was in a situation which made selling something personal – sex or a kidney – preferable to not selling, but in the meantime, completely prohibiting sale through market-inalienability may only make matters worse for the would-be sellers. Put differently, the prophylactic argument requires a corollary in welfare rights, an elimination of the need to sell, but until that is fully achieved, there is an imperative not to make matters worse for the would-be seller by putting her in the double bind of not being able to improve her situation by selling – and empowering herself at least to that extent. The thrust of this objection has been rehearsed by various academic commentators in support of a free market in living donor organs.[21] It is important to note, however, that in Radin's own analysis, the double bind issue is not taken to settle the commodification question either way in any of her exemplar contexts, but is treated only as an important consideration that may counsel in favour of some intermediate, incompletely commodified alternative. This is precisely her conclusion on prostitution, where the consideration that selling sex services might ameliorate the powerless-

[20] Radin, 'Market-Inalienability', above n 6.

[21] See J Radcliffe-Richards, AS Daar, RD Guttman, R Hoffenberg et al, 'The Case for Allowing Kidney Sales' (1998) 352 *Lancet* 1950–52.

ness and oppression of some women needs to be balanced against the propensity of the sex industry to generally legitimate and encourage women's oppression. In the non-ideal world, justice may demand that we tolerate a certain amount of the commercialisation of sex, while trying to change the circumstances which create the dilemma in the first place.

When it comes to organ sales, the double bind and possibility of empowerment through selling really is at issue, since it seems obviously true that only someone in already desperate circumstances could be prevailed upon to sell such a thing. However, particularly in existing kidney markets, it is a serious point of contention as to whether the selling class's poverty is truly ameliorated through sale, or instead only worsened by it. The application of the double bind problem does, after all, depend on it being true that selling actually *empowers* the vendor, leaving him materially better off in the non-ideal circumstances. Although there is no room to explicate it thoroughly here, some evidence exists to suggest that in the thriving kidney markets that are known, the vendors, far from being made better off, remain in just as bad, if not worse financial straits.[22] Steadily accruing debts, no change in socioeconomic status and, in many cases, the health consequences of selling, are all evidence of markets benefiting no-one except the organ recipients and the brokers. Added to this is the distinct possibility, aptly explained by Simon Rippon, that the mere existence of the option to sell might only increase the would-be vendor's likelihood of *needing* to sell, for example by placing him in a strategically worse bargaining position vis-à-vis existing or potential creditors.[23]

Organ-selling is clearly on the more extreme end of a market in the human body. It is possible that the prophylactic argument would not apply as forcefully to, for instance, the sale of gametes. The relative harmfulness of gametic donation is one possible distinguishing factor. Sperm donation is, of course, not harmful at all. The same is not quite true of ova donation, which carries the risk of ovary hyperstimulation, a potentially very serious condition. The process of egg donation also involves considerably more discomfort and labour: the woman concerned must undergo a series of injections before enduring an extraction procedure that can be quite painful.[24] The greater imposition involved in egg

[22] See M Goyal, RL Mehta, LJ Schneiderman, AR Segal et al, 'Economic and Health Consequences of Selling a Kidney in India' (2002) 288 *Journal of the American Medical Association* 1589–93; D Rothman, 'Economic and Health Consequences of Selling a Kidney' (2002) 288 *Journal of the American Medical Association* 1640–41; L Cohen, 'Where it Hurts: Indian Material for an Ethics of Organ Transplantation' (1999) 128 *Daedalus* 135–65; J Zargooshi, 'Quality of Life of Iranian Kidney "Donors"' (2001) 166 *Journal of Urology* 1790–99; MK Mani, 'Making an Ass of the Law' (1997) 10 *National Medical Journal of India* 242–43.

[23] S Rippon, 'Imposing Options on People in Poverty: The Harm of a Live Donor Organ Market' *Journal of Medical Ethics* (first published online on 28 June 2012) doi:10.1136/medethics-2011-100318. The standard answers to these sorts of objections argue that the negative consequences of sale are a hallmark of black markets only, that all such harms can be addressed with the right regulatory structure, and, sometimes, that organ-selling is no more exploitative a practice than numerous other activities the law allows people to undertake in an attempt to alleviate their poverty. I am largely unconvinced by such replies, and have explained my scepticism elsewhere.

[24] More detailed information about the process and risks of egg donation can be found in D Dickenson, *Body Shopping: The Economy Fuelled by Flesh and Blood* (London, Oneworld Publications,

donation may provide more reason to suspect that the choice to sell is an economically pressured one. Still, even egg donation does not typically involve as much risk and loss as donating a kidney; there is less reason to perceive it as a truly desperate exchange.

To what degree does the sale of gametes inculcate the 'purer' harms of objectification, captured by Radin's exploration of market rhetoric and the domino theory? In these respects, the outright sale of gametes arguably differs quite meaningfully from the property rights in gametes recognised in the *Yearworth*-type cases. I commented that the rights of possession and control of semen acknowledged in *Yearworth*, if anything, bolstered the conception of human genetic material as deeply personal, its special meaning for progenitors being a major ground of the right. Conversely, the symbolic meaning of gamete *sales* is to sever the anonymous progenitor from the material – to *de*-personalise it. At the same time, such a market has the propensity to encourage a commodified conception of the value of persons through the market value of their genes.

On this second point, an analogy might be drawn with Radin's exposition of market rhetoric and the domino theory in the context of prostitution and baby-selling: permitting gametes to be sold commodifies not just the material itself, but the human attributes that are thought desirable in a set of genes – skin colour, build, intellect, athleticism and so on. The market rhetoric risk is that the market value of these attributes, expressed through the relative value of genes, will infiltrate the way we conceive of and value each another and ourselves. The domino theory threat is that such widespread commercial thinking might eventually taint the value of some non-commercial interactions, such as choosing a partner.

None of this is to say that gamete sales will necessarily cause such 'harms to human flourishing' to any serious degree; what truth there is in market rhetoric and domino theory thinking as it applies here may be a price worth paying for optimal fertility solutions, or, following Radin's approach, it may simply be a reason to opt for a regime of incomplete commodification, where compensation but not payment to gamete providers is permitted (as is the case in the UK) and where donors and their attributes are kept anonymous.

With respect to selling things like blood or gestational services in commercial surrogacy arrangements (prohibited in England and Wales), the emphasis will probably fall on different considerations again. It is sometimes suggested that altruism has an important value in blood donation (as well as organ donation) and that commodifying the transfer will preclude that value. Of course, the existence of payment does not preclude anyone from donating rather than selling should they so wish, and it is here that, on Radin's account, the domino theory argument comes in. What if it is the 'altruistic experience' of an organ or a blood donor that encourages donation, an experience that might be withheld once market rhetoric enters the realm, even if the donor remains free to give freely? It is

2009) ch 1; and McLeod, 'For Dignity or Money: Feminists and the Commodification of Women's Reproductive Labour', above n 7.

possible that Radin is missing something here in her discussion of altruism. That is, one might think the non-commodified version of a transfer is sometimes *enhanced* by the existence of the commodified one. It is true that if blood and organs are saleable, I do not benefit a donee by giving him mine any more than I would if I simply transferred the cash equivalent. However, the fact that I *could* transfer in exchange for money might just doubly emphasise the gratuitousness of the pure donation.

In some respects, the commodification concerns over surrogacy for payment resemble those surrounding prostitution in ways which differ from organ-selling: it is the sale of a bodily service, not the separation and transfer of human material; it (typically) entails no permanent loss, and it risks objectifying women by commercialising a feature with which they are already, arguably, too much associated in many cultures: their reproductive capacities. Nevertheless, as Carolyn McLeod explains, the marketisation of reproductive labour has also been argued to have the opposite effect. By treating their reproductive capacities as an impersonal source of revenue, women may instead be challenging their traditional *social* role as breeders, a role which is more fully embraced when they perform reproductive labour for free. Radin notes that paid surrogacy also carries the potential of the double bind, but perhaps less so than in the case of prostitution and organ-selling, since surrogates do not tend to be the women most targeted by economic desperation. On the other hand, surrogacy may be detrimental to human flourishing if it is disempowering of surrogates (for example, if they have specific performance of contracts enforced against them), or indeed if it disempowers infertile women by placing a high market value on something which they lack. When the considerations are weighed up, the intermediate solution that English law adopts – facilitating surrogacy arrangements with compensation for expenses, but refusing to enforce surrogacy contracts *or* allow pure commercial remuneration – may strike the best compromise.

Conclusion

I started this chapter with some general remarks about the commodification and objectification of the human body. My suggestions about how the real harms of commodification and objectification might or might not bear out in a few instances of legal property rights in the human body (or potential legal rights) were also fairly general, but, I hope, effectively illustrated how the various considerations might be reasoned through in different cases. My discussion also testified to one of Radin's key propositions, that 'there is no algorithm or abstract formula to tell us which items are (justifiably) personal'; there are, rather, only an amalgam of relevant questions that ought to be asked of each case. Does the property right foster an inferior conception of personhood? Does it excessively objectify an individual, or a class of human beings? Does it encourage thoroughgoing market rhetoric about the human body? Does it endanger a valuable, *non-commodified* form of the same property right – such as altruistic transfer? If so, do the benefits of the property right outweigh possible damage to the non-commodified version? Finally, does the property right encourage 'desperate exchanges'? If it does, how does the possible harmfulness of the exchange balance against the threat of the 'double bind'?

Where the prophylactic argument has significant influence, as is often true of commercial transfer, it will usually represent the overwhelming consideration, albeit complicated by the problem of transition and the non-ideal world. Nevertheless, it seems to follow from my discussion here that the line between tolerable and intolerable property rights in the human body does not fall neatly between commercial transfer and less full-bodied rights of possession or control. The correct determination depends just as much on other features, particularly: the kind of body part or material at issue; whether the property right benefits the progenitor, and the social consequences and symbolic meaning of granting that right. Being cognisant of these differences will mainly mean applying a different standard of scrutiny to suggested property rights in the human body depending on the background considerations.

7

Property Rights in Human Biological Material

SIMON DOUGLAS

Introduction

The aim of this chapter is to examine two questions. First, can things such as blood and tissue samples, organs, corpses, hair clippings and other human biological material form the subject matter of a property right? This question is not an ethical one, but a purely doctrinal one that can be answered by looking at the rules of property law. We will see that anything which has a physical existence can, in principle, be made the subject matter of a property right. Having answered the first question in the affirmative, the second question this chapter considers is, *should* human biological material be made the subject matter of a property right? This chapter will argue that it should. It will be seen that if someone in possession of human biological material does not hold a property right in it, then he is vulnerable to being dispossessed of the material by another. This 'instability of possession', as David Hume called it, is something that the law tries to avoid and it does this by allocating property rights. For this reason, it will be argued, the law should recognise property rights in human biological material.

Defining Terms

Before asking whether human biological material can be made the subject matter of a property right, it is important to describe what is meant by the term 'property right'. We will also consider the notion of 'ownership', which is a type of property right.

Property Rights

'Property rights', sometimes called 'rights in *rem*', are typically contrasted with 'personal rights', or 'rights in *personam*'. Nicholas writes:

> The difference between the two is the difference between owning and being owed something. Thus a man's assets may be his house and his furniture, which he owns, his bank balance which, however much one may speak of 'having money in the bank', is a debt owed by the bank, and his right to his unpaid salary, which is likewise a debt.[1]

The difference between these two types of rights can be expressed as the difference between their 'exigibility'. The 'exigibility' of a right determines against whom the right can be enforced. A personal right can only be enforced against a single person. For example, if A enters into a contract with B, under which B is obliged to pay A a sum of money, A's right is a 'personal right' because the only person that A can enforce his right against is B. A cannot, for example, call on a stranger, C, to pay him. A's right is 'exigible' against an individual because he is owed a legal duty by one person only (B). Property rights, by contrast, are 'exigible' or 'enforceable' against all persons.[2] For example, if A owns a house, which is to say that he has a freehold title in land, then his right would be enforceable not just against B, but against all other third parties (C, D, E, etc): if B, C, D or E walk across A's land without A's consent, A will have a claim against each individual. Because all persons (B, C, D, etc) owe A a legal duty to stay off the land, we can say that A's property right in his land is 'exigible' against all persons. Property rights, as distinguished from personal rights, are rights that are exigible against all persons (sometimes expressed as being 'exigible against the world').

This definition of property rights needs to be refined because not all rights that are 'exigible against the world' are property rights. A good example is the right to a reputation: A's right to a reputation imposes a duty not upon an individual, but upon all persons (B, C, D, etc) not to defame A. Although reputational rights are exigible against the world we would not classify them as property rights. This means that we must identify a second characteristic which marks out certain rights as being property rights. This characteristic is that of 'thing-relatedness', in the sense that the right must relate to a physical thing (such as land, a painting, coins, cars, etc) before we can call it a property right.[3] A right to a reputation would fall outside this definition of property rights because such a right does not relate to a physical thing but an abstract concept. Pretto describes this feature of property rights in the following terms:

> Rights are all incorporeal. Those whose exigibility or demandability is defined by the existence and location of the thing to which they relate are rights *in rem*. *Res* is the Latin

[1] B Nicholas, *An Introduction to Roman Law* (Oxford, Clarendon Press, 1962) 99.

[2] W Hohfeld, 'Fundamental Legal Conceptions as Applied in Legal Reasoning' (1913) 23 *Yale Law Journal* 16, 32.

[3] B McFarlane, *The Structure of Property Law* (Oxford, Hart Publishing, 2008) 196–98.

for 'thing' and right *in rem* means 'right in the thing', or 'to the thing'. A right *in rem* is a right demandable against anyone who holds or is trying to hold the relevant *res*.[4]

All clear property rights, in addition to being exigible against the world, have a second characteristic of relating to a physical thing. Freehold of land, for instance, is both exigible against the word and relates to a physical thing (the land). Property rights, therefore, are those rights which have the two characteristics of being exigible against the world and relating to a physical thing.

Ownership

There are a number of different rights which share these two characteristics of exigibility against the world and 'thing-relatedness'. For example, in respect of land the law recognises freehold title to land (which is 'ownership' of land, in colloquial terms), as well as lesser use rights (such as easements and profits), rights which restrict the use of land (restrictive covenants) and rights which provide security (legal charges).[5] These are all 'property rights' because they are all exigible against the world and they all relate to a physical thing (the land). While we may have a number of different property rights, however, it is worth considering the best type of property right, 'ownership'. The reason for this is that in most cases involving litigation over human biological material, the right being claimed by a litigant is that of ownership.

As one would expect, there is a substantial amount of literature on the content of this right, and this is not the place to give a full account of this debate.[6] For present purposes it will suffice to say that case law clearly establishes that an owner of a thing, whether a chattel or land, has a 'right to exclude' others from the thing. A 'right', properly so called, is something which correlates with a legal duty on others.[7] In relation to an owner's 'right to exclude', this right correlates with a legal duty on others to refrain from interfering physically with the owner's thing (a 'duty of non-interference'). A simple illustration can be found in the case of *Vine v Waltham Forest Council*.[8] The claimant was the owner of a car that was clamped by the defendant local council and she was charged £108 to have the car removed. Because the clamp warning sign was not properly visible, the claimant had not consented to the interference with her car and she successfully sued for trespass to goods. This straightforward claim demonstrates that the defendant

[4] A Pretto, *Boundaries of Personal Property: Shares and Sub-Shares* (Oxford, Hart Publishing, 2005) 90. See also Bennett Moses, ch 12 in this volume for a helpful discussion on the difficulties in defining 'property'.

[5] See generally, S Bright, 'Of Estates and Interests: A Tale of Ownership and Property Rights' in S Bright and J Dewar, *Land Law: Themes and Perspectives* (Oxford, Oxford University Press, 1998).

[6] This debate is discussed in detail in S Douglas and B McFarlane, 'Defining Property Rights' in J Penner and H Smith (eds), *Philosophical Foundations of Property Law* (Oxford, Oxford University Press, 2013).

[7] Hohfeld, 'Fundamental Legal Conceptions as Applied in Legal Reasoning', above n 2 at 32.

[8] *Vine v Waltham Forest Council* [2000] 1 WLR 2383 (CA).

(and all other third parties) was under a legal duty to the claimant not to interfere physically with her car and, by attaching a clamp to the car, the defendant breached this duty. As owner of the car, therefore, the claimant had a 'right to exclude' others from the car.

According to this very brief account of ownership, the salient feature that singles out a person as an owner of a thing is that he or she has a 'right to exclude' and, consequently, he or she is owed a duty of non-interference by others.[9] This may seem to be a simplistic view of ownership. An alternative account of this right, which stresses its complexity, is the 'bundle of rights' theory,[10] which holds that 'ownership' does not consist of a single right, the 'right to exclude', but of other rights as well, such as the 'right to use' and 'right to control' the thing.[11] The 'bundle of rights' theory, in addition to having a number of doctrinal flaws, may be problematic in the present context for another reason. A concern that we may have in recognising property rights in human biological material is that it could lead to the use, exploitation and commercialisation of such material. The bundle of rights theory, with its focus on the owner's 'right to use' and 'control' his asset, may actually lend doctrinal support to the ability to exploit such material. This problem will be considered in detail in the final section of this chapter. It will be seen that if the law did recognise ownership of such material, this would not, contrary to the bundle of rights theory, import a 'right to use' this material. For present purposes it will suffice to say that an owner of a thing has a 'right to exclude' others from it.

Property Rights and the Body

So far we have considered property rights generally, and the right of ownership in particular. In this section we will ask whether or not human biological material can form the subject matter of this property right.

A Test for the Recognition of Property Rights

The definition of property rights set out above is controversial. The assertion that a right must have the characteristic of 'thing-relatedness', in that it must relate to

[9] For academic support for the 'exclusion' model of property rights, see F Cohen, 'Dialogue on Private Property' (1954) 9 *Rutgers Law Review* 357, and T Merrill, 'Property and the Right to Exclude' (1998) 77 *Nebraska Law Review* 730. The issue is discussed further in Wall, ch 8 in this volume. For the problems that the 'exclusion' model creates for so-called 'communal' or 'non-private' property, see J Harris, *Property and Justice* (Oxford, Oxford University Press, 2002) ch 7, although *cf* Dickenson, ch 11 and Herring, ch 13 in this volume.

[10] For a recent defence of this theory, see S Munzer, 'A Bundle Theorist Holds on to his Collection of Sticks' (2011) 8 *Econ Journal Watch* 265.

[11] AM Honoré, 'Ownership' in A Guest (ed), *Oxford Essays in Jurisprudence* (Oxford, Clarendon Press, 1961) 116. See also Harris, *Property and Justice*, above n 9, 30.

a physical thing, in order to be classed as a 'property right' means that it excludes other rights often thought of as 'property rights'. Intellectual property rights, as their name would suggest, are often classed as property rights. Rahmatian, for example, has recently argued, 'intellectual property is property, with all the advantages and dangers which originate from that quality. It is arguably even more accurate to say that the legal concept of property rights in general is more easily understood when looking at intellectual property rights first'.[12] However, because intellectual property rights relate to ideational entities[13] rather than physical things, they are not 'property rights' under the definition adopted in this chapter. Similarly, it is often the case that contractual rights, or 'choses in action', being a source of wealth, are labelled 'property rights'. Baroness Hale, in the recent case of *OBG Ltd v Allan*,[14] took this view when she argued that a contractual right to the payment of a sum of money was a 'property right' and, as such, could be stolen in much the same way that a physical asset could be.[15] Again, under the definition of 'property rights' adopted in this chapter, a contractual right to the payment of a sum of money does not count as a 'property right' because it does not relate to any physical thing, but merely correlates with the debtor's duty to pay.[16] The point being made here is that many rights that are frequently referred to as 'property', such as 'intellectual property' and 'contractual debts', fall outside of the definition of 'property rights' adopted in this chapter because they do not relate to physical things. It is necessary, therefore, to attempt to justify this definition of property rights, and the stipulation that they must relate to a physical thing. It is worth setting out this justification in some detail because, as we will see, the justification provides us with a method of asking whether or not human biological material can be made the subject matter of property rights.

There are a number of basic questions that all systems of property law need to be able to answer. The most important will include: what is the content of a property right; how are property rights created; how are property rights transferred; and how are property rights destroyed? Property law has developed a number of rules that provide answers to these questions. The important point in this context is that these rules usually presuppose the existence of a physical thing, and become incoherent when applied in a dispute not involving a physical thing. Take the first question: what is the content of a property right? We saw above, when considering the property right of ownership, that this right consists of a 'right to exclude' others from a thing. If A holds a property right in a thing, such as a car, he has a right to exclude others (B, C, D, etc) from the car. This means that B, C, D, etc are under a duty to A not to interfere physically with A's car. B will breach this duty if,

[12] A Rahmatian, 'Intellectual Property and the Concept of Dematerialised Property' in S Bright (ed), *Modern Studies in Property Law*, vol 6 (Oxford, Hart Publishing, 2011) 362.

[13] Harris, *Property and Justice*, above n 9, 43.

[14] *OBG Ltd v Allan* [2008] 1 AC 1.

[15] ibid, 309.

[16] See B Bouckaert, 'What is Property?' (1990) 13 *Harvard Journal of Law and Public Policy* 775.

for example, he scratches A's car,[17] attaches a clamp to it[18] or carelessly damages it. The important point for present purposes is that this duty – the duty not to interfere physically with the owner's thing – presupposes the physical existence of a thing. One cannot owe the same duty to the holder of an intellectual property right because there is nothing that one can physically interfere with: one cannot scratch, touch or physically damage an ideational entity. Consequently, intellectual property rights must have a different content, in that they must impose duties to refrain from other activities, such as imitation. In short, the rules governing the content of property rights can only be applied to rights relating to physical things.

Turning to the other questions – how is a property right created and transferred? – again, the rules developed by property law often presuppose the physical existence of a thing. These rules state that A will acquire a property right in a thing by taking physical possession of it;[19] further, once A has this property right, he can transfer it to B by physically delivering the thing to B.[20] These rules of acquisition make perfect sense when applied in a case involving a physical thing, let us say a lost gold bracelet.[21] A can take physical possession of the bracelet, thus acquiring a property right in it and, further, he can transfer this right to B by physically delivering the bracelet to B. When we turn to intellectual property rights, these acquisition rules become incoherent: A cannot take physical possession of an idea, nor make physical delivery of the idea to B in any intelligible sense. Intellectual property, therefore, must develop its own acquisition rules that are distinct from those found within the law of property.

This section has sought to justify the restriction of the label 'property right' to rights relating to physical things on the basis that much of the law of property only makes sense when applied to physical things. This is an important methodological point in the present context because it gives us a way of testing whether something can be made the subject matter of a property right. Anything which has a physical existence can, in principle, be made the subject matter of a property right because it will be possible to apply the rules of property law to the thing. When asking whether human biological material can be made the subject matter of a property right, therefore, we need only ask whether it has a physical existence. Before considering this question, however, a slight refinement must be made in light of the problem of 'self-ownership'.

Self-ownership

The claim of self-ownership occurs when a person, A, asserts that he holds a property right in his own body. Self-ownership, the notion that A has property in his

[17] *Fouldes v Willoughby* (1841) 8 M & W 540, 151 ER 1153.
[18] *Vine v Waltham Forest LBC* [2000] 1 WLR 2383.
[19] *Armory v Delamirie* (1722) 1 Strange 505, 93 ER 664.
[20] *Cochrane v Moore* (1870) 25 QBD 57.
[21] As in *Parker v British Airways Board* [1982] QB 1004.

own body, has attracted much academic attention,[22] mainly because of its perceived importance to Lockean labour theory.[23] Cohen describes self-ownership in the following terms:

> Each person has over himself, as a matter of moral right, all those rights that a slaveholder has over a complete chattel slave as a matter of legal right, and he is entitled, morally speaking, to dispose over himself in the way such a slaveholder is entitled, legally speaking, to dispose over his slave.[24]

As is well known, prior to the abolition of slavery a person, A, could hold property rights in relation to another person (a slave), in much the same way that he can hold property rights over other chattels or land. As Cohen explains, self-ownership involves the notion that A can hold identical rights over his own body as well. While there is no doubt that the language of self-ownership is important as a rhetorical or literary device, the important question is whether, as Cohen seems to suggest, it has doctrinal significance. Is there any case for saying that a right-holder, A, has rights in his own body that are legally identical to his rights in his car or his land? One objection sometimes expressed is that A's body is not a 'thing' in the same sense that his car and his land are, and hence cannot form the subject matter of a property right. Lord Bingham seemed to use this reasoning in *R v Bentham* where the defendant had carried out a robbery by concealing his fingers behind his jacket to give the appearance of a gun. [25] He was prosecuted for the 'possession of an imitation firearm'[26] and the question was whether he could be said to be 'in possession' of his own hand. Lord Bingham, finding for the defendant, said: 'What is possessed must under the definition [in the relevant Act] be a thing. A person's hand or fingers are not a thing.'[27] This reasoning is clearly wrong. A person's body and its parts have a physical existence in just the same way that cars, coins, paintings, ships and land do. One can see and touch a body, just as one can see and touch a car or hold a coin. A person's body is a 'thing' which has a physical existence.

In the previous section it was argued that in order for something to be made the subject matter of a property right, the only requirement that must be satisfied is that the thing should have a physical existence. Given that a person's body is a physical thing it may seem, in light of this argument, that a person, A, should be able to hold property rights in his own body. Such a conclusion would be

[22] For an account of this debate, see Harris, *Property and Justice*, above n 9 at 190–92. See also Goold and Quigley, ch 14 in this volume.

[23] Locke's labour theory for the acquisition of property rights is premised on the assumption that we have property in our own persons. From this starting point Locke argues that we must own our labour and, consequently, we acquire property rights in things when we 'mix' our labour with them. See J Locke, *Second Treatise of Civil Government* or *Two Treatises of Government*, 2nd edn (Cambridge, Cambridge University Press, 1967) ch V, 27.

[24] G Cohen, *Self-Ownership, Freedom and Equality* (Cambridge, Cambridge University Press, 1995) 68.

[25] *R v Bentham* [2005] 1 WLR 1057.

[26] Firearms Act 1968, s 17(2).

[27] *R v Bentham*, above n 25 at 1060.

problematic, however, as there are a number of convincing objections to the idea of self-ownership. Harris, for instance, pointed out that the notion that a right-holder, A, has 'property rights' in his own body would be superfluous.[28] We do not need to say A has property rights in his body in order to protect him from unlawful interferences with his person. Strict liability torts such as assault, battery and false imprisonment already protect us against bodily interferences. A further objection to the notion of self-ownership is made by Penner in his 'separability' thesis.[29] Penner observes that many of the things that we do with property rights, and consequently many of the problems which property law has to deal with, are not possible in relation to a person's own body: 'We do not trade out talents, give away our personalities, licence our friendships to others, or pay our taxes with our eyesight.'[30] These types of transactions are only possible with things that are, in Penner's words, 'separate' and therefore 'contingently ours'.[31] A car belonging to A is only 'contingently' A's car because it could, in principle, belong to B. The fact that the car is only contingently A's means that A is able to do things such as sell the car to B, gift it to him or license B to use it. These typical forms of property transactions are simply not possible in respect of a person's own body as it is not separate from the person. The inability to subject a person's own body to typical forms of property transactions leads Penner to argue, convincingly, that they fall outside the scope of property law. We can also link this to the methodological point, made above, that in order for a thing to be made the subject of a property right, we must be able to apply the rules that we collectively refer to as 'property law' to the thing. One such rule, it was noted above, is that a property right in a thing can be created by taking possession of the thing. Further, such a right can be transferred to another by making a physical delivery of the thing. The inability to apply these rules to, for instance, intellectual property rights, means that such rights cannot be called 'property rights'. The same point can be made in relation to one's body. One cannot, in any intelligible sense, take 'possession' of one's body in the same way that one can take possession of a coin or a painting. Nor, it is suggested, can one make a physical delivery of one's body in the same way that one can deliver a car or a bank note. 'Delivery' seems to presuppose that you are delivering something external to yourself. In short, the rules that constitute the law of property cannot be applied to a person's body in any intelligible sense. Consequently, a person, A, cannot hold a property right in his own body.

In order for something to be made the subject matter of a property right, it is still true to say that the thing must have a physical existence. However, the thing must also be separate from the right holder because he cannot, for the reasons set out here, hold property rights in his own body. When we ask whether a person, A, can hold property rights in human biological material, therefore, we are only concerned with material that is physically separate from A.

[28] Harris, *Property and Justice*, above n 9 at 185.

[29] J Penner, *The Idea of Property in Law* (Oxford, Oxford University Press, 1997) ch 5.

[30] ibid, 111–12.

[31] ibid, 112.

Separate Human Biological Material

The argument made so far is that anything which has a physical existence can, in principle, be made the subject matter of a property right, so long as the thing is separate from the right-holder. Under this approach, while it is not possible for a person, A, to hold property rights in his own body, it is possible for him to hold property rights in a human biological material separate from him. The reason for this is that such material – corpses, organs, tissue and blood samples, hair clippings, and so on have a physical existence and, therefore, it will be possible to apply the rules of property law to such material.[32] Take, for instance, the famous case of *Exelby v Handyside.*[33] This involved a claim in conversion brought by the father of conjoined twins, who had died shortly after their birth, against the male midwife who had taken away and kept their corpses. To establish a claim in conversion the claimant must establish that he has a property right[34] and, in a judgment that has proved difficult to interpret,[35] the court appeared to reject the claim on the basis that one could not have a property right in a corpse. This finding of 'no property' will be criticised in the next section, but the important point for present purposes is that the corpses in the case could, in principle, have been made the subject matter of property rights. Because the corpses had a physical existence and were separate from the person claiming property rights in them, it would have been possible to apply the rules of property law to them. Take the rules governing the acquisition of property rights: if a person, A, takes physical possession of a thing, then A will acquire a property right in it.[36] Further, A can transfer his property right to B by physically delivering the thing to B.[37] These rules could be applied to the corpses in *Exelby v Handyside.* Because the corpses had a physical existence, it would have been possible for a person, as a matter of fact, to have taken physical possession of them and have delivered them to another. The applicability of these rules of property law meant that there was no logical bar to recognising property rights in the corpses. Any objection, therefore, must have been for ethical and policy reasons (which, as we will see, are not particularly convincing in themselves).

The potential applicability of the rules of property was expressly recognised in the more recent case of *Washington University v Catalona.*[38] The defendant was a university researcher, initially employed by the claimant university, who had been involved in the collection of tissue samples over a number of years. When the defendant was appointed to a new university he wished to take the tissue samples

[32] A full account is given of the different types of human biological material in R Hardcastle, *Law and the Human Body* (Oxford, Hart Publishing, 2007).

[33] *Exelby v Handyside* (1749) 2 East PC 652.

[34] *Jarvis v Williams* [1955] 1 WLR 71 (CA).

[35] P Matthews, 'Whose Body? People As Property' (1983) 36 *Current Legal Problems* 193.

[36] *Armory v Delamirie* [1722] 1 Strange 505, 93 ER 664.

[37] *Cochrane v Moore* (1870) 25 QBD 57.

[38] *Washington University v Catalona* 490 F 3d 667 (2007).

with him, something which the claimant resisted. In the resulting case the court had no problem in applying basic property law rules to the tissue samples. The court began by stating the acquisition rule that one will acquire a property right in a thing by taking physical possession of it: 'Where, as here, personal property is of a type that is not subject to title, exclusive possession and control of such property creates a presumption of ownership.'[39] The claimants had, as a matter of fact, taken possession of the samples and, applying this acquisition rule, there was a presumption that the claimants had acquired property rights in the samples. The court was also able to apply a further rule of property law, namely that a property right in a thing can be transferred by the physical delivery of the thing.[40] They noted that claimants may also have acquired property rights in the tissue samples when the samples were physically delivered to them by the donors.[41] Because the tissue samples had a separate physical existence, it was factually possible for someone to take physical possession of them, and it was possible for someone to physically deliver them to another. Consequently, it was possible to apply the rules governing the creation and transfer of property rights to these samples, as the court did. Given the applicability of the rules of property law to such human biological material, there is no conceptual difficulty with the court recognising that it could be made the subject matter of a property right.

The Argument for Property Rights

So far we have seen that separate human biological material can, in principle, be made the subject matter of a property right. It is important to stress that this does not mean that such material *should* be made the subject matter of property rights, but rather that it *could* be made the subject matter of property rights. Whether it should be made the subject matter of property rights is essentially a matter of policy.[42] There are a number of arguments against it. The principle one, which will be considered in the next section, is that the law should not allow the commercialisation of human biological material and the recognition of property would be contrary to this policy.[43] Without commenting on whether the commercialisation of body parts is a good or bad thing, it will be argued in the next section that this would not automatically result from the recognition of property rights. However, before turning to this issue, the aim of the present section is to make the case for the recognition of property rights in human biological material in the first

[39] ibid, 5.

[40] ibid, 9–10.

[41] For the legal significance of a 'donation', or the view that a donor somehow 'abandons' his property right in the donated material, see Goold, ch 9 in this volume.

[42] For a helpful discussion of whether human biological material should be made the subject of property rights, see Goold and Quigley, ch 14 in this volume.

[43] See Greasley, ch 6 in this volume.

place. The argument is a simple one, which focuses on the law's need to protect a person's peaceful possession of a thing.

Vulnerability to Dispossessions

When a person, A, has possession of a separate physical thing, such as a car, coin or painting, he is vulnerable to being dispossessed of the thing by B; B may find it profitable to seize the thing from A and take it for himself. This vulnerability is unique to separate physical things. B cannot, for instance, dispossess A of A's ideas or A's body. This unique problem which attaches to separate physical things was articulated by David Hume:

> There are different species of goods, which we are possess'd of; the internal satisfaction of our minds, the external advantages of our body, and the enjoyment of such possessions as we have acquir'd by our industry and good fortune. We are perfectly secure in the enjoyment of the first. The second may be ravish'd from us, but can be of no advantage to him who deprives us of them. The last only are both expos'd to the violence of others, and may be transferr'd without suffering any loss or alteration.[44]

The principle attraction for B to attempt to dispossess A of A's car, coin or painting, is that, following the dispossession, B will be able to use and enjoy the thing for himself. As Hume says, the thing can be 'transferr'd [to B] without suffering any loss or alteration'. What adds to A's vulnerability to suffering such a dispossession is that separate physical things – cars, coins and paintings and so on – tend to be scarce, meaning that there are usually more people who wish to possess and make use of these things than there are things available. As Hume says when he continues his argument:

> [Separate physical things are] expos'd to the violence of others, and may be transferr'd without suffering any loss or alteration while at the same time, there is not a sufficient quantity of them to supply every one's desires and necessities. As the improvement, therefore, of these goods is the chief advantage of society, so the instability of their possession, along with their scarcity, is the chief impediment.[45]

Harris illustrates the problem of scarcity in his example of the fictional community of Forrest Land where the inhabitants need to make use of sticks and stones in order to live and thrive.[46] Fortunately there is an abundance of sticks and stones in Forrest Land. If A collects a bundle of sticks and stones then B, another inhabitant, is unlikely to try to dispossess A; because the supply of sticks and stones outstrips demand, B can easily acquire this resource elsewhere. As such, there is no real benefit to B in trying to dispossess A. Consequently, there is no need to recognise A as the holder of property rights in the bundle of sticks and stones that he

[44] D Hume, *A Treatise of Human Nature, Book III*, 2nd edn (Oxford, Clarendon Press, 1978) Part 1, Section 2.

[45] ibid.

[46] Harris, *Property and Justice*, above n 9 at 24.

has collected; there is not much point in imposing a duty on B to refrain from interfering physically with the sticks and stones in A's possession if B is unlikely to do this in the first place. As Harris says: 'Where a resource really is abundant, it will normally be pointless to carve out parcels of exclusivity through the operation of trespassory rules.'[47]

Let us say that due to a growth in population in Forrest Land the demand for sticks and stones starts to outstrip the supply. If this were to happen it would be correct to say that sticks and stones have become a scarce resource, and this creates a danger; inhabitants of Forrest Land, such as A and B, will now become rivals for this resource. If A has collected some sticks and stones it will now become profitable for B to try to dispossess A. As one property law textbook puts it, once a resource becomes scarce, 'those who want to make use of the resource will struggle for control of it, leading to friction and costly and dangerous conflict'.[48] The 'instability' of possession, the danger that B will try to dispossess A of his sticks and stones, is, according to Hume, the 'chief impediment' to society and, consequently, something that the law tries to prevent. The best way to do this is to invest one of the parties (let us say A) with a property right. If A is recognised as owner of the sticks and stones that he has collected, then it would mean that A is owed a duty by all others (including B) to refrain from physical interferences with them. While it may remain profitable for B to try to dispossess A of his sticks and stones, B is unlikely to do this if he is under a legal duty to refrain from this type of behaviour. In short, by investing A with a property right, the law, to a large extent, removes A's vulnerability to being dispossessed by B and, consequently, A's peaceful possession is protected.

A good illustration of this policy can be found in the concept of relative title. Under the common law it is possible for a number of different persons to be recognised as having ownership rights in the same thing. The best illustration of this is the case of *Armory v Delamirie*.[49] The claimant, a chimney sweep's boy, found a gold ring in a chimney which he took to the defendant to be valued. When the defendant discovered that the ring had been found, and hence probably belonged to some third party who had lost it (who we will call X), the defendant refused to return it. The court, finding for the claimant, held that the defendant had converted the ring. The basis of the decision was the finding that the claimant, in taking possession of the ring, had acquired a property right in it. This was despite the fact that there was almost certainly another person, X, who held a pre-existing property right in the ring. In short, more than one person can have a property right in a single thing.[50] The reason why the law is willing to recognise multiple titles in this way was explained in the subsequent case of *Jeffries v Great Western*

[47] ibid.

[48] A Clarke and P Kohler, *Property Law: Commentary and Materials* (Cambridge, Cambridge University Press, 2005) 60.

[49] *Armory v Delamirie* [1722] 1 Strange 505, 93 ER 664.

[50] The claimant's property right was 'relative' in the sense that it could not be enforced against X, but it could be enforced against the defendant.

Railway.[51] A person who owned a truck had been made bankrupt, which meant that his property right in the truck had vested in X, his liquidator. However, before X could take possession of the truck, the bankrupt sold and delivered it to the claimant (who was completely unaware of the vendor's bankruptcy). Subsequently, in an unrelated matter, the claimant was dispossessed of the truck by the defendant. In its defence to a claim in conversion, the defendant pointed out that because the truck had been purchased from a bankrupt vendor, ownership of the truck actually resided with X, the liquidator, not the claimant. Had this argument been accepted then it would have created a real vulnerability for the claimant (and others in his position) because it would have meant that the defendant could have seized the truck from him with complete impunity. This would have been contrary to the principle, stated by Lord Campbell CJ, that it is 'essential for the interests of society, that *peaceable possession should not be disturbed by wrongdoers*'.[52] To prevent this happening, and to protect the claimant's peaceful possession, the court held that the claimant had a property right in the truck as 'a person possessed of goods as his property has a good title as against every stranger, and that one who takes them from him . . . is a wrongdoer'.[53] By recognising the claimant as holding a property right in the truck, the court ensures that he is not completely vulnerable to being dispossessed by others, thus removing the problem of the 'instability of possession'.[54]

Application to Human Biological Material

What Hume and Harris demonstrate is that separate physical things, if they are scarce, need to be subject to legal regulation. In the absence of legal regulation, those in possession of such things are always vulnerable to being dispossessed by a more powerful party. This is something that the law tries to avoid, and it does this by allocating property rights in such things to individuals, thus imposing a legal duty on others to refrain from interfering with goods that are in a person's possession. This argument, it is suggested, can apply to human biological material in the same way that it applies to other separate physical things.[55]

This can be illustrated through the leading case on the issue, *Moore v Regents of University of California*.[56] The claimant visited the defendant's medical centre

[51] *Jeffries v Great Western Railway* (1856) 5 Ell & Bl 802, 119 ER 680.

[52] ibid, 805, 681.

[53] ibid.

[54] So important is this principle that the courts have even applied it to someone who had illegally acquired possession by theft: *Costello v Chief Constable of Derbyshire Constabulary* [2001] EWCA Civ 381.

[55] It is important to note that in the argument that follows it is not suggested that all human biological material should be made the subject matter of property rights, but only those that satisfy the criterion of scarcity. There is unlikely to be a dispute, for instance, over use of dandruff or a shed hair because such things are not scarce. There would be no point, therefore, in making such things the subject matter of property rights.

[56] *Moore v Regents of University of California* (1990) 51 Cal 3d 120.

after he had been diagnosed with leukaemia. The claimant consented to undergoing a splenectomy and to providing blood and tissue samples to the defendant over the subsequent years. However, the claimant did not consent to, nor was he informed of, the defendant's research into the claimant's tissue samples. The defendant developed a cell line from the tissue samples, which was then patented and used for the development of cancer drugs (making the cell line extremely valuable). When the claimant discovered the use that had been made of his cells he brought a number of actions against the defendants, including the tort of conversion. As Panelli J explained, in order to sue for the conversion of his cells taken from tissue samples, the claimant needed to establish that he 'retained an ownership interest in them'.[57] In rejecting this claim, Panelli J said that statute law regulates the use of biological material excised from a human body, rather than the law of property:

> [T]he laws governing such things as human tissues, transplantable organs, blood, fetuses, pituitary glands, corneal tissue, and dead bodies deal with human biological materials as objects sui generis, regulating their disposition to achieve policy goals rather than abandoning them to the general law of personal property. It is these specialized statutes, not the law of conversion, to which courts ordinarily should and do look for guidance on the disposition of human biological materials.[58]

By stating that human biological material lies outside of the law of personal property, Panelli J was clearly stating that such things cannot form the subject matter of property rights.

The problem with Panelli J's reasoning is that it cuts both ways. If the law does not recognise property rights in human biological material then not only is the claimant unable to hold property rights in the tissue samples, but also the defendant. This creates a serious vulnerability for the defendant. The tissue samples, as separate physical things are, in Hume's word, 'expos'd to the violence of others, and may be transferr'd without suffering any loss or alteration'. In other words, they are things that someone (such as the claimant or a rival researcher) would be able to seize and take away from the defendants. Further, it would be (potentially) very profitable for someone to try to dispossess the defendants. There is not an abundance of excised human tissue, with the claimant's particular genetic code, which can be successfully developed into an extremely valuable cell line. Given the scarcity of this resource, and the potential profitability in dispossessing the defendants of the tissue, the defendants are subject to a serious vulnerability. As explained above, when such vulnerability exists, the law tries to protect peaceful possession by allocating property rights in the thing to a particular person. Unless such a right is recognised in a case such as *Moore*, there would be nothing to stop someone, such as a rival researcher, from taking the tissue samples from the defendants with complete impunity.

[57] ibid, 136–37.
[58] ibid, 137.

The arguments advanced by Panelli J against the recognition of property rights do not deal with the vulnerability that a finding of 'no property' creates. First, Panelli J argued, as can be seen in the paragraph cited, that human biological material should not be made the subject of property rights because it is best regulated by statute law. However, this confuses the public regulation of this material by the creation of criminal offences, which is typically achieved by statute, with the protection of a person's peaceful possession of it, which is achieved by the law of property. The statutes referred to by Panelli J[59] are similar to the leading English statute, the Human Tissue Act 2004, in that they are silent on what happens in the case where one person is dispossessed of human biological material by another. Such statutes do not protect a person's peaceful possession of human biological material. The other argument used by Panelli J was that if property rights were recognised then this would hinder research, as claimants like Moore would always be able to sue research institutions for unauthorised uses of tissue samples:

> The second important policy consideration is that we not threaten with disabling civil liability innocent parties who are engaged in socially useful activities, such as researchers who have no reason to believe that their use of a particular cell sample is, or may be, against a donor's wishes.[60]

This conclusion would only follow, however, if the court, in addition to recognising that tissue samples could be made the subject matter of property rights, also allocated those property rights to the patients who have donated the samples.[61] It is only if such rights are allocated to patients (who could then control their use) that there would be adverse consequences for research. However, there is no logical reason why, if the law were to recognise property rights in tissue samples, such rights could not be allocated to the research institution instead. Indeed, if such property rights are not allocated to the research institution then this could positively disrupt research activities because, as we have seen, the research institution would always be vulnerable to being dispossessed of the material.

A case which appears to accept the need for property law to play a role in these circumstances is *Washington University v Catalona*.[62] As outlined above, the defendant, who had been involved in the collection of thousands of tissue samples during his employment with the claimant university, wanted to bring these samples with him to a different university he had been appointed to. The facts present a good illustration of the potential conflict over such materials. There is a limited resource of tissue samples of which the claimant wants to make one particular use (that is, to keep them at Washington University for research purposes), whereas the defendant wants to make a different and inconsistent use of them (that is, move them to a new university for research purposes). Unless these tissue samples are subject to legal regulation, in the form of being made the subject of property

[59] Primarily the California Health and Safety Code, s 7054.4.

[60] Clarke and Kohler, *Property Law: Commentary and Materials*, above n 48 at 143.

[61] See Goold, ch 9 in this volume.

[62] *Washington University v Catalona* 490 F 3d 667 (2007).

rights, then there is a likely to be a physical conflict as there is nothing to prevent one party from trying to physically dispossess the other of the material. To prevent this happening the court, in applying the normal rules of property law, held that ownership of the material resided in the claimant. The court held that because the patients, when donating the material, had delivered them to the claimant university, rather than the defendant personally, title vested in the claimant. Consequently, the defendant was under a legal duty to refrain from interfering with the materials. The presence of this duty means that the defendant would not have been able to dispossess the claimant of this material with complete impunity; he would have committed a legal wrong in so doing. The 'instability of possession' is avoided, therefore, by allocating a property right in the material to the claimant.[63]

The Problem of Use

In light of the arguments made in the last section, it is important to consider one of the difficult issues that may arise from recognising property rights in human biological material. At the beginning of this chapter a brief account was given of the content of property rights, particularly the right of ownership. The most important feature of ownership, it was argued, is that the owner of a thing has a 'right to exclude', meaning that he is owed a duty by all others to refrain from physical interferences with the thing. However, there is another view of ownership, referred to as the 'bundle of rights' view, which stresses not only the duty on others to refrain from interferences with the thing, but also the owner's ability to make positive uses of the thing himself. For example, Clarke has written:

> To say that the defining characteristic of my ownership of a book is my right to exclude you from it is an extraordinarily negative, and potentially misleading, way of putting it. On the whole, the importance to me of book-owning is that it gives me free use of the book I can read it whenever I want, or put it on the shelf to admire it.[64]

Under this approach, if a court recognised that a person, A, had an ownership right over a specific thing, then it would follow that A had a 'right to use' and 'control' that thing. An owner of a car, for instance, would not only be owed a duty of non-interference by others, but would also have the right to use the car himself: he would have a right to drive it, pick up friends in it, charge others for a lift, try to sell the car at a profit and so on. This 'right to use', argued for by Clarke and others, is what would allow the owner of a thing to exploit it. This is problematic in the context of human biological material. First, it is often argued that it

[63] See also *Pierce v Proprietors of Sawn Pont Cemetery* 10 RI 227, 14 Am Rep 667 (1872).

[64] A Clarke, 'Use, Time and Entitlement' (2004) 57 *Current Legal Problems* 239, 241–42. See also Honoré, 'Ownership', above n 11, 116. See also Harris, *Property and Justice*, above n 9 at 30.

should not be possible to exploit and commercialise human biological material.[65] If the law were to recognise ownership rights of such material, however, then this may actually import a 'right to use' such material, meaning that an owner may have a right to use and exploit it in much the same way that he can use and exploit his car.[66] This gives rise to an ethical objection to the recognition of property rights in human biological material. A separate, but related, objection to the recognition of property rights focuses on a doctrinal problem. Because the commercial exploitation of human biological material is often seen as a bad thing, there are a number of statutes which regulate the use, and largely prevent the exploitation, of such material. The leading English statute is the Human Tissue Act 2004, section 32 of which provides that a person will commit an offence if he 'gives or receives an award for the supply of, or for an offer to supply' certain types of human biological material. Should ownership rights of human biological material be recognised then the effect of this and similar statutes would be to deprive owners of their so-called 'right to use'. Some have seen this as presenting insurmountable doctrinal problems. For example, in *Moore v Regents of University of California* Panelli J discussed the effect of a statute which imposed similar restrictions on use as found in the Human Tissue Act 2004:[67]

> [O]ne cannot escape the conclusion that the statute's practical effect is to limit, drastically, a patient's control over excised cells. By restricting how excised cells may be used and requiring their eventual destruction, the statute eliminates so many of the rights ordinarily attached to property that one cannot simply assume that what is left amounts to 'property' or 'ownership' for purposes of conversion law.[68]

If a 'right to use' is a cardinal feature of ownership,[69] then it is arguable that it is impossible for anyone to own human biological material if they are deprived of the right to use it.

In order to answer these objections it is important to say something about the apparent 'right to use'. For one the label is a misnomer. The word 'right' is usually reserved for a legal relationship which imposes a duty upon another person to behave in a certain way.[70] An owner's 'right to exclude' is a 'right' properly so-called because it imposes a legal duty upon others to refrain from physical interferences with the owner's thing. A 'right to use', on the other hand, does not impose a legal duty upon others to behave in a certain way: there is no duty to refrain from interfering with an owner's ability to use his thing. A good illustration is the recent case of *D Pride & Partners (a firm) v Institute for Animal Health*[71] where the defendant research institute had carelessly caused the outbreak of foot

[65] For a summary of this argument, see J Herring, *Medical Law and Ethics*, 3rd edn (Oxford, Oxford University Press, 2010) 449.
[66] ibid.
[67] The California Health and Safety Code, s 7054.4.
[68] *Moore v Regents of University of California*, above n 56, 140.
[69] As Honoré terms it: 'Ownership', above n 11, 116.
[70] Hohfeld, above n 2.
[71] *D Pride & Partners (a firm) v Institute for Animal Health* [2009] EWHC 685 (QB).

and mouth disease. While the disease did not reach the claimant's land, in that none of his livestock were infected, he suffered substantial losses because of the environmental restrictions imposed upon the movement of livestock in order to contain the disease. The claimant was unable to move animals onto his land, nor remove animals from his land to the abattoir. The restrictions effectively caused his land to stagnate and he was unable to use it effectively as a commercial farm for a period. Despite this impairment of use, the court held that the defendant had committed no wrong. While the defendant was under a duty to the claimant to refrain from interfering physically with the claimant's land (which had not been breached), he was not under a further duty to refrain from impairing the claimant's ability to use his land. What this illustrates is that 'use' is not a 'right' because it is not directly protected by the law. Instead of saying that an owner has a 'right to use', it is more accurate to say that he has a 'liberty to use'.[72] This nomenclature was favoured by Cave J in *Allen v Flood*:

> [I]t was said that a man has a perfect *right* to fire off a gun, when all that was meant, apparently, was that a man has a freedom or *liberty* to fire off a gun so long as he does not violate or infringe any one's rights in doing so, which is a very different thing from a right the violation or disturbance of which can be remedied or prevented by legal process.[73] (emphasis added)

To say that an owner of a thing has a 'liberty' to use his thing is simply to say that his use is permitted; he is under no legal duty to others not to use his thing and, in the absence of such a duty, his use is permitted. It is this legal construct, a 'liberty to use', not a 'right to use', that a person would hold if the law recognised him as owner of human biological material.

We can now return to Panelli J's claim that by limiting the 'right to use' human biological material, statute law has eliminated 'so many of the rights ordinarily attached to property that one cannot simply assume that what is left amounts to "property" or "ownership"'.[74] According to this view, the 'right to use' is such an important element of ownership that if you deprive the owner of this right, you effectively deprive him of ownership completely. First, we should be sceptical of this claim given that 'use' is not, as we have seen, a 'right' but a mere 'liberty'. Because there is no legal duty to refrain from impairing an owner's use of his thing, we are forced to say that although 'use' is permitted by the law, it is not a 'right' directly protected by the law. In other words, because the 'bundle of rights' that makes up ownership does not include a 'right to use', a statute which limits an owner's use is not actually depleting the bundle. Evidence of this can be found in the numerous examples of statutes that have deprived owners of liberties to use their things without depriving them of ownership. A good example here is the position of a freeholder of land. Freehold of land which, as we have seen, effectively means 'ownership' of land, is subject to a number of statutes which restrict

[72] Hohfeld, above n 2 at 38.
[73] *Allen v Flood* [1898] AC 1, 29.
[74] *Moore v Regents of University of California* (1990) 51 Cal 3d 120, 177.

the freeholder's liberties to use his land. Under the Town and Country Planning Act 1990, and a raft of other environmental legislation,[75] any freeholder who wishes to carry out building, engineering, mining or other operations in, on, under or over his land, must first apply to the relevant local authority for planning permission.[76] Furthermore, a freeholder cannot materially change the use of his land, for example, from residential to agricultural use, without obtaining permission.[77] This is a huge restriction on a freeholder's freedom to use his land. He is not, for example, free to build a house on his land; if there is already a house on his land he is not free to build an extension to it, carry out a loft conversion or create more floor space without obtaining permission. However, this does not mean that freeholders do not have property rights for the simple reason that they continue to hold a right to exclude others from their land.[78]

This argument was accepted in the recent case of *Yearworth v North Bristol NHS Trust*.[79] The defendant in the case had carelessly stored semen samples, leading to their loss. The samples had been given by the claimants before they underwent treatment that affected their fertility. The question that the court had to decide was whether the claimants held property rights in their semen that would allow them to sustain a claim in negligence against the hospital. One objection to the recognition of such rights was that the Human Tissue Act 2004 had imposed a number of restrictions on the claimants' abilities to use their sperm: under the statute the claimants were prohibited, personally, from doing things such as storing the sperm,[80] testing, preparing or transporting the sperm,[81] and using their sperm to bring about the creation of an embryo outside of the human body.[82] These uses of the sperm could only be made by a licensed body (that is, a medical body). Despite the claimants being restricted in their use of their sperm, Lord Judge CJ said that they were still capable of owning it, noting that 'there are numerous statutes which limit a person's ability to use his property . . . without eliminating his ownership of it'.[83] The claimants may have been unable to use their sperm, but this did not mean that they could not be owed a duty of non-interference (or retain 'negative control', as Lord Judge CJ called it),[84] which is the primary feature of ownership. In short, recognising property rights in human biological material is possible despite the presence of statutes which have restricted the use privileges of such material. This also answers the ethical objection that the

[75] See generally, K Gray, 'Land Law and Human Rights' in L Tee (ed), *Land Law: Issues, Debate, Policy* (Cullompton, Willan Publishing, 2002).

[76] Town and Country Planning Act 1990, s 57.

[77] ibid, s 55.

[78] *cf* W Lucy and C Mitchell, 'Replacing Private Property: The Case for Stewardship' (1996) *Cambridge Law Journal* 566, 567.

[79] *Yearworth v North Bristol NHS Trust* [2010] QB 1.The case is considered in further detail by Krebs, ch 4 in this volume.

[80] Human Tissue Act, s 4(1)(a).

[81] ibid, s 4(1A).

[82] ibid, s 3(1).

[83] *Yearworth*, above n 79 at 20.

[84] ibid.

recognition of property rights in human biological material would lead to the commercialisation of such material. If the law does recognise property rights in human biological material, there is nothing to stop the law from legislating (as it has) against the use, exploitation and commercialisation of it.

Conclusion

The principal argument made in this chapter is that human biological materials must be subject to legal regulation. In the absence of regulation, possession of human biological material will never be secure because a person will always be vulnerable to being dispossessed of the material by a stronger party. Such a situation would be contrary to the law's clear policy of protecting peaceful possession. The best way to regulate this material, and to protect peaceful possession, is to allocate property rights in human biological material to particular individuals, thus imposing a duty on others to refrain from interfering with it. Furthermore, as we saw in the last section, recognising property rights in this way would not be inconsistent with some of the ethical concerns that have been expressed over the potential commercialisation of human biological material.

8

The Boundaries of Property Law

JESSE WALL

Introduction

We are a complex combination of *things*: genes expressing, cells dividing, neurons firing, muscles twitching. We are also more than a combination of things; we are a complex combination of preferences, emotions, experiences and relationships. To view ourselves only in terms of our physiological complexity is to overlook what gives value to our existence. We risk a similar oversight when we treat all items of bodily material as items of property; we risk overlooking why bodily material is valuable to some people. The purpose of this chapter is to explain why the wholesale application of property law to the use and storage of bodily material may be inappropriate and to suggest how the law can develop to avoid the overextended application of property law.

In the first section of this chapter I will briefly divide the analysis of 'property law' into three dimensions: the functional, conceptual and structural dimensions of property law. In the following two sections, I will explain how property rights are conceptually 'exclusionary' and 'contingent' rights, and identify the structural features of property rights that follow from these conceptual features. The concern that is developed in the next two sections is that property law is configured to protect preferences and choices that can exist independently of the rights-holder, and that there are many instances where the rights that people may have in bodily material represent preferences and choices that cannot exist independently of them. In such instances, a structure of rights and duties – that is distinct from the structure of property law – is required. An analogy with the law of confidentiality is drawn to illustrate the appropriate legal structure for rights in bodily material that cannot exist independently of the rights-holder.

Beyond Ownership and Beyond Things

We may be interested in the recognition of property rights in bodily material for different reasons. A healthcare institution or progenitor may be interested in what the law entitles them to do with bodily material; a philosopher may be interested in the assumptions that underlie the decision to place bodily material in the same category as other items of property; and a lawyer may be interested in the type of rights and duties that apply to the possession and use of bodily material. Our interest in property may be a *functional*, *conceptual* or *structural* interest.

I suggest that it is best to view property law as having these three dimensions. The *functional* dimension of property concerns the relationship between a person and a thing. When Matthew brushes his teeth, Mark determines how his artwork is exhibited, Lucy ploughs her field and Joanna discloses her medical history to her physician, they are exercising their entitlements in things. In other words, Matthew, Mark, Lucy and Joanna are exercising 'incidences of ownership'.[1] For reasons advanced elsewhere,[2] the exercise of 'entitlements' or 'incidences of ownership' is not necessarily the same as the exercise of property rights. A particular method of legal protection (a specific *structure* of rights and duties) needs to be applied to the ownership relationship in order for a thing to be an item of property.

In order to connect the exercise of entitlements in things (the functional dimension) with the specific set of rights and duties that represent property law doctrine (the structural dimension) we need to *conceptualise* property law. That is, we need to consider the social and moral assumptions about the relationship between a person and a thing on which property law is premised. Since the structure of property law is configured to particular types of relationships that arise between a person and a thing, in order to understand the structure of property law we must explore the concept of property law.

It is tempting to conceptualise property rights in terms of 'things-ness'. However, a definition of property rights as 'rights in things' must presuppose a definition of 'things' that is neither circular (that is, it avoids the danger of defining 'things' with reference to what we consider to be items of property) nor contestable (that is, it accounts for borderline cases, such as the 'attached' body, statutory codes and intellectual property). A wider approach is instead taken here. It will be assumed that all branches of law concern a rights-holder, a duty-bearer, a thing and an activity. Where branches of law differ is how these basic features of law are organised in relation to each other. Importantly, this provides a way of viewing multiple branches of law through a common and neutral framework.

Here, two conceptual distinctions will be drawn. First, where branches of law can differ is in terms of whether the *thing* or the *activity* is the focal point for the legal relationship between rights-holder and duty-bearer. 'Exclusionary rights' have the *thing* as the focal point of the legal relationship, whereas 'interactive rights' have the *activity* as the focal point of the legal relationship. The second conceptual distinction concerns the relationship between the right and the right-holder; 'contingent rights' are rights that can exist independently of the rights-

[1] AM Honoré, Ownership' in *Making Law Bind: Essays Legal and Philosophical* (Oxford, Clarendon Press, 1961).

[2] J Wall, 'The Legal Status of Body Parts: A Framework' (2011) 31 *Oxford Journal of Legal Studies* 783.

holder, whereas 'dependent rights' are rights that cannot exist independently of the rights-holder. I will explain how property rights are (conceptually) exclusionary and contingent rights, and explore the five structural features of property law that follow from the conceptual features of property law.

Hence, on the assumption that individuals and institutions will able to lawfully exercise 'entitlements' or 'incidents of ownership' in bodily material, the following analysis will concentrate on the conceptual and structural dimensions of the law. Given this conceptual and structural understanding of property law, it is then possible to articulate my concern with property law. I will argue that there may be many instances where entitlements in bodily material are (conceptually) exclusionary and contingent rights, and as such, it is appropriate for the (structure) of property law to be applied to such the rights in such instances. However, the essence of my claim here is that there are also instances where rights in bodily material are (conceptually) exclusionary and *dependent* rights. In such instances, a legal structure – that is distinct from the structure of property law – is needed to provide adequate protection of exclusionary and dependent rights.

Property Rights are Exclusionary Rights

Our first conceptual distinction concerns whether the *thing* or the *activity* is the focal point for the legal relationship between rights-holder and duty-bearer.[3] For property law, the focal point is the use of the *thing*. When an entitlement-holder has possession of an item of property, the right to possession *enables a set of activities* that the rights-holder may engage in. For example, if Lucy possesses land (thing), she is able to grow wheat on the land (activity); and if Matthew possesses a toothbrush (thing), he may brush his teeth with his toothbrush (activity). Although the use of things enables activities, property law treats such activities as an 'open-ended'[4] or 'undefinable'[5] set of activities insofar as the permissible uses of any item of property 'cannot be exhaustively listed'.[6]

Since the relationship between the rights-holder and the thing cannot be reduced to a set of activities that the thing enables, the law of property employs an 'exclusion strategy'.[7] The exclusion strategy communicates the simple message of 'keep out', so that an undefined set of activities is protected without 'officials needing to know what these activities may be'.[8] Hence, instead of identifying particular and preordained uses of property that are protected under the law, the

[3] HE Smith, 'Modularity and Morality in the Law of Torts' (2011) 4 *Journal of Tort Law* 1.

[4] JW Harris, *Property and Justice* (Oxford, Clarendon Press, 1996) 160; L Katz, 'Exclusion and Exclusivity in Property Law' (2008) 58 *University of Toronto Law Journal* 275, 280.

[5] JE Penner, *The Idea of Property in Law* (Oxford, Oxford University Press, 1997) 72.

[6] Harris, *Property and Justice*, above n 4 at 160; Penner, *The Idea of Property in Law*, above n 5 at 71.

[7] HE Smith, 'Property and Property Rules' (2004) 79 *New York University Law Review* 1719, 1753.

[8] ibid, 1728.

'contours' of a property right are provided by the exclusion of others from using the object or resource.[9] The property right operates to exclude all others from the use of the thing and, as a result, the 'rights-holder' becomes 'the last person standing after the exclusion of everyone else'.[10]

In contrast to exclusionary rights, the law may recognise that the entitlement-holder has an interest in an action or activity. Although the action may involve a thing, the action or activity remains the focal point of the relationship between the rights-holder and the duty-bearer. These rights are 'interactive rights'. For example, Lucy may sow seeds (activity) on her land (thing); Matthew may brush his teeth (activity) with his toothbrush (thing). Lucy may owe duties to her neighbour when sowing seeds and the manufacturer of Matthew's toothbrush may owe Matthew duties regarding his oral care. Where the focus is on the activity or interaction between the rights-holder and the duty-bearer, the law employs a 'governance strategy'.[11] The governance strategy 'takes more direct aim at acts and activities'[12] by specifying the entitlements and responsibilities of those who are engaged in an activity or interaction.

As I will explain, structural features follow from this conceptual distinction between 'exclusionary' and 'interactive rights'. Note, however, that the resulting structural divide is less clear where there are dual sources of law, such as *negligence* causing damage to *property*. In such cases, there is a structural hybrid that combines structural features from the exclusionary and governance strategies. Unfortunately, some of the subtlety of the many different property-based actions (such as conversion, trespass, bailment, reversionary injury and negligent damage to property) may be lost in this survey of the five structural features of property rights. The subtle differences do not, however, undermine the critical claim in the section discussing the boundaries of property law.

The Basis of the Right

Where the law focuses on the exclusion of others from the thing, the rights-holder's right is enforceable against the duty-bearer independently of the duty-bearer's conduct[13] and independently of any relationship between the rights-holder and the duty-bearer.[14] These are 'trespassory'[15] or 'pre-existing' rights.[16] In the context of property law, these are termed rights *in rem*. The structural feature here is that the right is enforceable against an open set of persons since the success of the action 'does not depend on there being a pre-existing relationship between

[9] Penner, above n 5 at 72.
[10] Katz, 'Exclusion and Exclusivity in Property Law', above n 4 at 277.
[11] ibid, 280; Smith, 'Property and Property Rules', above n 7 at 1753.
[12] Smith, 'Modularity and Morality in the Law of Torts', above n 3 at 1.
[13] B McFarlane, *The Structure of Property Rights* (Oxford, Hart Publishing, 2008) 20–22.
[14] Penner, above n 5 at 128.
[15] ibid.
[16] McFarlane, *The Structure of Property Rights*, above n 13 at 20–22.

the holder of the right and the person infringing it'.[17] In comparison, where the law focuses on activities or interactions, the law will identify the rights that arise 'against [the duty-bearer] because of [the duty-bearer's] own conduct'.[18] The *basis* of the right is the transaction or interaction between the rights-holder and duty-bearer. These are 'direct' or 'transactional'[19] rights (and in the context of property law are described as *in personam* rights).

For the court in *Moore*, it was this pre-existing basis of property rights that mitigated against accepting the claim in conversion.[20] The main concern expressed by the Supreme Court of California was that conversion

> imposes liability on all those into whose hands the cells come, whether or not the particular defendant participated in, or knew of, the inadequate disclosures that violated the patient's right to make an informed decision.[21]

However, because of the 'no-property rule', the claimants in *Greenberg* were unable to establish a pre-existing right to their bodily material. The court held that '[t]here is no automatic fiduciary relationship that attaches when a researcher accepts medical donations and the acceptance of trust'.[22] As a result, the claimants were forced to rely upon (ultimately unsuccessful) claims based in tort and fiduciary duties.[23]

We may consider pre-existing rights as being over-extensive, and transactional rights as being under-extensive, of the rights of a progenitor in their bodily material. If so, we may prefer an intermediate position between pre-existing and transactional rights; where the right to control the bodily material arises in circumstances where the duty-bearer knew, or ought to have known, of interest of the progenitor (discussed further below).[24]

The Content of the Right

If the exclusion strategy excludes others from the use of a thing (and thereby preserving an open set of activities for the rights-holder), it follows that the inference with the thing by another person amounts to interference with the rights of the rights-holder. As I will explain here, for exclusionary rights, claims are 'actionable per se' since the exclusion strategy protects both the 'original' and 'derivative' content of the right. In comparison, since interactive rights protect a particular action or activity, claims are actionable only upon proof of loss, protecting only the 'derivative' content of the right.

[17] Penner, above n 5 at 128.
[18] McFarlane, above n 13 at 20–22.
[19] Penner, above n 5 at 128.
[20] *Moore v Regents of the University of California* 51 Cal 3d (1990) 124, 144.
[21] ibid.
[22] *Greenberg v Miami Children's Hospital Research Institute* 264 F Supp 2d. 1064, 1066 (SD Fl 2003).
[23] ibid.
[24] See *Campbell v MGN* [2004] UKHL 22 [14].

The 'original' dimension of entitlement concerns the relationship between the rights-holder and the thing.[25] For instance, Matthew may have the right to have physical control over a painting; Mark may have the right to determine how the painting is stored and displayed, and Lucy may have the right to transfer all of the entitlements to the painting to another person. In terms of the Torts (Interference with Goods) Act 1977, these are rights *to* the good.[26]

When Matthew, Mark or Lucy is deprived of these entitlements, they suffer – generally speaking – a loss. The loss they suffer, however, is intangible. Depriving Matthew of his rightful possession of the painting, disregarding Mark's valid instructions as to the use of the painting or preventing Lucy from transferring the entitlements to another, are all instances of interference with the relationship between entitlement-holder and thing. Yet it is difficult to quantify the harm done, or loss suffered, that is caused by disrupting the relationship between Matthew, Mark or Lucy and the thing.

In such situations of interference, Matthew, Mark and Lucy will often be able to identify a tangible loss that follows from the deprivation of their entitlements; it is because Matthew was deprived of possession of the painting that he could not participate in the exhibition; it is because, contrary to Mark's instructions, the painting was exposed to regular sunlight that the painting is discoloured and has depreciated in value; and it is because Lucy could not transfer the painting overseas Lucy could not benefit from a lucrative contract.

These tangible losses are the 'derivative' dimensions of entitlements.[27] The tangible value of having entitlements consists of having derivative entitlements in the object, resource or asset, for example, the ability to display a painting, to preserve a painting, or to profit from the sale of a painting. In terms of the Torts (Interference with Goods) Act 1977, these are interests *in* the good.[28]

Protection of both the original and the derivative content of an entitlement follows from the entitlement being characterised as an exclusionary right. Since exclusionary rights protect the exercise of an open-ended set of activities, interference with the relationship between the person and thing is *itself* an intrusion into the sphere of protected activity. Depriving someone of their rights of possession or acting inconsistently with their instructions as to the use or care of the object, are actionable wrongs. As Stevens explains, 'there need be no loss *consequent* upon the defendant's interference'.[29] Rather, the law need only assess whether 'an individual has had a right infringed, or he has not'.[30]

In contrast, since interactive rights are concerned with a particular activity or interaction, a claim is only 'actionable upon proof damage'.[31] In other words, the

[25] S Green, 'Rights and Wrongs: An Introduction to the Wrongful Interference Actions' in D Nolan and A Robertson (eds), *Rights and Private Law* (Oxford, Hart Publishing, 2012) 538.

[26] ibid *cf* Torts (Interference with Goods) Act 1977, s 1(d).

[27] ibid.

[28] Torts (Interference with Goods) Act 1977, s 1(d).

[29] R Stevens, *Torts and Rights* (Oxford, Oxford University Press, 2007) 66.

[30] Green, 'Rights and Wrongs: An Introduction to the Wrongful Interference Actions', above n 25 at 536.

[31] D Nolan, 'New Forms of Damage in Negligence' (2007) 70 *Modern Law Review* 59, 60.

governance strategy only protects the 'derivative' content of the entitlement (the tangible losses that follow from interference with the thing).[32] The law assesses whether the right-holder's *interest in the activity or interaction* was interfered with by the defendant.[33] This structural distinction between the original and derivative content of the duty concerns what losses are sufficient to establish a cause of action. This, as Nolan notes, 'should not be confused with the harms for which recovery is permitted once the cause of action has been established'.[34] The 'harms for which recovery is permitted' (content of the remedial duty) is discussed below.

The recognition of property rights in *Yearworth* was motivated by the need to recognise the 'original' content of the chemotherapy patients' entitlements in the semen. Their claim in negligence causing injury or distress failed because they could not prove that, on the balance of probabilities, damage to the semen interfered with their ability to conceive a child.[35] That is, they could not prove a harm or loss in a *derivative* sense. With the recognition of property rights in the semen, it was then sufficient for them to show that their superior right to possession had been interfered with.[36] That is, an interference with the 'original' content of their right to possession. It is this feature of the exclusion strategy that also drives Nwabueze's recommendation to recognise quasi-property rights in bodily material if 'only to avoid the remedial hurdle of proving a contemporaneous . . . loss in negligence'.[37]

The Content of the Duty

The third structural feature concerns the content of the duty imposed on the duty-bearer. The duty on the duty-bearer may be a duty of non-interference or a duty of care. Duties of non-interference impose a singular duty not to undertake deliberate action that interferes with the rights of the rights-holder.[38] In contrast, a duty-bearer may satisfy their obligations under a duty of care by either not interfering with the rights of the rights-holder (avoiding the outcome), or by causing interference but doing so 'innocently' (taking the required steps in trying to avoid the outcome).[39] Duties of non-interference are concerned with the outcome of the duty-bearer's (deliberate) conduct, whereas duties of care are concerned with the combination of the outcome of the duty-bearer's conduct and the standard of conduct undertaken by the duty-bearer.

[32] Green, above n 25 at 538.

[33] ibid at 536.

[34] Nolan, 'New Forms of Damage in Negligence', above n 31 at 61.

[35] *Yearworth v North Bristol NHS Trust* [2009] EWCA Civ 37 [24].

[36] ibid at [25].

[37] RN Nwabueze, 'Donated Organs Property Rights and the Remedial Quagmire' (2008) 16 *Medical Law Review* 201, 205.

[38] P Cane, 'Causing Conversion' (2002) 118 *Law Quarterly Review* 544. See *Kuwait Airways Corp v Iraqi Airways Co and another (Nos 4 & 5)* [2002] UKHL 19, [2002] 2 AC 886 (Lord Nicholls) [39].

[39] J Gardner, 'Obligations and Outcomes in the Law of Torts' in P Cane and J Gardner (eds), *Relating to Responsibility: Essays for Tony Honoré* (Oxford, Hart Publishing, 2001) 10.

For instance, *Arora* concerned the breach of a duty of non-interference under the law of conversion: the respondent was liable since their total, albeit brief, control over the cell line was held to be wholly inconsistent with the claimant's right to possession.[40] However, the NHS Trust in *Yearworth* was liable for breach of bailment and negligent damage because the NHS Trust failed to avoid damage to the semen while also failing to take reasonable steps to safeguard the claimants possessory entitlements in the stored semen.[41] The difference between the two types of duties can be clearly seen in circumstances where a loss is caused by the conduct of the interferer despite the interferer taking the required precautionary steps. Where duties of non-interference are imposed the loss is shifted to the interferer regardless of fault. Where duties of care are imposed, and neither of the parties is at fault, the rights-holder bears the loss.[42]

This structural distinction between duties of non-interference and duties of care also follows from the conceptual distinction between exclusionary and interactive rights. Since exclusionary rights protect spheres of undefined activity, it follows that the interferer – the one that caused an intrusion into the sphere – ought to bear the loss (despite taking reasonable precautions). In contrast, where the legal strategy is to allocate entitlements and responsibilities to participants engaged in an activity or interaction, the care taken by each participant to avoid causing loss will be relevant in assigning responsibility for loss.

The exclusionary strategy of property law provides robust protection of entitlements *in things*. It is because property rights are 'pre-existing' and 'original' rights that impose 'duties of non-interference' that property law is an appealing candidate for the job of protecting entitlements in bodily material. Note that property law is not the only branch of law that protects exclusionary rights; rights of privacy and bodily integrity are also protected by 'pre-existing' and 'original' rights that impose 'duties of non-interference'. We must now turn to consider other conceptual and structural features of property law. This will enable us to differentiate property rights from other exclusionary rights as well as explain why there is a reluctance to apply property law to all instances of the possession and use of bodily material.

Property Rights are Contingent Rights

If we understand property rights solely as exclusionary rights (or as rights in things), we overlook an important conceptual distinction between the different types of relationships that can arise between a rights-holder and a right (in a thing). According to Baroness Hale in *OBG v Allan*:

[40] *US v Arora* 860 F Supp (1994) 1091, 1097–100.

[41] *Yearworth*, above n 35 at [13], [25], [45f].

[42] E Weinrib, *The Idea of Private Law* (Cambridge, MA, Harvard University Press, 1995) 174; see also AM Honoré, 'Responsibility and Luck' (1988) 104 *Law Quarterly Review* 530.

> The essential feature of property is that it has an existence independent of a particular person: it can be bought and sold, given and received, bequeathed and inherited, pledged or seized to secure debts, acquired (in the olden days) by a husband on marrying its owner.[43]

Penner's 'Separability Thesis' argues for a similar conceptual distinction:[44]

> Only those 'things' in the world which are contingently associated with a particular owner may be objects of property; as a function of the nature of this contingency, in theory nothing of normative consequences beyond the fact that the ownership has changed occurs when an object of property is alienated to another.[45]

I suggest that property rights are rights that can exist independently of any rights-holder. Where the exercise of a right (in the thing) gives rise to preferences and choices that can be exercised by any other potential rights-holder, then such rights are conceptually *contingent* to the rights-holder. In comparison, 'dependent rights' are rights that cannot exist independently of the rights-holder. Where the exercise of a right gives rise to preferences and choices that can only be exercised by the particular rights-holder, then such rights are conceptually *dependent* upon the rights-holder.

Note that the 'separability' or 'independence' of property is the separability or independence of the *rights* (rather than the separability of thing) from the rights-holder. Moreover, it is not clear to me why critics of the separability (of rights) thesis have prescribed the thresholds of 'substantial changes to constitutive parts of our personality' or complete deprivation 'of our status as persons' to the separability thesis.[46] Perhaps the direction of the dependency relationship has been misinterpreted. It is not that our personalities depend on dependent rights (so that the deprivation of a dependent right is a drastic event for our 'personalities' or 'status as persons'). Rather, the existence of dependent rights is dependent on the rights-holder (so that the change in rights-holder would be fatal to the existence and content of the dependent right). In short, *my* right to privacy is dependent upon *my existence* (as the rights-holder) but *my existence* is not dependent upon my right to privacy!

It follows that there where contingent rights are transferred or interfered with, there are no normative consequences above and beyond the (lawful or unlawful) reallocation of entitlements in the thing from Matthew to Mark. However, when the dependent rights of Lucy are obtained by Joanna, there are normative consequences above and beyond the shift of entitlements. These additional normative consequences can be understood as the loss suffered by Lucy that is incommensurate with any gain obtained by Joanna.

[43] *OBG v Allan* [2007] UKHL 21 [309].

[44] Penner, above n 5 at 111.

[45] ibid.

[46] M Quigley, 'Property in Human Biomaterials – Separating Persons and Things?' (2012) 32 *Oxford Journal of Legal Studies* 659, 672.

The Content of the Remedial Duty

The fourth structural feature, and the first that follows from the distinction between contingent and dependent rights, concerns how the law remedies interference with the rights of the rights-holder. For contingent rights, since there are no normative consequences above and beyond the misallocation of entitlements from the interference with the interest, it follows that law can remedy interference with contingent interests by reallocating entitlements to the entitlement-holder (or the cost of replacement *in lieu*).

In such instances, the wrongful interaction or transaction 'is reversed, undone or counteracted'[47] by restoring 'the notional equality with which the parties enter the transaction' or interaction.[48] In some contexts, the remedial obligation can easily be performed. For example, if Joanna had a perfectly good bicycle, which Lucy converted or negligently destroyed, the damages Lucy ought to pay is the cost of a replacing Joanna's perfectly good bicycle or repairing Joanna's bicycle to its original state. Damages can repair the loss because they are able to substitute for loss by either compensating for the loss in value or by restoring the damaged goods, thereby returning the parties to the initial allocation of entitlements. Hence, since the remedial aim of property law is corrective, damages are awarded to place 'the plaintiff . . . as far as money can do it, in the same place as if the loss had not been inflicted on him'.[49]

However, such an approach is inapplicable to dependent rights. This is because the reallocation of entitlements to the rights-holder does not address the normative consequences of the interference that are above and beyond the mere misallocation of entitlements. For example, Lucy may be deprived of possession or control of a miscarried foetus or deceased infant, Joanna may be unable to undergo assisted reproductive therapy due to inadequately stored ovum, or bone marrow donated by Matthew to Mark may be misdirected or destroyed. Here, for Lucy and Joanna at least, it is not possible to restore the allocation of entitlements. Moreover, monetary damages are unable to substitute for any of the preferences and choices that have been forgone because of the interference with their entitlements. In such circumstances, the corrective aim of property law is inapplicable.

Property law does recognise that interference with goods may harm personal interests and non-pecuniary loss may be recoverable where a claimant can succeed in his or her claim for psychiatric injury or emotional distress.[50] In order to succeed in a claim for psychiatric injury, two particular elements need to be established. 'The first hurdle,' according to Lord Bridge in *McLoughlin v O'Brian*, 'is to

[47] J Gardner, 'What is Tort Law For? Part 1. The Place of Corrective Justice' (2011) 30 *Law and Philosophy* 1, 9.

[48] EJ Weinrib, 'Corrective Justice in a Nutshell' (2002) 52 *The University of Toronto Law Journal* 349.

[49] NE Palmer and E McKendrick (eds), *Interests in Goods*, 2nd edn (London, Lloyd's of London Press, 1998) 548.

[50] JK Mason and GT Laurie, 'Consent or Property? Dealing with Body Parts in the Shadow of Bristol and Alder Hey' (2001) 64 *Modern Law Review* 710, 728.

establish that [the loss suffered is] not merely grief, distress or any other normal emotion, but a positive psychiatric injury'.[51] This means that the loss suffered must satisfy either the American Diagnostic and Statistical Manual of Mental Disorders or the International Statistical Classification of Mental and Behavioral Disorders.[52]

The second hurdle is foreseeability. Under the law of negligence, an award for damages in respect of a psychiatric injury is only recoverable subject to proof of causation and foreseeability.[53] Similarly, the damages awardable for breach of bailment are governed by contractual principles that require that the non-commercial loss be 'a major or important part of the object' of forming the bailment relationship.[54] This requirement, as applied by the Court of Appeal in *Yearworth*, amounts to a requirement that the psychiatric injury be 'foreseeable consequent upon the breach of duty' which the claimants in *Yearworth* were able to satisfy.[55] The foreseeability requirement may not always be easily satisfied. For example, in *Re Organ Retention*, Mrs Harris succeeded in establishing that the healthcare professionals owed her a duty of care (regarding the treatment of the body of her deceased infant), and succeeded in establishing that the duty of care was breached. However, the claim in negligence failed since it was held that the psychiatric injury that she suffered was not foreseeable.[56]

If a loss cannot satisfy the criteria for identifying a psychiatric injury for legal purposes, damages for emotional distress may be recoverable. Nonetheless, 'English law does not currently recognise the infliction of emotional distress as a separate cause of action';[57] rather, a claimant must satisfy the elements of another action and then attempt to add to the damages an award for emotional distress. In essence, where there is emotional distress or personal suffering, in order to obtain a remedy under property law, claimants must satisfy the additional elements of – what is treated as – an extraordinary remedial measure.

Compare the damages available under property law with the damages available under torts that concern an individual's personality, such as false imprisonment, assault, malicious prosecution and even trespass to land. Witzleb notes that as far as these 'general damages' are concerned: 'the law presumes that the defendant's wrongful conduct will cause some mental distress and claimants may be awarded substantial damages without being required to prove actual emotional harm'.[58]

[51] *McLoughlin v O'Brian* [1983] 1 AC 410 (HL) 431; R Mulheron, 'Rewriting the Requirement for a "Recognised Psychiatric Injury" in Negligence Claims' (2012) 33 *Oxford Journal of Legal Studies* 77, 80.

[52] Mulheron, 'Rewriting the Requirement for a "Recognised Psychiatric Injury" in Negligence Claims', ibid at 84.

[53] *Attia v British Gas* [1988] 1 QB 304; *Yearworth*, above n 35 at [55].

[54] *Farley v Skinner* [2001] UKHL 49, [2002] 2 AC 732 [24].

[55] *Yearworth*, above n 35 at [54].

[56] *AB and others v Leeds Teaching Hospital NHS Trust and another; Re: Organ Retention Group Litigation* [2004] EWHC 644 [259].

[57] R Hardcastle, *Law and the Human Body: Property Rights, Ownership and Control* (Oxford, Hart Publishing, 2009) 190.

[58] N Witzleb, 'Monetary Remedies for Breach of Confidence in Privacy Cases' (2007) 27 *Legal Studies* 430, 446.

The approach taken here is to presume that there has been a personal loss or suffering following from the interference with the rights of the rights-holder. These damages are therefore concerned with compensating the normative consequences of interference that go beyond the misallocation of entitlements in any given thing. As I will explain below, the use and storage of bodily material will often concern dependent rights, and in such instances I suggest that the content of the remedial duty ought to be similar to the remedial approach under torts that concern an individual's personality. Such an approach is responsive to normative consequences of interference that go beyond the misallocation of entitlements in any given thing.

The Transferability of the Right

If property rights are contingent rights (that represent preferences and choices that are not associated with any particular rights-holder), then it is possible for the property rights to be transferred and for the recipient of the right to exercise the same set of preferences and choices. In such instances, the parties themselves ought to be free to determine the content of the transaction.[59] In contrast, since dependent rights represent a set of preferences and choices that can only be exercised by the rights-holder, dependent rights are inalienable or non-transferable.[60] There also exists a middle ground. Even where a right can exist independently of the rights-holder (a contingent right), there may still be wider normative consequences to the transaction or interaction that require 'an organ of the state' to govern the transaction.[61] Such transfers are legally permissible but the content of the transfer is determined by liability rules.[62]

If entitlements in bodily material are viewed as property rights, there are few (if any) limits on the transferability of the property right. It is this feature of property law that explains the motivation towards treating stored semen as items of property in the circumstances that arose in *Hecht*,[63] *Bazley*[64] and *Re Edwards*.[65] In these cases, once the progenitor's entitlements in their semen were conceived as property rights, the progenitor's entitlements in their semen were transferable entitlements. The widows were then able to assert their rights to their husbands' property, which provided a legal basis for the transfer of the right to possession to the widows. More significantly, in *Re Edwards*, property law was used to enable

[59] G Calabresi and AD Melamed, 'Property Rules, Liability Rules and Inalienability' (1972) 85 *Harvard Law Review* 1089, 1092–111.

[60] ibid, at 1111–15.

[61] ibid, 1092–111.

[62] ibid.

[63] *Hecht v Superior Court of Los Angeles County* (1993) 20 Cal Rptr 2d 275; *Yearworth*, above n 35 at [40].

[64] *Kate Jane Bazley v Wesley Monash IVF Pty Ltd* [2010] QSC 118.

[65] *Jocelyn Edwards, Re the estate of the late Mark Edwards* [2011] NSWSC 478.

the transfer of possession of bodily material in order to *circumvent* liability rules that required the consent of the progenitor.[66]

In contrast to the permissible framework of property, 'liability rules' represent a restrictive framework for the transfer of entitlements. Consider, for instance, the restrictions on the transfer of human tissue or gametes under the Human Tissue Act 2004 and the Human Fertilisation and Embryology Act 1990 and the liability rules which: prescribe particular consent procedures,[67] limit the use of the transferred material to particular purposes,[68] and limit the content of the exchange to payments of compensation for expenses incurred and loss of earnings.[69] My concern here is that the recognition of property rights in bodily materials provides a permissive legal framework for the transfer of entitlements in bodily material, whereas there are many instances where the law ought to (and does under the Human Tissue Act and the Human Fertilisation and Embryology Act) restrict the transferability of entitlements in bodily material.

The Boundaries of Property Law

There are instances where the use and storage of bodily material gives rise to exclusionary and contingent rights. In such instances (which may be very frequent), the application of property law may be appropriate. There are other instances where the use and storage of bodily material gives rise to dependent rights, and in such instances the (wholesale) application of property law is inappropriate. The purpose of this final section is to demonstrate why the application of property law to all items of bodily material is troublesome, and suggest another way in which the law could develop.

On a conceptual level, we know that property is good at dealing with things, but sometimes our control of things is more about us (our personality, personhood or our relationships). Privacy is a useful example. We control our personal information in order to protect a feature of our personality, and when our control of our personal information is interfered with, the loss suffered is a loss that is particular to the rights-holder. Equally, when a parent is deprived of control of a miscarried foetus or the body of a deceased infant, when a patient's stored semen thaws, when directly donated bone marrow is misallocated, or when a widow is unable to continue with assisted reproductive therapy, progenitors are unable to exercise their entitlements as a parent, as a wife or as an embodied person. In other words, the parents, patients and widows stand in relation to the bodily material in their capacity as parents, wives or persons with bodily integrity. No

[66] See J Wall and J Lidwell-Durnin, 'Control, Over My Dead Body: Why Consent is Significant (and Why Property is Suspicious)' (2012) 12 *Otago Law Review* 314.

[67] Human Tissue Act 2004, s 5(1); Human Fertilisation and Embryology Act 1990, sch 3.

[68] Human Tissue Act 2004, s 8(1); Human Fertilisation and Embryology Act 1990, s 41.

[69] Human Tissue Act 2004, s 32(7); Human Fertilisation and Embryology Act 1990, s 12(1).

other person can stand in the same position as the parents, patients or widow with regard to the bodily material, and hence their rights to the bodily material represent preferences and choices that are necessarily associated with them as the rights-holder (that is, dependent rights).

On a structural level, two main concerns arise. First, where personal rights in bodily material arise (such as in the examples above) the law ought to presume that 'the defendant's wrongful conduct will cause some mental distress'[70] and award 'general damages'. The remedial aim of the law should be to compensate the wronged party for the incommensurable loss suffered, rather than to attempt to correct the wrong itself. Following the remedial path set by property law is to require claimants to clear the additional remedial hurdles for proving a non-pecuniary loss.

The second concern is that property law ought not to be used to as tool to circumvent liability rules or convert a non-transferable right into a transferable right. For instance, the court in *Re Edwards* was able to evade the requirement of progenitor consent by finding that the widow of the progenitor had a property right in the semen. The widow was then able to assert her property right to the bodily material, requiring the healthcare institution to 'relinquish' the semen, rather than the healthcare institution 'supplying' (since 'supply' without consent was prohibited).[71] The presumption, under property law, is that there are no normative consequences beyond the transfer of entitlements. Nevertheless, there will often be concerns with the transfer of bodily material and liability rules – such as the provisions under the Human Tissue Act and the Human Fertilisation and Embryology Act – exist to address these concerns.

These structural concerns reflect the underlying limit of property law: that it is poorly equipped to protect the preferences and choices that are necessarily associated with the rights-holder. The problem, briefly put, is that property law is overly restrictive in awarding remedies for non-pecuniary loss and overly permissive in allowing the transfer of entitlements.

I suggest that the law that ought to apply the exclusion strategy to the possession or use of bodily material. Hence, rights in bodily material ought to be 'pre-existing' or at least exercisable against those who ought to have known of the claimant's interest. The rights also ought to be actionable per se and impose duties of non-interference. The law ought also be to configured to the fact that many instances will arise where entitlements in the bodily material protect preferences and choices that can only be exercised by the particular rights-holder. In such instances, the law ought to presume that a defendant's wrongful conduct will cause a significant, but non-pecuniary, loss to the rights-holder. Moreover, the law ought to also be able to continue restrict (through liability rules) or prohibit (through inalienability rules) the transfer of bodily material to others.

[70] Witzleb, 'Monetary Remedies for Breach of Confidence in Privacy Cases', above n 58 at 446.

[71] Assisted Reproductive Technology Act 1997 (Qld), s 21: 'An ART provider must not supply a gamete or an embryo to another person (including another ART provider) except with the consent of the gamete provider and in a manner that is consistent with the gamete provider's consent.'

Hence, in instances where exclusionary and dependent rights arise in bodily material, a legal structure is required that is distinct from the particular sets of rights and duties provided by property law. Duties of confidentiality (with regards to personal information) are configured to protect exclusionary and dependent rights. As a result, the right to privacy: (a) is exercisable 'whenever a person receives information he knows or ought to know is fairly and reasonably to be regarded as confidential';[72] (b) is actionable per se;[73] (c) imposes duties of non-disclosure;[74] (d) remedies non-pecuniary loss through general damages;[75] and (e) is a non-transferable right. Bodily material, like personal information, may be freely abandoned, retained or entrusted to a healthcare professional (and healthcare institution). Although parts of our body may become separate from us, we may retain an interest in our bodily material. It is this interest – like our interest in privacy – that is inseparable from us.

If the common law is to apply this structure of rights and duties to protect personal interests in bodily material, it then becomes a question of labelling as to whether we call these rights in bodily material 'property rights'. In my opinion, these (exclusionary and dependent) rights appear to be more structurally analogous to the rights exercisable under the law of confidentiality. Moreover, on a conceptual level, I suggest that it is important to retain the boundary between rights that are contingently associated with the rights-holder and rights that are necessarily associated with the rights-holder. The recognition of property rights in all items of bodily material dissolves this boundary.

Conclusion

The attraction of property law as a solution to the uncertain legal status of bodily material is clear: we want the item of bodily material to be the focal point of the legal relationship between rights-holder and duty-bearer. But treating rights in bodily material as 'pre-existing' rights (that are exercisable against an open set of persons) or 'original' rights (that are actionable per se) that impose duties of 'non-interference', does not *necessitate* the application of property law. This is because property rights are not the only instance of exclusionary rights. Moreover, the use and storage of bodily material gives rise to instances of 'dependent rights':

[72] *Campbell v MGN*, above n 24 [14]; G Philipson, 'Transforming Breach of Confidence: Toward a Common Law Right to Privacy under the Human Rights Act' (2003) 66 *The Modern Law Review* 726, 746.

[73] *A-G v Guardian Newspapers (No 2)* [1988] UKHL 6 [256]; *Bluck v Information Commissioner* (2007) 98 *Butterworth's Medico Legal Reports* 1 [15]; R Arnold, 'The Protection of Confidential Information in the Human Rights Era: Two Aspects (2007) 2 *Journal of Intellectual Property Law & Practice* 599.

[74] *A-G v Guardian Newspapers*, above n 73 at [34].

[75] *Archer v Williams* [2003] EWHC 1670 [76]; *Cornelius v de Taranto* [2001] EMLR 12 [66]; Witzleb, above n 58 at 549.

rights that protect preferences and choices that can only be exercised by the rights-holder. I have argued here that property law is unable to provide adequate legal protection of dependent rights. The problem with property law is that it is overly restrictive in awarding remedies for non-pecuniary loss and overly permissive in allowing the transfer of entitlements. I have also suggested that there are branches of law that provide adequate protection for exclusionary and dependent rights. The contention here is that when we consider the legal status of separated bodily material, there are not only limits to property law, there are also alternatives to property law.

9

Abandonment and Human Tissue

IMOGEN GOOLD

Introduction

In the debate over how we should regulate human biomaterials, and specifically whether we ought to deal with them as legal property, reference is often made to the notion of 'abandonment', both in the legal and the lay sense (and sometimes, unhelpfully, interchangeably). Despite these references to the concept of abandonment, there has to date been little fine-grained analysis of how the legal concept of abandonment, as part of the law of property, would actually operate if applied to human tissue. This chapter presents such an analysis. It begins by providing an account of the doctrine of abandonment in English law, as well as some comparison with the positions in other jurisdictions. A focal issue in this account is whether it can be said that such a doctrine operates in these jurisdictions at all. The chapter then outlines and critically appraises some of the ways in which this concept has been deployed in the body-as-property debate. It argues that this deployment is often marked by shifts between the legal and lay senses of abandonment, and a lack of grounding in the relevant case law. Both are considered serious problems given the vital role abandonment plays in some conceptions of how the law of property might apply to human biomaterials. Given this, the chapter then turns to an analysis of how the doctrine of abandonment might operate in relation to discarded human biomaterials, if such a doctrine indeed exists. In doing so, it explores whether deeming biomaterials property will necessarily render 'innocent' or 'legitimate' uses of biomaterials legally problematic, and why an accurate application of the concept of abandonment in the body-as-property debate is so important, with a particular focus on its implications for dealings with so-called 'waste' tissue, and the acquisition of biomaterials for research.

The Doctrine of Abandonment at Common Law

What is Abandonment?

In general parlance, to abandon something is to give it up, and we often talk of abandoning something when we mean we are no longer interested in it. In relation to things, we could call this simply 'discarding'. For the common law, 'abandonment' has a particular meaning that differs in some ways from the non-legal sense in which it is used day to day. To abandon, in the legal sense, means something stronger than merely to discard. It means to give up ownership or possession of the thing entirely and irrevocably. Andrew Simester and Robert Sullivan define abandonment as follows:

> Abandonment of ownership requires a giving up of the owner's physical control of an item, accompanied by the cessation of any intention to possess that item and of any intention to exclude other persons from its possession – i.e. a deliberate relinquishing of all rights over the item.[1]

In some situations 'discarding' and 'abandoning' will amount to the same thing, but in others they will not. Whenever a person merely discards something but would expect to retain some right to it, or some control over it (to prevent its use by others), this would not equate to abandonment at common law, merely to giving up possession. For clarity in this chapter then, merely throwing something away in the lay sense will be referred to as 'discarding', while the expression 'abandonment' will refer to the act of giving up legal ownership of an item.[2]

An example will draw out the distinction. If I throw away, say, a letter from an unkind friend in a fit of pique, I might want to take it back a little later when I have cooled off, or perhaps never see it again and expect that it will be destroyed. If I go to remove the scrunched up sheets from the rubbish bin, it is probable that I do not doubt that the sheets remain mine, at least in many circumstances. If someone else had taken possession of those sheets and then asserted that they belonged entirely to him and that he could exclude me from them, I would probably both be surprised and would find this quite unreasonable. In this latter example, we would say I discarded the letter, but if it were clear that I did not

[1] As quoted in S Thomas, 'Do Freegans Commit Theft?' (2010) 30 *Legal Studies* 98, 108. FH Lawson and Bernard Rudden take a similar view, stating 'it is the sum of all that can be done with it that constitutes the consent of ownership': FH Lawson and B Rudden, *The Law of Property*, 2nd edn (Oxford, Clarendon Press, 1982) 8. While there are, of course, some problems with the term 'ownership', as there are with 'property', and indeed 'title' might be preferable, in this chapter the usual terminology of 'ownership' will be used. See further, AS Burrows, *English Private Law*, 2nd edn (Oxford, Oxford University Press, 2007) (WJ Swadling) 4.131.

[2] Possession can also be abandoned at law, but this is not relevant to us in this context as the new possessor would not gain the rights to use, manage and so on that are assumed to be gained by new possessors of abandoned tissue in the accounts given here and elsewhere in the body as property literature.

intend to give up any and all interest in the letter, then we would not say I had abandoned the letter. That is, we would not say I had divested myself of ownership, but only of possession. If I expected someone else to take away my discarded letter and dispose of it, this would not be abandonment but rather a transfer of ownership. This is what occurs when one puts rubbish in the bin, or leaves items for collection by a charity shop.[3]

Why is it important to be clear about when an item has been abandoned? It is important because once the owner divests herself of all the rights associated with (or comprising) her ownership, the item becomes ownerless. The next person to take it into his control will become the owner and will thereby gain a right to possession against all others. *Goode on Commercial Law* explains that ownership encompasses the residue of legal rights in an asset remaining in a person, or in persons concurrently, after specific rights over the asset have been granted to others.[4]

Other possessors do hold a range of important rights, but between the owner (O) and the mere possessor (P), even though both may have title to the absolute interest in the item, O's title is the strongest. Indeed, O's title is indefeasible, while P can usually defend hers usually against all others except that of O.[5] Further, P's rights against others are relatively vulnerable, as her title will be extinguished if she loses possession, while O's title (and therefore O's rights) would not be so extinguished.[6]

Another reason it is important to be clear about abandonment is that we must distinguish abandoned items from those that are merely lost, as this distinction has legal consequences for the person who takes such items into her control. We have seen that the next person to control an unowned item will become the owner; however, this is not the case with an item that has simply been lost but not abandoned. The finder of a lost item will gain possessory rights against all but the true owner, except in cases where the finder might be guilty of theft 'by finding'.[7] These rights do not entitle her to do as she pleases with the item. She will hold the item under the terms of what Bridge argues is a 'fictitious bailment', which places a duty on the finder not to act so as to so seriously deny the rights of the true owner as to constitute a conversion.[8] This, as we shall see, has implications for those who come into possession of so-called 'waste' tissue.

[3] *R (Rickets) v Basildon Magistrates' Court* [2011] 1 Cr App R 15.

[4] R Goode and E McKendrick, *Goode on Commercial Law*, 4th edn (London, Penguin, 2010) 34.

[5] A possessor gains a right to exclusive possession by the act of taking possession. It can be defeated by the owner or someone else with a better right to exclusive possession. An example of the latter would be a dispute over an item found on land, where the landowner would have a better right to possession of the item than the finder if the landowner had manifested his intention to control things found on his land: *Armory v Delamirie* (1722) 1 Strange 505; *Parker v British Airways Board* [1982] 1 QB 1004 (QB); and Burrows, *English Private Law*, above n 1, 4.414–4.419.

[6] See further, Goode and McKendrick, *Goode on Commercial Law*, above n 4, 36.

[7] M Bridge, *Personal Property Law*, 3rd edn (Oxford, Oxford University Press, 2002) 23. Theft by finding occurs when a person takes seemingly lost or abandoned goods, but fails to take reasonable steps to find the owner and also has the requisite dishonest mental state required by the law of theft.

[8] Bridge cites *Gilchrist Watt & Sanderson Pty Ltd v York Products Pty Ltd* [1970] 1 WLR 1262 and *Moffatt v Kazana* [1969] 2 QB 152 in support of this view: Bridge, *Personal Property Law*, above n 7, 23.

The finder will also be under a duty to make reasonable efforts to find the true owner, although fulfilling this duty is not a condition of retaining title (it merely protects her from liability in conversion).[9] Eventually, however, the true owner will no longer be able to claim against a finder as the Limitation Act 1980 will bar a tort action six years after the initial conversion.[10] Once that period has run out, the original owner's title is extinguished unless, again, it is a case of 'theft by finding'.[11] Theft by finding occurs when a person takes seemingly lost or seemingly abandoned goods dishonestly. Taking will not be dishonest if the person 'appropriates the property in the belief that the person to whom the property belongs cannot be discovered by taking reasonable steps'.[12] Therefore, a person who takes possession of seemingly lost or seemingly abandoned goods and then takes the necessary steps to find the owner, or reasonably believes that the owner cannot be found, will not be guilty of theft.

Anthony Hudson has made the point that a doctrine of divesting abandonment is a useful one in part because it accords with ordinary people's expectations, and also avoids the need for the courts to resolve some situations by 'providing devious explanations for non-liability in situations which could more straightforwardly be called cases of divesting abandonment'.[13] There are times when we want to have nothing further to do with an item, have neither rights over it, nor responsibilities in relation to it. A doctrine of abandonment facilitates this. As James Penner has put it:

> Abandonment is purposeful, unlike loss. It normally involves relinquishing possession of something that is no longer wanted, in respect of which the right of exclusive use is no longer of any value to the owner. Abandonment is a permanent decision not to take advantage of the general duty *in rem* prohibiting interference in respect of a particular thing abandoned.[14]

Property law is in large part concerned with protecting the interests people have over items that they want for themselves because of the value they hold. It is for this reason that much of the law of property is about protecting people's capacity to exclude others from their possessions. But just as property is about protecting this aspect of a person's will in relation to a good, so it should be, in Penner's

[9] *Parker v British Airways Board*, above n 5, per Donaldson LJ.

[10] Limitation Act 1980, s 3(1). Where two parties claim possession of a lost chattel where neither is the true owner, the first to take legal possession will have the better title. The situation is complicated, however, when the owner of the land on which an item is lost claims possessory rights as well as the person who finds it. The decision in *Parker v British Airways Board* confirmed that the owner of the land will only have better title than the finder if he manifested an intention to control the premises and the things upon or in it. Such possessory intention will generally be evident if the landowner demonstrates both physical control of items on the land and an intention to exclude others from controlling them. See *Parker v British Airways Board*, above n 5.

[11] Limitation Act 1980, s 3(2).

[12] Theft Act 1968 (UK), s 2(1)(c).

[13] A Hudson, 'Abandonment' in Norman Palmer and Ewan McKendrick (eds), *Interests in Goods*, 2nd edn (London, Lloyd's of London Press, 1998) 613.

[14] J Penner, *The Idea of Property in Law* (Oxford, Oxford University Press, 2000) 79.

view, about allowing them to divest themselves of the relationship with that good when they no longer want to continue with it. He states:

> It is surely part of a right to determine how a thing is to be used that one may make no use of it at all, for evermore. One ought not to be saddled with a relationship to a thing that one does not want, and an unbreakable relation to a thing would condemn the owner to having to deal with it. It would indeed be a funny turn of events if the norms serving our interest in property in essence gave the things a person owned a power over him.[15]

It might seem at this juncture self-evident that the law would allow me to abandon an item of property. However, under the English common law the matter is not so clear-cut as one might expect. There has been, in fact, considerable doubt as to whether divesting abandonment is possible under English law, although the preferred view is now in favour of its existence. In Australia, the matter is also fairly murky, while the US case law suggests that abandonment is in fact possible. As this chapter focuses on the English position, this section will examine this in detail, followed by an outline of the Australian and American positions for comparative purposes, with particular attention paid to the American authorities that have been cited in the literature on human tissue.

Can Property be Abandoned?

The English Position

That the doctrine of abandonment is at best unclear, and most likely exists in only the most limited form, if at all, is widely recognised. As Michael Bridge has commented, 'the law on abandonment is obscure and difficult to relate to modern conditions'.[16] Anthony Hudson and *Goode on Commercial Law* support the existence of a doctrine of abandonment, as do Bridge et al in *The Law of Personal Property*, where it is argued that abandonment of property is possible if a clear intention to do so can be demonstrated.[17]

However, other sources, such as *English Private Law*, doubt that abandonment is possible at all under English law:

> Suppose that, when love cools, a ring is cast away with an appropriately unequivocal adieu. Does the ring become *res nullius*? This is a controverted question. The stronger school of thought denies that divesting abandonment of personal property rights has ever been possible . . . [although] authority cited in support is weak . . . By the same token, authority in favour of the view that divesting abandonment is possible is fairly thin on the ground.[18]

[15] ibid, 79.

[16] Bridge, above n 7, 22.

[17] M Bridge, L Gullifer, G McMeel and S Worthington, *The Law of Personal Property*, (London, Sweet & Maxwell, 2013) 8-034. See further *Moffatt v Kazana* [1969] 2 QB 152; *Robot Arenas v Waterfield* [2010] EWHC 115 (QB).

[18] Burrows, *English Private Law* (WJ Swadling), above n 1, 4.568. See in favour Hudson, 'Abandonment', above n 13; Goode and McKendrick, *Goode on Commercial Law*, above n 4; and also

This section first examines what abandonment is in a general sense, before turning to a detailed exploration of the relevant law.

What is clear is that it is not easy to define a clear rule determining when abandonment will have occurred beyond the need to identify a clear intention to abandon on the part of the owner. Rather, we must turn to clusters of cases dealing with highly fact-specific situations, as well as the few recent cases such as *Robot Arenas v Waterfield* that suggest a general approach. This difficulty in identifying when abandonment will occur is compounded by the fact that while there is some authority on abandonment in the context of charges of theft, there is very little authority on abandonment in the context of tort claims for trespass to goods or conversion.

Before the case law is explored, it is worth considering *why* the English courts have been reluctant to find property to have been abandoned. One reason the law can be said to abhor a vacuum in the context of ownership of property is that with title comes responsibility as well as rights. Consequently, there may be public policy reasons for prohibiting abandonment in some cases, such as where it might have a damaging effect on the environment to simply divest oneself of both rights and responsibilities in relation to an object. In being reluctant to find that property has been abandoned, the law is ensuring that a title-holder remains the person in whom responsibility for the item will vest. This may be the original owner, who cannot divest herself of her responsibilities, or it may be someone to whom title has been passed who then takes on this responsibility. It avoids the problems associated with things becoming unowned, and thereby no-one's particular responsibility.[19] The other main reason for the law's reluctance to find property abandoned is a facet of its commitment to protecting ownership – it will not lightly presume an intention to divest ownership precisely because ownership of many objects is so important to people. To take that ownership away without being very sure that this is what the owner wanted would undermine the protection of that owner's rights and interests.

The main authority in support of a doctrine of divesting abandonment in English law comes from a range of sources: the very specialised law of wreck, a few cases of conversion, and a number of cases concerning theft of items thought to have been abandoned. It is sometimes thought that the civil and criminal laws deal with abandonment in separate, distinguishable ways. For example, Penner states that that property cannot be abandoned *de jure* under the civil common

A Bell, 'Bona Vacantia' in N Palmer and E McKendrick (eds), *Interests in Goods*, 2nd edn (London, Lloyd's of London, 1998) 211. See further, R Hickey, *Property and the Law of Finders* (Oxford, Hart Publishing, 2010) 68 especially n 89.

[19] As James Penner puts it: 'The rules of title, specifically the rule that one's title is not extinguished unless another takes possession and acquires his own title, either gratuitously or for a fee, provide a means of ascribing responsibility to a person for the harms which his property may cause, even though he might wish to sever his relation to it': Penner, *The Idea of Property in Law*, above n 14, 79–80. See also Thomas, 'Do Freegans Commit Theft?', above n 1, 100–101 on how this point might be used to justify the actions of 'freegans' in taking discarded food that would otherwise be disposed of at an environmental cost.

law, but that abandonment is recognised in the criminal law of theft. Robin Hickey, however, has suggested that this may not be the case and that a uniform approach to abandonment across civil and criminal cases can be supported.[20] As the authorities are somewhat distinct, we will examine these areas separately.

One of the best authorities in support of a doctrine of abandonment outside the context of theft is *Pierce v Bemis (The Lusitania)*.[21] The case concerned a passenger ship named *The Lusitania*, which was abandoned by her crew and passengers when torpedoed by a German U-boat in 1915 off the southern coast of Ireland. The ship sunk within 18 minutes, and those leaving the ship did so to save their lives. Sixty-seven years after the sinking, an attempt to salvage items from the cargo and the passengers' personal possessions from the ship was made. Sheen J found on that the crew and passengers had no hope or intention of returning to the ship. This, together with the lapse in time before the salvage attempt, meant that the owners of these items had abandoned their property.

However, while *The Lusitania* is possibly good authority for abandonment in the context of wreck, as William Swadling has pointed out, any comments on abandonment generally were obiter, since the very particular law of wreck governed the decision.[22] In that context, there is a strong argument to say that divesting abandonment is necessary to facilitate salvage, as otherwise those attempting to rescue objects from the ship have only a finder's right to possession.[23] There are strong policy reasons to support facilitating such salvage. Providing salvagers with the possibility of acquiring ownership of what they salvage creates an incentive to invest in reclaiming otherwise wasted resources. Alternatively, we might still criticise the conceptualising of even this sort of situation as one of 'abandonment' for, as Swadling points out, the kind of intention evinced in such a situation is not really anything to do with abandonment: 'there is a great difference between an intent positively to be rid of the thing and a despairing acceptance that it has probably gone for good'.[24]

Stronger authority for a doctrine of abandonment is found in the cases concerning the theft of seemingly abandoned goods. As Hickey explains, it is not surprising that the question of abandonment would arise in the context of theft: 'since theft requires the dishonest appropriation of property belonging to another, it can never be theft to take goods in which no proprietary interest is subsisting at the time of the taking'.[25] For example, in *R v Reed*, Coleridge J said: 'If property be found when it is abandoned by the owner, it is his who finds it.'[26]

[20] R Hickey, 'Stealing Abandoned Goods: Possessory Title in Proceedings for Theft' (2006) 26 *Legal Studies* 584.

[21] *Pierce v Bemis (The Lusitania)* [1986] 1 All ER 1011 (QB). See, eg Burrows, *English Private Law*, above n 1, 4.569.

[22] Burrows, *English Private Law*, above n 1, 4.569.

[23] S Dromgoole, 'Interests in Wreck' in N Palmer and E McKendrick (eds), *Interests in Goods*, 2nd edn (London, Lloyd's of London Press, 1998) 164.

[24] Burrows, *English Private Law*, above n 1, 4.569.

[25] Hickey, *Property and the Law of Finders*, above n 18, 68–69. Also Theft Act 1968, ss 1, 5.

[26] *R v Reed* (1842) Car & M 307.

Abandonment is relevant to the determination of both the *actus reus* and *mens rea* in proceedings for theft. On *actus reus*, it goes to whether goods owned by someone else have been taken; on *mens rea*, it is relevant to taker's belief (or otherwise) in her legal right to the property (the dishonesty aspect).[27]

Given the difficulty in such cases of determining whether the goods have in fact been abandoned, it is not surprising that issues around *mens rea* have received greater judicial attention. In both *R v White* and *Ellerman's Wilson Line Ltd v Webster*, the court made statements to the effect that an accused would not be guilty of theft if he had genuinely believed the goods to have been abandoned.[28] This accords with the dishonesty requirement now laid down in the Theft Act 1968, which provides that if the taker honestly believes she has a right to the item, would have the owner's consent to appropriate it, or that the person to whom the property belongs cannot be discovered by taking reasonable steps, then she will not be guilty of theft.[29] Whether or not the goods are in fact abandoned is not relevant to the charge of theft (though it remains relevant to conversion claims).

Hickey cites the convincing (and more modern) authority of *R v Small* in support of this perspective. In that case, Small was charged with the theft of a car. He argued that he had found the car 'dumped', and the evidence suggested his view was at least understandable – the car had been left by the side of the road unlocked with the keys in the ignition, it had a flat battery and flat tyre, its windscreen was smashed and the petrol tank was empty.[30] Hickey argues that in this case these facts were relevant to the honesty of the defendant's belief that it was dumped, and that therefore ostensible abandonment is relevant to *mens rea*.[31] However, these cases are not evidence that abandonment of property is possible, only that facts that *suggest* abandonment has occurred will be relevant to the state of mind of an alleged thief.

As to *actus reus*, the courts have displayed considerable reluctance to find goods allegedly stolen to have been abandoned. A clear intention to divest on the part of the owner must be shown, and we know from the cases that this will not be found where a householder has left rubbish on the street for collection, nor where the carcasses of diseased pigs have been buried to prevent the spread of infection.[32]

Two cases dealing with theft appear to hold goods to have been abandoned, but on closer viewing do not. Both concern the taking of golf balls 'abandoned' by their owners on a golf course. In each case, the golf balls had been lost during play, and left by the players. The defendant in each case had come onto the course and collected these balls, probably with the intention of selling them, and were subse-

[27] Theft Act 1968, s 2(1).

[28] *R v William White* (1912) 7 Cr App R 266, 268; *Ellerman's Wilson Line Ltd v Webster* [1952] 1 Lloyd's Rep 179, 180 per Lord Goddard CJ.

[29] Theft Act 1968, s 2(1).

[30] *R v Edwards and Stacey* (1877) Cox CC 384. That belief need only be subjectively held: *R v Small* [1987] Crim LR 777.

[31] Hickey, *Property and the Law of Finders*, above n 18, 70.

[32] *Williams v Phillips* (1957) 41 Cr App Rep 5; *R v Edwards and Stacey*, above n 30.

quently apprehended by the police and charged with stealing the balls.[33] We need only explore the first of these cases for our purposes. In *Hibbert v McKiernan*, the trial justices found that the players had abandoned the balls and hence the question was whether the accused could be said by finding the balls to have gained title that could be sustained against the owner of the golf course on which they were found.[34] They found that in taking steps to exclude and apprehend people who might take lost balls, the owner of the course had exercised sufficient control to be said to be in possession, hence an owner was determined and Hibbert was duly convicted. On appeal, however, the Divisional Court felt that these aspects of the facts were largely irrelevant, as it was clear that Hibbert had taken the balls dishonestly and that they belonged to someone other than him.[35] For this reason, the higher court declined to take a view on whether or not the players had abandoned the balls, although at least one doubted that this was the case.[36] They did, however, seem at some level to agree that the golf club had at least a possessory interest in the balls.[37] What we can take from this case is that it provides some support for the possibility of abandonment, but only from a lower court.

There is, however, one very recent case on theft that supports the possibility of divesting abandonment. In *R (Rickets) v Basildon Magistrates' Court*, the Queen's Bench Divisional Court considered whether a man who took bags left outside a British Heart Foundation charity shop could rightly be charged with theft.[38] Having sought judicial review after he was committed for trial for the alleged theft, Rickets argued that there was no evidence to support the requirement that he had appropriated the property of another.[39] Mr Justice Wyn Williams stated that the issue before the court was 'whether or not the only inference open to the justices at the time of the committal was that the unknown would-be donors had abandoned their property'.[40] Dismissing the application, it was his view (with which Lord Justice Moses agreed) that this was not the correct analysis of the facts. Rather, the court found that until the British Heart Foundation took delivery of the bags, they acquired no proprietary interest in them, but that 'until that time, although the unknown would-be donor had divested himself of possession

[33] *Hibbert v McKiernan* [1948] 2 KB 142 (the charge was larceny); *R v Rostron* [2003] EWCA Crim 2206, [2003] All ER (D) 269 (the charge was theft).

[34] *Hibbert v McKiernan*, above n 33, 148–49.

[35] Their Honours held varying opinions on the matter, but in general focused on the dishonesty rather than the ownership question. See, eg the opinion of Lord Goddard CJ: 'this court . . . is of opinion that these interesting questions [of ownership] do not in this case arise': ibid, 149.

[36] ibid, 151 per Humphreys J.

[37] Both Robin Hickey and Sean Thomas have rightly commented that there was a need in that case to consider questions of ownership, but that the larceny charge could have been easily supported simply by finding that the club had a sufficient possessory interest in the balls. Interestingly, this *was* the approach taken in the later case on theft of human anatomical specimens in *R v Kelly* [1998] 3 All ER 741. See Hickey, 'Stealing Abandoned Goods', above n 20, 589–93; Thomas, 'Do Freegans Commit Theft?', above n 1, 110.

[38] *R (Rickets) v Basildon Magistrates' Court* [2010] EWHC 2358 (Admin).

[39] A requirement of theft under Theft Act 1968, s 5(1).

[40] *R (Rickets) v Basildon Magistrates' Court* [2010] EWHC 2358 (Admin) [18].

of the items, he had not given up his ownership of the items'.[41] The decision seems, then, to be some authority for the possibility of divesting abandonment, which the court apparently considered conceivable but not an accurate description of what had occurred in the situation before it. For this reason, however, there is only quite scant discussion of the doctrine of abandonment and no real consideration of the cases on abandonment, rendering the decision only a weak authority in support of the doctrine. Overall, then, it appears that the theft cases provide very little authority for the existence of a doctrine of abandonment.

Outside the context of theft and wreck, the authority for abandonment in English law is slim.[42] The matter might have been resolved in the recent case of *Robot Arenas Ltd v Waterfield*, in which abandonment was raised as a defence to a claim of conversion, but the plaintiffs did not challenge the assertion by the defence that abandonment was possible. Accordingly, Edelman QC, as a Deputy Judge of the Queen's Bench Division, proceeded on the basis that there could be abandonment and applied the test of whether there had been both an intention to abandon and some physical act of relinquishment.[43] The other main case in support is *Bentinck Ltd v Cromwell Engineering Co*, which is examined below. The case concerned a claim for conversion of a car, and the Court of Appeal accepted that the car could be said to have been abandoned (and hence not converted).[44]

It seems, on balance, that there is sufficient authority to assume that abandonment may be possible in the right circumstances, but that these circumstances will be very limited indeed. Having made this assumption, we then meet the main difficulty with the doctrine of abandonment: finding a clear, unequivocal intention to divest ownership in addition to physical relinquishment. In *Ellerman's Wilson Line Ltd v Webster* Lord Goddard was of the view that it must be shown that the property had been 'abandoned in the sense or under circumstances which would show that the owner had definitely abandoned it and did not intend to retrieve it'.[45]

Very often the original owner will not be available to question, and so the only option will be to infer such an intention from the circumstances. It is evident from the case law that the courts will be very wary of inferring such intention. How will such an inference be drawn? The wide variety of situations in which property might be regarded as abandoned makes it difficult to say with certainty, but we do know that the value of the good will be relevant. For the most part, in the absence of substantial evidence otherwise, an intention to abandon will be found only if the value of the item is minimal. Where the item has value, the court will presume that the owner did not mean to abandon it.[46] This is true even of

[41] ibid, [13].

[42] Indeed, Anthony Hudson, in one of the most thorough surveys of the English law on abandonment, turns largely to Australian authorities when discussing trespass to goods and conversion: Hudson, 'Abandonment', above n 13, 612–14.

[43] *Robot Arenas Ltd v Waterfield, Newton Nottingham LLP* [2010] EWHC 115 (QB) [14].

[44] *Bentinck Ltd v Cromwell Engineering Co* [1971] 1 QB 324, [1970] 3 WLR 1113, [1971] 1 All ER 33.

[45] *Ellerman's Wilson Line Limited v Webster* [1952] 1 Lloyd's Rep 179, 180 per Lord Goddard CJ.

[46] See, eg, *Moffatt v Kazana* [1969] 2 QB 152 in which it could not be presumed that money hidden

items dropped and left in the street. As Rolfe B stated in *R v Peters*: 'If I had an apple and dropped it, it might be presumed that I had abandoned it, but if I drop £500 the presumption is that I do not mean to abandon it.'[47]

Value, however, is subjective, and may also be contextual, and hence value alone will not be a sufficient indicator of whether an item has been abandoned. Goods may have economic value, sentimental value, or personal value in terms of the person wanting them to remain private or the information they contain confidential. The relevance of value will have particular importance in the context of discarded human biomaterials.

Mere inaccessibility of an item will not automatically render it abandoned and hence *res nullius*. In fact, in the context of cases concerning shipwrecks, Anthony Hudson goes so far as to state that it 'does not seem to raise even a presumption of abandonment'.[48] It will depend on the facts. In *The Egypt*, Langton J was not convinced that the mere fact that a cargo of gold had sunk to the bottom of the sea meant that it was *res nullius*.[49]

The context will also be important, and may provide indications of the state of mind of the owner. In *Bentinck Ltd v Cromwell Engineering Co* we see Penner's reasoning in support of the doctrine at play. The case concerned whether a car, acquired on hire purchase, had been abandoned. Having been damaged in a crash, it was taken to a garage and left. The defendants were the employers (and indemnifiers) of the hirer, Mr Faulkner, who could not be found after the car was left. The Court of Appeal found that the car had been abandoned, with Lord Denning reasoning:

> Here was a car with all the costs running up. Mr. Faulkner would not want to shoulder the liability. He disappeared altogether. The judge was quite entitled to find that he had abandoned it in the real legal sense as abandoning all rights whatever which he had in the car.[50]

Particularly pertinent in the context of human tissue will be the cases on intention to abandon waste. In the two main cases, abandonment was not found due to a lack of clear intention to abandon. In *Williams v Phillips*, two refuse-collectors who took items from bags of rubbish left out for collection were convicted of larceny. In such cases, the Court of Appeal held, the rubbish is not abandoned but rather put out 'so that it may be collected and taken away by the local authority, and until it has been taken away by the local authority it is my property . . . because I intended to pass it from myself to them, it becomes their property'.[51]

In *R v Edwards and Stacey*, policy concerns about public health appear to be the basis for finding that the carcasses of pigs that had been buried to prevent the

in a biscuit tin, which was itself concealed in a house that was then sold, had been abandoned (nor conveyed as part of the house to the new owner).

[47] *R v Peters* (1843) 1 Car & K 245.

[48] Hudson, 'Abandonment', above n 13, 608.

[49] *The Egypt* (1932) 44 Ll LR 21, 39 as discussed in Hudson, 'Abandonment', above n 13, 608.

[50] *Bentinck Ltd v Cromwell Engineering Co* [1971] 1 QB 324.

[51] *Williams v Phillips* (1957) 41 Cr App R 5, 8 per Lord Goddard CJ.

spread of disease had not been abandoned, and remained within the control of the owner.[52] How these decisions might apply to human tissue will be explored below.

On balance then, it appears that while there is support for the existence of a doctrine of abandonment, and it is considered possible for someone to divest herself of ownership of an item, the situations in which a sufficiently clear intention to do so can be found are few. Therefore, it can at least be said that even if abandonment is possible under English law, it will not lightly be found.

Comparative Positions: Australia and the United States

The Australian Position

There is arguably some Australian authority in support of a doctrine of abandonment. In *Johnstone & Wilmot v Kaine* Clarke J felt himself bound to 'adopt the rule that the intentional abandonment of a chattel by the owner of it does not divest him of his ownership'.[53] However, this approach was neither confirmed nor rejected in the later New South Wales Court of Appeal decision in *Moorhouse v Angus & Robertson*, in which the Court declined to provide a determination on whether divesting abandonment was possible. At best, they were prepared to say that if abandonment were to be found, then a clear and unequivocal intention to abandon had to be shown.[54]

Janine Baker-Griffiths identifies four cases that suggest the doctrine may exist. In *Re Jigrose Pty Ltd*, Kiefel J stated: 'I do not consider that there is difficulty at law with the notion of abandonment divesting ownership', and in that case found that the terms of a contract did effect a divesting abandonment.[55] Approval followed in *Keane v Carter*, with Ipp J stating that abandonment could occur where the specific intention to relinquish ownership could be shown.[56] Baker-Griffiths also identifies *Stewart v Gustafson* (a Canadian authority from the Saskatchewan Court of Queen's Bench) as a somewhat similar authority that allowed divesting abandonment to have occurred where the plaintiff had shown an intention to relinquish ownership, and also where an intention to abandon could be inferred in the case of worthless property.[57] The final authority in support cited by Griffiths-Baker is *Munday v Australian Capital Territory*, in which it was held that a person who leaves rubbish at a tip 'may be assumed to intend to the [managing authority] possession of deposited material . . . The deposit of such materials and the

[52] *R v Edwards and Stacey*, above n 30.

[53] *Johnstone & Wilmot v Kaine* (1923) 23 Tas LR 43 as discussed in Hudson, 'Abandonment', above n 13, 612.

[54] *Moorhouse v Angus & Robertson* [1981] 1 NSWLR 700, 702 (Hutley JA), 706–707 (Samuels JA), and 712–13 (Mahoney JA) as discussed in Hudson, 'Abandonment', above n 13.

[55] *Re Jigrose Pty Ltd* [1994] 1 Qd R 382 as discussed in J Griffiths-Baker, 'Divesting Abandonment: An Unnecessary Concept?' (2007) 36 *Common Law World Review* 16, 24.

[56] [1994] 12 WAR 20. Griffiths-Baker, 'Divesting Abandonment: An Unnecessary Concept?', above n 55, 4.

[57] ibid, 4. [1999] 4 WWR 695.

leaving of them at the tip face would prima facie evidence abandonment.'[58]

However, as Baker-Griffiths points out, in each case the same result could have been achieved without reference to abandonment. In *Re Jigrose*, ownership could have passed due to the contractual terms, and in *Munday* there was a contractual arrangement between the ACT and those tipping rubbish as they paid a fee to do so. They were not abandoning it; they were transferring it. In *Stewart*, again, what had actually occurred was a transfer because on the facts the plaintiff had not abandoned the chattels to just anyone, but to the defendant specifically. This is better conceptualised as a gift, argues Baker-Griffiths, even though the court used the language of abandonment. For some of the other chattels, the doctrine of estoppel would protect the defendant from a claim of conversion in this sort of context where the owner failed to remove his chattels in circumstances where the landowner had shown an intention to treat left items as abandoned. Klebuc J accepted this role for estoppel as a possibility in that case.[59]

The United States Position

Unlike the English and Australian positions, the law on abandonment in the US is relatively clear: abandonment of personal property is possible. The Supreme Court of Arkansas stated in *Eads v Brazelton* that 'property is said to be abandoned when it is thrown away, or its possession voluntarily forsaken by the owner, in which case it will become the property of the first occupant'.[60]

Similarly, the US Airforce Court of Military Review stated: 'Abandoned property is property the owner has thrown away. The former owner has relinquished all right or title to, and possession of the property with no intent to reclaim it.'[61]

It is clear, too, that human tissue can be abandoned in the US, as the decision in *Venner* (examined in detail below) indicates.[62]

[58] ibid, 4. [2000] FCA 653.

[59] ibid, 5.

[60] *Eads v Brazleton* 22 Ark 499 (1861), 509.

[61] *US v Wiederkehr* 33 MJ 539 (AFCMR 1991) 541. In *Ex parte Szyzcgiel*, the Supreme Court, Oneida County, New York said obiter: 'The abandonment of property is the relinquishment of all title, possession or claim to or of it — a virtual intentional throwing away of it': *Ex parte Szczygiel* 51 NYS 2d 699 (Sup Ct 1944), 702.

[62] Although it should be noted that most of the jurisprudence is not easily extrapolated to other jurisdictions as the case law deals largely with seizure of property without a warrant and the protection of privacy by the Fourth Amendment of the US Constitution. Property that has been abandoned can be seized without warrant as it falls outside the Fourth Amendment, but abandonment in this context does not mean complete abandonment of ownership permanently. Instead, it seems to mean something less and the owner can sometimes regain ownership or possession. What is clear is that if property is discarded, then the owner loses any reasonable expectation of privacy in it (*US v Veatch* 674 F2d 1217, 1220 (9th Cir 1981); *State v Walker* 119 Ariz 121, 126, 579 P2d 1091, 1096 (1978)). Property has been abandoned in this context when there is an intention to abandon and a physical act supporting this intent (ibid). A denial of ownership, when questioned, also constitutes abandonment in this context (ibid).

Abandonment in the Body-as-Property Debate

As the preceding section evidences, the notion of abandonment at law is complex, and the circumstances in which an owner will be said to have divested herself of all rights are highly circumscribed. Despite this, abandonment is often referred to in the literature on whether human biomaterials can and should be dealt with as legal property. This section describes and critically appraises some of these references with a view to highlighting both the role the concept has played in the debate, and the problems associated with its use.

One way in which the concept is sometimes used in the debate over the regulation of biomaterials is as a means to avoid concerns about liability of subsequent, legitimate users of tissue. In discussions of whether property law is the preferable legal mechanism for regulating human tissue, it is often noted that human tissue is regularly discarded, often seemingly as waste. For some, this is one of the difficulties with a property approach, as it (arguably) means that anyone touching, taking or otherwise dealing with that tissue might be liable in conversion or for wrongful interference with goods.[63] It is also sometimes suggested that taking such discarded tissue might amount to theft. On this view, the very strength of the control given to the owner of tissue becomes a problem for the property approach, as to avoid any possible legal implications of what will very often be acceptable or innocuous dealings with tissue, clear authority to use would need to be obtained. Regarding such discarded tissue as having been abandoned is sometimes, therefore, raised as a means to get around the potentially problematic consequences of deeming biomaterials property, as it would (it is said) mean that the next intentional possessor becomes the owner and may largely do with that tissue as he or she wishes. Similarly, those who take possession of this abandoned tissue would not be open to claims of conversion or charges of theft, nor would their use be constrained by the obligations placed on finders. This use of the concept will be called the 'response to absurd consequences' argument.

The second use of the language of abandonment in the debate, which will be explored here, is as a means to show how tissue can pass into the control of someone else, usually a medical researcher, who is then legitimately allowed to use it as she wishes. Sometimes, this invocation of abandonment arises in the context of arguing for a property approach, but it also used by some who reject property yet still draw on concepts like 'abandonment' as part of their proposed schema for regulating human tissue. This use of the concept will be called the 'legitimating transfers' argument.

The predominant use of the concept comes in examinations of what happens to human tissue that is removed during a surgical procedure, and for reasons of

[63] The Nuffield Council on Bioethics recognised this in its 1995 report: Nuffield Council on Bioethics, *Human Tissue: Ethical and Legal Issues* (1995) 9.13. See also *Moore v Regents of the University of California* (1990) 51 Cal 3d 1990, 144 per Panelli J.

scope this context will be the focus of discussion in this chapter. In their 1995 report, *Human Tissue: Ethical and Legal Issues*, the Nuffield Council on Bioethics (Nuffield Council) considered this question, asking: 'Does the person retain any right of control over [removed tissue] or is the consent to removal to be regarded as implying abandonment of the tissue?'[64] Two further questions followed: 'Is [the removed tissue] abandoned absolutely or only on terms, for example, that it be destroyed?'[65] and: 'If on terms and these terms are not complied with, does any sort of dominion revert to the person from whom the tissue was removed?'[66]

The Council rejected a property approach to tissue regulation, preferring a model based on consent alone. In its view, any claim in relation to excised tissue 'should . . . proceed on the basis of the consent given to the removal rather than any claim in property'. By this it meant that conflicts about control should be resolved by reference to whether consent had been given for use, rather than by the application of property principles. Consent to removal entailed abandonment, or it would otherwise be prima facie presumed.[67]

Given the account of the legal position on abandonment in the previous section, the numerous problems with these sorts of comments should be immediately apparent, and they will be given particular attention because they are indicative of the ways in which the concept of abandonment is used in the debate and the problems that attend this. They will be briefly appraised here, and discussed in greater detail in later sections.

First, abandonment at law does not (and cannot, by definition) occur 'on terms'. When one divests oneself of all rights and interests via abandonment, there can be no terms as a result of that action alone that will mean it can later revert to oneself. This is precisely why the courts have been (rightly) so reluctant to find objects to have been abandoned. However, it is not clear whether the Nuffield Council was using the term 'abandonment' here in the strict legal sense, and perhaps it meant merely 'discarding', as is often the case in the debate. This, however, raises its own problems, demonstrating how the loose use of terms with a particular legal meaning can lead to poorly-founded legal arguments, and also further muddying of already murky waters about what we can say happens when someone discards something. Even in the lay sense, to discard means to give something up. To suggest this is done 'on terms' is confusing even in that sense.

The second problem, which is one that attends many uses of abandonment in the debate, is the suggestion that abandonment might be implied. As we have seen, for good reasons the courts do not lightly imply abandonment, and indeed the case law suggests that almost invariably only a clear, unequivocal intention to abandon will be sufficient for ownership to have been divested under English law.

The Council described a number of ways we might legally conceptualise what happens when tissue is retained following a procedure for removal but is

[64] Nuffield Council on Bioethics, *Human Tissue: Ethical and Legal Issues*, above n 63, 2.17.

[65] ibid, 2.17.

[66] ibid, 2.17.

[67] ibid, 6772.

subsequently returned to the patient at his request. For example, a boy wants to keep his appendix after it has been removed. The Council suggested that one approach might be that consent to the operation could entail that the patient had abandoned any claim to tissue removed during the procedure. Another could be that:

> Tissue once removed becomes the property of the person from whom it was removed. This is to say that consent to removal does not *entail* an intention to abandon. The tissue may well, in fact, be abandoned or donated, but these imply a prior coming into existence of a *res* and the exercise of rights over it.[68]

The patient could then either 'waive' their right to it, or retain it. Here, by 'waiver' the Council presumably meant 'divesting abandonment'. It reasoned that in the appendix example, the tissue would have always been that of the boy. At this point, it turned to the US case of *Venner v State of Maryland*, from which they quoted Powers J's statement in the Court of Special Appeals:

> By the force of social custom . . . when a person does nothing and says nothing to indicate an intent to assert his right of ownership, possession, or control over [bodily] material, the only rational inference is that he intends to abandon the material.[69]

From this the Council concluded that the legal presumption is in favour of abandonment, and that abandonment can be prospective, but that when abandonment could not be presumed, in the absence of consent (or a conditional consent), property rights would not pass.[70] Again, as the previous section on the law of abandonment would suggest, such a presumption is very unlikely to be supported by the courts. The *Venner* approach has little traction in the law of England, and this conceptualisation is therefore not likely to reflect what would happen in such a scenario.

The third problem with the Council's use of the term 'abandonment' in much of its report, and particularly the quoted sections above, is the use of a term that has a specific legal meaning outside the legal context in which it is applicable. That is, 'abandonment' at law means the divesting of ownership. Ownership is a property concept, therefore to use it as part of a framework in which a property approach is explicitly rejected is legally nonsensical and confusing. This confusion is exacerbated by the shifts in the report between suggestions that consent to treatment 'will entail the abandonment of any claim to the tissue',[71] and sometimes that tissue removed during treatment will be regarded 'as having been abandoned by the person from whom it was removed'.[72] If the tissue were property, then both could be true, but given that the property approach was rejected, this cannot be so. This is more than a merely semantic criticism; it demonstrates that precision in the use of terms is important to avoid a lack of clarity about the kinds

[68] ibid, 9.7.
[69] ibid, 9.8 quoting *Venner v State of Maryland* 30 Md App 599, 354 A2d 483 Md App 1976, 627.
[70] Nuffield Council on Bioethics, ibid, 9.8.
[71] ibid, 67.
[72] ibid, 9.14.

of claims (and defences) that might be open when conflicts arise. To achieve the meaning the Council was aiming at, the term 'discarding' of the tissue would have avoided this confusion, while still capturing the lay sense of giving up an object. This point will be explored in greater depth below (The Operation of Abandonment in a 'Tissue as Property' Model).

Academic commentators have also delved into the role of abandonment in regulating human tissue. Gerald Dworkin and Ian Kennedy, for example, explore a number of analyses of how we can conceptualise what happens legally when tissue is removed and subsequently retained for use in research. Having rightly pointed out that the difference a property approach makes is that 'should the law regard rights in human tissue as property rights, issues relating to ownership and title could affect those who directly or indirectly acquire such tissue',[73] they go on to first argue that the standard lay understanding of a medical procedure includes the belief that tissue removed from the body will be destroyed, and that this implies consent to such destruction. They then state that

> [a] comparable legal analysis would be that although property does not come into existence until the tissue is removed, the consent to removal ensures that, upon removal, the property becomes vested *in the person removing it.*[74]

They offer an alternative analysis via the doctrine of abandonment:

> In most cases where a patient has consented to medical procedures without more, the presumption of abandonment of all property or other rights in the removed tissue could apply, leaving the patient with no further legal interest in the material, whatever may subsequently be done to it.[75]

While what might then be done would probably be inhibited by ethical or professional constraints, they emphasise that this aside, at this point the patient would lack any *legal* control of the tissue. They add that patient's consent to some uses might be required (although they do not specify when or why) and that only in some very rare cases would such consent be withheld, or conditions on use be demanded. In such cases, they suggest, 'such reactions may modify the nature of the abandonment or gift which has taken place', as a person is free 'to reserve a right to revoke a gift or to impose conditions upon a donee'.[76] They go on to argue that in the *Moore* case,[77] Moore might have expressly abandoned the tissue (via a consent form) or impliedly abandoned it when he consented to medical treatment. On either analysis (which they say is an application of English law), ownership of the tissue would have passed to the medical authorities, who could then decide to destroy it or to use it. They further argue that:

[73] G Dworkin and I Kennedy, 'Human Tissue: Rights in the Body and its Parts' (1993) 1 *Medical Law Review* 291, 302.

[74] ibid, 302.

[75] ibid, 303–304.

[76] ibid, 304.

[77] *Moore v Regents of the University of California*, above n 63.

> In most circumstances, the mere fact that the physician failed to disclose any research or economic potential of discarded tissue is unlikely to affect the analysis: the norm of implied abandonment is likely to prevail.[78]

This alternative analysis is a version of the 'legitimating transfers' argument noted at the beginning of this chapter. As should be evident from the outline of the English legal position described above (The Doctrine of Abandonment at Common Law), the 'norm of implied abandonment' is not a legal norm, but is probably an assumed norm in the context they describe, as well as reflecting lay belief in the norm of discarding biomaterials in this context.[79]

Bernard Dickens and Loane Skene have offered analyses of how abandonment could play a role if human tissue were deemed property that bear many similarities with one another. For Dickens, the preferable approach

> may be to consider the human source as having an inchoate right of property in materials issuing from his body, which right he may expressly or by implication abandon to another, or similarly make prevail over a contending claim.[80]

On Dickens's view, the person from whom the tissue is taken has the superior right to it over any other person, but this inchoate right is lost just as it crystallises, for the tissue is to be 'deemed abandoned, perhaps to a hospital, very soon after it is first isolated'.[81] His approach does, as he puts it, preserve 'traditional jurisprudential tests of, for instance, intention, possession, and control as affecting ownership' by affording the source individual the initial, 'superior right', but then allowing it to be lost via explicit or presumed abandonment.

Like the Nuffield Council, Dickens turned to the decision in *Venner* for support due to the lack of direct common law authority on abandonment of human tissue. The case is an appealing authority as it concerned the abandonment of faeces. The defendant had swallowed balloons containing hashish oil, and while in hospital nurses had taken bedpans used by the defendant to enable the police to retrieve the balloons from the patient's waste and use these in evidence. At the time, the patient made no protest, but he later asserted that he had a property right in his faeces, on the basis of which he could exclude the nurses and police from confiscating his excrement. It was held that he would be deemed to have abandoned his waste products, and hence their subsequent retrieval by the police was lawful.

In *Venner*, the Court of Special Appeals held:

> It could not be said that a person has no property right in wastes or other materials which were once a part of or contained within his body, but which normally are dis-

[78] Dworkin and Kennedy, 'Human Tissue: Rights in the Body and its Parts', above n 73, 311.

[79] Dworkin and Kennedy do note that the situation is different if the patient *expressly* addresses the issue of what will happen to the tissue post-removal. If the patient does so, then prima facie, they suggest, the patient would have a right to control the tissue and if the recipient (such as the hospital) acts outside the wishes of such a patient who allows them to use the tissue, they will be open to an action for conversion: ibid, 311–12.

[80] BM Dickens, 'The Control of Living Body Materials' (1977) 27 *University of Toronto Law Journal* 142, 183.

[81] ibid, 183.

carded after their separation from the body. It is not unknown for a person to assert a continuing right of ownership, dominion, or control, for good reason or for no reason, over such things as excrement, fluid waste, secretions, hair, fingernails, toenails, blood, and organs or other parts of the body, whether their separation from the body is intentional, accidental, or merely the result of normal body functions . . . But it is all but universal human custom and human experience that such things are discarded – in a legal sense, abandoned – by the person from whom they emanate, either 'on the spot', or, if social delicacy requires it, at a place or in a manner designed to cause the least offense to others.[82]

Powers J went on to make it clear that

> [b]y the force of social custom, we hold that when a person does nothing and says nothing to indicate an intent to assert his right of ownership, possession, or control over such material, the only rational inference is that he intends to abandon the material.[83]

Dickens agrees with this perspective, arguing that where the person from whom tissue is taken is 'passive' he may be 'deemed in principle to have abandoned his legal interest in it'. He does suggest, however, that there would be benefits to referencing future use of removed tissue on hospital admissions or consent to treatment forms as this 'might overcome problems of using material immediately upon its origination from the source, perhaps while he is still under anaesthetic'.[84]

While Dickens' approach (like Skene's below) might be pragmatic, and even reflective of community views about the fate of tissue removed in this context, it does not reflect the law in England. Far from being ready to 'deem' objects to have been abandoned, the case law suggests quite the opposite – that the courts are deeply reluctant to find something has been abandoned in the absence of very clear evidence of such an intention.

Skene's view is somewhat less problematic. For her, if we were to take a property approach to tissue regulation (which she does not entirely support), where tissue has been removed during treatment, any property interest the patient might have had 'would be regarded as abandoned by their intention, stated or implied, to claim no future interest in it'.[85] The current state of the law would most probably allow for an express abandonment of the kind she suggests, and if the evidence were sufficiently clear could accept an implied abandonment. The case law demonstrates, however, that the evidential requirements will be stringent on this point.

Skene's argument is founded on the view that the patient's interest is in the treatment alleviating their symptoms, and once performed, they no longer have an interest in the offending tissue.[86] She goes on to say that: 'Philosophers might say that the issue cannot be so simply resolved', as they would want us to look at

[82] *Venner v State of Maryland*, above n 69, 626–27.

[83] ibid, 627.

[84] Dickens, 'The Control of Living Body Materials', above n 80, 186. Dickens does later comment that abandonment must be into the legal control of another, 'as opposed to constituting the property *res nullius*'. This will be examined later in this chapter.

[85] L Skene, 'Ownership of Human Tissue and the Law' (2002) 3 *Nature Reviews: Genetics* 145, 147.

[86] ibid, 147.

what the patient's expectations actually were. In her example, the patient has a tooth removed to alleviate toothache. In this scenario, if the tooth had some value (perhaps it contained a gold filling), the patient might have different expectations than the patient who sees the tooth merely as garbage and who says 'throw it out'.[87] That may be an accurate description of the lay sense of discarding, but a lack of ongoing interest is not sufficient for the legal divesting of ownership. Indeed, this takes us back to Penner's point – there is more to abandonment than a lack of interest, but at the same time there is need for people to be able to shed their rights (and attendant responsibilities) to property. But as the case law shows, this intention must be clear. A mere seeming or presumed absence of ongoing interest is not likely to be sufficient for the English courts.

Skene discusses abandonment to explain how a property approach could work if taken, but in general she does not support such a regulatory approach. Her point is that if we *did* go down the property route, we could use the concept of abandonment to manage situations such as those she outlines. Sophie Mills deploys abandonment in a similar way, but for slightly different reasons. On her view, the provision within property law for abandonment is a reason in support of taking a property approach. Where a patient lacks strong views on the use of her tissue, then a property approach 'would facilitate gift or abandonment of rights in it' by clarifying its status as property and would consequently 'help prevent and resolve any subsequent legal disputes'.[88] Following Paul Matthews, she argues that the flexibility of property allows the source individual to control her tissue in 'a manner consistent with her own concept of self' by either taking advantage of the protective power of property to prevent use by others, or by relinquishing control 'through gift or abandonment'.[89] For Mills, such an approach is supported by the fact that studies of patient views demonstrate that the majority of patients from whom tissue is removed are happy to donate it for research purposes.[90]

Mills' (and to a degree Skene's) position is another variant of the 'legitimating transfers' argument, but might be better termed the 'facilitating transfers' argument. They deploy the concept to allow for subsequent possessors to gain ownership, particularly Skene who advocates a pragmatic approach that supports medical research and treatment practices. Seemingly, they are referring to abandonment in the legal sense of 'divesting abandonment', where the owner gives up ownership of an item and thereby gives up all of her rights in relation to it. However, this is not strictly what is meant by abandonment in English law, because divesting abandonment means that the item becomes ownerless, and then the next intentional possessor, or the person controlling the land on which it

[87] ibid. Others, such as Lyria Bennett Moses, have also taken the view that if human tissue is property, tissue collected in the course of a medical procedure would be regarded as abandoned by the patient: L Bennett Moses, 'The Applicability of Property Law in New Contexts: From Cells to Cyberspace' (2008) 30 *Sydney Law Review* 639, 645.

[88] S Mills, 'Owning My "Self": A Reconcilliation of Perspectives on the Body' (1999) 6 *UCL Jurisprudence Review* 191, 204.

[89] ibid, 209.

[90] ibid, 204.

is left, can become the owner. This may cover some of the instances to which they refer, but abandonment in this, its proper legal sense, does not 'facilitate gift', because a gift is a transfer of ownership, not a mere relinquishment without concern for who will gain that ownership.

In many of the situations of biomaterials being discarded in a hospital, a more apt characterisation would be as gift (perhaps conditional) to the hospital. 'Abandonment' is sometimes used in the sense of 'abandoning to' another person in discussions about using property principles to regulate human tissue, but this is an unhelpful and inaccurate use of the term. If the patient is happy for the tissue to be used by the hospital or researchers, she is not giving up all claim to it, she is giving up her claims on the understanding that the hospital or researchers are taking control of it. This is not abandonment in the strict sense; it is a transfer of ownership.

Mark Pawlowski has used the term in a similar manner. He argues initially that the Human Tissue Act 2004 implicitly recognises a 'presumption of abandonment' with regard to tissue removed during a medical operation, as the legislation permits it to be treated as waste.[91] He then further suggests that the patient has 'implicitly licensed [the tissue's] destruction or disposal as an integral part of the medical procedure to which he (or she) has validly consented'.[92] Having used the language of abandonment, Pawlowski then makes clear that he does not mean abandonment in the sense of divesting abandonment, but rather abandonment 'into the legal control of another, as opposed to rendering the property a *res nullius*'.[93] It would be better to term this a transfer, a donation or a gift, rather than 'abandonment' as it obscures the more particular meaning of that term in law.

Finally, a note on the 'absurd consequences' argument and abandonment. Jonathan Herring has, in this volume, made points about the possible absurd or problematic consequences of a property approach to regulating biomaterials, asking:

> [I]f all your body is property you are committing the offence of littering if you leave property in a public place. Dropping hair on a pavement as the wind blows through your hair could be a criminal offence. If you leave property in someone else's property they are entitled to ask you to remove it; the dandruff you leave at your restaurant could result in a phone call from the restaurant asking you to remove your property. . . Is a hospital to ensure there is consent to dispose of bodily waste, if it is the patient's property? What if the patient wishes to keep their bodily waste and material, if we see it as their property? Would a hospital be entitled to charge patients for storage or removal of their bodily property? Can relatives claim ownership rights over the organs of a deceased?[94]

[91] Human Tissue Act 2004, s 44.

[92] M Pawlowski, 'Property in Body Parts and Products of the Human Body' (2009) 30 *Liverpool Law Journal* 35, 46.

[93] ibid, 47.

[94] See Herring, ch 13 in this volume. He notes that the first cluster of examples is implausible: 'Now I agree these examples seem implausible. But the implausibility works both ways: it is implausible that these would result in legal actions, but that is because it is implausible these body parts are property.'

Skene has also raised this concern in response to ownership of body parts, commenting that if biomaterials were property, then

> beneficiaries would inherit not only the possessions of the deceased but also the deceased's body and stored body parts and tissue. A bequest of 'all my property to my son' would entitle the son to stored tissue on slides, severed limbs and other 'surgical waste'. He could, of course, waive this right but the hospital would be legally obliged to consult him about the matter before disposition.

Further, she comments:

> Hospitals could not dispose of bodies and body parts without permission, even if the hospital was being closed. . . . The hospital would have no legal right to retain tissue that might be vital in defending claims against it; the 'owner' would be entitled to remove and destroy the stored tissue unless restrained by injunction.[95]

Skene's arguments about explicit and implied abandonment would alleviate some of these concerns, but not all (moreover her arguments are not well founded in the law of England). Herring, understandably and reasonably, eschews a property approach in part due to these potential problems.

This is only a brief outline of the use of the concept of abandonment in the literature on how we should regulate the use of human tissue, but it demonstrates that the concept has clearly been drawn on to explain (and sometimes justify) what might be happening, in a legal sense, when tissue is removed and retained. As the role ascribed to the concept in these accounts suggests, whether one has the capacity to abandon rights in tissue could be (and probably should be) an integral part of arguments both for, and against, a property-based approach. It has been shown that some uses of the term in the context of human biomaterials have not been sufficiently well grounded, or at least would not apply in the English context given the stringency of the intention requirements in this jurisdiction. They might, however, find more favour in Australia and the US, as their positions are more accepting of the possibility of divesting abandonment.

This chapter now turns to a detailed exploration of how the concept of abandonment could be applied in relation to regulating human biomaterials. This is broken into two sections. The first teases out an important misconception about legal abandonment that has been touched upon above, namely, that abandonment is a property concept and as such it is incoherent to deploy it in a regulatory model that does not permit human tissue to be property. It argues that there is a need for clarity and precision in the use of abandonment in a debate over the best legal approach to regulating biomaterials. In the second section, the chapter works through the implications of the status of the doctrine of abandonment as part of that model.

[95] L Skene, 'Arguments against People Legally "Owning" Their Own Bodies, Body Parts and Tissue' (2002) 2 *Macquarie Law Journal* 163, 1.3.

Abandonment is a Property Concept

Abandonment is by its very nature a property concept. It must be, because to abandon something at law means to divest oneself of one's ownership of an item. To own an item means holding all the residual rights to it that are not held by others. Giving up ownership means giving up all of those rights. Where ownership is about rights in relation to things, abandonment is the divesting of these rights. It is therefore a necessary component of abandonment that one has ownership in the first place, otherwise one has nothing to give away (except possession, and that is not abandonment). Therefore, any mention of 'abandonment' in the legal sense must presume that the item in question is property, and that the person doing the abandoning is the owner.

For this reason, it does not make sense to talk of abandonment of human tissue (in the legal sense) if that tissue had no owner and was not property. If it was not property, there would be no rights to give up. This is why the Nuffield Council's approach was incoherent and attracted such criticism.[96] The Council had rejected taking a property approach, yet used the language of property, suggesting that what was happening when a person no longer wanted their excised tissue was an abandonment of their rights in it. But as the Council would not permit that person to own their tissue, they had no such rights to abandon. The invocation of notions of 'abandonment' might simply have had the lay meaning of discarding had the Nuffield Council not specifically stated that this was how such tissue was to be 'regarded in law'.[97] It is true that might have meant in the lay sense of discarding, but regardless, there is need in this debate for precision in the use of terms with a particular legal meaning.

The Council's approach exemplifies another problem with failing to use abandonment in its proper legal sense. They shifted between talking of 'abandonment of any claim'[98] and abandoning the tissue itself. If one abandoned the tissue, then one would have no claim in conversion for an interference, nor could the tissue be stolen. However, this is a much narrower implication than 'abandoning any claim'.[99] Failing to use the concept in a way that accords with its meaning in law both creates confusion, and can lead to saying more than one actually means to

[96] For example, Ken Mason and Graeme Laurie have argued that the Nuffield Council 'was not able to divorce itself completely from the property model', as it recommended that tissue removed during treatment should be regarded in law as 'having been abandoned', while donated tissue should be regarded as 'a gift'. They rightly make the point that that the terms 'gift' and 'abandonment' 'imply an underlying property interest': JK Mason and GT Laurie, 'Consent or Property? Dealing with the Body and its Parts in the Shadow of Bristol and Alder Hey' (2001) 64 *Modern Law Review* 701, 725; Nuffield Council on Bioethics, above n 63, 9.14.

[97] Nuffield Council on Bioethics, ibid, 9.14.

[98] ibid, 67.

[99] The confusion of terminology is compounded in the report by references to 'gifts' of tissue, another property concept deployed in a model that expressly rejected tissue having the status of property.

say. We need to ask what the Council was actually intending. It seems they wanted to say that the individual whose tissue is 'abandoned' gives up any say about the future of her tissue. This is what both 'abandoning any claim' and abandoning in the property sense both mean. But this might actually be saying too much, particularly for some sorts of tissue, given the importance of some tissue to some people in certain contexts. Given also the informational content of tissue, asserting that someone abandons any claim might also say too much if they will have legitimate continuing interests in how that tissue is used. However, it is important to note that the Council was writing before the passage of the Human Tissue Act, and some of their concerns are now dealt with via its provisions, particularly the prohibition on non-consensual analysis of DNA.[100]

The Operation of Abandonment in a 'Tissue as Property' Model

If we take a property approach, we need to be clear on the role the concept of abandonment plays in our model, and the implications for the workability (or otherwise) of such a model. Achieving such clarity will require the exploration of a number of issues. First, we need to address the question of original ownership. We need to be clear on how the current law on abandonment (such as it is) would apply to human tissue. We need also to be clear on what the implications of this application will be for our model and to critically evaluate them.

Original Ownership: The Necessary Prior Question Must Be Resolved

Examining the treatment of abandonment in the literature reveals some of the deeper issues (and problems) in discussions of whether human tissue should be property. As we have seen, for tissue to be abandoned it must first have an owner. It is this owner's intentions and actions that largely determine whether that tissue has been abandoned, or indeed transferred by gift or sale. If we do not know who the owner is, it is very difficult to sustain a property analysis. This is not the place to delve into this thorny question, but it is important to note that if we choose to take a property approach, this necessitates knowing who holds rights before we can consider to whom they may have been transferred, or when they may have been given up altogether.

Such an examination is also revealing of in whom commentators consider ownership will vest. The Nuffield Council presented its range of possible analyses, which variously suggested that newly excised tissue might be *res nullius* (owned by

[100] Human Tissue Act 2004, s 45.

no-one) or owned but then abandoned by the person from whom it was taken. Dickens' and Skene's accounts of a possible property approach also took this latter approach, with Dickens arguing in favour of the individual holding an inchoate right that would crystallise on excision. Mills, Matthews, Bennett Moses and Pawlowski all also admit the possibility that initial ownership would be vested in the source individual, although no-one other than Matthews has delved into the matter in much depth.

Whether in fact this is the approach the law would (and should) take remains open to debate. Certainly the decision in *Yearworth* suggests the courts might find the source of the tissue to be the owner in some cases,[101] but there is much in the Court of Appeal's decision on this point with which to take issue, although again this is not the place for that discussion. What we should draw from this observation about the assumptions in relation to initial ownership is that there is still work to be done to determine just who, if anyone, the law of property would find to be the first owner.[102] This issue needs further, and fuller, exploration and we should not simply proceed by assuming ownership will vest in the source individual and then presume she has abandoned her tissue to avoid the consequences of this if they are unwanted. This is particularly important given the difficulties in finding tissue to have been abandoned that will now be described.

Evaluation of the Role of Abandonment in a 'Tissue as Property' Model

The debate over its existence aside, if the doctrine of abandonment does exist, we can now ask whether human tissue taken from the body could be abandoned, and if so, how? Three requirements emerge from the foregoing explanation of the case law: an original owner of the tissue, a physical relinquishment of the tissue, and a clear, unequivocal intention on the part of the owner to divest herself of all rights in relation to the tissue. Any property model put forward for the regulation of human biomaterials needs to take account of this, and either demonstrate how abandonment will play a role in that model, or work around any problems that might arise if biomaterials generally cannot be regarded as abandoned (as the case law would suggest).

In evaluating the role abandonment might play in a 'biomaterials as property' model, we should keep in mind what is wanted of an effective model of regulation for human tissue. It is relatively uncontroversial to say we would want our model to protect the privacy and autonomy interests of the person from whom the tissue was taken, but that this protection would need to be balanced with enabling researchers and doctors to use tissue for beneficial purposes such as research and treatment.

[101] *Jonathan Yearworth and others v North Bristol NHS Trust* EWCA Civ, [41]–[45].

[102] Rohan Hardcastle has so far offered the only in-depth analysis of this question: R Hardcastle, *Law and the Human Body: Property Rights, Ownership and Control* (Oxford, Hart Publishing, 2007).

Assuming first that tissue could be abandoned, both useful and problematic consequences might flow, depending on the goals we have for our model. Assume that, unlike much of the case law, an intention to abandon would be found essentially when we might say a person had discarded their tissue or expressed no interest in it, as they might following surgery – the *Venner* position. What would the beneficial consequences of abandonment be? For one, it would provide researchers and medical practitioners who take intentional possession of abandoned tissue with the security of ownership. If they came into possession of tissue abandoned by a patient in a clinical context, they would, within the limits of the law, be permitted to use it as they wished, and hence could use it in research, clinical audits and the like as they do now. There would be no concern about losing access or even dealing with complaints from the source individual, who would have no claims to the property (the tissue). The source individual could only bring a claim or raise a legal complaint where the law had specifically provided a basis. The offence of non-consensual testing under the Human Tissue Act would be an example, and would not be affected by the research or doctor now owning the tissue, as the offence would operate just as prohibitions on other uses of property do. For example, I am still guilty of grievous bodily harm for stabbing someone if I use a knife of which I am the owner.

Allowing for abandonment of tissue would not only provide security, but would also produce a clear explanation of how researchers and other subsequent possessors of tissue could legitimately deal with it if a property model were adopted. Without allowing abandonment, any such uses of tissue would be potential conversions unless some clear indication of a transfer of rights (such as via gift) could be demonstrated.

A property model allowing for abandonment would also avoid some of the other dealings with tissue that Justice Higgins suggested in *Doodeward v Spence* were 'winked at' by the law.[103] Transfers of tissue discarded by patients to commercial companies producing cell lines, primary culture tissue, and treatments are all on a sounder legal footing if we conceptualise them as an initial abandonment, followed by a hospital or other taking possession, becoming the owner and then transferring or even selling that tissue. The same could be said of hair left at a hairdressers that is later used in wigs or extensions.

There are, however, significant objections to be made in response to these suggested benefits. First, very often a sufficiently clear indication that a patient or other source of tissue has no further interest in her tissue may not have been obtained nor be obtainable in the clinical context, or if it can be, only at significant administrative cost.[104] It was demonstrated above (The Doctrine of Abandonment at Common Law) that an intention to abandon will not lightly be

[103] *Doodeward v Spence* (1908) 6 CLR 423.

[104] See, eg a number of studies analysing the realities of obtaining consent to research use of tissue as cited in K Liddell and A Hall, 'Beyond Bristol and Alder Hey: The Future Regulation of Human Tissue' (2005) 13 *Medical Law Review* 170, 214–15.

found, and hence researchers and others would be very unwise to assume they have gained ownership of biomaterials without very clear evidence of abandonment.

It would be possible to create an assumption of abandonment in a property model. It could be argued, as some of the commentators discussed in the previous section indicated, that this would accord with many patients' usual wishes. It would also enable a property model to afford users, such as researchers, security without the difficulties associated with ensuring that a clear gift has been made in every situation. Indeed, we might also argue that a property model that includes abandonment is a more transparent means of promoting research access to tissue than the consent model of the Human Tissue Act, as it might afford researchers greater access and more security. Coupled with the offence of non-consensual testing, it might also better align with people's actual feelings about their tissue, as most people do regard tissue taken during surgery as waste and have no further interest in it. A property model might then better support research, which is beneficial to the community as a whole.

However, one might object that presuming abandonment too lightly might lead us back to the practices that led to the organ retention scandals of the early 2000s. It might also lead to situations in which individuals lose control of their biomaterials in a way that later causes them unwanted (and probably unforeseen) harms. For example, a patient might honestly believe she cares not about the fate of her tissue, but then feels differently if it is subjected to genetic testing, or sold, or otherwise used in a manner to which she would object if she later knew. A hospital using her tissue for clinical audit purposes might be unobjectionable, but she might feel differently about it being sold on to a commercial venture.

Presuming abandonment, or finding it easily, may also *not* coincide with people's feelings about their tissue, and so the presumption of abandonment would be simply another fiction. In some contexts we can already see that the presumption of abandonment is not as obviously in line with individual's views as some would suggest. As Sheelagh McGuinness and Margaret Brazier rightly point out, bodily material has several values.[105] One person may wish to protect her privacy – from family, from insurers, from an employer, or from many others. She might not want the state to collect it for analysis, nor indeed want the risk of someone planting it at a crime scene. Some will have religious reasons for wanting to determine their tissue's fate, such as an Orthodox Jew who wants his amputated limb buried with him. Others will simply want the tissue for themselves. McGuiness and Brazier give the example of a boy wanting to take home his appendix in a jar. Jean McHale gives the example of a placenta, which many women want to take home with them following a birth.[106] And what of the woman who suffers a missed miscarriage and must have the foetus removed? Many do not want the 'tissue'

[105] S McGuiness and M Brazier, 'Respecting the Living Means Respecting the Dead Too' (2008) 28 *Oxford Journal of Legal Studies* 297, 299–301.

[106] J McHale, 'Waste, Ownership and Bodily Products' (2000) 8 *Health Care Analysis* 123, 124.

used for research, nor simply incinerated. Indeed, some choose to bury what they often consider a child at home.[107]

Some tissue is clearly valuable to people generally – this is not in doubt in relation to transplantable organs. Some tissue has obvious emotive value, whether due to the nature of the tissue (the precious symbolism of a heart), or contextual value (tissue taken in highly emotional circumstances). And then in some circumstances, people are not aware of the value of something until they have lost it. As the abandonment cases, particularly the theft cases, make it clear, there are good reasons why, when an item has value, abandonment will not (and should not) easily be shown. As the law currently stands, it is clear that the courts are even more reluctant to find abandonment of property that has value, demonstrating themselves to be acutely mindful of both the value of the good and the circumstances in which it was relinquished in finding an intention to abandon, and there is little doubt they would act with similar care in relation to human tissue. In many situations regarding biomaterials there would be some indication that the tissue held value and the courts would very likely not find it had been abandoned, and would be rightly reluctant to support a presumption otherwise.

Setting aside the option of an automatic presumption of abandonment, and leaving the matter to the assessment of value taken in some of the cases, a further problem emerges given the complexity of determining the value of biomaterials. Such an approach would rely on the courts accurately evaluating individual sensitivities as part of a determination of value, which may not always be successful. The real difficulty in the context of abandonment, then, is determining when waste really is unwanted. McHale makes an excellent observation about the notion of waste when she states that 'what constitutes waste is a highly relative notion. It cannot be effectively seen in the abstract, we need to consider it in the particular context'.[108]

Like placenta, cord blood is also subject to individual sensitivities, but in that case the value or otherwise arises for different reasons. It is generally useful to the community as a potential health resource, but might be crucially important to a parent wanting it for a child who suffers from an illness for which it might provide treatment. Other parents give it barely a thought.

Sometimes value will also be contingent on the intended actions of another. A piece of tissue might be regarded by its source as valueless until he learns of the intentions of someone else to put it to use in a commercial venture. He might then see it in a different light; it is no longer waste (that is, something without a use), but now a resource, of which he is owner and which he now may have the option to exploit. Conversely, knowledge of such an intention might lead the source individual not to value the tissue per se, but to want control of its fate precisely to prevent its being used in a commercial venture.[109] All of these

[107] McGuiness and Brazier, 'Respecting the Living Means Respecting the Dead Too', above n 105, 300.

[108] McHale, 'Waste, Ownership and Bodily Products', above n 106, 128.

[109] For example, McHale notes John Moore's claim that had he known of the commercial exploitation of his tissue intended by Golde and Quan, he would not have consented to its removal (and, therefore, effectively would not have consented to its use in this way): ibid, 128.

complexities make the task of finding, or presuming, abandonment fraught with complexity.

Given this, an approach that ensures consent is obtained, whether via a property approach or not, goes much of the way to avoiding these problems; the notion of abandonment, however, undermines this notion of consensual, informed giving that emerged as being so important following the incidents at Alder Hey Hospital. Therefore, it seems that deeming biomaterials to have been abandoned is not a desirable path to resolving the concerns around subsequent use.

A final problem with automatically, or more easily presuming abandonment of biomaterials is that it potentially gives too much control to subsequent possessors, leaving the source of the tissue without the recourse they did not realise they might want until it was too late. As has been emphasised throughout this chapter, divesting abandonment means the owner gives up all rights to the object. It prevents a more nuanced approach, such as a detailed consent procedure, and in fact removes much of the incentive to ensure that clear, considered consent is provided. It similarly removes the incentive to apply a more useful gift-based approach, wherein we might either use a consent-based framework, or deploy the law of gifts, and even trust concepts argued for both in this collection and elsewhere.

Let us assume now that tissue cannot be abandoned, or at least that the courts will only very rarely find sufficiently clear intention to do so. Effectively, then, the safe presumption would be that tissue had not been abandoned without strong evidence to the contrary. Given the case law, this is the likely scenario. If such were to be the case, it would ensure that whoever had been deemed the initial owner (probably but not certainly the individual from whom it was taken) would retain significant rights to that tissue. Given the intimate connection between a person and their tissue, informational and also sometimes emotional or psychological, such control would reflect the importance we place on promoting autonomy.[110] Throughout the law we already aim to support individual choice and control as an aspect of respecting autonomy, and if tissue were property that was not easily abandoned, then this would mean individuals would not lightly lose control over their tissue. It is true that many problematic uses of tissue could be addressed through legislation, and many (such as non-consensual analysis of DNA) are.[111] However, there may be situations in which having ownership over tissue as property, and retaining the rights that come with ownership unless we choose to divest ourselves of them will be important. That the Court of Appeal resorted to a property analysis in *Yearworth* indicates as much. Retention of ownership might also enable individuals to prevent (or be compensated for) unwanted

[110] For example, Mason and Laurie comment that 'it is not true . . . that we lose all interest in materials surrendered for research. The moral significance of body parts remains, even after they have been separated from their original source': Mason and Laurie, 'Consent or Property? Dealing with the Body and its Parts in the Shadow of Bristol and Alder Hey', above n 96, 726.

[111] Human Tissue Act 2004, s 45.

uses of tissue that currently fall outside the Human Tissue Act, such as taking tissue discarded in the normal course of daily life, and taking it to another jurisdiction for testing. Presuming that ownership is not lightly lost also supports individuals having the bargaining power to negotiate what is done with their tissue in some circumstances if this is the approach we support.[112] Such an approach also creates further incentives to obtain proper consent to use or to permanently transfer. In doing so, greater clarity about the nature of the transfer when tissue is donated or sold is achieved – it would be a bailment (potentially via contract), a gift or a sale, and so be governed by the relevant existing rules.

There is, however, a range of negative consequences that flow if tissue is property that cannot be abandoned easily. The most important would be the opening up of researchers and other subsequent users to potential liability for conversion. While it is true that items of relatively low value are regularly taken and no-one finds themselves in court for taking a colleague's pencil, human tissue is not so fungible as a pencil and there may be instances where source individuals are unhappy. If they are, then all to the good – they can bring a claim. However, the public policy in support of medical research speaks against allowing such claims too easily and researchers need security to know that they can use samples without impunity. Also we ought not to establish a system in which the law works only because it is often not invoked.

If excised tissue, particularly waste tissue, is deemed property and so creates potential liability in conversion, this might also act as a disincentive to valuable uses to which such waste is put. Commercial ventures supplying needed tissue for research and treatment depend in part on access to such tissue, and in fact, as Nik Brown and others have explored, the deeming of that tissue waste.[113] There is a case to be made for supporting this industry as it feeds into research and treatment that benefit us all. Similarly, hospitals that use for treatments tissue that would otherwise be destroyed need to be supported. We need to carefully walk a line between protecting individual interests in their tissue, and treating waste as waste where this is appropriate and reasonable.

Conclusion

Abandonment is a rather obscure area of law, but a potentially important one in the context of human tissue regulation. This chapter has presented an overview of that law with the goal of elucidating why it is important that analyses of how tissue should be regulated take account of the particularities of the law on abandonment. If abandonment is possible under English law, it is only possible in very

[112] In support of this aspect of ownership, see Mason and Laurie, 'Consent or Property? Dealing with the Body and its Parts in the Shadow of Bristol and Alder Hey', above n 96, 726.

[113] N Brown, 'Contradictions of Value: Between Use and Exchange in Cord Blood Bioeconomy' (2013) 35 *Sociology of Health and Illness* 97.

limited circumstances, and very clear evidence of an intention to abandon will be necessary if the next possessor is to gain ownership. The authority of *Venner* does not apply in England, but is likely to be influential if the courts are called upon to determine whether discarded human tissue can be said to have been abandoned. Whether such a case will arise is doubtful, but even taking *Venner* into account, the informational content of almost all human tissue, and the subjective value of some of it, coupled with the English law's reluctance to find property has been abandoned suggest it is unlikely that human tissue will be found abandoned in any but the clearest circumstances. Those arguing for a property approach need to take account of this likelihood if their account relies on human tissue being capable of being abandoned. Alternatively, they must argue for an expectation of how the courts will deal with discarded tissue that is more conductive to the success of their model.

Those who eschew a property approach may find support for their view here. The difficulty of finding abandonment suggests that we cannot rely on tissue being seen as abandoned to legitimate the subsequent possessor acting as an owner. This potentially undermines the property approach, as it means that subsequent possessors (such as researchers) have only possessory title and cannot, legitimately, use or use up the tissue of which they have gained possession. They should, by rights, wait six years until the original owner's title has been extinguished, otherwise they risk being liable for conversion. A non-property model based on consensual use does not face such problems, and so can allow for easier transfer and use of discarded tissue. These points might suggest that our policy goals might be better supported by a non-property system if abandonment cannot resolve these difficulties.

10

Cadavers, Body Parts and the Remedial Problem

REMIGIUS N NWABUEZE*

Introduction

This chapter explores the hypothesis that most of the critical questions (or controversies) that arise in relation to the right of use and control over cadavers and body parts are, in a way, an acute expression of the more fundamental remedial problems encountered in the context of interferences with body parts and dead bodies. For instance, only a few people can deny a person's right to defend the corpse of his/her ancestor against mutilation or violation, but there is no agreement as to the legal bases upon which such a right (or defence) could be asserted. What is the appropriate remedy for such brutal interference with an ancestor's body? The same applies to the body parts of the living. Does, and should, the patient have continuing control over a blood or tissue sample, taken with consent for, say, a test on diabetes but, contrary to consent, tested for HIV?[1] By looking at the available legal remedies for interference with cadavers and excised body parts, I will argue that the law is arbitrary, selective and discriminatory against sources of body parts and relatives of deceased persons. Thus, I will argue for a harmonised remedial framework, one which puts all remedial options on the table and seeks to achieve justice among all interested parties.

* This chapter was completed during my time as a Visiting Professor of Law at the Faculty of Law, Thompson Rivers University, Kamloops, British Columbia, Canada. Many thanks to my students, Curtis Simmonds and Kendall Cholak, JD candidates at the Faculty of Law, Thompson Rivers University, Canada, for their excellent research assistance.

[1] By analogy consider the complaint of parents, in the Alder Hey scandal, that the body parts of their deceased children were harvested, retained or used without their consent: *The House of Commons, The Royal Liverpool Children's Inquiry* (2001) available at: http://webarchive.nationalarchives.gov.uk/20111202162649/http:/www.rlcinquiry.org.uk/.

Architecture of Current Remedies

It might be argued that the amplitude and latitude of current remedial categories used for unauthorised interferences with cadavers and body parts render the argument for a proprietary remedification framework a work in supererogation. However, that sort of hypothesis is difficult to justify. Not only does such argument reflect some romanticism with existing remedies, but it also reposes much faith in the ability of current remedies to do justice in a case involving the mutilation of a relative's remains, or the unauthorised use of a separated body part. On closer scrutiny, however, it is possible to unpack the limitations and deficiencies that characterise the current remedial frameworks. As a result of such deficiencies, the current remedial frameworks are most often completely useless to sources complaining about the unauthorised use of their excised tissues, as well as claimants who allege the mistreatment of their relatives' cadavers. Three hypothetical scenarios may help to generalise the gaps in the remedies applicable to interferences with the human body:

- D, a medical researcher, clandestinely performs an unauthorised autopsy or dissection on the corpse of P's relative;[2]
- D obtains P's blood sample with P's consent for a test on diabetes. However, contrary to authorisation, D performs an additional test for schizophrenia;[3] and
- D removes a diseased organ from P; the surgery is medically indicated and necessary to save P's life. However, without P's knowledge and consent, D uses the separated body part to develop an innovative and lucrative therapeutic product. D holds tightly to the profits.[4]

Could P succeed in any claim in the three scenarios above? Note that these examples are comprehensive, encompassing cadavers, body parts and products of the body. Shockingly, absent a proprietary framework, P might not succeed in any claim in the above examples,[5] a situation that obviously provokes some concern in view of D's outrageous and morally indefensible conduct.[6] Worse still, the

[2] As in *Davidson v Garrett* [1899] CCC 200; *Christensen v Superior Court*; 54 Cal 3d 868 (Su Ct Cal 1992) and, to some extent, *AB v Leeds Hospital NHS* [2005] 2 WLR 358 (Gage J).

[3] As in *Havasupai Tribe v Arizona Board of Regents* (consolidated suit numbers 1 CA-CV 07-0454 and 1 CA-CV 07-0801) (Ca App Ariz 2008); also, *Norman-Bloodsaw v Lawrence Berkeley Laboratory*, 135 F 3d 1260 (9th Cir 1998).

[4] As in *Moore v Regents of the University of California*, 793 P 2d 479 (Cal S Ct 1990) and, to some extent, *Greenberg v Miami Children's Hospital Research Institute* 264 F Supp 2d 1064 (SD Fl 2003).

[5] More detailed comments are provided below regarding the pre-trial success of claimants in *Moore v Regents of the University of California*, 793 P 2d 479, (Cal S Ct 1990) (breach of fiduciary duty and informed consent); and *Greenberg v Miami Children's Hospital Research Institute* 264 F Supp 2d 1064 (SD Fl 2003) (unjust enrichment).

[6] Harris would not object to the conduct in the first scenario if the dissection was performed to achieve a public good, such as organ transplantation: J Harris, 'Law and Regulation of Retained Organs: The Ethical Issues' (2002) 22 *Legal Studies* 527.

Human Tissue Act 2004 provides only criminal sanctions for breach of its consent provisions and, thus, it does not directly apply to the hypothetical scenarios above, which focus on civil remedies. However, to the extent that the Human Tissue Act 2004 could undergird a civil action for non-consensual interference with body parts, such an action will sound in negligence as argued below. A similar quandary presented itself in *Ritter v Couch*,[7] but with a hint of frustration at the remedially parlous position of the claimant, Brannon P asked:

> The world does not contain a tribunal that would punish a son who should resist, even to death, any attempt to mutilate his father's corpse, or tear it from the grave for sale or dissection; but where would he find the legal right to resist, except in his peculiar and exclusive interest in the body?[8]

Certainly, *Ritter* was about a buried cadaver, but the case is still instructive. There, a disused cemetery belonging to the local authority was sold to the defendant. Under the deed of sale, the defendant was free, after four months of the sale, to disinter corpses buried in the cemetery, or otherwise deal with the buried corpses as he desired. Unsurprisingly, the claimants (who were relatives of the buried persons) sought to have the sale annulled, and to restrain the defendant from disinterring the corpses. The defendant challenged the claimants' standing to bring the action.

Brannon P was dismayed to learn that existing legal categories, other than a proprietary approach, could not justify the claimants' suit. Tort law could not apply as the defendant had not yet interfered with the buried corpses. Contractual action was also unavailable because the claimants were not a party to the deed of sale, and the transaction was not made for their benefit. However, the claim in that case touched the 'deepest and most unerring instincts of human nature', which justified judicial intervention.[9] In the end, Brannon P turned to natural law, underpinning the claimants' standing on 'a self-evident right of humanity', so 'sacred and precious' that the support of an existing precedent was not needed.[10] A property law approach could have reasonably constituted the fulcrum of Ritter's claim, but its application was obviated by the anachronistic no-property rule for dead bodies – a doctrine that Brannon P vilified in no uncertain terms:

> The dogma of the English ecclesiastical law, that a child has no such claim, no such exclusive power, no peculiar interest in the body of its parent, is so utterly inconsistent with every enlightened perception of personal right, so inexpressibly repulsive to every proper moral sense, that its adoption would be an eternal disgrace to American jurisprudence.[11]

Ritter should not be dismissed as a relic of history. More modern cases in the law relating to the human body evince a similar remedial imbroglio. Consider, for

[7] *Ritter v Couch*, 76 SE 428 (Sup Ct App 1912).
[8] ibid, 430.
[9] *Ritter v Couch*, 76 SE 428, 430 (Sup Ct App 1912).
[10] ibid.
[11] ibid.

example, the tort claims of negligence, intentional tort and battery. In essence, analysis of the remedial problems associated with the causes of action below is intended to provide a vivid specification of the three hypothetical scenarios above.

Negligence

As a cause of action, negligence is used here to embrace causes of action known in American jurisprudence as the breach of fiduciary duty, and lack of informed consent. In the law of England and Wales, however, there are no freestanding or independent causes of action in tort known as 'breach of fiduciary duty'[12] and 'lack of informed consent'; interests protected by them are vindicated through the general action in negligence.[13] For instance, although the Human Tissue Act 2004 does not provide a civil remedy for breach of its consent provisions, any conceivable civil action based on the Act will be grounded in negligence, rather than 'lack of informed consent'. Even in the US where breach of fiduciary duty and lack of informed consent are recognised as independent causes of action (as in *Moore*), they are not only interchangeable and, therefore, practically one and the same cause of action,[14] but they are also mainly an action in negligence in a different guise, entailing similar elemental requirements. Justice Mosk's dissenting judgment in *Moore* gave vivid expression to that issue when he endorsed the observation of Martin and Lagod[15] to the effect that 'an action based on the physician's failure to disclose material information sounds in negligence'.[16] Thus this section's criticism of a negligent action in relation to cadavers and body parts equally applies (*mutatis mutandis*) to an action for breach of fiduciary duty, and lack of informed consent.[17]

By way of compensation, negligence punishes a party responsible for substandard conduct. Negligence is full of promises in litigations over dead bodies and excised body parts. But can it deliver on such promises? Alas, there is no special category of negligence applicable to dead bodies or separated body parts,[18] therefore, despite the uniqueness of that field, a claimant must still establish all of the traditional elements of negligence: a duty of care, a breach of duty, causation and

[12] However, in the context of fiduciary relationships, equity recognises the cause of action for breach of fiduciary duty: *Boardman v Phipps* [1967] 2 AC 46 (HL).

[13] See, generally, *Chester v Ashfar* [2005] 1 AC 134 (HL), relating to a negligent action based on lack of informed consent.

[14] For instance, writing for the majority in *Moore*, Panelli J observed that Moore's allegations in relation to the non-disclosure of relevant information to him stated a cause of action which 'can properly be characterized either as the breach of a fiduciary duty to disclose facts material to the patient's consent or, alternatively, as the performance of medical procedures without first having obtained the patient's informed consent'. *Moore v Regents of the University of California* 793 P 2d 479 at 483, (Cal S Ct 1990).

[15] PA Martin and ML Lagod, 'Biotechnology and the Commercial Use of Human Cells: Towards an Organic View of Life and Technology' (1989) 5 *Santa Clara Computer & High Technology Law Journal* 211 at 222.

[16] *Moore v Regents of the University of California*, 793 P 2d 479 at 519, (CalS Ct 1990).

[17] For the defence of a negligent action, see Krebs, ch 4 in this volume.

[18] However, the same observation applies to other subject matters.

damages. It would be incongruous to undertake a disquisition into the elemental constituents of negligence in this chapter as such information can be obtained easily in standard treatises on the subject. Nonetheless, a cursory comment on those elements might illumine the potential struggles of negligence with the hypothetical scenarios above.

A duty of care in negligence is a teleological concept. Duty of care limits a wrongdoer's potential liability, ensuring that liability is not disproportionate to the fault.[19] Consequently, not all victims of a wrong can recover compensation for their injuries – only those in a legally recognisable relationship of duty can do so. But what relationships give rise to a duty of care? The answer to that question shows that negligence is not an exact science; it trenches on value judgements and is immersed in policy discourse. The US jurisprudence readily accepts this characterisation, prompting the declaration in *Tarasoff v Regents of University of California*: 'Legal duties are not discoverable facts of nature, but merely conclusory expressions that, in cases of a particular type, liability should be imposed for damage done.'[20] Equally poignantly, Prosser and Keeton observed that a duty of care is 'not sacrosanct in itself, but is only an expression of the sum total of those considerations of policy which lead the law to say that the plaintiff is entitled to protection'.[21] In the same vein, Lord Bridge, in the often quoted case of *Caparo Industries v Dickman*, observed that a duty of care analysis requires that 'the situation . . . be one in which the court considers it fair, just and reasonable that the law should impose a duty of a given scope upon the one party for the benefit of the other'.[22] What *Tarasoff* suggests is that, in certain circumstances, the judiciary erects an artificial roadblock undergirded by policy considerations, on the claimant's road to recovery in negligence. In the area of dead bodies, no case illustrates this judicial attitude better than *Christensen v Superior Court*.[23] The defendants' conduct in *Christensen* was outrageous; they clandestinely mutilated the cadavers of claimants' relatives, and the harvested body parts were subsequently sold to a biotechnology company (as in the first hypothetical scenario above).

Christensen was grounded in negligence; the obstacle involved in that case was the requirement that an action for the negligent infliction of emotional distress, arising from injury to a third party, can only be brought by a direct percipient witness to that injury (this is otherwise known as the 'bystander's rule'). In *Christensen*, however, the injury was to corpses (about 16,500 of them), and was done furtively; this proved problematical for the claimants. It is a remarkable defendant, with the impudence of the devil, who can desecrate a corpse in the presence of living relatives. As it was, the *Christensen* claimants only learned about the cadaveric mistreatments in a media report. The corpses had been given to the

[19] PH Winfield, 'The History of Negligence in the Law of Torts' (1926) 42 *Law Quarterly Review* 184.

[20] *Tarasoff v Regents of University of California*, 17 Cal 3d 425 at 434 (1976).

[21] W Page et al (eds), *Prosser and Keeton on the Law of Torts*, 5th edn (St Paul, MN, West Publishing Co, 1984) 358.

[22] *Caparo Industries v Dickman* [1990] 2 AC 605 at 617–18.

[23] *Christensen v Superior Court*, 54 Cal 3d 868 (Su Ct Cal 1992).

mortuary and crematory defendants for cremation. However, those defendants colluded with another defendant, a North Carolina biological supply company, to mine and harvest various body parts from the corpses for commercial gain. The defendants brought a preliminary objection challenging the standing of claimants, other than those who had the statutory right of burial and those who contracted for the funeral services.[24] It was alleged that the affected class of claimants had no standing to sue because they were not percipient witnesses to the defendants' outrageous conduct. This type of objection attaches to any potential claim analogous to the first category of the hypothetical example given above. Baxter J, for the majority, appreciated the implications of the bystander's rule in litigations over dead bodies, observing that the effect of the objection was to create 'an immunity protecting [the defendants] from liability for the serious emotional distress caused by such egregious, but clandestine, misconduct',[25] and that 'it would be the exceptional case in which any family member would observe misconduct of the type alleged in the complaint'.[26] Thus, Baxter J dismissed the preliminary objection and ordered a full trial. No further proceedings on the case have been reported.[27]

Even if *Christensen* had gone on to a full trial, the claimants would most certainly have lost, being unlikely to scale the hurdle of causation, which would require them to establish a causal link between the wrong and their alleged injury. The claimants would have needed to show that, based on the media report, they were reasonably certain that their decedents were among those mutilated by the defendants – an inference which led to their emotional distress. Such a Herculean task entails reliance on the accurate records of the defendants. Unfortunately, as might be expected, the defendants had not kept an accurate record of their outrageous and unlawful activities. In *Christensen*, Baxter J appreciated this causation test and the potentially enormous difficulties it posed for the claimants, but he did not dwell on it as the matter was not yet ripe for trial.[28] In his concurring and dissenting opinion, Kennard J observed that the claimants were most likely to fail on causation, so that in endorsing the causation test of the majority, above, a situation arises where what 'the majority gives with one hand, it takes with the other'.[29]

Christensen was not unique in that sense; *Moore v Regents of the University of California* had also struggled with the causation requirement.[30]As is well known, Moore had undergone a medically indicated splenectomy; his physician had surreptitiously used Moore's excised spleen, and other body parts deceptively obtained in the name of post-operative procedures, to invent a lucrative cell line valued at over three billion US dollars. Moore, in addition to protecting his autonomy interests, arguably wanted a share of the profits derived from his body

[24] There were more than 6,000 claimants.
[25] *Christensen*, above n 23 at 887.
[26] ibid.
[27] A search on Westlaw and the Internet did not reveal any further proceedings in the case.
[28] *Christensen*, above n 23 at 900–902.
[29] ibid, 919.
[30] *Moore v Regents of the University of California* 793 P 2d 479, (Cal S Ct 1990).

parts. A preliminary objection saw to the dismissal of his claims, with the exception of his cause of action in negligence based on lack of informed consent. Fortunately, the case was settled out of court before trial, as if it had not Moore would have lost on causation. Moore would have been required to show that, had he been informed of his physician's research and economic interests in his body parts, he would have declined the life-saving splenectomy procedure,[31] and this would have been very difficult.[32] Moreover, Moore's subjective opinion would have been irrelevant given that the causation inquiry is an objective exercise.[33] Thus, Moore could not have convinced the court that a *reasonable* patient in his position would forego a life-saving therapy if informed that their physician had some research and economic interests in their excised tissues. The little window of a negligent cause of action that was opened in *Moore* was rudely shut in the later case of *Greenberg v Miami Children's Hospital*,[34] where it was held that a physician-researcher had no duty to disclose their personal and economic interests in the excised tissues of their patients.

Thus, in the area of dead bodies and body parts, an action in negligence offers very little hope of recovery. In relation to the hypothetical situation described above, a negligence action is not a sure peg on which to hoist a claimant's remedy.

The US position is not significantly different from the situation in England and Wales, where it is similarly difficult to see how an action in negligence would assist a claimant in the above hypothetical situation. As in the US, such a claim is hedged with control mechanisms evident in the tort jurisprudence of England and Wales. A quintessential example is *Alcocks v Chief Constable of South Yorkshire Police*,[35] arising from the Hillsborough stadium disaster. In *Alcocks* the House of Lords imposed significant limitations on recovery through policy factors that required the claimants to show a close tie of love and affection with the primary victim (such as exists between a husband and wife, and parent and child). Claimants were also required to establish proximity to the accident in time and space (by being within sight and sound of the accident or coming upon its immediate aftermath, as well as showing that they directly perceived the accident, rather than merely being informed of it by third parties. As each of the claimants lacked one or more of the factors above, their action was dismissed. Of course, primary victims are not subject to *Alcock's* control mechanisms,[36] but that is little consolation to a claimant in the first situation who will irrefutably be a secondary victim.

[31] ibid, 519 (Mosk J dissenting) – this can only be on the basis that Moore's physicians acquired knowledge of the economic value of his tissues, before the actual splenectomy procedure, during the pre-surgery tests; for a similar causation test, see *Cobbs v Grant*, 8 Cal 3d 229 at 245 (1972).

[32] However, note Justice Broussard's suggestion (in concurring and dissenting judgment) that Moore would have succeeded on causation by simply showing that he would not have consented to the unnecessary postoperative procedures had he been informed of the defendants' research and economic interests and motivations: ibid, 500.

[33] *Cobbs v Grant* [1972] 8 Cal 3d 229.

[34] *Greenberg v Miami Children's Hospital Research Institute* 264 F Supp 2d 1064 (SD Fl 2003).

[35] *Alcocks v Chief Constable of South Yorkshire Police* [1992] 1 AC 310 (HL).

[36] *Page v Smith* [1996] AC 155 (HL).

Damages in Negligence

The element of *damage* equally produces its own problems for a claimant involved in litigation over dead bodies or separated body parts. Unfortunately, only damage to the person or their property is recognised in negligence. While this type of damage is easily established in the ordinary negligence case, it assumes a complex dimension in cases relating to dead bodies and excised body parts. Consider *Yearworth v North Bristol Health Care Trust*,[37] in which the claimants had deposited samples of their sperm with the defendant for preservation before undergoing chemotherapy treatment for cancer. Due to the defendant's negligence, the samples were irretrievably damaged, prompting the claimants to sue in negligence (although the Court of Appeal also received submissions on bailment).[38] Of course, the claimants needed to prove damage in order to succeed. Since damage to the sperm samples was not tantamount to damage to the (persons of the) claimants, their only option was to show that it was damage to their property. However, there were two difficulties with this argument – the no-property rule, and the lack of any previous precedent (in the UK) acknowledging the existence of proprietary interests in sperm samples. Fortunately, the Court of Appeal held that the claimants had a proprietary interest in their sperm samples.[39] Beyond negligence and products of the body, it is not clear that *Yearworth* has a broader application.[40] If it is of narrow application *Yearworth's* proprietary framework might not be applicable to the first and third hypothetical examples above.

Intentional Tort Action

The cause of action for intentional infliction of emotional distress is no different. In England and Wales, the status of this tort is even controversial, in contrast to the US where the tort is much more developed. Although *Wilkinson v Downton* was initially thought to have established an intentional tort category in England and Wales,[41] the House of Lords dispelled such assumptions in *Wainwright v Home Office*, where Lord Hoffman firmly observed that *Wilkinson* was rather a case of negligence.[42] As all the categories of the hypothetical example above involve intentional misconduct on the part of the defendant, an unreflecting analyst would think that an intentional tort action would certainly be the route to

[37] *Yearworth v North Bristol Health Care Trust* [2010] QB 1.

[38] L Skene, 'Proprietary Interests in Human Bodily Material: *Yearworth*, Recent Australian Cases on Stored Semen and their Implications' (2012) 20 *Medical Law Review* 227.

[39] Elsewhere the author has provided a justification of the judgment in *Yearworth*: see RN Nwabueze, 'Death of the No-Property Rule for Sperm Samples' (2010) 21 *King's Law Journal* 561.

[40] Quigley was optimistic: M Quigley, 'Property: The Future of Human Tissue?' (2009) 17 *Medical Law Review* 457. For a less optimistic view, see RN Nwabueze, 'Death of the No-Property Rule for Sperm Samples', above n 39.

[41] *Wilkinson v Downton* [1897] 2 QB 57.

[42] *Wainwright v Home Office* [2004] 2 AC 406.

take; such reasoning would be good common sense, but would bear no relation to reality.

In the US, there are three elements of this tort: (1) extreme and outrageous conduct with the intention of causing, or reckless disregard of the probability of causing, emotional distress; (2) the claimant suffered severe or extreme emotional distress; and (3) the defendant's outrageous conduct caused the claimant's emotional distress.[43] This tort was also alleged in *Christensen*. Interestingly, the majority observed that the relevant question was not whether the defendants' outrageous misconduct was intentional, but rather, whether the defendants' misconduct was directed at the claimants. In other words, was it the intention of the defendants to inflict emotional distress on the claimants? Accordingly, Baxter J observed that 'it is not enough that the conduct be intentional and outrageous. It must be conduct directed at the plaintiff, or occur in the presence of a plaintiff of whom the defendant is aware'.[44] Put in this way, the question easily resolved itself; the claimants lost on this claim because the intention of the defendants was simply to make monetary profits. The only way for the claimants to succeed was to prove recklessness on the part of the defendants. However, this could only have been done by establishing the claimants' presence at the scene of the misconduct, something not practically possible in view of the facts. In this way, the presence requirement underpinning the bystander's rule in negligence resurfaces in an intentional tort action. Returning to the hypothetical example above, this obstacle is surely insurmountable because the interferences therein are carried out either for commercial gain or in pursuit of academic research; in addition, the interferences occurred surreptitiously. Furthermore, the problem is tellingly exacerbated for the second hypothetical scenario above (unauthorised use of blood sample).[45] For instance, an action in battery, privacy or contract against the unauthorised test on the blood sample might fail (for reasons highlighted below). Negligence would have been the next best claim, but is not possible here since the interference was intentional rather than negligent, and negligence does not redress mere mental distress.

Battery

Battery safeguards a claimant's right to their bodily integrity, thus indirectly protecting their autonomy.[46] As can be surmised, battery protects the interests of living human beings, and not of dead bodies or separated body parts. Since the dead have no interest in their physical integrity, a battery action cannot be brought against the mutilation of a cadaver. Thus, the first hypothetical scenario is not remediable under this action. Neither can an action in battery be brought over a

[43] *Davidson v City of Westminster* [1982] 32 Cal 3d 197 at 209.

[44] *Christensen*, above n 23 at 903.

[45] This might warrant a criminal prosecution under the Human Tissue Act 2004, s 45, as well as a claim under the Data Protection Act 1998.

[46] Marjorie Shultz, 'From Informed Consent to Patient's Choice: A New Protected Interest' (1985) 95 *Yale Law Journal* 219.

separated part of the body, as in the second and third hypothetical scenarios above.[47] The separated bodily tissues in those examples were obtained with consent, and thus the grievance can only be directed against the test itself and the relevant invention. This means that a battery action does not adequately protect the interests of tissue sources.

Privacy and Human Rights

Privacy is not an independent tort in England and Wales but, nevertheless, it is vindicated by the cause of action for breach of confidence which,[48] in turn, has been invigorated by the principles underpinning the protection of private and family life under Article 8 of the European Convention for the Protection of Human Rights.[49] In contrast, the tort of privacy is more fully developed in the US. Under the analytical framework developed by Prosser and Keeton, the tort of privacy falls into four distinct categories: (1) intrusion upon seclusion; (2) appropriation of name and likeness; (3) public disclosure of private facts; and (4) putting a claimant in a false light.[50] Obviously, these categories do not capture many circumstances involving an unauthorised interference with a cadaver or a separated body part. For example, it has been held in the US that the tort of privacy has no application to allegations concerning the mistreatment of a dead body,[51] or to an unauthorised test on blood samples taken from a dead body.[52]

In terms of human rights, privacy might not be a significant remedy in the contexts of the hypothetical example above. First, the right of privacy dies with the person;[53] secondly, privacy protects relationships among the living rather than the dead.[54] Consequently, no action in privacy can be brought over the interference in the first hypothetical scenario above. Nonetheless, under Article 8 of the convention, there are a few circumstances in which the living might assert certain privacy interests in relation to a corpse, such as the right of a bereaved to attend the funeral of a deceased family member,[55] and the right to mourn the death of a close relative.[56] Furthermore, a person's wishes regarding their own burial or cremation might not be disregarded under article 8 of the convention.[57]

[47] *Doe v Dyer-Goode*, 389 Pa Super 151 (Pennsylvania Sup Ct 1989); *Hecht v Kaplan*, 221 AD2d 100 (Sup Ct New York 1996).

[48] *Coco v AN Clark (Engineers) Ltd* [1969] RPC 41.

[49] *Campbell v MGN Ltd* [2004] 2 AC 457 (HL).

[50] WP Keeton et al, *Prosser and Keeton on Torts*, 5th edn (St Paul, MN, West Publishing Co, 1988) 849–68.

[51] *Armstrong v H & C Communications*, 575 So 2d 280 (Dist Ct App 1991); *Waters v Fleetwood*, 212 Ga 161 (1956).

[52] *Hubenschmidt v Shears*, 270 NW 2d 2 (Sup Ct Mich, 1978).

[53] *Silkwood v Kerr-McGee Corporation*, 637 F 2d 743 (1980).

[54] *Jones v United Kingdom*, App no 42639/04 (ECtHR, 13 September 2005).

[55] ibid.

[56] For a similar view, see Harris, 'Law and Regulation of Retained Organs: The Ethical Issues', above n 6.

[57] *Burrows v HM Coroner for Preston* [2008] EWHC 1387; *R (Ghai) v Newcastle City Council* [2010] 3 WLR 737 (Cranston J).

The protection of privacy is, however, more relevant to the second category of the hypothetical situation (unauthorised test of blood). A quintessential example is the Icelandic Supreme Court case of *Ragnhilder Gudmundsdóttir v The State of Iceland*.[58] In that case, it was held that a daughter could prevent the transfer of the body parts of her deceased father to an Icelandic biobank because a genetic analysis of the cadaveric parts might disclose private and intimate information concerning the daughter, in violation of her constitutionally protected privacy interests. Similarly, in *Norman-Bloodsaw v Lawrence Berkeley Laboratory*,[59] an employer collected their employees' blood and urine samples for a stipulated purpose but, contrary to the employees' consent, the employer tested the samples for sickle cell anaemia and syphilis. The Ninth Circuit of the US Court of Appeals held that the unapproved test was a violation of the employees' privacy. So too was the situation in *Doe v High-Tech Institute, Inc*,[60] where a student consented to his school testing his blood sample for rubella but, contrary to consent, the school tested the sample for human immunodeficiency virus. It was held that the unauthorised test was a violation of the student's privacy interest in his blood sample, and that the 'additional unauthorized test . . . can be sufficient to state a claim for relief for intrusion upon seclusion'.[61]

The types of cases described above apply where the genetic analysis of a biological sample was intended to obtain some private information about the claimant, hence their relevance to the second hypothetical scenario. The law of privacy might not be very helpful to a claimant outside this type of genetic context.

Unjust Enrichment

Through restitution, the law of unjust enrichment reverses enrichment obtained by a defendant at the expense of the claimant. Birks observed that the law of unjust enrichment is analogical to situations where payment is made for a non-existent debt.[62] As a legal category, unjust enrichment trenches on monetary benefits,[63] which makes its application to matters over dead bodies and body parts counterintuitive.[64] A claim in unjust enrichment must establish that: (1) the defendant was enriched; (2) the enrichment was at the expense of the claimant; and (3) it is unjust for the defendant to retain the benefit.[65] A restitutionary claim over an interference with a cadaver or excised body parts must also establish those elements. *Moore v Regents of the University of California*-type of cases (exemplified by the third hypothetical scenario) attracts the application of unjust enrichment

[58] *Ragnhilder Gudmundsdóttir v The State of Iceland* No 151/2003 (Sup Ct 2003).
[59] *Norman-Bloodsaw v Lawrence Berkeley Laboratory*, 135 F 3d 1260 (9th Cir 1998).
[60] *Doe v High-Tech Institute, Inc*, 972 P 2d 1060 (1998).
[61] ibid, 1064; *US v Comprehensive Drug Testing, Inc* 513 F 3d 1085 (9th Cir 2008).
[62] P Birks, *Unjust Enrichment*, 2nd edn (Oxford, Oxford University Press, 2005) 3.
[63] S Stoljar, 'Unjust Enrichment and Unjust Sacrifice' (1987) *Modern Law Review* 603 at 606.
[64] Especially in the contexts of the first and second hypothetical scenarios described.
[65] Birks, *Unjust Enrichment*, above n 62 at 39.

theory of liability.[66] It is significant that Moore's tissues had been surreptitiously harvested by his physicians, and were applied in commercially lucrative and innovative research. Interestingly, Moore's claim in unjust enrichment was not considered by all the courts that heard the matter as they focused on the claim for conversion and breach of informed consent. In contrast, an unjust enrichment claim was considered in *Greenberg v Miami Children's Hospital*,[67] a case involving research collaboration between the defendant-scientists and the claimants (parents of children suffering from Canavan disease and charitable organisations that fund research on Canavan disease). The collaboration was fruitful, leading to the identification, isolation and patenting of the Canavan gene, as well as the development of a genetic test for diagnosing the abnormality. However, the defendants' commercialisation of the fruits of the research was contrary to the expectations of the claimants. Worse still, the claimants were denied a share in the profits from the patented results of the research. Moreno J held that the claimants had stated a sufficient cause of action in unjust enrichment. Therefore, we can see that unjust enrichment might be appropriate for cases within the last hypothetical scenario.

An action in unjust enrichment is not applicable to the types of cases characterised by the first and second hypothetical scenarios because the cases lack the monetary character that triggers an unjust enrichment action.[68] Moreover, the relevant enrichment must be 'at the expense' of the claimant, meaning subtracted from the claimant, in the sense that it came directly from them. A broader conception of that phrase is not relevant to the action for unjust enrichment.[69] This difficulty is particularly acute for cases that come within the first hypothetical scenario above. For instance, even if a defendant's interference with a dead body engendered some monetary benefits, the claimant cannot say that the 'enrichment' was at their expense; rather, it was subtracted from the corpse.

Contractual Claims

Interferences with a dead body or an excised body part might occur within the context of a contractual relationship. For instance, the mistreatment of dead bodies in *Christensen* arose in the course of providing some mortuary services under a funeral contract. Where such a contract is breached by an undertaker-defendant, a bereaved claimant who contracted for the services of the undertaker should be able to claim some damages. In *Christensen*, the majority even held that close relatives of the deceased who were not contracting parties themselves were entitled to

[66] *Moore v Regents of the University of California* 793 P 2d 479 (1990).

[67] *Greenberg v Miami Children's Hospital Research Institute* 264 F Supp 2d 1064 (SD Fl 2003).

[68] J Beatson, *The Use and Abuse of Unjust Enrichment* (Oxford, Clarendon Press, 1991) at 29–32. But it has been argued that 'enrichment' should include non-monetary benefits, such as receipt of services; see G Virgo, *The Principles of the Law of Restitution*, 2nd edn (Oxford, Oxford University Press, 2006) at 62–64; also, *Rowe v Vale of White Horse DC* [2003] EWJC 388; *McDonald v Coys of Kesington* [2004] 1 WLR 2775.

[69] Birks, *Unjust Enrichment*, above n 62 at 74.

sue on the funeral contract because it was made for their benefit. Usually, the remedy for a breach of contract is the award of compensatory damages to a wronged claimant, that is, compensation sufficient to bring the claimant to the position they were in before the breach. Thus, damages awarded are restricted to losses arising directly from the breach of contract. Generally, damages are not awarded for mental or emotional distress experienced in connection with the breach of a contract. Paradoxically, the breach of a contract for the provision of funeral services is only likely to give rise to emotional distress.[70] Thus, a strict application of the general rule would leave many claimants without a remedy.

The law adopts a sensitive and unique approach to the interpretation of funeral contracts because such contracts are usually concluded at a time when the bereaved-claimant is most vulnerable.[71] In consideration of this vulnerability, the law allows a claimant to recover for emotional distress arising from the breach of a funeral contract. The principle was given the clearest expression in *Lamm v Shingleton*:

> The tenderest feelings of the human heart center around the remains of the dead. When the defendants contracted with plaintiff to inter the body of her deceased husband in a workmanlike manner they did so with the knowledge that she was the widow and would naturally and probably suffer mental anguish if they failed to fulfil their contractual obligation in the manner here charged. The contract was predominantly personal in nature and no substantial pecuniary loss would follow its breach. Her mental concern, her sensibilities, and her solicitude were the prime considerations for the contract, and the contract itself was such as to put the defendants on notice that a failure on their part to inter the body properly would probably produce mental suffering on her part. It cannot be said, therefore, that such damages were not within the contemplation of the parties at the time the contract was made.[72]

The role of contract law is more contestable in the types of cases illustrated by the second and third hypothetical scenarios above. Admittedly, those scenarios (involving, respectively an unauthorised test and tissue obtained in the course of a surgical procedure) are rooted in contract, at least initially. Interestingly, in *Grimes v Kennedy Krieger Institute*,[73] the Maryland Court of Appeals has confirmed that the physician–researcher–patient relationship (as in the two categories above) is grounded in contract, as well as in tort. However, a claimant alleging the use of their blood sample for an unauthorised test must establish that an express or implied term of the contract prohibited the test. Such express terms are not usually embodied in standard form contracts for diagnostic tests on blood samples, and it is unlikely that physician-researchers will accede to such express terms. Consequently, a claimant is most unlikely to convince an adjudicator that such terms should be implied in the contract for the provision of diagnostic

[70] J Leavitt, 'The Funeral Director's Liability for Mental Anguish' (1964) 15 *Hastings Law Journal* 464.

[71] Generally, *Vigers v Cook* [1919] 2 KB 475.

[72] *Lamm v Shingleton*, 55 SE 2d 810 at 813 (1949).

[73] *Grimes v Kennedy Krieger Institute*, 782 A2d 807 (Md Ct App 2001). B Dickens, 'Contractual Aspects of Human Medical Experimentation' (1975) 25 *University of Toronto Law Journal* 406.

services; the same argument applies to any contract alleged in relation to the invention in the last category of the hypothetical situation above.

Proprietary Claims

A proprietary claim relatively easily solves most of the problems in the hypothetical example above.[74] Unlike causes of action, a proprietary interest gives a tissue source a continuing control over the separated parts of their body.[75] Thus, a claimant in the second hypothetical scenario can bring an action in conversion for the unapproved test on their blood sample. Surely, conversion applies when property given for a particular purpose is used for another purpose.[76] Similarly, the recognition of some proprietary interests in dead bodies and body parts would enable a claimant to succeed in cases analogical to the first and third categories of the hypothetical example above, because the interferences therein would amount to a conversion of property. Why is it that despite this utility of the proprietary framework, there has been a marked reluctance to apply property concepts to the human body and excised body parts?

Some suggestions might be made. First, the anachronistic no-property rule in corpses and body parts has bedevilled this area of law for over 200 years. While the rule has an uncertain origin,[77] its authority has been confirmed by the Court of Appeal in England and Wales.[78] Second, it is believed that the human body and its parts are sacrosanct and, thus, should not be degraded with the application of property concepts, something that is best reserved for application to *things*. In *Moore*, Arabian J gave acute expression to this moral concern when he observed that Moore had entreated the court to 'regard the human vessel – the single most venerated and protected subject in any civilized society – as equal with the basest commercial commodity. He urges us to commingle the sacred with the profane.'[79] Third, and following from this, there is the perception that to treat the human body as a *thing*, an object of property, is to render it alienable and commercially transferable.[80] Fourth, the courts in England and Wales conceive their role as the declaration of pre-existing property rights, and not that of creating new property rights where none existed in the past, something that only the legislature can do.[81]

[74] See, generally, R Hardcastle, *Law and the Human Body: Property Rights, Ownership and Control* (Oxford, Hart Publishing, 2007); RN Nwabueze, *Biotechnology and the Challenge of Property: Property Rights in Dead Bodies, Body Parts and Genetic Information* (Aldershot, Ashgate Publishing, 2007).

[75] GT Laurie, *Genetic Privacy: A Challenge to Medico-Legal Norms* (Cambridge, Cambridge University Press, 2002) 316.

[76] *All Cargo Transport, Inc v Florida East Coast Railway Co*, 355 So 2d 178 (Fla 3d DCA, 1987).

[77] PDG Skegg, 'Human Corpses, Medical Specimens and the Law of Property' (1975) 4 *Anglo-American Law Review* 412; P Matthews, 'Whose Body? People as Property' (1983) 36 *Current Legal Problems* 193.

[78] *R v Kelly* [1998] 3 All ER 741.

[79] *Moore v Regents of the University of California*, 793 P 2d 479 at 497 (1990).

[80] L Skene, 'Arguments Against People Legally "Owning" Their Bodies, Body Parts and Tissue' (2002) 2 *Macquarie Law Journal* 165.

[81] C Rotherham, *Proprietary Remedies in Context* (Oxford, Hart Publishing, 2002) 33–39.

As the common law does not generally recognise a proprietary interest in cadavers and excised body parts, the courts are understandably reluctant to confer new proprietary status on such biological materials.[82] Fifth, it has been argued that the human genetic materials are generally shared by all humanity. Thus, it is wrong for an individual to claim any part of the human body as their property. Herring and Chau captured this perspective in their argument that human bodies are interconnected and interdependent and, thus, should not be subject to proprietary claims.[83] Panelli J expressed a similar sentiment in *Moore* when he disavowed a conversion claim on the ground that it 'include[ed] the genetic code for chemicals that regulate the functions of every human being's immune system'.[84]

While this debate merits further attention, some of the objections are arguably inattentive to the theoretical understanding of property and its implication for dead bodies and excised body parts. Although a layperson may understand property as a *thing*,[85] the theoretical conception of property projects it as *a bundle of rights* that creates a relation between persons.[86] Metaphorically, property can be seen as a bundle of sticks, with each stick in the bundle representing a proprietary interest and a proprietary relation; the greatest aggregation of such sticks amounts to ownership. Thus, Wilson observed that *ownership* is 'the largest bundle that any one person can have at any time as regards one thing, according to the rules of the particular legal system'.[87] Accordingly, *property* and *ownership* are two interrelated but distinct concepts. While ownership is made up of congeries of rights in the bundle, an aggregation or permutations of certain sticks in the bundle as determined by a particular legal system, a phenomenon that Waldron identified as the *conception* of property,[88] property could be constituted by a single stick in the bundle of rights. Such a stick gives rise to a protectable proprietary interest.

Furthermore, a single stick of proprietary interest does not need to be coextensive with the incident of alienation, which is commonly (although mistakenly) associated with the existence of a proprietary interest. This means that I can have a recognised proprietary interest in the corpse of my relative or in the separated part of my body without having, at the same time, the incident (or stick) of alienation which would entitle me to alienate, sell, transfer for value, or otherwise commercialise the corpse or my excised body part. Thus, Justice Arabian's concurring judgment in *Moore* missed this character of proprietary interests by misconceiving Moore's claim in conversion as necessarily entailing the 'recogni[tion] and enforce[ment of] a right to sell one's own body tissues for profit',[89] and to

[82] This reluctance was evident in *Ainsworth v National Provincial Bank* [1965] AC 1175, where the House of Lords refused to recognise a new sort of deserted wife's equity.

[83] J Herring and P Chau, 'My Body, Your Body, Our Body' (2007) 15 *Medical Law Review* 34.

[84] *Moore v Regents of the University of California*, 793 P 2d 479 at 488 (1990).

[85] KJ Vandevelde, 'The New Property of the Nineteenth Century: The Development of the Modern Concept of Property' (1980) 29 *Buffalo Law Review* 325.

[86] SR Munzer, *A Theory of Property* (Cambridge, Cambridge University Press, 1990) 23.

[87] GP Wilson, 'Jurisprudence and the Discussion of Ownership' (1957) *Cambridge Law Journal* 216 at 222.

[88] J Waldron, *The Right to Private Property* (Oxford, Oxford University Press, 1988) at 28.

[89] *Moore v Regents of the University of California*, 793 P 2d 47 at 497 (1990).

permit 'a marketplace in human body parts'.[90] This type of reasoning exaggerates and universalises the stick of alienation; it attributes to alienation a conceptually imperialistic role in the definition of property. More perceptively, Justice Broussard's concurring and dissenting judgment acknowledged that Moore's right to 'determine, prior to the removal of his body parts, how those parts would be used after removal' was a proprietary interest,[91] despite the alleged 'right of control' not being necessarily grounded in commerciality or alienability.

Honoré has contributed much to property scholarship by developing and analysing 11 incidents of ownership.[92] As the title of his seminal essay suggests, Honoré was concerned about *ownership* rather than *property*; thus, he focused on the aggregations of property interests that can constitute ownership. Consequently, Honoré did not examine the question of whether or not a single incident of ownership could constitute a protectable proprietary interest.[93] Similarly, Gray's seminal essay was concerned about ownership rather than property.[94] Gray hypothesised that the most definitive character of ownership is *excludability*, that is, the owner's right to exclude others. Excludability was thus the irreducible minimum content of ownership. Even then, Katz has doubted the overriding and definitive status attributed to *exclusion* (Gray's excludability) in the definition of ownership, suggesting that the relevant element is *exclusivity*, an owner's supreme position and agenda-setting authority with respect to property.[95] The framework of exclusivity allows owners to share a resource with others.

Hohfeld developed an analytical scheme that is more germane to the conceptualisation of *property*.[96] Hohfeld observed that when *property* is said to exist in X, it is technically an assertion of eight jural relations among persons with respect to X. Hohfeld delineated four pairs of the jural relations as elements and correlatives:

Elements	**Correlatives**
Claim-right	Duty
Privilege (liberty)	No-right
Power	Liability
Immunity	Disability

The Hohfeldian framework above underscores not only the multiplicity of proprietary interests, but also the potentially infinite range of proprietary relations

[90] ibid, 498.

[91] ibid, 501.

[92] AM Honoré, 'Ownership' in AG Guest (ed), *Oxford Essays in Jurisprudence* (Oxford, Oxford University Press, 1961) 107–47.

[93] For a useful application of Honoré's incidents of ownership to body parts, see I Goold, 'Sounds Suspiciously Like Property Treatment: Does Human Tissue Fit Within the Common Law Concept of Property?' (2005) 7 *University of Technology Sydney Law Review* 62–85; M Quigley, 'Property and the Body: Applying Honoré' (2007) 33 *Journal of Medical Ethics* 631.

[94] K Gray, 'Property in the Thin Air' (1991) 50 *Cambridge Law Journal* 252.

[95] L Katz, 'Exclusion and Exclusivity in Property Law' (2008) 58 *University of Toronto Law Journal* 275.

[96] WN Hohfeld, 'Some Fundamental Legal Conceptions as Applied in Judicial Reasoning' (1911) 23 *Yale Law Journal* 16; WN Hohfeld, 'Some Fundamental Legal Conceptions as Applied in Judicial Reasoning' (1917) 26 *Yale Law Journal* 710.

and, more importantly, the potential for a single pair of jural relations to create a protectable proprietary relation. While, for example, C might have a *claim-right* in X which imposes a *duty* on D with respect to X; a *power* over X might inhere in another person, Y, thereby creating *liability* in yet another person, Z. Legal *power* is the ability to alter a person's own legal position or that of another. *Liability*, on the other hand, is a person's susceptibility to having their legal position altered.[97] Thus, while the claim-right over X belongs to C, Y might be given a power over X which enables Y to alter their legal position by, for instance, transferring X to him or herself or to Z who, by receiving X, has become liable to having their status altered, by, for instance, becoming a new property owner. As such, the bundle of rights picture of property is conceptually different from the Blackstonian definition of property as an absolute right over a physical thing.[98] Under the Hohfeldian framework, therefore, an interest in a relative's corpse or in the excised part of a person's body could qualify as a protectable proprietary interest. As highlighted above, it is immaterial that such an interest does not approximate to the level which a given legal system would recognise as ownership. Thus, however correct he might be as regards ownership, Panelli J was certainly inaccurate as regards property when he observed in *Moore* that the 'statute eliminates so many of the rights ordinarily attached to property that one cannot simply assume that what is left amounts to "property" or "ownership" for purposes of conversion'.[99] Apart from eliding the two concepts of ownership and property, Panelli J's observation mistakenly assumes that the existence of *property* requires some irreducible minimum content of rights or interests.

Interestingly, Wall has argued that to qualify as *property* it is not enough that an interest should be found within an ownership spectrum.[100] In addition, he argued, the interest must be capable of protection with a property rule; thus, ownership is a necessary but insufficient condition of property. Wall deployed the analytical framework developed by Calabresi and Melamed (otherwise known as trespassory rules), in which the authors analysed the different regimes that are available for the protection of an entitlement.[101] Calabresi and Melamed suggested that an entitlement is protected by property rules if it can only be transferred voluntarily, and at a subjectively determined value. On the other hand, liability rules protect an entitlement that could be taken from the owner without their consent, subject to the payment of an objectively determined compensation. Rules of inalienability protect an entitlement to which transfer is prohibited by the state, or where the state imposes some conditions precedent to the transfer of such entitlements. Accordingly, Wall argued that since current interests recognised over dead bodies and excised body parts are more commonly protected by liability rules, such

[97] Munzer, *A Theory of Property*, above n 86 at 18.

[98] W Blackstone, *Commentaries on the Laws of England*, vol 2 (London, A Strahan, 1809).

[99] *Moore v Regents of the University of California*, 793 P 2d 479 at 492 (1990).

[100] J Wall, 'The Legal Status of Body Parts: A Framework' (2011) 31 *Oxford Journal of Legal Studies* 783.

[101] G Calabresi and AD Melamed, 'Property Rules, Liability Rules, and Inalienability: One View of the Cathedral' (1972) 85 *Harvard Law Review* 1093.

interests should not be regarded as proprietary in nature. However, Wall cannot be suggesting that X ceases to be your property simply because a new legislation prohibits the alienation thereof, thereby protecting your interest in X with rules of inalienability (rather than property rules); that sort of outcome is surely contrary to the way property is understood in practice, and is inconsistent with the analysis above.

Arguably, Wall misconceived the remedial nature of trespassory rules by projecting them as part of the calculus for the conceptualisation of property. In other words, trespassory rules are remedial in nature, and are not part of the meaning of property. As such, trespassory rules play a significant role in selecting the remedial category that would govern a case. Harris captured this role of trespassory rules in his insightful observation that trespassory rules mean 'any social rules' by which entitlements in the ownership spectrum are protected.[102] Harris even went further to highlight the extensiveness of such rules, by including criminal law protections within their remit. Obviously, such criminal protections go beyond the three-dimensional trespassory rules analysed by Calabresi and Melamed, and could hardly be said to be part of the *meaning* of property. It is suggested that trespassory rules have some significant connection with the institution of property but only in the remedial role highlighted above. Arguably, Calabresi and Melamed equally deployed trespassory rules as an analytical remedial framework. Note that the operationalisation of trespassory rules involves a consideration of important policy factors. Thus, Calabresi and Melamed suggested that liability rules are preferable to property rules where market valuation of an entitlement is deemed inefficient.[103]

All of this implies that the recognition of a proprietary interest in a corpse or excised body part does not inexorably yield the protection of a property rule. Put differently, it is one thing to recognise the existence of a legally protectable proprietary interest over the human body or excised parts of the human body, but another thing to determine whether an interference with that interest should be remedied on the basis of a property rule, a liability rule or a rule of inalienability; that level of analysis depends on a host of relevant policy factors.[104] Thus there is no inevitability in the deployment of a property remedy over interferences with recognised legal interests in cadavers and separated body parts.

Conclusion

The analysis above is not so much a paean for the proprietary remedial framework as it is for a multidimensional remedial approach involving the integration

[102] JW Harris, 'Who Owns My Body' (1996) 16 *Oxford Journal of Legal Studies* 55 at 59.

[103] Calabresi and Melamed, 'Property Rules, Liability Rules, and Inalienability: One View of the Cathedral', above n 101 at 1110.

[104] For examples of such factors, see B Bjökman and SO Hansson, 'Bodily Rights and Property Rights' (2006) 32 *Journal of Medical Ethics* 209.

of a proprietary framework into the remedial armamentarium applicable to interferences with cadavers and excised body parts. Such an approach would be vastly superior to the current system that generally excludes a remedial proprietary framework in relation to cadavers and excised body parts. As we have seen, the recognition of a proprietary interest in cadavers and body parts does not necessarily entail an interference with the interest being remedied on the basis of a property rule; that stage of litigation involves important policy considerations which, in the end, might lean in favour of a liability rule rather than a property rule.

Pressure to apply a proprietary framework to cadavers and excised body parts is usually avoided in the mistaken belief and assurance that consent-oriented remedies will adequately do the job. But the analysis of negligence, battery and intentional tort above shows that such consent-oriented approaches often turn out to be illusory. This adds to the failure of the Human Tissue Act 2004 to provide civil remedies for breach of its consent provision. As Justice Mosk opined in his dissenting judgment in *Moore*, the gaps in the law of negligence in relation to excised body parts are such that the 'remedy is largely illusory',[105] and, as a potential deterrence to interferences with cadavers and excised body parts, the law of negligence is 'largely a paper tiger'.[106] Similar limitations were highlighted above in relation to other private law causes of action. However, the idea is not to dismiss or undermine the importance of non-proprietary causes of action, but to argue that a proprietary framework should be used in conjunction with other private law remedies in order to render the claim of a tissue source more efficacious.

[105] *Moore v Regents of the University of California*, 793 P 2d 479 at 519 (1990).
[106] ibid, 520.

11

Alternatives to a Corporate Commons: Biobanking, Genetics and Property in the Body

DONNA DICKENSON

Introduction

In this chapter I argue that the old common law concept of the commons can make a major contribution to how we regulate human tissue and genetic information in the twenty-first century. But if we want to use this concept, we will have to act fast, because private corporate interests have already realised the relevance of the commons for holdings in human tissue and genetic information. Instead of a commonly created and commonly held resource, however, they have sought to create one derived from many persons' mutual labour but owned privately: what I call, with deliberate irony, a 'corporate commons'. Unlike the traditional commons, this new form of the commons does not allow specified rights of access and usufruct to those whose labour has gone to establish and maintain it. (Indeed, contributors to one emblematic 'corporate commons' have actually paid to contribute.) This new 'corporate commons' is also different from an 'anticommons', in which multiple owners hold the effective rights of exclusion in a scarce resource';[1] in the case of the corporate commons, a single owner holds monopoly rights.

Whether the notion of the commons could apply to human tissue and genetic information has been debated since Howard Hiatt published 'Protecting the medical commons' in 1975 (although his discussion was mainly confined to organs).[2] The original vision of property in the human genome was communitarian, envisioning it as the common property of humanity in the spirit of the 1997 UNESCO

[1] MA Heller, 'The Tragedy of the Anticommons: Property in the Transition from Marx to Markets' (1998) 111 *Harvard Law Review* 621, 668.

[2] H Hiatt, 'Protecting the Medical Commons: Who is Responsible?' (1975) 293 *New England Journal of Medicine* 235. Subsequent discussion includes: P Ossorio, 'Common-Heritage Arguments against Patenting Human DNA' in A Chapman (ed), *Perspectives on Gene Patenting: Religion, Science and Industry in Dialogue* (Washington DC, American Academy for the Advancement of Science, 1997) 89–108; RS Eisenberg, 'How Can You Patent Genes?' (2002) 2 *American Journal of Bioethics* 3; H Thorsteindottir et al, 'Commentary: Genomics – A Global Public Good?' (2003) 363 *Lancet* 9361; R Mitchell, 'Registered Genes: Patents and Biocirculation', paper presented at the London School of Economics and Political Science, BIOS Centre, September 2003; Y Joly, 'Open Source Approaches to Biotechnology: Utopia Revisited' (2007) 57 *Maine Law Review* 385.

Declaration.[3] Likewise, the 'Bermuda statement' of 1996 declared that: 'All human genome sequence information from a publicly funded project should be available in the public domain'.[4] Many academic analysts have argued for a property regime recognising the genome as a whole as common property not subject to patents (although some have distinguished between the entire genome and individual genes).[5] Governance of the commons has also received substantial attention and analysis in terms of common property in land and the environment.[6]

James Harris distinguishes between the interpretation of common property as 'no property' and the traditional concept of the commons in English law, referring to land which is subject to rights of common for a defined class of persons.[7] A commons is not a cooperative, which is owned mutually. In the traditional concept of the commons there is more typically a single owner of the land, which in modern terms often translates to a public authority vested with a quasi-ownership interest, subject to certain rights of public access. This interpretation is also similar to Carol Rose's notion of 'inherently public property', all assets to which there is a public right of access regardless of whether formal ownership is vested in a public agency or private hands.[8] Essentially, I am advocating a similar right of public access to the inherently public property of the human genome, with strictly limited rights of exclusion for the formal owner – so that the resource is open for widespread use, substantially free of patent or licensing restrictions.

The political–theoretical basis of the argument against restrictive genetic patenting is convincingly laid out by Seana Valentine Shiffrin, who reverses the usual direction of a Lockean argument by requiring justification for the trespass on the commons entailed by any act of appropriation. With tangible property, she argues, the justification is that unless an individual appropriates an item, for example by eating an apple, the object cannot be enjoyed, as God willed it should

[3] UNESCO Universal Declaration on the Human Genome and Human Rights (1997) art 1: 'The human genome underlines the fundamental unity of all members of the human family, as well as the recognition of their inherent dignity and diversity. In a symbolic sense, it is the heritage of humanity ... [and] in its natural state, shall not give rise to financial gain.'

[4] First International Strategy Meeting on Human Genome Sequencing, Bermuda, February 1996, www.wellcome.ac.uk/About-us/Policy/Policy-and-position-statements/WTD002751.htm. These principles were agreed by officers from, and scientists supported by, the Wellcome Trust, the UK Medical Research Council, the National Institutes of Health National Center for Human Genome Research Institute, the US and UK Departments of Energy, the German Human Genome Programme, the European Commission, the Human Genome Organization and the Human Genome Project of Japan.

[5] S Munzer, 'Property, Patents and Genetic Material' in J Burley and J Harris (eds), *A Companion to Genethics* (Oxford, Blackwell, 2002) 438–54.

[6] For example, E Ostrom, *Governing the Commons: The Evolution of Institutions for Collective Action* (Cambridge, Cambridge University Press, 1990); H Daly and J Cobb Jr, *For the Common Good: Redirecting the Economy Toward Community, the Environment, and a Sustainable Future* (Boston, Beacon Press, 1989); H Dagan and MA Heller, 'The Liberal Commons', ch 8 in H Dagan, *Property: Values and Institutions* (New York, Oxford University Press, 2011). Although Dagan and Heller note briefly at the start of their chapter that biomedical research is one of several areas which could benefit from their analysis of the commons, the rest of their chapter largely concerns land.

[7] JW Harris, *Property and Justice* (Oxford, Clarendon Press, 1996) 109.

[8] CM Rose, 'The Comedy of the Commons: Custom, Commerce, and Inherently Public Property' (1986) 53 *University of Chicago Law Review* 711.

be. But with intellectual property there is no need for individual appropriation; intellectual advancement is actually best served by leaving intellectual property as a commons, not by subjecting it to patenting.[9] The practical ramifications of this argument were played out in the Supreme Court decision in the *Myriad Genetics* case, where plaintiffs successfully argued that good clinical care and research progress depended on overturning restrictive genetic patents. [10]

However, elsewhere in biomedicine, particularly in the rapid establishment of private property-holding in genetic biobanks and the increased publicity surrounding personalised medicine based on individual genetic profiles,[11] an individualised and privatised model is becoming predominant, even in publicly funded banks.[12] Yet new alternatives to that model also vie for position, for example the notion of the scientific commons or the charitable trust for biobanks. The latter model, originally developed by academics, has already been consciously adopted by a biobank, demonstrating that such proposals are eminently practical. We need to build further on those alternatives, rather than simply accept the 'new enclosures' embodied in the corporate commons. I begin with a case study illustrating just such a puzzlingly private commons.

The Corporate Commons: A Case Example

The direct-to-consumer genetic testing firm 23andMe, established to provide customers with genetic profiles suggesting their statistical propensity to a limited number of illnesses, also set up a research arm called 23andWe. When they logged in to their accounts after sending their tissue (spit) sample and receiving their results, customers were invited to fill out online surveys about their lifestyle, family background and health, adding epidemiological value to the genetic data and creating a sizeable biobank.[13] About 60 per cent of 23andMe customers agreed to

[9] SV Shiffrin, 'Lockean Arguments for Private Intellectual Property' in S Munzer (ed), *New Essays in the Legal and Political Theory of Property* (Cambridge, Cambridge University Press, 2001) 139–67.

[10] *Association for Molecular Pathology et al v Myriad Genetics et al* (decided 13 June 2013) 569 US 12–398.

[11] D Dickenson, *Me Medicine vs. We Medicine: Reclaiming Biotechnology for the Common Good* (New York, Columbia University Press, 2013). Contrary to the very vocal claims of its proponents, however, the personalised approach has not yet delivered a paradigm shift in medicine. A 2012 Harris poll of 2,760 US patients and physicians found that doctors had recommended personal genetics tests for only 4 per cent of patients. See UnitedHealth Center for Health Reform and Modernization, 'Personalized Medicine: Trends and Prospects for the New Science of Genetic Testing and Molecular Diagnosis' Working Paper 7 (March 2012).

[12] Similarly, public umbilical cord blood banks, which receive their samples from women who have donated altruistically, are now engaging in a commodified international trade in cord blood units, resulting in what has been called 'the economisation of life'. See N Brown, L Machin and D McLeod, 'The Immunitary Bioeconomy: The Economisation of Life in the International Cord Blood Market' (2011) 30 *Social Science and Medicine* 1.

[13] The firm's privacy statement stipulates that '23andWe Research only uses Genetic and Self-Reported Information from users who have given consent according to the applicable Consent

provide this information, resulting in a database that numbered over 100,000 individuals by June 2011 . The company's target is 500,000, equivalent to the size of UK Biobank. Given that the US decided not to create a national biobank like the one in the UK because of the high cost of setting it up – estimated at about a billion dollars – 23andMe regarded its data biobank as saving the firm an outlay of a similar magnitude and as providing a resource of at least equivalent value.[14] 'The long game here is not to make money selling kits, although the kits are essential to get the base level data,' according to 23andMe board member Patrick Chung. 'Once you have the data, [23andMe] does actually become the Google of personalized health care.'

True, this business strategy was thrown into doubt when in November 2013 the US Food and Drug Administration ordered the company to stop marketing its retail genetic testing kits. After what it termed years of 'diligently working to help you comply with regulatory requirements', FDA sent a scathing letter to 23andMe CEO Anne Wojcicki. It stated baldly that the 23andMe Personal Genome Service (PGS) was being marketed without their approval and in violation of Federal law, because six years after they began marketing the kits, the firm still hasn't proved the tests actually work. In a separate development, a California woman, Lisa Casey, filed a $5 million class action lawsuit against 23andMe, alleging false and misleading advertising[15]. This action has been followed by several others, still in early stages at the time this article went to press.[16] Because their outcome is uncertain, and because the firm insists it wants to work with the FDA to overcome the regulatory hurdles, it is still worth examining the 23andWe biobank as the first attempt to create a corporate genetic commons.

The company prides itself on what it calls its 'participant-led' paradigm, distinguishing it from conventional academic research. Of course, it is also distinguished from conventional research in another way: in conventional research, research participants generally either volunteer or are paid; they do not pay to take part. With the exception of programmes such as Roots Into The Future, in which the

Document'. Less prominently displayed on the page is this qualifier: 'If you do not give consent for your Genetic and Self-Reported Information to be used in 23andWe Research or your individual-level Genetic and Self-Reported Information to be used in the Research Portal, we may still use your Genetic and/or Self-Reported Information for R&D purposes as described above, which may include disclosure of Aggregated Genetic and Self-Reported Information to third-party non-profit and/or commercial research partners who will not publish that information in a peer-reviewed scientific journal.' The statement defines this as 'Information that has been stripped of Registration Information and combined with data from a number of other users sufficient to minimize the possibility of exposing individual-level information while still providing scientific evidence', available at: www.23andme.com/about/privacy/. Thus commercial use of non-identifiable information is still allowed without donors' explicit consent.

[14] Julian Cockbain, personal communication, 1 July 2013.

[15] *Casey et al v 23andMe, Inc. and Does 1-100,* Case No 13-cv-2847, S D CA.

[16] *Spreter et al v 23andMe, Inc,* Case No 14-cv-0487, SD CA; *Dilger et al v 23andMe, Inc,* Case No 14-cv-00296, SD CA; *Guthrie et al v 23andMe, Inc,* Case No 14-cv-01258, WD PA; *Stanton et al v 23andMe, Inc,* Case No 14-cv-00294, ND CA; *Martin et al v 23andMe, Inc,* Case No 14-cv-00429, ND CA; *Stefani et al v 23andMe, Inc,* Case 1:13-cv-13206-GAO. My thanks to Andelka Phillips for providing these citations.

firm has offered free genetic tests to 10,000 African Americans, and free kits for particular genetic conditions including Parkinson's disease or the rare blood and bone marrow cancers called myeloproliferative neoplasms, 23andMe customers are just that: customers, not research participants. Their tissue and the data they willingly provide does constitute the raw material for research, but that does not necessarily make them equal participants in scientific progress. There is no element of communal benefit-sharing, even though that notion became suggested policy in genetic research at the start of the twenty-first century when the ethics committee of the Human Genome Organization recommended that between one and three per cent of profits should be returned to research participants.[17]

However, 23andMe lays a strong emphasis on communality of production: on working together for the benefit of scientific research and creating a valuable tool for genomewide analysis. Customers who fill out the additional epidemiological questionnaires can also take part in surveys about what future research directions the firm should pursue. They receive badges or stars proclaiming them 'research pioneers', 'research trailblazers' or 'research captains', depending on their level of participation. As the firm's advertising puts it: 'We believe research is a two-way process, where participants are valued as partners in scientific discovery.'[18] That partnership, however, does not translate into any form of property rights for participants. It is this appeal to communal values in production of the resource, combined with unrestricted proprietary rights of exclusion for 23andMe and its real partners – the other major corporations with which it has investment and management connections, including Johnson & Johnson, Google and Roche[19] – that leads me to call the 23andWe biobank a new thing, a 'corporate commons'.

While some commentators worry that benefit-sharing might constitute an undue inducement to participate in research,[20] obviously that argument does not apply where participants already pay to participate. By contributing not only their tissue but also the figurative sweat of their brow – the labour they put into completing repeated questionnaires – 23andMe customers create corporate 'biovalue'.[21] Information from the spit samples on customers' genotypes would be of lesser value without the additional phenotype information about the medical conditions from which customers and their relatives have suffered. That 'added

[17] Human Genome Organization (HUGO) Ethics Committee, *Statement on Benefit Sharing* (Geneva, World Health Organization, 2000). For the argument that the HUGO Ethics Committee was motivated by the notion of the genome as the common heritage of humanity, see C Hayden, 'Taking as Giving: Biopolitics, Exchange and the Politics of Benefit-Sharing' (2007) 37 *Social Studies of Science* 729.

[18] spittoon.23andme.com/2011/06/16/23andme-research-findings-from-you-back-to-you, (archived by WebCite® at www.webcitation.org/60MeO68xr).

[19] A Harris, S Wyatt and S Kelly, 'The Gift of Spit (and the Obligation to Return It): How Consumers of Online Genetic Testing Services Participate in Research' (2012) 16 *Information, Communication and Society* 236; J Cockbain and S Sterckx, 'The Phenotype Goldmine', paper delivered at workshop on 'Biocapital and Bioequity', University of Bristol (UK) October 2012.

[20] Hayden, 'Taking as Giving: Biopolitics, Exchange and the Politics of Benefit-Sharing', above n 17.

[21] R Mitchell and C Waldby, 'Clinical Labor, Risk Production, and the Creation of Biovalue' (2010) 35 *Science, Technology, and Human Values* 330; G Palsson, 'Spitting Image' (2009) 1 *Anthropology Now* 1.

value' is particularly important for genome-wide association studies and epigenetic research.

The firm's commercial strategy rests on a loyal, recontactable customer base and the ongoing aggregation of the data provided altruistically by these participants.[22] Their labour is altruistic in the sense that it is unpaid. Indeed, most participants pay the firm for their genetic analyses, with the exception of the free programmes for Parkinson's disease patients and African Americans. However, there is also an element of narcissism in surveys entitled 'Ten things about you' and 'Ten more things about you', as well as in the injunction to 'Find out which traits make you stand out from the crowd'. Some commentators consider that 23andMe is appealing to an 'entrepreneurial self', a new model for research participants, motivated primarily by self-aware curiosity rather than by altruism.[23] Self-interest is certainly targeted by promises such as: 'The more active you are in the community, the more you'll get out of it.'[24]

On the whole, however, the emphasis is on communality and sharing; as the 23andMe blog 'The Spittoon' puts it: 'Wikipedia, YouTube and MySpace have changed the world by empowering individuals to share information. We believe this same phenomenon can revolutionize healthcare.'[25] Theorists of the commons have noted that people value cooperation as a benefit in itself, in addition to its importance in facilitating economic success.[26] It appears that 23andMe is aware of this psychological penchant, which it gratifies by providing online fora and other opportunities for participants not only to share personal information, but also to develop a common identity, increasing their likelihood of continued participation. These mechanisms, probably unconsciously, parallel the procedural norms for democratic self-governance of successful commons regimes.[27]

Although the value of the 23andMe database is largely created by its customers, excluding the analyses performed by the company, the database and any patents associated with it will remain a private commercial resource.[28] The value of the

[22] Harris, Wyatt and Kelly, 'The Gift of Spit (and the Obligation to Return It', above n 19.

[23] R Tutton and B Prainsack, 'Entrepreneurial or Altruistic Selves? Making Up Research Subjects in Genetic Research' (2011) 33 *Sociology of Health and Illness* 1081.

[24] Harris, Wyatt and Kelly, 'The Gift of Spit (and the Obligation to Return It)', above n 19 at fn 12.

[25] ibid at fn 9.

[26] Dagan and Heller, 'The Liberal Commons', above n 6 at 165.

[27] M McKean, 'Success on the Commons: A Comparative Examination of Institutions for Common Property Resource Management' (1992) 4 *Journal of Theoretical Politics* 247.

[28] 23andMe had a US patent granted for a Parkinson's assay in June 2012 but as of July 2013 had not yet filed in its own name for an equivalent patent in Europe. (Its close association with pharmaceutical companies, however, means that other firms may be mining the 23andMe database for their own patent applications.) A 'continuation' application in the US, seeking patent protection for further aspects of the 'invention', was withdrawn in March 2013, leaving no outstanding US application, which indicates that the firm does not intend to proceed any further with the US patent. It is noteworthy that 23andMe actually withdrew the application, rather than merely letting it lapse, as is the usual procedure if a company is no longer interested. The granted patent, moreover, may well be invalid following the US Supreme Court ruling in *Mayo v Prometheus* (Julian Cockbain, private communication, 1 July 2013). However, on 24 September 2013 the company was granted a patent in quite a different area: 'a method for gamete donor selection' through a computerised comparison of the genotypic data of the egg provider and the sperm provider. See S Sterckx et al, '"I Prefer a Child with. . .": Designer Babies, Another

old agricultural commons was likewise largely created and maintained by the labour of the commoners, who undertook cultivation of fields, maintenance of culverts, coppicing of forests and pasturing of animals to keep the land from reverting to the wild state. In return, they eked out a living from the rights to graze their geese and cows, gather wild rushes for basket-making and roof-thatching, pick nuts and berries, and dig for peat as fuel. Under the old system, the ownership of the commons vested in a landlord but the commoners had rights of usage and management[29] – which 23andMe customers lack, no matter how much the company encourages them to think of themselves as 'research partners'. Commoners could even enforce these rights against their landlord: for example, in Selbourne Woods the landlord was not allowed to fell beech trees, even if he replanted them with another tree of lesser value to the commoners, who needed the beech mast (acorns) for their pigs.[30]

The 23andMe biobank is that modern anomaly, what I call a 'corporate commons' – created in substantial part by the labour, cash and bodily materials of thousands of individuals, who are nevertheless excluded from any ownership or management rights. But although that combination seems anomalous, huge numbers of the 20 million new entries in biobanks annually belong to private companies.[31] The argument that the human genome is the common heritage of humanity only prevents genomic information from being appropriated by any nation state, but in the absence of a binding international treaty, does not rule out appropriation by biotechnology firms.[32] Using the doctrine of the finality of gifts *inter vivos*, as in the case of *Washington University v Catalona*,[33] biobanks can exclude even those who laboured to create the biobanks from the right to determine ongoing use of their tissue. The *Catalona* court, viewing the issue primarily in terms of consent, remained silent on the question of any property interest vesting in the research participants.[34] Many of the men who had contributed their tissue samples testified that they wanted the biobank to go with the lead researcher, Professor William Catalona, when he changed institutions, rather than being retained by his original employer. However, the court held that the original consent document that they had signed did not give them any say in the disposition of the biobank.

Controversial Patent in the Arena of Direct-to-Consumer Genomics' (2013) *Genetics in Medicine*, doi:10.1038/gim.2013.164.

[29] P Linebaugh, 'Enclosures from the Bottom Up' (2010) 108 *Radical History Review* 11. My thanks to my daughter, Pip Lustgarten, for alerting me to this article, which contains a lengthy case study about resistance to the enclosure of Otmoor, common land adjoining our village, Beckley, near Oxford. In this century, Beckley has in fact re-established a commons in an orchard maintained by volunteer villager labour, and an RSPB bird reserve has been established on Otmoor, with reedbeds planted again by volunteers.

[30] R Mabey, *The Common Ground: A Place for Nature in Britain's Future?* (London, Hutchinson Books, 1980).

[31] L Andrews, 'Harnessing the Benefits of Biobanks' (2005) 33 *Journal of Law, Medicine & Ethics* 22.

[32] BM Knoppers, 'Biobanking: International Norms' (2005) 33 *Journal of Law, Medicine & Ethics* 7.

[33] *Washington University v Catalona* 437 F Supp 2d, (ED Mo 2006).

[34] RA Charo, 'Body of Research – Ownership and Use of Human Tissue' (2006) 355 *New England Journal of Medicine* 1317.

Even in the twenty-first century, it is not unknown or impossible for large-scale genetic biobanks to be more communal in character. True, UK Biobank (UKBB) is legally constituted as a corporation, and its contributors own neither the original samples that they have contributed nor the additional epidemiological data that they supply. But the biobank's ownership of its samples is constrained by a legal obligation as a non-profit entity to act consistently with its charitable purpose, by the fiduciary duties of its directors and by their legal position as charitable trustees as well as company directors under UK corporate law.[35] Its Ethics and Governance Framework states that UKBB will not exercise all the possible rights of ownership; for example, it will not sell samples outright.[36] Donors also have the right to withdraw their samples, although that possibility was not originally mooted because it would entail a level of unpredictability that might undermine the scientific and commercial value of the collection.

During the consultation in 2002 leading up to the establishment of UK Biobank, the British public expressed concern that the new biobank would focus on 'profitable diseases' rather than on public health.[37] It does seem that some of their concerns have been taken on board, as is appropriate for a national resource developed with public funding and from NHS patients' crucial contributions – even though the UK Biobank model still falls short of full communal ownership. It has been argued that UK Biobank can be seen as a form of the charitable trust,[38] but it might also be seen as a revival of the notion of the property model embodied in the traditional commons: not as sole and despotic dominion by the owner, but as a bundle of sticks in which some rights of management and control also accrued to the commoners. In the next section I will show that it is not the only such model, and that the commons is even enjoying a new heyday in modern biotechnology.

The Public Commons Revived

Governance of the commons has received substantial attention and analysis in terms of common property in land and the environment.[39] Against considerable

[35] DE Winickoff, 'Partnership in UK Biobank: A Third Way for Genomic Governance?' (2007) 35 *Journal of Law, Medicine & Ethics* 440. I would argue that the decisions in *Dobson v North Tyneside Health Authority* [1996] 4 All ER 474, 33 BMLR 146 and *R v Kelly* [1998] 3 All ER 741 would imply that the intentionality and work performed by UKBB on the tissue samples are sufficient to ground a property right, since the intention is clearly to retain the sample for research purposes and labour has been performed in setting up and administering the biobank. See JK Mason and GT Laurie, *Mason and McCall Smith's Law and Medical Ethics*, 8th edn (Oxford, Oxford University Press, 2011) 14.45.

[36] My thanks to Imogen Goold for pointing out that the samples would have had to be sufficiently processed to fall under s 32(9) of the Human Tissue Act 2004. I argue in the previous footnote that they would meet the standard for intentionality and labour set in the *Dobson* and *Kelly* cases.

[37] Winickoff, 'Partnership in UK Biobank: A Third Way for Genomic Governance?', above n 35.

[38] ibid.

[39] For example, Daly and Cobb, *For the Common Good: Redirecting the Economy Toward Community, the Environment, and a Sustainable Future*, above n 6; Ostrom, *Governing the Commons: The Evolution*

resistance, new commoners have bought out landholders and established communal ownership rights on such places as the Inner Hebridean Isle of Eigg.[40] The pessimistic view of the 'tragedy of the commons'[41] – that the commons is inherently open to abuse because everyone who has common rights in an object is tempted to overuse it – is not a threat in the case of the genome: it is hard to see how anyone could overuse that. But the no-property-in-the-body rule in law has limited the applicability of the idea of the commons in the case of the genome or human tissue. (One exception is James Boyle's parallel between the agricultural enclosures movement, which limited or abolished the traditional rights of commons in Great Britain over a period between the sixteenth and the nineteenth centuries, and the 'enclosure' of the genetic commons by restrictive patenting.)[42]

The no-property rule, however, arose in a period when excised human tissue was considered to be of no commercial value, because it was generally diseased – an amputated gangrenous limb or a kidney stone, for example – or because the technology did not exist to make use of it. In our modern era of 'biovalue', with the widespread commodification of human gametes, other tissue and genes, that is manifestly no longer the case. While in the *Yearworth* case the plaintiffs were found to have a property interest in their sperm,[43] no commercial interests were involved, and many commentators view the court's finding as quite limited.[44] However, that case might still be an encouraging precedent for the success of measures aimed at limiting the exclusionary rights of biobank owners, making a chink as it does in the no-property rule regarding tissue donors.

I have argued elsewhere for a property-based approach to governance of the human genome and human tissue as an effective way to 'fight fire with fire': using the concept of property as a variegated bundle of rights explicitly to counter the commodification of the body. [45] As Mason and Laurie have written:

of Institutions for Collective Action, above n 6; V Shiva, *Biopiracy: The Plunder of Nature and Knowledge* (Boston, South End Press, 1997); M Hardt and A Negri, *Commonwealth* (Cambridge, MA, Harvard University Press, 2011).

[40] P Kingsley, 'Doing Things Differently: Hatching a Nest on Eigg', *Guardian* (London, 18 September 2012) 9, s 2; A McIntosh, *Soil and Soul: People versus Corporate Power* (London, Aurum Books, 2004).

[41] G Hardin, 'The Tragedy of the Commons' (1968) 162 *Science* 1243.

[42] J Boyle, 'The Second Enclosure Movement and the Construction of the Public Domain' (2003) 66 *Law and Contemporary Problems* 33.

[43] RM Nwabueze, 'Death of the "No-Property" Rule for Sperm Samples' (2010) 21 *King's Law Journal* 561.

[44] For example, Timothy Caulfield, who views the decision as delivering no more than a qualified right in negligence on the basis that sperm possesses sufficient attributes of property to ground such an entitlement (in 'How Does "The Law" Handle Human Reproductive Tissue?', paper delivered at conference on 'The Uses of Human Reproductive Tissue in Research and Treatment: Principles and Practice', PEALS Centre, Newcastle-on-Tyne, UK, February 2011).

[45] For example, D Dickenson, *Property, Women and Politics* (Cambridge, Polity Press, 1997); 'Property and Women's Alienation from Their Own Reproductive Labour' (2001) 15 *Bioethics* 205; 'Commodification of Human Tissue: Implications for Feminist and Development Ethics' (2002) 2 *Developing World Bioethics* 55; 'Consent, Commodification and Benefit-Sharing in Genetic Research (2004) 4 *Developing World Bioethics* 100; *Property in the Body: Feminist Perspectives* (Cambridge, Cambridge University Press, 2007).

> For many, it is the logical consequence that given a commodity model, one could buy and sell body parts and this is what lies at the heart of repugnance to the concept in that it shows a fundamental disrespect for the status of the human body.[46]

Winickoff and Neumann likewise say that: 'The rejection of "property in the body" in certain jurisdictions limits the free alienability of bodily entities integral to personhood, and is based on the visceral and ethical disdain for commodification of the human body.'[47] I share this repugnance, but I disagree that a property approach necessarily entails unregulated buying and selling of body parts.

Although both opponents *and* proponents of commodifying tissue often argue that a property approach necessitates accepting tissue markets,[48] I have consistently argued the opposite: in my view, giving contributors of tissue some limited property rights is actually the best and most practical way to avoid the excesses of those markets. Hanoch Dagan likewise maintains that property law can underpin commons-like structures, which facilitate sharing rather than the exclusion rights associated with property in the popular understanding: 'Thus, alongside exclusion and exclusivity, property is also a proud home for inclusion and for community.'[49]

Winickoff and Neumann argue that 'recognizing the existence of property-like interests in human tissue is not tantamount to endorsing a full spectrum of alienable property rights, for example the right to sell tissue at any time for cash compensation'.[50] Like me, they rely on a differentiated model of property, reflecting the dominant Hohfeldian view that has largely replaced Blackstone's conception of property as 'sole and despotic dominion'.[51] In Hohfeld's model, we can possess some, all or none of the rights in the property 'bundle of sticks', which are 'strikingly independent'.[52] These 'sticks' in the bundle may include:

[46] Mason and Laurie, *Mason and McCall Smith's Law and Medical Ethics*, above n 35 at 14.03.

[47] DE Winickoff and LB Neumann, 'Towards a Social Contract for Genomics: Property and the Public in the "Biotrust" Model' (2005) 1 *Genomics, Society and Policy* 8.

[48] For a view that this all-or-nothing argument militates against allowing property rights in tissue, see L Skene, 'Proprietary Rights in Human Bodies, Body Parts and Tissue: Regulatory Contexts and Proposals for New Laws' (2002) 22 *Legal Studies* 102, and Herring, ch 13 and Skene, ch 15 in this volume; for the view that if we allow transfer by gift we must also allow transfer by sale, which to my mind assumes that property is undifferentiated, see J Harris and CA Erin, 'An Ethically Defensible Market in Human Organs' (2002) 325 *British Medical Journal* 114. The Roman concept of property as undifferentiated dominium, still influential in civil law countries, may also be linked to this all-or-nothing view of property. Blackstone's model of 'sole and despotic dominion' is, of course, a major influence (W Blackstone, *Commentaries on the Laws of England* (Chicago, University of Chicago Press, 1979)). For further discussion, see J Christman, *The Myth of Property: Towards an Egaliarian Theory of Ownership* (Oxford, Oxford University Press, 1994) 5 ff.

[49] Dagan, *Property: Values and Institutions*, above n 6 at xviii.

[50] Winickoff and Neumann, 'Towards a Social Contract for Genomics: Property and the Public in the "Biotrust" Model', above n 47 at 13. See also JD Mahoney, 'The Market For Human Tissue' (2000) 86 *Virginia Law Review* 16.

[51] Dagan, *Property: Values and Institutions*, above n 6 at xii; Blackstone, *Commentaries on the Laws of England*, above n 48; WN Hohfeld, *Fundamental Legal Conceptions as Applied in Judicial Reasoning* (New Haven, CT, Yale University Press, 1919). One leading critic of the Hohfeldian model is James Penner, in his *The Idea of Property in Law* (Oxford, Clarendon Press, 1997).

[52] Hohfeld, *Fundamental Legal Conceptions as Applied in Judicial Reasoning*, above n 51 at 747, cited in Dagan, *Property: Values and Institutions*, above n 6 at 11, fn 23.

1. A right to the physical possession of object X;
2. A right to its use;
3. A right to its management, that is, to determine the ways in which others can use it;
4. A right to the income that can be derived from its use by others;
5. A right to its capital value;
6. A right to security against its being taken by others;
7. A right to transmit or alienate it to others by gift or bequest;
8. A right to transmit or alienate it to others by sale;
9. A permanent right to these other rights, without any limit or term; and
10. A duty to refrain from using X in a way that harms others.[53]

In a traditional commons, commoners only possess some rights in the property bundle, but those are crucial ones: the rights of use (2), income (4) and security against being taken by others (6). In collaboration with other commoners, they also hold rights of physical possession (1) and management of the resource for the common good (3). (This latter right also entails communally enforceable duties (10), for example, not to exhaust the commons by overgrazing, for which a fine could be levied on offenders.)

Commoners typically lack both the right to transmit or alienate part of the communally held resource by sale or gift to outsiders (8) and the right to the capital value realisable by sale (5). Those two rights are arguably the ones of most concern to private corporations amassing biobanks. However, because they are generally of lesser concern to the original tissue contributors than the rights of security, management for the common good and the duty to refrain from harmful uses, it would be feasible for both parties to come to an agreement on dividing up the rights along those lines, at a minimum. Marie-Claire King, whose work underpinned the discovery of the BRCA1 gene, said in a recent interview:

> I think there is one issue that many geneticists don't appreciate, which was germane during this whole period, and that was that it's not really the patent per se that is the problem: it's the exclusivity of the licensing of the patent.[54]

Some patenting and licensing restrictions to prevent rival corporations from developing copycat products, for example, could co-exist with the rights of 'commoners' to access genetic tests at a reduced rate. Indeed, we saw in the case of UK Biobank that the public 'commoners' even succeeded in placing limitations on the untrammelled right of sale, which is important in the case of a biobank that becomes bankrupt or falls prey to asset-strippers.

Furthermore, modern genetic commoners have a weapon in their armoury that their agricultural forebears lacked: without their contribution of genetic material and labour, the potential commons would not exist. Enclosure of the agricultural

[53] AM Honoré, 'Ownership', in *Making Law Bind: Essays Legal and Philosophical* (Oxford, Clarendon Press, 1987) 161–92.

[54] J Gitschier, 'Evidence Is Evidence: An Interview with Mary-Claire King' (2013) 9 *PLoS Genetics* 9: e1003828. doi:10.1371/journal.pgen.1003828.

commons began when landowners realised they could make more profit from their lands for sheep farming than from arable use if they expelled their tenants, in the ostensible name of progress and the national interest.[55] However, while the land went on existing with or without its human inhabitants, there would be no biobanks without the contributions of tissue and epidemiological data made by individuals.

There are already signs that disgruntled biobank contributors are beginning to realise their potential power and are threatening to withdraw their aid unless some concessions are made to their interests. After 23andMe announced in June 2012 that it had taken out a commercial patent on a genetic variant (G2019S) that appears to protect against a high-risk mutation for Parkinson's disease – a patent deriving from tissue and additional survey information voluntarily provided by its customers – one contributor wrote angrily to the firm: 'I had assumed that 23andMe was against patenting genes and felt in total cahoots all along with you guys. If I'd known you might go that route with my data, I'm not sure I would have answered any surveys.'[56] This attitude increasingly extends beyond 23andMe customers to research participants more generally, as has become evident in the *Greenberg* case (discussed below) and in attitudinal research.[57]

Even if genetic commoners' rights began to be better recognised, there would still, of course, be conflicts about how to allocate the sticks in the bundle. I have suggested that the sticks of most concern to the commoners are generally of less concern to the companies, and vice versa. That conveniently neat fit may not hold in every case: for example, the commoners' security of tenure would be under threat if companies were allowed unrestricted rights to sell the biobank without consulting those who contributed to it. Yet it cannot be beyond the considerable wit of commercial lawyers to come up with some sort of prioritisation of contributors' rights to consultation and compensation, perhaps of the sort that underpins existing bankruptcy legislation. Bills under consideration in some US state legislatures attempt a balancing of that sort, giving contributors to genetic databases ongoing property rights in their data while at the same time viewing human genomic information as a public commons.[58]

Progress on practical proposals has been going on for 15 years already with the charitable trust model, which can be seen as making a similar distinction between the rights of management and of capital value.[59] Although it does not give bio-

[55] For a fictionalised account of a Scottish landlord's decision along these lines, see NM Gunn, *Butcher's Broom* (Edinburgh, Polygon, 2006) 231–32.

[56] Anonymous contributor to 'The Spittoon' blog, 12 June 2012, quoted in D Dickenson, *Me Medicine vs. We Medicine: Reclaiming Biotechnology for the Common Good*, above n 11 at 191. See above n 28 for a fuller discussion of the patent.

[57] AF Cook and H Hoas, 'Trading Places: What the Research Participant Can Tell the Investigator about Informed Consent' (2011) 2 *Journal of Clinical Research Bioethics* 121; M Levitt and S Weldon, 'A Well Placed Trust? Public Perceptions of the Governance of Research Databases' (2005) 15 *Critical Public Health* 311.

[58] For example, 18 Vermont State Acts 9330. A similar bill is under consideration in Massachusetts.

[59] See, inter alia, K Gottlieb, 'Human Biological Samples and the Law of Property: The Trust as a Model for Biological Repositories' in RF Weir (ed), *Stored Tissue Samples: Ethical, Legal and Public*

bank contributors full ownership rights, the trust model protects them by giving them the same status as beneficiaries of a personal trust. Just as trustees are restricted in what they can do with the accumulated wealth in a trust by the requirement to act in the interest of the beneficiaries, this model would limit the rights of biobank managers to profit as they please from the resource or to sell all or part of it to commercial interests. The key point of the trust is to provide donors with robust governance mechanisms for their input and participation, rather than vague assurances of stewardship or dedication to scientific progress. As one of the main developers of this model, David Winickoff, has put it: 'We should be moving from individual consent to rethinking governing institutions. Shareholding and voting is only one of many mechanisms that could be imagined – although this one seems the most controversial for biobank insiders!'[60]

The Winickoff model has served as the 'touchstone' for the Michigan Biotrust for Health (an infant heelprick blood spot bank), which promulgates proprietary rights and obligations, collaborates with a community advisory body set up for this explicit purpose, and provides accountability mechanisms between the science and the community boards.[61] Such provisions are particularly crucial because this form of screening is mandatory, so that the notion of voluntary 'gift' is untenable. Therefore, we cannot apply the *Catalona* view that a gift *inter vivos* is complete and irrevocable, giving the 'donor' no further management rights. Under Michigan law the biobank only has 'qualified ownership' in the tissue, requiring it to fulfil specific fiduciary duties. The trust views its duties as incompatible with any purpose that does not directly serve public health, for example, allowing the samples to be used for commercial production of cosmetics.

The charitable trust model gets round many of the objections against people having any rights in their tissue or genetic data, once contained in a public or private biobank. The contribution of any individual donor of a tissue sample to a biobank is often minimal – although the ongoing labour put into answering further questionnaires or providing epidemiological data should also be acknowledged – and the case law in *Kelly* and *Dobson* has left some uncertainty about how much labour on a tissue sample is required to ground a property right.[62] Some commentators have argued that for similar reasons, biobank donors should only have limited powers of consent or veto over future research.[63] Additionally, there

Policy Implications (Iowa City, University of Iowa Press, 1998) 183–97; DE Winickoff and RN Winickoff, 'The Charitable Trust as a Model for Genomic Biobanks' (2003) 349 *New England Journal of Medicine* 1180; Winickoff and Neumann, above n 47; A Boggio, 'Charitable Trusts and Human Research Genetic Databases: The Way Forward?' (2005) 2 *Genomics, Society and Policy* 41.

[60] DE Winickoff, personal communication, 19 September 2013.

[61] D Chrysler et al, 'The Michigan Biotrust for Health: Using Dried Bloodspots for Research to Benefit the Community While Respecting the Individual' (2011) 39 *Journal of Law, Medicine & Ethics* 98.

[62] Mason and Laurie, above n 35 at 14.45.

[63] MG Hansson et al, 'Should Donors Be Allowed to Give Broad Consent to Future Biobank Research?' (2006) 7 *Lancet Oncology* 288.

may be problems about recontacting donors[64] (although 23andMe would have fewer problems because it has consciously created mechanisms to encourage the people whom it calls its 'active genomes' to stay active).

Furthermore, the charitable trust model sets out a far more precise roster of duties and entitlements than the rather vague notions of 'stewardship' and 'custodianship' found in some biobanks' literature. The trust model includes the requirement that full disclosure of all pending commercial interests must be made to the tissue donor. In Winickoff and Neumann's version, a 'donor approval committee', drawn from shareholder models in corporate law, would be elected periodically through proxy voting.[65] If the biobank fails or goes bankrupt, a very real risk in the 'easy come, easy go' world of modern biotechnology,[66] charitable trust status could prevent its altruistically donated assets from simply passing to the highest bidder or to a creditor, since the trustees of the biobank would have a legal fiduciary duty to use the income or capital of the trust solely for the benefit of the beneficiary, rather than for third parties.

Donors would presumably retain a right to withdraw their tissue in the event of a takeover to which they did not consent, since they retain an equitable interest. As part of their duty to manage the trust assets faithfully, trustees are generally barred from entering into transactions adverse to the trust, which would presumably include 'asset stripping' by outsiders. The charitable trust model also builds in a social structure aimed at fostering communal participation, representation and trust in genetic governance:[67] what might be termed a sense of loyalty to the commons. (We have seen that 23andMe also recognised the value of participant loyalty in creating a recontactable database of individuals willing to submit the further lifestyle and epidemiological data that gives the biobank most of its commercial value.)

The charitable trust model builds imaginatively and painstakingly on the differentiated notion of property as sticks in a bundle. As Winickoff and Neumann write:

> The creation of a charitable trust would not require a general property right in the body, but something much narrower: the recognition that personal rights of control, and use, and access in pieces that can be extracted without harm (indisputably held by the person prior to donation) may form the basis of a legal trust. In fact, the charitable trust is a legal tool for effecting this norm of non-commodification. The structure relies on the recognition of a property-like interest in donated materials only for the narrow purposes of creating an enforceable trust relationship, one that embeds control of tissue in a managed network of non-commodity exchange: samples must be used according to the terms of the trust, and the trustee enforces this use.[68]

[64] C Johnson and J Kaye, 'Does the UK Biobank Have a Legal Duty to Feedback Individual Findings to Participants?' (2004) 12 *Medical Law Review* 239.

[65] Winickoff and Neumann, above n 47.

[66] For example, the for-profit genomics bank Framingham Genomics Medicine, whose collapse is discussed by Winickoff, 'Partnership in UK Biobank: A Third Way for Genomic Governance?', above n 35.

[67] Winickoff and Neumann, above 47 at 14.

[68] ibid, 15.

Another model which uses a property-based approach in order to limit excessive corporate power over biobanks is joint patenting between patients and researchers. This method was pioneered by an advocacy organisation, the PXE International Foundation, established by families of children with the inherited connective tissue disorder *Pseudoxanthoma elasticum*.[69] Set up in 1995, this registry and biobank funds its activity through private and NIH grants and ploughs back into further research all profits from its co-discovery of the gene associated with PXE, for example, from diagnostic kits licensed to a private company (Transgenomic).[70] Disease-specific advocacy groups have existed for a long time, of course, and some, such as the Hereditary Disease Foundation, have spearheaded successful research efforts such as the Venezuela Collaborative Huntington's Disease Project.[71] However, in the founding of PXE International there was a greater element of conscious effort not only to initiate, conduct and accelerate translational research – although those goals were central – but also to put right 'a market failure with respect to the value added to the research enterprise by patient and subject groups'.[72]

The PXE founders rejected what they saw as the institutional orientation of private and charitable funders alike: as they put it, they aimed

> to achieve positive health outcomes for their members – to 'work until we turn the lights off and go home' – rather than focusing on the wealth and longevity of the organization. Most organizations that the PXE International founders had met with until this point were focused primarily on building a strong organization as an end point, rather than as a means to an end.[73]

The PXE founders actually embraced the notion of commodification, but only if it could be consciously subordinated to the needs and control of a community, which had to be established first. As the founders' account puts it:

> Early on, the founders of PXE International knew that there was a need to incentivize research into PXE by leveraging the available resources. It seemed that this would be best achieved by establishing a community, developing a commodity through this community, making the foundation an essential part of the academic enterprise, and aiming

[69] Formally the body was set up not as a charitable trust but as a private foundation; it is a not-for-profit entity with tax-exempt status under s 501c(3) of the US Internal Revenue Code. See also Y Shi et al, 'Development of a Rapid, Reliable Genetic Test for Pseudoxanthoma Elasticum' (2007) 9 *Journal of Molecular Diagnostics* 105.

[70] SF Terry et al, 'Advocacy Groups as Research Organizations: the PXE International Example' (2007) 8 *Nature Reviews Genetics*, available at: www.pxe.org/advocacy-groups-as-research-organizations-pxe-international-example.

[71] JF Gusella et al, 'A Polymorphic DNA Marker Genetically Linked to Huntington's Disease' (1983) 306 *Nature* 234; PA Locke et al, 'A Genetic Linkage Map of the Chromosome 4 Short Arm' (1993) 19 *Somatic Cell Molecular Genetics* 95; NS Wexler et al, 'Venezuelan Kindreds Reveal that Genetic and Environmental Factors Modulate Huntington's Disease Age of Onset' (2004) 101 *Proceedings of the National Academies of Science of the USA* 3498.

[72] JF Merz et al, 'Protecting Subjects' Interest in Genetic Research' (2002) 70 *American Journal of Human Genetics* 965.

[73] Terry et al, 'Advocacy Groups as Research Organizations: the PXE International Example', above n 70 at 3.

> towards the industrialization of a treatment or technology, with the goal of improving the lives of affected individuals. They determined that biological samples would serve as the commodity, and established the PXE International Blood and Tissue Bank as an important first step.[74]

This innovative attempt rooted in a strong communal loyalty has largely succeeded: as Winickoff writes, 'PXE International has become a well-known model for the way it has leveraged its control of the biobank *qua* biocapital in order to achieve collective goals'.[75]

Sharon Terry, who was instrumental in creating the foundation, is now CEO of a broader group, the Genetic Alliance, whose remit is not limited to any particular disease. In June 2013 the Genetic Alliance, together with the University of San Francisco, patient advocates and a private corporation (InVitae), announced the formation of an innovative initiative called 'Free the Data'.[76] They plan to encourage women to upload their genetic data directly into a searchable public database, building on but transcending the US Supreme Court decision of that same month in the *Myriad* case that human DNA in its naturally occurring form cannot be patented or monopolised by any one firm. Terry has written that while the *Myriad* decision brought restrictions on sharing genetic information to national attention, it does not in itself provide immediate better public access to shared genetic information for diagnostic and care purposes. Property rights in the 'Free the Data' resource will be differentiated, with ownership vesting in the public–private alliance but limited by the management rights of 'commoners'. While the charitable trust model was originally conceived in relation to tangible property in biobanks, there seems no inherent reason why it should not also apply to intangible property in information. Granting management rights to those who provide genetic data is very much in that spirit.

The work of Genetic Alliance has been called 'part of a growing movement to unlock medical secrets by empowering patients to gather, control and even analyze their own health data'.[77] A similar movement, although spearheaded by scientists rather than patients, is Science Commons (now integrated with the Creative Commons movement), which focuses on getting scientists to collaborate by signing agreements to exchange research data.[78] Its first project will bring together rheumatoid arthritis patients who have agreed to share their genetic data – provided the investigator also shares the results with both the patients themselves and other scientists – and a commercial firm, which has agreed to sequence the patients' entire genomes for free.

[74] ibid, 4.

[75] Winickoff, 'Partnership in UK Biobank: A Third Way for Genomic Governance?', above n 35 at 450.

[76] Anon, 'Free the Data! International Initiative Applauds the Supreme Court Decision Eliminating Gene Patents and Announces the Launch of a Database for Hereditary Gene Mutations' available at http://www.free-the-data.org/.

[77] AD Marcus, 'Citizen Scientists', *Wall Street Journal* (New York, 3 December 2011) available at: https://online.wsj.com/article/SB10001424052970204621904577014330551132036.html.

[78] Anon, 'Towards a Science Commons', available at: sciencecommons.org/about/towards.

Likewise, Cancer Commons, founded by melanoma survivor and computer scientist Marty Tenenbaum, has 'set out to create a "commons" that collects diagnoses, biomarkers, treatments and outcomes' in 'a patient-centred nonprofit [body] uniting patients, clinicians and researchers in rapid learning communities'.[79] 'Health hackers' or 'citizen scientists', as they call themselves, seek to facilitate the flow of patients' data to researchers in exchange for open access to the results for those who contributed samples and for others in a similar position.

These developments would bypass the norm established by the poignant case of *Greenberg v Miami Children's Hospital*.[80] Here the plaintiffs were parents who had contributed their dead children's tissue, as well as their own assistance with raising funds and developing a list of other Canavan disease parents for a database. Without their knowledge, the lead researcher and the hospital where he worked took out a comprehensive patent (US patent number 5,679,635) covering the gene coding for Canavan disease, diagnostic screening methods and kits for carrier and antenatal testing. The hospital then began to collect royalties from the patented test, claiming that as a non-profit-making body it needed to recoup its outlay on research – although the seed money had actually been provided by the parents and the charitable Canavan Foundation. Previously the foundation had offered free testing, which had reduced the incidence of the disease by 90 per cent, but now it was blocked from doing so. Furthermore, the hospital attached a number of additional conditions, limiting the number of laboratories that could perform the tests and the total number of tests that could be performed annually. Many laboratories stopped offering the diagnostic test to parents trying to establish whether they were carriers of this recessive genetic disorder.

In response, the Canavan families, together with associated charities including the Canavan Foundation and the National Tay-Sachs and Allied Diseases Association, filed a lawsuit alleging breach of informed consent, breach of fiduciary duty, fraudulent concealment and unjust enrichment (the only claim on which they won). The plaintiffs alleged that had they known that the lead researcher and hospital intended to commercialise the discovery, they would either have withheld the tissue samples and funding they provided or found another researcher who was less commercially minded. Clearly, they were primarily seeking the right to manage the genetic test derived from the tissue in such a way as to help other parents of children with the same disease, not the right to profit from the discovery. In terms of the property bundle, they were most concerned with rights 3 (management) and 10 (duty to refrain from harmful uses, which consisted of price increases for the diagnostic tests and restrictions imposed by the respondents on who was allowed to administer them). The final confidential settlement exempted research scientists and some licensed laboratories from having to pay a royalty fee, but in return the plaintiffs had to agree not to

[79] Anon, 'About Cancer Commons,' available at: www.cancercommons.org/about.

[80] *Greenberg et al v Miami Children's Hospital Research Institute Inc*, 208 F Supp 2d 918 [2002], 264 F Supp 2d 1064 [2003].

challenge the hospital's full and exclusive ownership of all the rights for the gene patent that it had been granted.

The *Greenberg* decision, like the previous *Moore* case,[81] did not accept that the plaintiffs had any property interest in the body tissues and genetic material that they had originally donated to the hospital and its research team. Behind this judgment lies the traditional common law doctrine of *res nullius*, the no-property rule concerning excised tissue to which courts in English-speaking countries have generally adhered.[82] The *Greenberg* court denied the conversion claim because it maintained that the plaintiffs could have no property interest in excised body tissues or genetic material; therefore, as in *Moore*, the respondents could not be guilty of interfering with any property right.

However, another assumption was also at stake in *Greenberg*, one not at issue in *Moore*: the dyadic nature of the doctor–patient relationship. Although he lost his action in conversion because of the no-property rule, Moore did achieve a partially favourable judgment on the narrower grounds of breach of fiduciary duty between doctor and patient, because the standards of informed consent had been breached by the physician. But the *Greenberg* court held that informed consent did not obtain in this case, because none of the plaintiff parents had actually been patients of the principal doctor involved.

In the instance of a biobank created by healthy volunteers (including paying customers, such as 23andWe participants) or at a remove through donation of tissue and data by guardians or parents, this limitation can be substantial. No doctor–patient relationship is involved in any of those scenarios. The consent model, widely seen as the leading alternative to the property model for regulation of human tissue, cannot easily handle these common situations in biobanking, as exemplified by the *Greenberg* case.[83] Under a property model using the concept of the commons, by contrast, we can conceive of the *Greenberg* parents as commoners claiming partial rights of control over a resource, which they had helped to create communally, but which had then been enclosed or privatised by the hospital. The individualistic slant of medical law, with its narrow focus on the doctor–patient dyad, is ill-equipped to deal with the realities of modern research medicine, on which the seemingly archaic notion of the commons actually has more purchase.

Conclusion

The practical examples in the previous section illustrate innovative permutations and combinations of rights in the property bundle, just as the 23andMe example

[81] *Moore v Regents of the University of California*, 51 Cal 3d 120, 793 P 2d, 271 Cal Rptr 146 [1990], cert. denied 111 SCt 1388.

[82] J McHale, 'Waste, Ownership and Bodily Products' (2000) 8 *Health Care Analysis* 123; M Quigley, 'Property: The Future of Human Tissue?' (2009) 17 *Medical Law Review* 457.

[83] See Mason and Laurie, above n 35 at 14.01.

illustrates an innovative if somewhat contradictory combination of exclusive ownership rights for the firm and communally-minded values for the participants. The ingenuity represented by all these instances is impressive but not altogether surprising, because the 'contested commodities'[84] of biobanks, cell lines and genetic patents often represent tremendous commercial value. The principal asset in the portfolio of many biotechnology companies lies in the 'promissory capital' stored in their patents and databases.[85] Reasserting public interests and rights in that value is the objective of the genetic commons.

In the *Myriad* decision – concerning two patented genes from which the firm involved did indeed derive the great bulk of its profits[86] – the coalition of plaintiffs succeeded in establishing that 'DNA would now be able to be used as part of a "public commons" instead of being the subject of a patent'.[87] In obiter dicta the Court offered some compensation to the firm by suggesting that a synthetically created version, cDNA, would, however, be patent-eligible. Together with the alternative forms of regulating biobanks sketched in this chapter, such as the charitable trust, the commons approach has been ratified by this latest decision, even though both parties are claiming victory.

That is actually a rather optimistic sign: it shows that everyone can get some of the sticks in the bundle through applying the concept of the commons to regulating modern biotechnology. It is also encouraging that the coalition of 'commoners' who took on the company was so far-reaching, extending from medical professional bodies through the American Civil Liberties Union to the Southern Baptist Convention. The commons makes for strange bedfellows, but that is one of its many strengths.

[84] MJ Radin, *Contested Commodities: The Trouble with Trade in Sex, Children, Body Parts and Other Things* (Cambridge, MA, Harvard University Press, 1996).

[85] M Cooper, *Life as Surplus: Biotechnology and Capitalism in the Neo-Liberal Era* (Seattle, WA, University of Washington Press, 2007).

[86] Estimated by *Bloomberg Business News* at over 80 per cent of the firm's revenues in the third quarter of 2012.

[87] LB Moraia and J Kaye, 'An Historical Turning Point? The Implications of the Myriad Decision on the Patentability of Human Genes' *Bionews* (London, 24 June 2013).

12

The Problem with Alternatives: The Importance of Property Law in Regulating Excised Human Tissue and *In Vitro* Human Embryos

LYRIA BENNETT MOSES*

Introduction

Although in some cases property law has been applied to sensitive subject matter such as excised human tissue (including gametes) and *in vitro* human embryos, the idea of property in such things often causes discomfort.[1] Thus, while in some cases property doctrines are applied, others contain statements to the effect that such things fall outside the scope of property law. While commentators are divided, much of this division stems from different conceptions of what property entails. Those in favour of property rights focus on the suitability of property remedies and the narrow scope of *in personam* rights through the law of torts and contract; those against property rights focus on the harms caused by commodification or full rights of 'ownership'.[2]

This chapter argues that we ought to recognise property rights in excised human tissue and *in vitro* human embryos. The recognition of such rights is important because it is the most appropriate category for ensuring that rights of control over such things are protected and leaving such things outside any legal category would give rise to both uncertainty and legal gaps. The option of creating *sui generis* legal rules for the regulation of human tissue and embryos outside the human body, while possible, has its own disadvantages. Importantly, and

* The author would like to thank Nicola Gollan for her excellent research assistance, as well as the editors and other contributors to this volume for their helpful comments and suggestions. She is also grateful for feedback received when an earlier version of the paper was presented at Kings College London. All outstanding errors remain the responsibility of the author.

[1] In this paper, I do not discuss the position of intact bodies or parts thereof, in relation to which see, eg G Calabresi, 'An Introduction to Legal Thought: Four Approaches to Law and to the Allocation of Body Parts' (2003) 55 *Stanford Law Review* 2113.

[2] Compare references in n 3 with eg Nwabueze, ch 10 in this volume.

contrary to the suggestions of some,[3] the recognition of property in something does not necessarily entail the right to do whatever one wishes with it or the power to sell it. Accordingly, by arguing that people ought to have property rights over *in vitro* embryos, I am not advocating baby markets[4] or the possibility of embryo earrings. Rather, I am arguing that a failure to treat excised human tissue or embryos as a potential object of property rights is problematic, and that the moral concerns can be sidelined through a better understanding of what property, in its modern sense, entails.

This chapter brings together two distinct ideas – the problems associated with *sui generis* legal regimes generally and the modern meaning of property – to justify the extension of property law to controversial subject matter. After a discussion about the importance of broad legal categories such as property,[5] there is a short summary of the jurisprudence in the UK, the US and Australia concerning treatment of excised human tissue (including gametes) and *in vitro* human embryos. Using examples from cases that did, and did not, make it to court, one can see both the advantages of a property approach and the gaps revealed where courts insist on treating tissue and embryos outside a human body as *sui generis*. The chapter then examines the concept of 'property', explaining how a 'thin' conception of property enables the application of property law to excised human tissue and *in vitro* embryos without negative consequences sometimes associated with 'commodification' and 'ownership'. Finally, the chapter concludes with a call to reframe the debate about property in these contexts in light of a clear understanding of property's meaning and the disadvantages of limiting property's scope. These arguments sit alongside others in this collection to make the case for property rights in controversial subject matter.[6]

[3] See, eg L Skene, 'Proprietary Interests in Human Bodily Material: *Yearworth*, Recent Australian Cases on Stored Semen and their Implications' (2012) 20 *Medical Law Review* 227, 227–45; M Brazier, 'Organ Retention and Return: Problems of Consent' (2003) *Journal of Medical Ethics* 30, 32. Other articles that suggest a link between property and commodification include, CH Harrison, 'Neither *Moore* nor the Market: Alternative Models for Compensating Contributors of Human Tissue' (2002) 28 *American Journal of Law and Medicine* 77, 78 ('The creation of a market in human tissue, which appears to follow inevitably from a private property model . . .'); R Rao, 'Property, Privacy, and the Human Body' (2000) 80 *Boston University Law Review* 359. See also B Dickens, 'The Control of Living Body Materials' (1977) 27 *University of Toronto Law Journal* 142, 180 (linking property and value).

[4] *cf* EM Landes and RA Posner, 'The Economics of the Baby Shortage' (1978) 7 *Journal of Legal Studies* 323.

[5] This section is based on earlier work that formed part of the 'Pacing Law and Ethics with Science and Technology' project based at Arizona State University; see L Bennett Moses, 'Sui Generis Rules' in GE Marchant, BR Allenby and JR Heckert (eds), *The Growing Gap Between Emerging Technologies and Legal-Ethical Oversight: The Pacing Problem*, vol 7, International Library of Ethics, Law and Technology (New York, Springer, 2011) 77.

[6] *cf* Goold and Quigley, ch 14, Nwabueze, ch 10 and Douglas, ch 7 in this volume.

The Importance of Legal Categories

Law is filled with categories and sub-categories that determine how things, relationships, people and activities are treated. Broad categories such as property, tort, and so forth allow many legislative and common law rules to be expressed at a high level of generality. As this section will argue, the advantages of relying on generalisations rather than specifics usually outweigh the costs.

Law includes both rules that apply to a broad range of activities and rules that apply to a more narrow range of contexts. Examples of the latter include legislation designed either to regulate some specific activity due to a particular health, environmental or social harm associated with that activity or to promote some specific activity deemed to be of benefit. While there are general rules about negligence and product liability, there are also specific regulations that apply in narrower contexts. The degree of narrowness is variable – laws can apply to a relatively wide range of activities (such as industrial chemical production) or a relatively narrow range of activities (such as the manufacture of nanomaterials). The generalist–*sui generis* dichotomy is thus revealed as a scale, from broadly applicable rules to more narrowly applicable rules. Laws can be described as *sui generis* to the extent that they do not treat something (whether an entity, activity or relationship) as part of a broader class.

It is fairly easy to make a prima facie argument that a particular activity, relationship or thing ought to be treated differently and made subject to a *sui generis* legal regime. One need merely point to differences between a particular thing or activity and things or activities covered by the more general category. In the context of intellectual property, for instance, the rate of invention, the speed with which products can be brought to market, the extent to which discoveries build on earlier discoveries and the importance of invention vary across different industries. Thus one often sees arguments for special treatment for particular industries – longer patent rights, lower innovation thresholds and so forth.[7] Sometimes, as in the case of the treatment of semi-conductor chips, governments are persuaded to adopt a *sui generis* approach. In some ways, arguments that excised human tissue or *in vitro* embryos ought to be excluded from the ambit of property laws are similar. Like particular industries, sensitive subject matter is 'different' from other things that are subject to property law. Such differences include their link with human life (stronger in the case of embryos), their symbolic value, and the different feelings people have towards them. The real question is not, however, whether differences exist, but the extent to which such differences are relevant, and the extent to which relevant differences are outweighed by other factors.

While it is relatively easy to articulate how a particular activity, relationship or thing is distinct, the argument for treating something within a broader class,

[7] Bennett Moses, 'Sui Generis Rules', above n 5.

despite differences, is rarely made explicit. To some extent, it is too obvious, as the following quote from Oliver Wendell Holmes makes clear:

> There is the story of a Vermont justice of the peace before whom a suit was brought by one farmer against another for breaking a churn. The justice took time to consider, and then said he had looked through the statutes and could find nothing about churns, and gave judgment for the defendant.[8]

The reason we do not need a law of churns in common law systems is that we have the law of property and tort which, among other things, gives a person whose owned thing is damaged by another a right to damages.[9] If the lack of a law of churns meant that there was no remedy where one person broke another's churn, then the 'gap' in the law (which might also be described as a case of under-inclusive legal rules) would be ridiculous. That is not to say that there might not be some churn-specific laws that might be justifiable. For instance, it might be thought that churns made of certain materials could contaminate the butter, and such materials could be banned in churn production. However, even if a specially crafted 'law of churns' were created, that would not eliminate the need for property law to apply to churns. After all, while one could enact churn-specific law of what happens when one person damages another's churn, and could make it more specifically applicable than the general law of property (with specific damages provisions based on prices nominated by experts for instance), it would not be efficient do so. Regulating churns specifically might add to the oft-bemoaned phenomenon of over-regulation, but it would be easier to justify churn-specific regulation than to justify taking churns outside the law of property (and contract and tort) entirely. That would be the case even if the legislature attempted to fill the void with churn-specific rules.

In other words, while *sui generis* legal rules enable a more finely tuned approach to law making, there are also drawbacks. These are: (1) the problem of completeness (or the creation of 'gaps' in the law); (2) the problem of administrative costs associated with creating (and amending and interpreting) multiple legal regimes, possible additional bureaucracy, and the need for the community (especially the legal profession) to navigate multiple legal regimes; (3) the risk that a *sui generis* regime might be overtaken by technological change to the extent it makes assumptions based on the technological landscape at the time of its creation; and (4) the risk that *sui generis* legislation will be distorted by special interest politics. Each of these is of varying importance in different contexts. In the context of excised human tissue and *in vitro* human embryos, the first concern is dominant,[10] though problems associated with ongoing technological change may also arise, leading to under-inclusiveness or uncertainty.[11]

[8] OW Holmes, 'The Path of the Law' (1897) 10 *Harvard Law Review* 457, 457–78.

[9] Other legal systems might deal with similar problems in different ways which may or may not be tied to a concept of 'property', but that is beyond the scope of this chapter.

[10] *cf* PA Martin and ML Lagod, 'The Human Preembryo, the Progenitors, and the State: Toward a Dynamic Theory of Status, Rights, and Research Policy' (1990) 5 *High Technology Law Journal* 257.

[11] Such as the uncertainty that arose in *R (on the application of Quintavalle) v Secretary of the State for Health* [2003] UKHL 13, [2003] 2 WLR 692.

Property is the law's primary mechanism for identifying who is allowed to interact with a 'thing' as well as civil and criminal consequences for those who interfere with things without such rights. While there are debates as to whether property law works through rights of use, rights of exclusion or exclusive rights,[12] the point here is merely that property law is the only generally operable 'law of things'. Property law operates *in rem*, which means that even people with whom a person has no specific legal relationship are discouraged from certain types of interference. At the same time, the law offers no general remedy for interfering with, damaging or destroying 'things that are not property', unless a specific law exists that regulates those interactions with that particular thing or that specific conduct. Legal categories such as property are important for a range of reasons, but one of them is that they create default rules that can be applied in diverse contexts not all of which can be anticipated by legislators creating a *sui generis* legal regime.[13] It is for this reason that, despite some general statements denying property rights in human tissue and embryos, courts have often turned to property law to resolve actual disputes.

While some have argued that other legal principles such as privacy or consent could replace property law in the context of tissue or embryos, these do not fulfil the same functions as property law once the tissue or embryo exists outside a human body.[14] The applicability of the law of privacy will depend on both context and jurisdiction, but does not always protect a person's interest in control of the physical thing.[15] The law of consent remains important within its sphere – it is the law of consent that determines the circumstances in which a particular person can remove particular tissue from the body of another person. However, to ensure completeness and avoid legal gaps after excision, both the law of consent and the law of property need to operate in tandem.[16] The law of consent does not protect a person's right to place limits on what might be done with their tissue after excision (in particular where it falls into the hands of third parties). Property law offers originators more control over the fate of their tissue and embryos through the rules around conditional gifts.[17] Of course, it is open to researchers to accept

[12] *cf*, eg T Merrill, 'Property and the Right to Exclude' (1998) 77 *Nebraska Law Review* 730; L Katz, 'Exclusion and Exclusivity in Property Law' (2008) *University of Toronto Law Journal* 58; A Mossoff, 'What is Property? Putting the Pieces Back Together' (2003) 45 *Arizona Law Review* 371; JE Penner, *The Idea of Property in Law* (Oxford, Oxford University Press, 1997) ch 4; and H Dagan, 'Inside Property' (2013) 63 *University of Toronto Law Journal* 1.

[13] *cf* KR Guzman, 'Property, Progeny, Body Part: Assisted Reproduction and the Transfer of Wealth' (1997) 31 *University of California, Davis Law Review* 193.

[14] M Quigley, 'Property: The Future of Human Tissue?' (2009) 17 *Medical Law Review* 457, 457–66; M Macilotti, 'Reshaping Informed Consent in the Biobanking Context' (2012) 19 *European Journal of Health Law* 271, 271–88.

[15] It has been argued that the US law of privacy is a useful means of protecting some interests (R Rao, 'Property, Privacy, and the Human Body', above n 3) but these are both jurisdiction- and context-specific.

[16] JK Mason and GT Laurie, 'Consent or Property? Dealing with the Body and its Parts in the Shadow of Bristol and Alder Hey' (2001) 64 *Modern Law Review* 710.

[17] JK Mason and GT Laurie, *Mason and McCall Smith's Law and Medical Ethics*, 8th edn (Oxford, Oxford University Press, 2011) at 14.27; *cf* R Magnusson, 'The Use of Human Tissue Samples in Medical

only tissue donated without restrictions – they would be able to refuse any conditional gift. But the main point here is that the protection offered by the law of privacy or consent is distinct from that offered by property law. There needs to be a legal regime (either a general regime such as property law or a *sui generis* regime) that specifies who can do what to a physical thing (such as tissue or embryos) that is physically outside a human body.

Rather than arguing for a *sui generis* legal regime, one could also argue that there is a legal category more suitable than 'property' that should be applied to sensitive subject matter. For example, perhaps *in vitro* embryos ought to be treated as 'persons' (or 'children') rather than objects of 'property'. While such a classification would be morally attractive to some, the fit is contingent on society being willing to live by its implications. Currently, unwanted *in vitro* embryos are routinely destroyed and have no 'right to life' – a reversal of that policy (while beyond the scope of this article) would be momentous and unlikely. Even those who regard embryos as having a high moral status do not necessarily equate them with living human beings (although a minority may). While treating embryos as persons might resolve the completeness problem, the solution seems less well suited than property, as described below.

Tissue and Embryos in the Courts

Historically, the failure to treat excised human tissue as a potential object of property is closely linked with the law of corpses, pursuant to which dead bodies could not be owned.[18] While the precise origins of this rule are obscure, it is now a well-established principle of law that a corpse cannot be an object of property rights or the subject of larceny.[19] This rule is subject to the proposition that an executor or administrator may have rights of possession of a body prior to burial for limited purposes,[20] and remedies (including mandamus) may be

Research: Legal Issues for Human Research Ethics Committees' (2000) 7 *Journal of Law and Medicine* 390, 394; Australian Law Reform Commission, *Essentially Yours: The Protection of Human Genetic Information in Australia*, Report No 96 (2003) at 529–30.

[18] P Matthews, 'Whose Body: People as Property' (1983) 36 *Current Legal Problems* 193; Quigley, 'Property: The Future of Human Tissue?', above n 14; SHE Harmon and GT Laurie, '*Yearworth v North Bristol NHS Trust*: Property, Principles, Precedents and Paradigms' (2010) 69 *Cambridge Law Journal* 476, 476–93.

[19] *Haynes's Case* (1614) 12 Co Rep 113, 77 ER 1389; *R v Lynn* (1788) 100 ER 394; *R v Sharpe* (1857) 169 ER 959 (no property in a corpse); *R v Kelly* [1998] 3 All ER 741, 749 (human corpses 'not in themselves and without more capable of being property'); *Doodeward v Spence* [1908] HCA 45, 45 (per Griffith J). See generally, PDG Skegg, 'Human Corpses, Medical Specimens and the Law of Property' (1976) 4 *Anglo-American Law Review* 412.

[20] *Dobson v North Tyneside Health Authority* [1997] 1 WLR 596, 600; *Smith v Tamworth City Council* (1997) 41 NSWLR 680, 688. See also, P Vines, 'The Sacred and the Profane: The Role of Property Concepts in Disputes about Post-Mortem Examination' (2007) 29(2) *Sydney Law Review* 235.

available to 'compel delivery of a corpse to the person charged with the duty of burying it'.[21]

The 'no property in a corpse' rule was weakened in the Australian case of *Doodeward v Spence.*[22] In that case, the preserved body of a 'two headed baby' was treated as an object of property rights due to the work and skill that had been lawfully applied to it. The case stands for the principle that a person who lawfully applies 'work and skill' to such an object will have property in the result, even though it may not have been property otherwise.[23] This exception has been criticised,[24] and although it has been incorporated into UK human tissue legislation, it has received a mixed reception in British cases.[25] What is clear is that, whether through the breadth of the work and skill exception, or through a preparedness to recognise property in human tissue in a broader range of circumstances, property law has been applied in the UK and Australia in a broad range of cases involving human tissue, including stored human gametes.[26] Thus the law of corpses no longer poses a practical barrier to the recognition of property rights in treated samples of excised human tissue in the UK and Australia.

In the US, a common starting point for discussion concerning property rights in human tissue is the Californian Supreme Court decision in *Moore v University of California.*[27] While Moore was entitled to some remedies as a result of the use of his excised spleen without his consent, he was not entitled to rely on the law of conversion as the spleen was held not to have been his property. At least in some contexts, however, the US courts are prepared to recognise property in human tissue: in *US v Arora*, an action for conversion was recognised in relation to cultured human cells held by the National Institute of Health;[28] in *Washington University v Catalona*, tissue could be donated to a university[29] effectively transferring property

[21] *Doodeward v Spence* [1908] HCA 45, 45 (per Griffith J).

[22] *Doodeward v Spence* (1908) 6 CLR 406.

[23] The relevance of the nature of the object differs among the judges. While Griffith CJ treats the object as a 'human body', it was relevant for Barton J that the object was a 'dead-born fœtal monster', a curiosity rather than a corpse in the ordinary sense. However, Barton J also agreed with Griffith CJ's reasons for decision.

[24] For example, R Hardcastle, *Law and the Human Body* (Oxford, Hart Publishing, 2007) 125–44; *Yearworth v North Bristol NHS Trust* [2009] 3 WLR 118.

[25] Human Tissue Act 2004 (UK), s 32(9)(c); *R v Kelly* [1998] 3 All ER 741 (expressing the view that human tissue may one day be recognised as property where they have a 'use or significance beyond their mere existence'); *Re Organ Retention Group Litigation* [2005] QB 506, 566; *AB v Leeds Teaching Hospital NHS Trust* [2004] EWHC 644. *cf Yearworth v North Bristol NHS Trust* [2009] 3 WLR 118.

[26] *Bazley v Wesley Monash IVF Pty Ltd* [2010] QSC 118; *Jocelyn Edwards; Re the estate of the late Edwards* [2011] NSWSC 478; *Re H, AE (No 2)* [2012] SASC 177; *Yearworth v North Bristol NHS Trust* [2009] 3 WLR 118; *Roche v Douglas* [2000] WASC 146. See also *Re Section 22 of the Human Tissue and Transplant Act 1982 (WA); ex parte C* [2013] WASC 3.

[27] *Moore v University of California* 793 P2d 479 (Cal Sup Ct, 1990).

[28] *US v Arora* 860 F Supp 1091 (D Md, 1994).

[29] To say that a person can donate or give away a thing implicitly assumes that the thing is property: Mason and Laurie, 'Consent or Property? Dealing with the Body and its Parts in the Shadow of Bristol and Alder Hey', above n 16, 701, 725. While one can talk of 'giving' time to someone, this is a different use of the term as there is there is no consequence for control of any 'thing', *cf* Skene, ch 15 in this volume.

rights;[30] in *Brotherton v Cleveland*, corneas from a corpse were held to be property for the purposes of the *United States Constitution*;[31] and in *Venner v State of Maryland*, human waste could be abandoned, which implies a property analysis.[32] The majority decision in *Moore*, which was strongly critiqued by the dissenting judges for its internal inconsistencies and is contrary to other decisions, need not be an insurmountable doctrinal obstacle to the argument made here.[33]

There are, however, more significant doctrinal hurdles to overcome in the context of human embryos. In the US, it was held in *Davis v Davis* that 'preembryos are not, strictly speaking, either "persons" or "property"' but occupy an 'interim category that entitles them to special respect because of their potential for human life'.[34] It is not clear whether this implies: (1) that embryos are property but subject to requirements that they be treated with respect; or (2) that embryos are neither people nor objects of property rights for legal purposes. Because the case is one of many in the US dealing with the disputes concerning the fate of embryos created by a couple following separation or divorce, the court did not need to concern itself with this distinction. The case could be decided based on balancing the reproductive liberty rights of the parties (the right not to reproduce being held in the context of that case to outweigh the right to reproduce). This way of determining the fate of embryos in the context of divorce or separation has been adopted in other US states,[35] although the extent to which an earlier agreement will be held to bind the parties varies.[36] In the UK, the rules as to the need for consent from those whose genetic material contributed to an embryo and the circumstances in which consent can be withdrawn are set out in legislation.[37]

However, even if embryos were to be the object of property rights, the rules as to their fate on divorce, separation or disagreement between progenitors could in any event be *sui generis*, whether through legislative design (as in the UK) or judicial development (as in the US). If the factors identified in family law or relationships legislation for division of property are unsuitable in the context of embryos, then embryos can be taken out of the general property distribution regime (as was done in *Davis*), or subjected to a different *sui generis* regime (as in the UK). There is no difficulty with *sui generis* (legislative or judicial[38]) rules specifying the dispo-

[30] *Washington University v Catalona* 490 F 3d 667 (8th Cir, 2007).

[31] *Brotherton v Cleveland* 923 F 2d 477 (6th Cir, 1991).

[32] *Venner v State of Maryland* 354 A2d 483 (1976) at 498–499 (Md Ct of Spec Apps). See Goold, ch 9 in this volume.

[33] See also M Goodwin, 'Formalism and the Legal Status of Body Parts' (2006) *University of Chicago Legal Forum* 317.

[34] *Davis v Davis* 842 SW2d 588 (Tenn Sup Ct, 1992). See also *Janicki v Hospital of St. Raphael* 46 Conn Supp 204 (Conn Superior Court, 1999).

[35] For example, *Reber v Reiss*, 42 A 3d 1131 (Pa Superior Court, 2012).

[36] *cf*, eg *Kass v Kass*, 696 NE 2d 174, 179 (NY Ct App, 1998); *AZ v BZ*, 725 NE2d 1051 (Mass, 2000). For a summary of the different approaches in the United States on this issue, see *Szafranski v Dunston* (2013) 993 NE2d 502 (Ill App).

[37] Human Fertilisation and Embryology Act 1990 (UK), as amended.

[38] As to the advantages of judge-made rules generally, see L Bennett Moses, 'Understanding Legal Responses to Technological Change: The Example of In Vitro Fertilization' (2005) 6 *Minnesota Journal of Law, Science and Technology* 505, 505–618.

sition of embryos where the progenitors (who would otherwise be the owners) disagree. However, this does not require that embryos be taken outside the law of property entirely. There are other things that fall generally under the law of property, but are subject to *sui generis* legal rules. Poisons and explosives can be owned, despite limits on their use and transfer.[39] Given that special rules would be required *in any event* to determine the fate of an embryo where progenitors disagree, the decision as to which law ought to apply in other circumstances remains open.

Despite some judicial statements that human tissue or human embryos cannot be objects of property rights, there are cases where property law has been used to resolve disputes concerning allocation of, damage to or destruction of embryos. In many of these cases, the decision to treat the tissue or embryo as a potential object of property rights enabled the plaintiff to access a remedy that would not otherwise have been available. They are cases where, had property law not been applied, it would have left a 'gap' in the law. They demonstrate that property law can facilitate sensible and predictable results. This is particularly obvious with the less controversial examples of blood, hair and urine which are capable of being stolen,[40] and ownership claims over samples of excised human tissue by research institutions.[41] Even in the most sensitive context of embryos, there have been many US cases where property law has been applied. In *York v Jones*,[42] patients of a fertility clinic were able to use the law of detinue to force a fertility clinic to send their embryos to a different clinic where they wished to pursue treatment. In *Frisina v Women and Infants Hospital*,[43] a claim alleging emotional distress following the loss of embryos was allowed to proceed to the extent that it was based on the loss or destruction of irreplaceable 'property'. In *Jeter v Mayo Clinic Arizona*,[44] embryos were recognised as 'things' and thus litigation based on breach of bailment and breach of an undertaking to protect 'things' was allowed to proceed. In *Dahl v Angle*,[45] rights of control over embryos were classed as 'personal property' so the court had jurisdiction to make an order respecting the embryos on dissolution of marriage.

While there are no UK or Australian cases recognising property rights in embryos, there are cases in the US, UK and Australia where property law has been applied to stored semen. In the US, semen has been recognised as an object of property for the purposes of succession[46] and the coverage of an insurance policy.[47] In the UK case of *Yearworth v North Bristol NHS Trust*,[48] stored semen

[39] For example, Poisons and Therapeutic Goods Act 1966 (NSW); Explosives Act 2003 (NSW).

[40] *R v Rothery* [1976] Crim LR 691; *R v Welsh* [1974] RTR 478; *R v Herbert* [1961] JPLGR 12.

[41] *Washington University v Catalona* 490 F 3d 667 (8th Cir, 2007); *US v Arora* 860 F Supp 1091 (D Md, 1994).

[42] *York v Jones* 717 F Supp 421 (ED Va, 1989).

[43] *Frisina v Women and Infants Hospital* LEXIS 73 (RI Superior Court, 2002).

[44] *Jeter v Mayo Clinic Arizona* 121 P 3d 1256 (Ariz Ct App, 2005).

[45] *Dahl v Angle* 222 Ore App 572 (Or Ct App, 2008).

[46] *Hecht v Superior Court of Los Angeles County*, 20 Cal Rptr 2d 275 (Cal Ct App, 1993).

[47] *Kurchner v State Farm Firm Arm and Casualty Co*, 858 So 2d 1220 (Fla Ct App, 2003).

[48] *Yearworth v North Bristol NHS Trust* [2009] 3 WLR 118.

was held to be property for the purposes of the law of tort and bailment. This gave men who had stored their semen a remedy when the storage failed. In particular, the fact that the men concerned could not do anything they wished with 'their' semen was held not to prevent semen being 'property'.[49] In Australia, three cases have treated semen as property. The first, *Bazley v Wesley Monash IVF Pty Ltd*,[50] recognised that stored semen is property and can be subject to a bailment, so that the storing facility was required to provide the stored semen to the personal representative of the deceased client upon request. In *Edwards; re the estate of Edwards*,[51] a woman was able to obtain possession of her dead husband's semen.[52] In *Re H, AE (No 2)*, which involved similar facts to *Edwards*, there was a similar result except that the court retained the power to place conditions on the use of the semen.[53] Although ultimately decided on other grounds, the idea of a property right in semen was also approved in *Re Section 22 of the Human Tissue and Transplant Act 1982 (WA); ex parte C*.[54]

In all of the cases where sensitive subject matter has been treated as an object of property rights, the use of property law enabled the appropriate resolution of disputes according to well-understood general rules. There are rules about jurisdiction, possession, destruction and so forth that are tied to the notion of 'property', either through statute or common law. There is no *sui generis* regime covering the same ground and, while one could be created, it would be unlikely to deal with all the situations covered by these cases.

This can be seen in the aftermath of a situation that arose in California. Despite the volume of academic and policy voices on the questions of what rules ought to govern *in vitro* human embryos, the absence of a suitable legal regime for embryos proved to be problematic. Reportedly, a doctor accused of using embryos in fertilisation procedures and research without the consent of the genetic contributors was not charged with theft by prosecutors (due to concerns about the fact that embryos were not property) and was charged instead with mail fraud related to errors on insurance billing forms.[55] The lack of an appropriate criminal offence for what ought (if true) to be criminal was due to the disinclination to apply property law to human gametes and embryos. At the time, California had no enacted *sui generis* regime protecting progenitors' rights in their embryos. Even the *sui generis* rule created after the scandal dealt only with the requirement of consent for use, not with other issues (such as unauthorised destruction of embryos) that

[49] This is similar to the Australian High Court's flexible understanding of property in *Yanner v Eaton* (1999) 201 CLR 351, discussed in the following section.

[50] *Bazley v Wesley Monash IVF Pty Ltd* [2010] QSC 118.

[51] *Jocelyn Edwards; Re the estate of Edwards* [2011] NSWSC 478.

[52] The *Edwards* case turned on the fact that 'work and skill' had been applied to the semen, making it property pursuant to *Doodeward v Spence* (1908) 6 CLR 406.

[53] *Re H, AE (No 2)* [2012] SASC 177.

[54] *Re Section 22 of the Human Tissue and Transplant Act 1982 (WA); ex parte C* [2013] WASC 3.

[55] Tracy Weber and Julie Marquis, 'In Quest for Miracles, Did Fertility Clinic Go too Far?' *Los Angeles Times* (Los Angeles, 4 June 1995) A1; John McDonald and Kim Christensen, 'No Jail: Fertility Doctor Gets Home Detention, Fine' *Orange County Register* (Orange County, 12 May 1998) B2.

would be managed by a general property law regime.[56] It is, of course, possible to create *sui generis* rules to deal with this or any number of other specific situations (as the UK has done).[57] The point is that such rules only work to create a complete legal framework if they are similarly exhaustive to property law.

As the cases demonstrate, where property law does apply, those with the strongest claim to an object are protected from interference from others. None of the cases in which property was recognised led to disrespectful treatment towards or enable the sale of tissue, embryos or semen. This gives rise to the question – can one keep the benefits of property law in these contexts without bringing in the harms said to be associated with commodification?

The Meaning of Property

Thus far, this chapter has explained the benefits of defining legal categories such as 'property' broadly as well as the specific advantages of such an approach in the context of human tissue and embryos. One question remains: why some judges and commentators have been reluctant to use the term 'property' in relation to sensitive subject matter. To answer this, it is necessary first to take a step back and look at the term 'property', in order to investigate the basis for this reluctance.

It would be ambitious to suggest that one could fully explain 'what property is' in a section within a chapter within a book. The definitions offered as to the meaning of property, which have shifted over time,[58] are as diverse as they are incompatible. In a previous article,[59] I gave examples of refusal to recognise property outside of established categories,[60] the test in *National Provincial Bank Ltd v Ainsworth*,[61] the link between property and the existence of a market,[62] excludability,[63] the link between property rights and *in rem* rights,[64] and the notion of there being a core list of rights or a core right.[65] Others prefer to test whether property rights ought to exist in a particular thing by reference to the existence of

[56] California Penal Code § 367g (2008).

[57] Human Fertilisation and Embryology Act 2008 c 22 (UK) sch 3.

[58] KJ Vandevelde, 'The New Property of the Nineteenth Century: The Development of the Modern Concept of Property' (1980) 29 *Buffalo Law Review* 325, 327.

[59] L Bennett Moses, 'The Applicability of Property Law in New Contexts: From Cells to Cyberspace' (2008) 30 *Sydney Law Review* 639, 639–62.

[60] *Victoria Park Racing and Recreation Grounds Co Ltd v Taylor* (1937) 58 CLR 479, 509; *Moore v University of California* 793 P2d 479 (Cal Sup Ct, 1990).

[61] *National Provincial Bank Ltd v Ainsworth* [1965] AC 1175, 1247–48.

[62] For example, *Halwood Corporation Ltd v Chief Commissioner of Stamp Duties* (1994) 33 NSWLR 395, 403. See generally, FH Lawon and B Rudden, *The Law of Property*, 4th edn (Oxford, Oxford University Press, 2002) 21.

[63] For example, K Gray, 'Property in Thin Air' (1991) 50 *Cambridge Law Journal* 252.

[64] For example, D Jackson, *Principles of Property Law* (Sydney, Law Book Co, 1967) 10, 44.

[65] For example, *Potter v Commissioners of Inland Revenue* (1854) 156 ER 392, 396; *Milirrpum v Nabalco Pty Ltd* (1971) 17 FLR 141.

justifications for allocating particular rights to particular people.[66] On the latter front, many arguments for property rights in particular things fall back on standard arguments in property literature (references to Locke, utilitarianism, or the importance of property for liberty or self-development) to justify particular recognitions or allocations of property rights.[67] The dispute about what 'property' means cannot be resolved with brevity.

The reason there are so many conflicting definitions of property is that they each address different questions. This can be illustrated by examining one definition of property, being that proffered in *National Provincial Bank Ltd v Ainsworth*:

> Before a right or interest can be admitted into the category of property, or of a right affecting property, it must be definable, identifiable by third parties, capable in its nature of assumption by third parties, and have some degree of permanence or stability.[68]

Ainsworth itself concerned whether the right of a wife to accommodation provided by her husband was proprietary and thus enforceable against a third party. The test, whether or not one agrees with it, is at least capable of answering that question. However, it would be relatively unhelpful to debate the treatment of controversial subject matter (such as human tissue) by reference to the *Ainsworth* test. On the one hand, interests in *in vitro* human embryos can be defined and identified, are theoretically capable of being controlled by another and have 'some degree' of permanence (albeit not until the end of time). Certainly, those arguing against recognising such things as objects of property do not, to my knowledge, make such arguments on the basis that rights are indefinable, unidentifiable, conceptually limited to one owner or have a short life span. Similarly, a test such as 'excludability' would not explain the reluctance to recognise property in *in vitro* embryos or excised body parts, at least those that are stored in secure conditions.[69]

In fact, discussion about whether human tissue or embryos ought to be treated as objects of property only rarely refer to a canonical test (such as that in *Ainsworth*) against which such a question could be answered. The result is that arguments are made based on assumptions about property that may in fact be contestable. For example, if two people agree that human embryos ought not to be objects of commerce, can one of them still argue that human embryos ought to treated as potential objects of other property rights? To answer this, we need to know whether property necessarily entails commercial alienability, in other words whether labelling a control right as property automatically gives the owner a

[66] H Dagan, 'The Craft of Property' (2003) 91 *California Law Review* 1517. In the context of human tissue, see A George, 'Is "Property" Necessary? On Owning the Human Body and its Parts' (2004) 10 *Res Publica* 15.

[67] See, eg J Berg, 'Owning Persons: The Applicability of Property Theory to Embryos and Fetuses' (2005) 40 *Wake Forest Law Review* 159; J Wall, 'The Legal Status of Body Parts: A Framework' (2011) 31 *Oxford Journal of Legal Studies* 783. See generally, L Becker, *Property Rights: Philosophic Foundations* (London, Routledge and K Paul, 1977). Utilitarian concerns played an important role in the majority decision in *Moore v University of California* 793 P2d 479 (Cal Sup Ct, 1990).

[68] *National Provincial Bank Ltd v Ainsworth* [1965] AC 1175, 1247–48.

[69] It may be otherwise for dead skin cells.

power to transfer that right to another for consideration. This leads us back to the question of what 'property' entails. Recent cases in Australia and the UK support the idea of a 'thin' conception of property pursuant to which something can be an object of *some* property rights even if other rights or powers commonly associated with property are denied.[70] This is similar to Dagan's position, discussing US law, that property is 'a set of institutions bearing a family resemblance'.[71] If this is correct, knowing that something can be an object of property does not tell which rights over that thing will be recognised. The label 'property' is important, not because it will give you particular rights in a thing, but because those rights that do exist will operate *in rem*. It is this *in rem* character that differentiates the kind of protection offered by property from the kind of protection offered by tort or contract.[72] If this description of 'property' is correct, then one cannot argue whether particular subject matter ought to be an object of property rights by reference exclusively to the appropriateness or justifiability of *particular* rights or powers.

Adopting a 'thin' conception of property does not deprive the term property of any meaning. A property right only makes sense in the context of a physically or conceptually definable thing with which more than one person might interact.[73] Aligned with this are variously worded restrictions on the definition of property designed to exclude rights related to things intrinsically linked to a person such as intact components of a living body or elements of personality.[74] A property right operates *in rem*, that is, against those with no pre-existing duty (for example in contract or tort) to an owner. It is protected by various rules of civil and criminal law, the content of which may vary according to the type of property concerned, the different rules for real and personal property being an example of such variance. Such laws generally operate through requiring others to exclude themselves from a thing, which has led some commentators to treat exclusion as part of a core notion of property.[75] One can go further and argue that the property rights entail at least a right to abandon or give away, as Penner does,[76] although I would argue that there is nothing in the idea of property inconsistent with restrictions on such rights (for example, environmental laws concerning abandonment in particular locations, or gun safety laws that require people to surrender guns they

[70] L Bennett Moses and N Gollan, '"Thin" Property and Controversial Subject Matter: *Yanner v Eaton* and property rights in human tissue and embryos' (2013) 21 *Journal of Law and Medicine* 307–11.

[71] H Dagan, *Property: Values and Institutions* (New York, Oxford University Press, 2011) xi, 42.

[72] *cf* Krebs, ch 4 in this volume.

[73] CA Arnold, 'The Reconstitution of Property: Property as a Web of Interests' (2002) 26 *Harvard Environmental Law Review* 281. Note that the object need not be tangible: AS Weinrib, 'Information and Property' (1988) 38 *University of Toronto Law Journal* 117, 120.

[74] *R v Bentham* [2005] UKHL 18, [2005] 1 WLR 1057 [8] ('One cannot possess something which is not separate and distinct from oneself'); *Yearworth v North Bristol NHS Trust* [2010] QB 1 [30]. See also J Penner 'The Bundle of Rights Picture of Property' (1996) 43 *University of California Los Angeles Law Review* 711; R Hardcastle, *Law and the Human Body*, above n 24; M Quigley, 'Property in Human Biomaterials – Separating Persons and Things?' above n 74, 659–83.

[75] TW Merrill and HE Smith, *Property: Principles and Policies* (New York, Foundation Press, 2007). Compare with references at n 12 above.

[76] Penner 'The Bundle of Rights Picture of Property', above n 74, 711.

no longer wish to own through particular channels, or laws restricting the transfer of embryos).

According to a thin conception of property, there is no *need* to add more requirements, in particular a power to alienate, at a definitional stage. It may be appropriate for different objects to be associated with different rights and duties because of differences in the personal and cultural meanings of an object.[77] There is a need in property scholarship to differentiate between general arguments justifying alienability of property rights and definitional questions such as whether a lack of full alienability prevents a particular right being classified as proprietary. One can have default rules (for instance, that unless the law says otherwise a property right is fully alienable) without making this a component of a definition. The debate as to the circumstances in which rights over sensitive subject matter ought to be transferable, if at all, is thus separable from the debate about whether such sensitive subject matter ought to fall within the scope of property law. This chapter does not attempt to engage in the former debate, about which much has been written.[78] The point is rather that, whether or not one believes that there ought to be restrictions on alienability, one can embrace property.

A thin definition of property allows for property law to have a broader scope. It allows for the possibility that certain things can be the subject of some property rights but not others. In particular, it makes possible inalienable property rights. Of course, reducing or eliminating the alienability of something will have an impact on the value of owning that thing.[79] However, in circumstances where economic value is not the rationale for recognising property rights, as is the case with human embryos, this is not problematic.[80] A right to possession and control of a human embryo with limited or no alienability can, on the thin conception, operate *in rem* and be backed up by civil and criminal laws concerning 'property'. In the case of human tissue which has commercial value, questions around who ought to benefit are more complex, and are dealt with in other chapters.[81] My point here is merely that one *can* have property without commerce.

The recognition of inalienable property rights is consistent with the law in other areas. An unassignable lease and unassignable shares in a private company are still classified as property. Similarly, laws restricting the sale of firearms or restricted substances do not mean that guns and pharmaceuticals are not objects of property.[82] As other commentators have pointed out, commerce and property

[77] CA Arnold, 'The Reconstitution of Property: Property as a Web of Interests' (2002) 26 *Harvard Environmental Law Review* 281.

[78] For example, *cf* MJ Radin, 'Market-Inalienability', (1987) 100 *Harvard Law Review* 1849 with H Horsley, 'Note: Reconsidering Inalienability for Commercially Valuable Biological Materials' (1992) 29 *Harvard Journal on Legislation* 223, and S Brown and S Then, 'Commercialisation of Regenerative Human Tissue: Regulation and Reform in Australia and England, Wales and Northern Ireland' (2007) 14 *Journal of Law and Medicine* 339.

[79] HE Smith, 'Property as the Law of Things' (2012) 125 *Harvard Law Review* 1691.

[80] HE Smith, 'Property is Not Just a Bundle of Rights' (2011) 8 *Econ Journal Watch* 279.

[81] For example, Dickenson, ch 11, Stewart, Lipworth, Aparicio, Fleming and Kerridge, ch 3 and Goold and Quigley, ch 14 in this volume.

[82] See, eg Firearms Act 1996 (NSW), pt 6; Poisons and Therapeutic Goods Act 1966 (NSW).

are distinct, albeit related, fields – not all property can be sold and not everything that can be sold is property.[83]

Inalienable property rights in excised human tissue and *in vitro* embryos would operate in conjunction with existing regulations. The sale of human tissue and human embryos is illegal or severely regulated in most jurisdictions.[84] Decisions such as *Yearworth, Bazley* and *Edwards* have not led to a judicial repeal of such provisions. Further, to the best of my knowledge there is no empirical evidence that decisions recognising property rights in tissue or embryos have made statutory restrictions on sale or mistreatment less effective. So long as statutory restrictions on sale are operative and enforced, we need have no concern about the application of the 'bona fide purchaser for value' doctrine, the applicability of personal property securities legislation or people legally profiting from facilitating trade in bodily material, contrary to the concerns of Skene.[85] While some people will break the law and illegal sales may occur, the property label will make little difference. If anything, the illegal nature of the transaction will preserve pre-existing property rights which will be able to be enforced *in rem,* providing a disincentive for potential 'purchasers'.

Similarly, recognising the proprietary character of existing rights of possession and control does not mean that people can do 'anything they like' with 'their' embryos. The fact that a person has property rights in a dog does not make animal cruelty legal. One could give other examples, from zoning in land law to the somewhat obvious point that ownership of a weapon is not a defence to murder or assault. If human embryos were recognised as objects of property, we could still have laws that, directly or indirectly, prohibited the creation of embryo earrings.[86] A legislature can impose laws that require people to treat embryos with respect without discarding the property label.[87] Similarly, the property label will not prevent the articulation of ethical guidelines for medical practitioners and researchers.[88] Further, contrary to Herring's concerns,[89] the label 'property' is besides the point for laws around littering which operate whether or not the 'litter' is an object of property rights, or owned by the litterer.[90] Whatever concerns about the property label one may have need to be based on the necessary features of a property label, not common associations.

[83] Penner 'The Bundle of Rights Picture of Property', above n 74, 711.

[84] For example, Human Tissue Act 1983 (NSW), s 32; Human Tissue Act 2004 (UK), s 34. See also Council of Europe's Convention for the Protection of Human Rights and Dignity of the Human Being With Regard to the Application of Biology and Medicine, ETS 1997, no 164, art 21; Additional Protocol of the Convention on Human Rights and Biomedicine Concerning Transplantation of Organs and Tissues of Human Origin, ETS 2002, no 168, arts 21, 22.

[85] Skene, 'Proprietary Interests in Human Bodily Material: *Yearworth*, Recent Australian Cases on Stored Semen and their Implications', above n 3, 227–45.

[86] For example, *R v Gibson* [1990] 2 QB 619 (CA).

[87] *cf* Martin and Lagod, 'The Human Preembryo, the Progenitors, and the State', above n 10.

[88] For example, Medical Research Council, Human Tissue and Biological Samples for Use in Research: Operational and Ethical Guidelines (2001).

[89] See Herring, ch 13 in this volume.

[90] For example, *Protection of the Environment Operations Act 1997* (NSW) s 144A (definition of 'litter'), s 145.

If I am right that one can have limited inalienable rights to human tissue and embryos, there is still one important dignitarian argument that remains to those who oppose the idea of human tissue or embryos becoming objects of property rights.[91] This is the concern that the property label itself might cause harm, encouraging people to think less of the 'specialness' or sacred value of human tissue, human embryos and, ultimately perhaps, human beings themselves. This is distinct, and certainly less severe, than concerns that around the impact of actual market-alienability, which relate to reduced human flourishing as a result of suggesting an equivalence between personhood and money.[92] The impact of actual market alienability will depend on metaphysical perceptions, in particular the extent to which people see their body as separate from 'themselves'.[93] The risk associated with a mere 'property' label is to some extent unknown, and depends in part on whether popular conceptions of property's meaning embrace notions of commodity and market, even where this is excluded from a legal definition. This dignitarian concern is related to a concern that property creates a presumption of alienability and that this may be a slippery slope.[94] If one thinks of property in activities rather than things, treating assisted reproduction through *in vitro* fertilisation as a property-protected activity may raise fewer eyebrows than describing *in vitro* embryos as owned.[95] This reduces the impact of property language on human dignity, although it does not necessarily eliminate these kinds of concerns. Politically, property language in the context of *in vitro* embryos in particular may be considered too risky even if, legally, it does not have the implications that some fear. Questions around the impact on perceptions, and the political impact, of employing property language in this sensitive field cannot be determined in the absence of empirical evidence. The argument in this paper is thus contingent on an assumption that issues around the scope of property law in this area would either be limited to legal audiences who understand its (minimal) impact or be explained to the public in ways that illustrated its (limited) purpose and confirmed the ongoing prohibitions on sale of human tissue and embryos.

[91] R Brownsword, *Rights, Regulation, and the Technological Revolution* (USA, Oxford University Press, 2008).

[92] Radin, 'Market-Inalienability', above n 78.

[93] H Horsley, 'Note: Reconsidering Inalienability for Commercially Valuable Biological Materials' (1992) 29 *Harvard Journal on Legislation* 223.

[94] For example, D Beyleveld and R Brownsword, 'My Body, My Body Parts, My Property?' (2000) 8 *Health Care Analysis* 87; J Nedelsky, 'Property in Potential Life? A Relational Approach to Choosing Legal Categories' (1993) 6 *Canadian Journal of Law and Jurisprudence* 343 ('And if potential life is designated as property, there will be strong pressures against regulation to control the disturbing possibilities of genetic engineering and competitive markets in "reproductive material"'); SHE Harmon, 'A Penny for Your Thoughts, A Pound for Your Flesh: Implications of Recognising Property Rights in Our Own Excised Body Parts' (2006) 7 *Medical Law International* 329, 330 ('Although a property model need not inevitably lead to commerce, the likelihood of it doing so is overwhelming'); Mason and Laurie, *Mason and McCall Smith's Law and Medical Ethics*, above n 17, 14.13 ('[Property] carries a particular message – one of the potential for commerce or trade...').

[95] See generally, H Breakey, 'Two Concepts of Property: Ownership of Things and Property in Activities' (2011) 42 *Philosophical Forum* 239.

Property rights in excised human tissue and *in vitro* human embryos would not be the same as property rights in ordinary objects such as cars. Alienability and use would be restricted by existing laws.

Further, the changing nature of the property rights which attach to wild animals provides a useful example of the status of how the law of property can apply to things whose status changes over time. Under the common law, the qualities of the animal and its relationship with its surroundings govern when property rights initially vest and are ultimately extinguished. Particularly, in order for an individual to *obtain* a property right to a wild animal, the animal must be 'reduced into possession',[96] which means that the animal must be caught or killed.[97] Further, the property in the wild animal will only subsist for 'so long as they remain tame, for if they do attain their natural liberty . . . the property is *lost*'.[98] Excised human tissues and *in vitro* embryos could be treated in much the same manner, with property rights only vesting upon their extraction from the body and extinguishing at the point of any later implantation. Treating *in vitro* embryos as objects of property rights need not imply that the babies born from such embryos can be owned. The precise point at which human tissue becomes (and ceases to be) property may be hard to define,[99] but the difficulty of drawing lines ought not prevent the operation of property law in clear cases.

Conclusion

Because property is a flexible concept, what matters in the debate about whether embryos or tissue can be objects of property is not what rights are granted, but how they are classified. As explained above, property classification offers many advantages. It provides appropriate remedies where a 'thing' is stolen, destroyed, misappropriated, harmed or used by others without the consent of those who have rights in the 'thing'.[100]

One could create a non-property legal regime that mirrored the *in rem* rights and remedies available to those whose rights are proprietary.[101] However, as was the case with the law of churns, one has to have good reasons for doing this that outweigh the disadvantages associated with *sui generis* legal regimes, in particular the risk of under-inclusiveness. Many of the arguments put against the idea of property in excised human tissue or property in an *in vitro* human embryo rely on a particular conception of property that has more in common with Blackstone's

[96] *Kearry v Pattinson* [1939] 1 KB 471; 1 All ER 65, 69.

[97] *Blades v Higgs* (1865) 11 HL Case 621; 11 ER 1474, 1478.

[98] *The Case of Swans* (1592) 7 Co Rep 15b; 77 ER 435, 438 (emphasis added).

[99] M Quigley, 'Property in Human Biomaterials – Separating Persons and Things?' (2012) 32 *Oxford Journal of Legal Studies* 659.

[100] On the question of remedies, see Nwabueze, ch 10 in this volume.

[101] An example would be the *sui generis* statutory regime proposed by Herring, ch 13 in this volume.

idea of a person's 'sole and despotic dominion'[102] than more nuanced modern views.

Rather than arguing for a *sui generis* legal regime, one could also argue that there is a legal category more suitable than 'property' that should be applied to sensitive subject matter. As explained above, alternative categories either do not address the same issues (for example, the requirement for consent) or are a poor fit (which I would argue is the problem with treating embryos as children). The law of property, on the other hand, does not require any major policy reversal, and will not prevent the operation of existing restrictions on the use and sale of tissue and embryos. It is unique as a general legal category in protecting the interests that people have in 'things' that are not part of or intrinsic to themselves. While there may be some discomfort with the word 'property', the practical implications are more targeted than most people believe. It is the rights of control over embryos that would be 'property', not the embryos themselves.

To the extent that excised human tissue and *in vitro* human embryos are special (and they are special in different ways), *sui generis* rules can be created. As explained in section I, there is a difference between relying generally on a broad category (such as property), supplemented by *sui generis* rules, and relying entirely on *sui generis* rules. For instance, one can prohibit or restrict the sale of human tissue (or embryos or gametes) to address concerns around commodification, one can control how embryos are created (if one wishes to deal with concerns around hybrids, for instance), one can regulate laboratories, and one can restrict what can be done with embryos. Such laws are required anyway (if one wants them) whether or not property law operates as the default regime. Whatever rules are thought desirable (and this chapter makes no comment on that question), we ought also to rely on the default broadly applicable legal regime of property law.

Allowing human tissue and *in vitro* embryos to be objects of property rights does not have the effects often attributed to it. It does not mean that such things can be sold (or charged), where these are otherwise prohibited. It does not permit one to do something (such as create embryo earrings) provided respectful treatment is enshrined in law. What it does do is ensure that there is a well-established default legal regime for dealing with situations involving damage, destruction, theft or, in some cases, ownership disputes.[103] Provided we do not create barriers to prevent this, property law will operate in a technologically neutral manner, regardless of changes in medical technology as to the types of excised tissue that are useful or the procedures for creating *in vitro* embryos. Arguments contrary to such a position should be based on clearly articulated and justified assumptions about the nature of property and should take account of the disadvantages of a *sui generis* approach.

[102] W Blackstone, *Commentaries on the Law of England* (Chicago, Callaghan and Cockcroft, 1871) vol 2, ch 1, 329.

[103] As explained above, a *sui generis* regime may be required to resolve disputes between progenitors over the fate of *in vitro* embryos.

13

Why We Need a Statute Regime to Regulate Bodily Material

JONATHAN HERRING

Introduction

Nearly everyone agrees that the current legal regime dealing with bodily material is inadequate. It is opaque, inconsistent and lacks a coherent basis. Reform there must be. But at that point consensus breaks down. This chapter will present the case for a legal regime based on statute, rather than one based on property rights. It will make two primary points.

First, a property model fails to protect important social, communal and relational interests in bodies. Moreover, it does not capture important personal interests in body parts. These interests could be recognised under a statutory approach. I will explore shortly more precisely what these interests are. I accept that a property approach could be adapted to take account of such interests. We could, as Donna Dickenson suggests in her chapter in this book, adopt a communal model of property. Alternatively, we could create statutory exceptions to take account of these. However, in doing so we would soon be departing so far from the standard property paradigm that it would barely resemble property as it is currently understood. More importantly, and this is a key point for this chapter, if we take property as our starting point that skews the debate about the treatment of bodily parts in a particular way. Property models, at least as understood in common law jurisdictions, are largely based on individualistic values that protect rights of exclusion and control.[1] Simon Douglas' chapter highlights this and indeed regards it as the primary benefit of the property approach. By contrast, relying on a statute gives us a starting point of unbiased scales with which to compare the different individual and social claims that may arise. While, of course, a statute can when drafted reflect a certain set of values, if we start our analysis with a statute we start with a clean slate. Furthermore, we have the flexibility to strike the balance between competing values in different contexts. I will also argue that property

[1] I don't make explicit reference here to consent-based models as they are not really candidates for an over-arching framework for body parts.

language misrepresents the nature of bodies and body parts. It is based on an image of the body as bounded and self-contained, which is simply false. A statute, by contrast, will enable us to weigh the broad range of interests and better reflect the complex nature of our bodies.

Secondly, the property approach claims that all our bodily material is property and in so doing imagines that we have similar interests in all parts of our bodies. We don't. We have utterly different attitudes towards different kinds of bodily material in different contexts. A statutory approach enables us to distinguish between the significance attached to different body parts and in different contexts. A property approach subjects the urine flushed down the toilet and the egg frozen for reproductive purposes to the same core legal regime. A statute enables us to provide a subtle nuanced response depending on the circumstances of the removal and retention of the body part, rather than using property as a one-size-fits-all concept that responds to all cases.

The chapter will conclude by examining two leading cases used by proponents of the property approach to demonstrate the benefit of their analysis. It will be argued that, in fact, on a close analysis, a response based on a statutory regime is hugely preferable.

Individualised Values

As Jesse Wall has argued, a useful starting place in the debate over the proper legal regulation is to identify the interests that people have in bodies and separated body parts.[2] Having done so we should then assess which set of legal rules best protect those entitlements. There are, I suggest, multiple interests. As argued later, these will vary greatly depending on the nature of the body part and the circumstances of its removal and/or storage. Property rights protect one particular set of legal interests: those of control, exclusion and transfer. It is not surprising that these interests receive so much attention from property rights supporters because in the legal context it is these kinds of rights that individuals are likely to claim. People rarely bring proceedings on behalf of the communal interests. Larissa Katz has captured the nature of property interests well. She writes:

> First, familiar property law doctrines . . . carve out a position of authority for owners that is neither derived from nor subordinate to any other's. These and other rules create the institutional structure that permits the owner to function as the supreme agenda setter for the resource.[3]

This favouring of the interests of the individual, and allowing the owner to 'set the agenda', is at the heart of property rights.

[2] J Wall, 'The Legal Status of Body Parts: A Framework' (2011) 31 *Oxford Journal of Legal Studies* 783.
[3] L Katz, 'Exclusion and Exclusivity in Property Law' (2008) 58 *University of Toronto Law Journal* 275.

But we should not be blind to the importance of other interests that are found in bodies and body parts. These include the interests of communities, society and those in relationship with the individual. These interests are not easily captured by a common law property regime. They could, however, be recognised and given weight under a statutory regime. I am not saying property is not a subtle enough legal tool to be able to capture these more societal, relational or communal values. My claim is that property law is particularly well honed to protect individual interests and to prioritise those interests. It is not naturally designed to protect communal interests.[4]

So what are these values that I am concerned will be sidelined in a property analysis? There is not enough space to set these all out. I will therefore summarise some of the ones that are particularly significant. First, the property approach does not capture the 'me-ness'[5] of our bodily material. As Jesse Wall writes:

> The problem is, that although property is good with things, sometimes our control of things is more about us (our personality, personhood or our relationships).[6]

Our bodies can represent us to others and play a role constituting our identity. This is evident in complaints of those with a disability who complain that their disability is used by others to define them. While this me-ness is especially true in relation to intact body parts, it can still apply in relation to separated body parts. This is reflected in the uneasy relationship between family and a donated heart. A good example is the story of the mother of a 13-year-old girl who had died in an accident and whose heart was donated, asking the recipient if they could listen to their 'daughter's heart'.[7] It is also reflected in the response of many of the families in the retained organs scandals.[8] There would have been nothing like this outcry had doctors been keeping, say, pieces of clothing from the children.

Some commentators have put this argument in terms of dignity interests.[9] Charles Foster has produced a number of examples of situations where he claims a property analysis does not capture all the interests in the body part. Here are two:

1. The human-ear ashtray: Medical students steal an ear from the cadaver they are dissecting. They varnish it and use it as an ashtray. The cadaver was donated for the purposes of medical education. Liberal though he was, the donor did not regard use of an ear as an ashtray as one of those purposes.

[4] See JW Harris, *Property and Justice* (Oxford, Oxford University Press, 2002) for an imagination of a property regime which is much more attuned to communal interests. It is a very different regime from the one we have.

[5] I first heard this phrase in a lecture given by Jesse Wall and am grateful for his permission to use it.

[6] J Wall, 'The Trespasses of Property Law' (2013) *Journal of Medical Ethics*, published online 10 July 2013: doi: 10.1136/medethics-2013-101439.

[7] www.today.com/id/39456266/#.UoCv0XDIYUs.

[8] The Retained Organ Commission, *Remembering the Past, Looking to the Future* (London, The Stationery Office, 2004).

[9] C Foster, *Human Dignity in Bioethics and the Law* (Oxford, Hart Publishing, 2011).

2. The head of an unknown person: Children play football in the street. They are using, not a football, but the head of an unknown and untraceable person which a dog has retrieved from a mediaeval cemetery.[10]

He argues in such cases, 'most of the wrongness is not that there was an inappropriate dealing with property per se, but that there was an inappropriate dealing with "property" of this kind'.[11] Foster acknowledges that dignity as a concept is problematic because it is difficult to produce a precise definition, but he believes that dignity is involved in protecting interests in thriving as a person. There is not space here to fully explore the benefits and difficulties of dignity and competing understandings of it, but at the very least what supporters of dignity are identifying is the sense of value many people recognise in body parts which is beyond the physical type captured by a property analysis.

The notion of property is based on the assumption that the owner has control over the thing which he or she uses to achieve their ends. It does not capture the idea that the thing may have the value of representation for others. We do not regard some parts of our body as a 'thing'. Simon Douglas in this volume explains that to be the subject of property something must be 'a thing'. But we don't (or at least not always) think of our bodies or their products or the bodies of others in that way. As Wall notes:

> [W]here a parent, patient, donor or a widow, is deprived of their entitlements in bodily material, they are being deprived of the opportunity to exercise their rights as a parent, as a wife or as an embodied person. Their interest in the bodily material represents a very personal interest.[12]

It is true that property interests can protect that interest while it is in the possession of the individual, but as the retained organ scandal shows, once the property is owned by someone else property fails to recognise the interests of the originator, and indeed, helps protect the new owner from claims from the originator.

Second, the best understandings of health are communal.[13] Health is typically understood as a subjective matter. It is a matter of how my body is functioning. However, this overlooks the fact that our bodies are highly dependent upon other bodies. There is great wisdom in the statement of the National Aboriginal Health Strategy Working Party:

> Aboriginal health is not just the physical well being of an individual but is the social, emotional and cultural well being of the whole community in which each individual is able to achieve their full potential thereby bringing about the total well being of their community.[14]

[10] C Foster, 'Dignity and the Use of Body Parts' (2014) 40 *Journal of Medical Ethics* 44.

[11] ibid.

[12] J Wall, 'The trespasses of property law' (2014) 40 *Journal of Medical Ethics* 19, 20.

[13] C Foster and J Herring, 'What is Health?' in M Freeman, S Hawkes and B Bennett (eds), *Law and Global Health* (Oxford, Oxford University Press, 2013).

[14] National Aboriginal Health Strategy Working Party, 1989, quoted in P Boddington and U Raisanen, 'Theoretical and Practical Issues in the Definition of Health: Insights from Aboriginal Australia' (2009) 34 *Journal of Medicine and Philosophy* 49.

The health of each of us is related to the health of those in our community. This is most obviously true in the case of infectious diseases and in the context of a national health system with rationed health care. In more subtle ways our bodily well-being is dependent on the health of a broader community.

In a powerful article Kate Lindemann contrasts the emphasis that is paid to the accommodations for disabled people so as to minimise the impact of their disability, with the lack of appreciation of the accommodations made for the able-bodied:

> Colleagues, professional staff members, and other adults are unconscious of the numerous accommodations that society provides to make their work and life style possible. ATM's, extended hours in banks, shopping centres and medical offices, EZpass, newspaper kiosks, and elevators are all accommodations that make contemporary working life possible. There are entire industries devoted to accommodating the needs of adult working people. Fast food, office lunch delivery, day time child care, respite care, car washing, personal care attendants, interpreters, house cleaning, and yard and lawn services are all occupations that provide services that make it possible for adults to hold full time jobs.[15]

We highlight the special provisions disabled people need to integrate into society, but ignore the facilities everyone needs. All of this indicates that we clearly do have interests in each other's bodies. Genetics too teach us how linked our bodies are. The difference between each body in genetic terms is minute. We are so much more alike than we differ. As Isabel Karpin puts it:

> The individual in the age of the gene is fundamentally connected and vulnerable. The individual in the age of the gene always contains a trace of the other; not-one but not-two.[16]

A proper understanding of evolutionary processes shows that evolutionary development is not simply a matter of individual pursuit. As Mary Midgley explains, Darwin's work shows: 'Like other social animals, [humans] are not shaped for heroic solitude but for profound cooperation with others, living interdependently in friendly association.'[17]

Third, more broadly, the self is a relational concept. It is in, with and through our communities and relationships with others that we understand our selves.[18] This is because our identity is found in our relationship with others, from our beginning to our end and beyond. This is not just in psychological terms. Vulnerability and dependency are central, essential, defining aspects of humanity. Caring for others is an essential part of life. We are cared for or are caring for other bodies throughout our lives. In caring, the division between 'you' and 'me'

[15] K Lindemann, 'The Ethics of Receiving' (2003) 24 *Theoretical Medicine and Bioethics* 501.

[16] I Karpin, 'Genetics and the Legal Conception of Self' in M Shildrick and R Mykitiuk (eds), *Ethics of the Body* (Cambridge, MA, MIT Press, 2005).

[17] M Midgley, *The Solitary Self* (London, Aucumen Publishing, 2010) 24. See further, C Foster, *The Selfless Gene* (London, Thomas Nelson, 2010).

[18] R Saltonstall, 'Healthy Bodies, Social Bodies: Men's and Women's Concepts and Practices of Health in Everyday Life' (1993) 36 *Social Science and Medicine* 7.

becomes lost. The vulnerability of the one becomes the vulnerability of the other; the disability of the one becomes the disability of the other.[19] The division between the body of one and the body of other makes no sense in relationships of intimacy or our psychological conception of the self. All of this clashes sharply with the claims of one person seeking ownership of their bodies with the corresponding rights to exclude others. This is not to say that the law is needed to allow exclusion of inappropriate invasions (such as the involvement of the criminal law), but it also has a role of enabling beneficial interactions to flourish. The law needs to be based on a norm of interlocking mutually dependent relationships, rather than an individualised vision of property or other rights.[20]

Fourth, in a series of articles P-L Chau and I have challenged the assumptions that commonly surround our bodies.[21] I will not repeat those arguments in detail here. We emphasise that our bodies are not in a straightforward way 'ours'. Bodies are constantly interacting with and dependent upon other bodies. In biological terms our bodies are constantly changing and are home for a host of different biological organisms which are creatures in their own right. Our bodies continually change with cells dying and falling off, and new cells being created. By the time we die there is little of us that is biologically the same as when we were born. Whenever people are in proximity bodily material can be passed through the air. As Kenneth Gergen, in his important book on the nature of the self, writes:

> [T]he idea of the skin as a container seems inappropriate. The metaphor of a sieve might be more relevant, with material moving in both directions. On the one hand we could say that nothing that passes through me is distinctly mine (my body); all that I call 'my body' belongs to the larger world out of which it is but a transient conglomerate.[22]

With everyone we meet we take a bit of their bodies and give a bit of ours. This means that the property approach based on rights of exclusive control over our bodies has more than an air of unreality. By their very nature bodies are things that cannot be controlled. Nor can we claim that bodily material is something we have created through our efforts. They are not things we have produced. They are constantly interacting and mixing with other bodies and the wider environment.

None of this is reflected in the language of property. Simon Douglas in his chapter in this book argues that for something to be a property right it must be a 'thing': it must be capable of being transferred and need protection from physical interference. He admits this is a controversial understanding, noting the example of intellectual property, which he doubts is properly property. I do not want, and

[19] S Whitney, 'Dependency Relations: Corporeal Vulnerability and Norms of Personhood in Hobbes and Kittay' (2011) 26 *Hypatia* 544.

[20] R West, *Caring for Justice* (New York, New York University Press, 1997) 356.

[21] J Herring and P-L Chau, 'My Body, Your Body, Our Bodies' (2007) 15 *Medical Law Review* 34; P-L Chau and J Herring, 'Interconnected, Inhabited and Insecure: Why Bodies Should not be Property' (2014)44 *Journal of Medical Ethics* 39; J Herring and P-L Chau, 'Relational Bodies' (2013) 29 *Journal of Law and Medicine* 214.

[22] L Gergen, *Relational Being* (Oxford, Oxford University Press, 2009) 97.

indeed lack the skills, to enter that debate, but he does capture a popular understanding of property: as a bounded, self-contained and constant thing. As just argued, the biological reality of bodies is very different.

Fifth, some of what has been said might sound fanciful but the next two points are more concrete. The notion of the body being owned ties strongly into a particular stream of political thought. Donna Dickenson has recently published a book entitled *Me Medicine vs. We Medicine: Reclaiming Biotechnology for the Common Good*.[23] This is not the place to describe its significant arguments, but her book describes a shift in some political philosophies to see health as an individual concept. People are encouraged to seek a personalised medical scheme. Typically, this is provided through private health insurance. This notion that we should each seek to promote our own 'me medicine' overlooks the importance of public health initiatives. It emphasises private health-care insurance over public health provision. The language of body ownership and the emphasis on 'my body is mine', often unwittingly, plays into the hands those who wish to promote individualised health as a political ideal. It has been used powerfully by large commercial enterprises to control and manipulate donated bodily material. Dickenson's chapter in this book (Chapter 11) provides a powerful discussion of that. Indeed, she calls for a radical rethinking about the nature of property in that context to protect individuals from corporate interests.

Finally, there are the more obvious social and communal interests in body parts as organs that can save the lives of others; of material that can be used for crucial medical research for the benefit of all; of material that can be used for the education of future medical practitioners; for information that is essential for the boring, but important, task of audit.[24] As Loane Skene and others have emphasised, it is crucial that the regulation of use of bodily material is carried out in a way that promotes medical treatment and research for the benefit of all.[25]

The property model of bodies is a comforting one. It conveys a message that many find reassuring. It tells us our bodies are secure and bounded. It tells us we have control over our bodies and can decide what happens to them. It tells us we can exclude others and be independent. This may be comforting, but it is false. Our bodies are constantly changing, dependent on others for survival and subject to environmental factors.

The 'leakiness', the interconnections, the interchanges between bodies are central aspects of our humanity, in the biological, social and psychological senses. These are lost in the reduction of our bodies to property. Our true sense of self and identity is not found in our bounded, owned body, but in the breaking, mixing, and interaction of our bodies with others and with the wider environment.[26]

[23] D Dickenson, *Me Medicine vs. We Medicine: Reclaiming Biotechnology for the Common Good* (New York, Columbia University Press, 2013).

[24] For broader issues see T Murray, 'The Gift of Life Must Always Remain a Gift' (1986) (March) *Discover* 90.

[25] L Skene, 'Proprietary Rights in Human Bodies, Body parts and Tissue: Regulatory Contexts and Proposals for New Laws' (2002) 22 *Legal Studies* 102.

[26] L Irigaray, *An Ethics of Sexual Difference* (New York, Cornell University Press, 1993).

We need a statute that does not emphasise control but rather acknowledges our leakiness; that does not emphasise individualist concerns but acknowledges the communal and familial nature of our bodies; that does not emphasise a right to profit but rather the common good. Our bodies are not property. They are far more interesting than that.

I do not for a moment claim that bodily material cannot at a theoretical level be property. Simon Douglas' chapter in this book (Chapter 7) provides a convincing argument it can be. However, his chapter displays precisely my concerns. A person needs property rights over their bodily material, we are told, because without a property right 'he is vulnerable to being dispossessed of the material by another', and we need property to 'impos[e] a duty on others to refrain from interfering with it'. Perhaps in some contexts this is true, but in others we need law to enable material from bodies to be exchanged and to recognise their interdependence. We sometimes need laws that bring bodies together, not keep them apart.

As the quotation from Larissa Katz referred to earlier shows, calling a body property is not a legal technicality. It is introducing a set of legal rules well-honed to prioritise the values of exclusion and control. What I find striking about much of the writing in favour of property interests is that there is no attempt to explain how the property approach sufficiently balances the individual and societal interests in bodies and body parts. Especially given, as Katz notes, that property makes the owner the agenda setter. Imogen Goold is a notable exception.[27] She accepts that it is 'relatively uncontentious that we need to develop an approach that supports medical and scientific research'. She adds:

> Much of the complexity in determining which approach to adopt in regulating the use of human bodily material arises from the variety of both uses and users of that material; and the contexts and reasons for its use. These may lead to conflicts between the person from whom the material was taken, the person who uses it or transfers it, and subsequent users. Add to this the need to promote more general goals such as supporting medical research, enabling effective health protection and promotion, encouraging investment in drug production while still avoiding an approach that produces absurd consequences, and the task of choosing an approach is understandably a vexed one. The law cannot make everyone happy all of the time.[28]

I agree with this. Yet the property model does not provide a good way of balancing these interests. Property rights, as explained above, prioritise the rights of control and exclusion. The mere fact of something being our property gives you *in and of itself* a claim to which others need to provide a very strong justification for interference. It gives very strong priority to just one of the interests we need to weigh up. True, your land can be compulsorily purchased if required in the public interest but there would need to be need extremely strong justification for doing

[27] I Goold, 'Property or Not Property? The Spectrum of Approaches to Regulating the Use of Human Bodily Material' (2013) 21 *Journal of Law and Medicine* 299.

[28] She cites K Liddell and A Hall, 'Beyond Bristol and Alder Hey: The Future Regulation of Human Tissue' (2005) 13 *Medical Law Review* 170.

so.[29] By granting property interests we not ignoring the state interests, but making it very difficult for them ever to outweigh the property interests.

You might not be convinced by my arguments in favour of recognising societal interests and think that we should give special protection to the individual interests. However, is that true for all body parts and in all circumstances? With a statute we can give special protection to individual interests in some cases, while recognising the interests of the state in others. The property argument gives special priority to the individual interests in all parts and all times. I will develop this argument in the second half of this chapter.

Parts of Bodies and Circumstances

A legal framework to govern bodies and body parts through a statutory scheme can distinguish between our response to different parts of our bodies, the circumstances of their removal and context of their retention. Further, such a scheme can recognise the competing social and individual interests that exist in bodies and body parts and produce a sophisticated balancing of those interests, which may differ depending on the context. A statute can do this far more effectively than an overarching property, autonomy or dignity based approach can. For example, under a property approach, the body of a deceased person should pass to their executors under the will or law of intestacy, as does all their property. There is no room for an argument based on communal interests in the organs of a deceased.[30] A statute could determine that if the organs are appropriate for transplant they can be used because the communal interests outweigh the concerns of the family.

The point made in this section is a straightforward one. We do not have the same attitude towards all the parts of our bodies. Our attitude towards our dandruff is very different to the attitude towards our reproductive material. Why is that?

First, there are instrumental values. There are some parts of a body, both while intact and once separated, that can be used for specific purposes. It may be it has commercial value or it can be used in the treatment of others or the self.[31] Other parts have no use. Dried skin and waste products are rarely of interest.[32] Indeed, not only do we have no use for them, we positively do not want to have control of them.

[29] The right to peaceful enjoyment of property is protected in human rights instruments such as Art 1 of the First Protocol of the European Convention on Human Rights.

[30] Of course, there could be an opt-out or opt-in scheme for the donor's interests to be considered.

[31] See Wall, 'The Legal Status of Body Parts: A Framework', above n 2, for a sophisticated analysis of these.

[32] For a rare example, see *Venner v State*, 30 Md App 599, 354 A2d 483 (1976).

Second, as argued above, there are expressive values. Some parts of body represent who we are in a special way. When people see that part or when a person thinks about that part they feel a special attachment to it. Perhaps the best-known example is parenthood, where many biological parents feel a strong attachment to their children as a result of the biological connection.[33] Another example is the unease people feel about face transplants, as compared with other types of transplants.[34] This is in part due to the identifying nature of the face, unlike, say, a kidney that does not normally have expressive value. Notably organ donation systems allow people to select which organs they wish to donate, recognising, for example, that some people will feel differently about their eyes than their pancreas.

These different interests have been explored elsewhere, most subtly by Jesse Wall.[35] However, the point I want to emphasise is that these values will differ depending on the body part in question. I would go further and suggest that in fact most separated body parts lack instrumental or expressive values for most people. We let go waste products and bodily material that is surgically removed with no thought. Does anyone really want to keep the excised cyst the doctor removes during an operation? True, there are a few body parts in some circumstances (on which more shortly) where we have interests, but not many. To claim that we need property rights in all our bodies and separated body parts seem excessive, if there are very few circumstances in which we would wish to exercise those rights.

An obvious response to the above is to question whether it matters. If there are cases where you need property rights to protect your interests then what would be wrong in treating all body parts as property, even if much of the time people will not want to exercise them. The answer lies in the fact that calling something property carries burdens as well as rights.

To give some examples: if all your body is property you would be committing the offence of littering if you leave parts of your body in a public place. Dropping hair on a pavement as the wind blows through your hair could be a criminal offence; if you leave property in someone else's property they are entitled to ask you to remove it; the dandruff you leave at a restaurant could result in a phone call from the restaurant asking you to remove your property. Now, I agree these examples seem implausible. But the implausibility works both ways: it is implausible that these would result in legal actions, but that is because it is implausible that these body parts are property.

Those examples seem absurd, but other examples may be less far-fetched. Is a hospital to ensure there is consent to dispose of bodily waste, if it is the patient's property? What if the patient wishes to keep their bodily waste and material, if we

[33] This is baffling: surely there are better reasons to find links with a child, but clearly this is an important issue to many people.

[34] See the discussion in R Huxtable and J Woodley, 'Gaining Face or Losing Face? Framing the Debate on Face Transplants' (2005) 19 *Bioethics* 505.

[35] Wall, 'The Legal Status of Body Parts: A Framework', above n 2.

see it as their property? Would a hospital be entitled to charge patients for storage or removal of their bodily property? Can relatives claim ownership rights over the organs of a deceased? If there were property rights in bodies, could a person direct to whom an organ is given?

There may be answers to these issues. However, it would appear that giving property rights over all body parts carries serious dangers. Contrast the alternative of using a statute to give rights in relation to particular body parts in particular contexts and to focus the attention of the law where it is needed.

The kinds of interests and rights we would claim or wish to claim vary not only according to the nature of the body part, but also the circumstances of the separation of the bodily material and its retention. A man normally seeks no claim over the sperm that is 'spilled on the ground' to use the biblical phraseology,[36] but the men in *Yearworth*, whose sperm was stored for use in case their cancer treatment rendered them infertile, had very particular interests in the sperm.[37] Similarly, a man would object if his semen was 'stolen' and used without his consent to produce a child for whom he would be financially responsible. Again, it is the context of the separation and storage and the nature of the material that generate a special interest in it. It is not the nature of the substance itself which generates claims in the material, but the circumstances of its removal and retention.

Consider, for example, the issues raised in *Evans v UK*,[38] which concerned a couple who had donated their gametes to produce stored embryos, but then disagreed on how they should be used. The case raised complex issues over rights to reproduction, efficiency and consistency in state regulation of assisted reproduction, interests of the embryo, gender discrimination and so on.[39] Whether the sperm and egg were property or not becomes insignificant in that case. Quite clearly the case would be completely different if the two individuals had donated hair that had been reduced to a piece of art. Even if you do support accepting property interests, this example shows that property could only ever be the first tiny step in the dealing with the legal issues raised by body parts and does not begin to deal with the host of other issues raised.

The circumstances of the removal can create responsibilities of trust and particular expectations. These will work out differently in different contexts. The statute can acknowledge these. It may be that in some cases the statute would give rights that will look very much like property rights, and societal interests will be protected. In other cases, the proper balancing of the interests will have nothing equivalent to a property interest. The Human Tissue Act 2004 is a fine example of a statute which seeks to balance the competing interests of individuals, family members, researchers, educators, doctors and the wider public. It provides a far more sophisticated approach than a straightforward property approach ever could.

[36] Genesis 38:8–10 (sometimes taken to constitute a prohibition on masturbation).

[37] *Yearworth v North Bristol NHS Trust* [2009] EWCA Civ 37.

[38] *Evans v UK* (2006) 43 *EHRR* 21.

[39] C Lind, 'Evans v United Kingdom – Judgments of Solomon: Power, Gender and Procreation' (2006) Child and Family Law Quarterly 576.

Applications

How might these ideas play out in some real cases? I choose the following two examples not because they are the best examples to promote my case, but because they are selected by supporters to illustrate the benefits of a property approach.[40]

Organ Retention

The first is the example of the scandals in England over the retention of children's organs after surgery.[41] Imogen Goold explains:

> The experience of organ and tissue retention revelations at the turn of the millennium, and the ensuing public outcry and suffering of the parents involved, made it clear that human bodily material matters to people. They care about how it is treated by others. Any framework for regulating the use of bodily material should therefore take account of these concerns and ensure that individual autonomy is promoted to a sufficient degree.[42]

She explains that this shows 'it is highly important to protect individual autonomy and choice in this context' and argues that property does this well.

This is not convincing. First, is it right that in this case describing the children's bodies and organs as 'property' will be comforting to parents? Does it accurately describe the interests the parents have?[43] Surely what we are talking about is not analogous to the kind of relationship a parent has to their deceased child's savings account. We have here a fine example of the kind of personal interests mentioned earlier that are not well represented by property. Of course, people can regard something as property, but also acknowledge that its value is not simply found in property terminology. A wedding ring might be a good example of something people will regard as property, but value in relational terms. However, the problem there is the law that should also reflect the broader values. Criminal law would do this crudely in the wedding ring example by, at the sentencing stage, recognising that the theft of a wedding ring was not simply the theft of property. Second, the remedy for property loss is, typically, financial compensation designed to purchase a replacement property. That again shows the bizarre consequences of a property model. With a statute a range of options from formal apologies, appropriate disposal of the body part, a memorial event or plaque could be given. These would not 'right the wrong' but enable a more imaginative response to the wrong done.

[40] For example, Goold, 'Property Or Not Property?', above n 27.

[41] See, eg V Sheach-Leith, 'Consent and Nothing But Consent? The Organ Retention Scandal' (2007) 29 *Sociology of Health and Illness* 1023.

[42] Goold, 'Property Or Not Property?', above n 27, 301 .

[43] It may be argued that it is more important if the rights protect the interest, than describe them. However, the language used is important when borderline cases arise.

So how could a statute provide a more effective response? It could recognise that the essential wrong here is a relational one; that in caring for a sick child the parent's identity has become integrated with their child's body. Mavis Maclean, who sat on the panel hearing the Inquiry at the Bristol Royal Infirmary and reported that the parents did not talk of 'parental rights to the body of their child as property' but instead as an interference in their responsibilities as parents.

> The only immediate form of care which a parent can offer their child after death is to arrange the funeral. When this event is based on lack of information about the physical state of the child, this final act of care may for some families seem to be somehow be devalued and damaged.[44]

The wrong here can only be understood in the context of the child–parent relationship. What was done in the organ-retention cases was not a property wrong – it was a relational wrong. At least through a statute we can find a language which recognises the true nature of the harm done. We might then find a remedy that is more appropriate. That remedy might be an apology, the hospital organising a memorial or paying money to a children's charity of the parent's choice, or ensuring a respectful disposal of the material. A statutory option opens up a far broader range of alternative remedies and appropriate language than does the property approach.

Yearworth

The other case that is cited in favour of the property approach is *Yearworth*.[45] Here, through what is widely accepted to be opaque reasoning, the court recognised the men had a property interest in the sperm and this enabled the court to find a remedy through bailment. Supporters of the property approach would wish this case to be used to achieve a more general acceptance that we have property in our bodily material.

But does that follow? Is the damage to the sperm in this case the same as the damage when a nurse throws away a urine sample without checking with the patient first? It is true that a different kind of bodily material is involved and perhaps less loss flowing from it, but should the law classify these losses as essentially the same loss? A property harm? This completely fails to capture the nature of the wrong that has taken place. Unless we place the harm within the context of the men's plans and hopes for a family, for the precious child–parent relationship which was to come; unless we see it in the context of the special trust between a patient and a hospital committed to care for things beyond value; unless we see it in the context of the hopes and plans of the partners of the men, we cannot really understand the nature of what has happened. A statute can find a response

[44] M Maclean, 'Letting Go. Retention of Human Material after Post Mortem' in A Bainham et al, *Body Lore and Laws* (Oxford, Hart Publishing, 2001).

[45] M Quigley, 'Property: The Future of Human Tissue?' (2009) 17 *Medical Law Review* 457, 466.

tailored to acknowledge the particular circumstances of the storage of sperm by a medical establishment to enable assisted reproductive technology.

Summarising the Benefits of a Statute

It has been argued in this chapter that we do have interests in body parts and bodily material. However, these are complex and depend on the nature of the body part and the nature of the circumstances of the removal and retention. We cannot expect one legal category – property – to deal with the different interests we have which are so dependent on the circumstances and nature of the body part.

The correct legal response to issues do not simply depend on the nature of the bodily part and circumstances of its removal, but also on a balance between the individual, relational and broader societal interests mentioned in this chapter. This is precisely the kind of balance we see, for example, in the Human Tissue Act 2004. There we see recognition of interests in control through the requirements of consent, but these are outweighed by the public interest in, for example, education and audit.

Objections to a Statutory Model

There are objections to a statutory model, which will now be explored. First, it might be said that it would be enormously complex to create a statute. If we look, for example, at the Human Tissue Act 2004 or the Human Fertilisation and Embryology Acts of 1990 and 2008, the legislation is lengthy and sophisticated and the Acts cover only a small portion of the issues that might arise if legislation for all bodily material was created. This is true but I would make two points. First, the two pieces of legislation just mentioned cover two major areas: those relating to the storage of bodily material in a hospital setting and reproductive material. Much of the work has been done. Second, even if a property analysis were used we would need statutes to regulate these property rights. Thus there is enormous work to do whichever route to reform is taken.

Second, it may be said that property would give us a clear, well-established set of rules to deal with difficult cases. If there were no clear statutory provision, courts would be left in the dark as to how to balance the competing claims and would not have the depth of jurisprudence that has developed around property to rely on. However, this concern assumes that property covers all of the interests that we have. In other words, the concern is one of 'proofing'. Property has a well-established set of rules that can provide us with the answers in any scenario. However, a statute does not provide a reasoning process that can point us in the right direction if a scenario is created, which was not thought of by the drafters. This is especially concerning in a fast moving area such as use of bodily material, where novel situations regularly arise. My response to this is, in part, that I suspect that the certainty produced by a property approach is exaggerated. Even supporters of the property approach accept there will need to be exceptions or additional remedies required. As Goold's chapter in this book (Chapter 9) demonstrates, the law on abandonment, which will be central to a property-based model, is highly complex and unclear. Furthermore, the idea that a statute does not have principles can be questioned. Occasionally a statute sets out some general principles which will guide its interpretation (see, for example, Family Law Act 1996, section 1). On many other occasions commentators or judges are able to detect principles underpinning a statute. These principles will provide as much guidance as the principles of property law.

Third, property provides a clear principle that we can declare: 'You own your body and separated body parts.' This can easily be communicated to the public and doctors. I accept that the kind of statute I have mind proposes a balancing between the competing interests involved and so cannot be reduced to a catchy slogan. But clarity is not everything, especially in such a sensitive area.

Conclusion

This chapter has sought to present a case in favour of a statutory response to the issue of the legal regulation of separated body parts. This is in preference to the currently popular approach of allowing property law to provide the solutions. I prefer a statute for the following reasons.

First, a statute provides a way of balancing the interests of the individual, others and society when determining how to deal with issues around bodily tissue. The property approach, I suggest, in its nature prioritises the interests of the individual over the interests of others and broader societal interests. I have argued in this chapter that property law fails to adequately acknowledge the communal nature of bodies and the strength of the communal interest in body parts.

Second, balancing of the different interests depends on the nature of the body part and its removal. Property lacks the subtlety to deal with the range of interests that can arise in different cases. The idea that the property interests in the hair that drops off our head is the same as in the egg removed for donation to an infertile sister is extraordinary. The interests are very different and these can be captured in a statute in a far more effective way than by using a property approach.

14

Human Biomaterials: The Case for a Property Approach

IMOGEN GOOLD and MUIREANN QUIGLEY

Introduction

Protecting living and deceased persons, their bodies, and parts therein from wrongful intrusions, interferences, appropriation, and (ab)uses is not a new realm of activity for the law. The tort of battery and the crime of assault protect the person from unauthorised touchings. The tort of negligence protects the individual where the actions of others (who have a duty of care) cause them (actual) harm. The Coroners and Justice Act 2009 prohibits slavery and forced labour.[1] Meanwhile, the Human Tissue Act 2004, using appropriate consent as its cornerstone, ostensibly protects a person's interests in, and control over, their biomaterials both before and after their death.[2] In offering such a panoply of protections, whether or not biomaterials could be considered property was once a largely inconsequential question for the law, and throughout the nineteenth century the legal system addressed a variety of interferences and transgressions without recourse to property principles. In the face of new challenges that emerged in the twentieth century, the law responded in some cases by utilising property discourse, albeit in a highly circumscribed manner due to a fundamental resistance to treating human biomaterials as property. However, recent legal developments suggest that the recognition of property in biomaterials is no longer the complete anathema that it once was. These developments, which are outlined in Loane Skene's contribution to this collection,[3] include cases in which biomaterials have been held to be property 'as a means of permitting remedial action and

[1] Section 71. The Human Rights Act 1998 gives domestic effect to Art 4 of the European Convention of Human Rights, which prohibits slavery and forced labour. Historically, the Slavery Abolition Act 1833 abolished slavery throughout the British Empire. It was repealed by the Statute Law (Repeals) Act 1998, although elements of the Slave Trade Acts 1824, 1843 and 1873 remain in force.

[2] Note that the Human Tissue Act 2004 governs the removal, storage, and subsequent use of tissues from the deceased: but in relation to the living, only storage and use (this is governed by the common law). The Human Tissue Act (Scotland) 2006 governs these matters in relation to the deceased in Scotland. This chapter does not deal with the Scottish Act or the relevant common law there.

[3] See Skene, ch 15 in this volume.

compensation for damage done, and, most recently, in order to permit possession of sperm for the purposes of *in vitro* fertilisation'.[4] Yet even outside of these specific legal circumstances, the ever-increasing set of uses of biomaterials for medical treatment, biomedical research, and industry activities has irrevocably altered the context within which the body and its parts are situated (scientifically, legally and ethically). We already deal with body parts and biomaterials as we do many other things that are accepted as property. Blood, organs and various biomaterials are donated to others for transplant, and to researchers for use in studies.[5] They are sometimes sold, sometimes stolen, and often stored. Given the breadth of transactions involving biomaterials, it is perhaps not surprising that a range of problems arises when we try to resist dealing with those biomaterials within a proprietary framework.

In the course of making our case for a property approach, this chapter identifies and examines some of the problems that are caused by eschewing property. Recognising that there are alternative legal approaches to dealing with the challenges posed by the use of human bodily materials, we examine whether property law provides the *right* and *best* mechanisms for dealing with these challenges.[6] Using theft as the exemplar, we tease out how attempting to avoid a property analysis causes legal difficulties. Via this analysis, and that outlined in later sections, we elucidate the legal lacunae that resistance to according property status to biomaterials creates. We also demonstrate that a property analysis best captures what occurs when bodily materials are donated, and consequently argue that the legal difficulties that can arise (and have arisen) when materials are donated are best addressed by mechanisms already in place to deal with interferences with chattels. Similarly, we argue that where biomaterials are damaged or lost, these harms are most fittingly dealt with as interferences with property, enabling those with an interest in the materials to obtain an appropriate remedy. We therefore make the overarching argument that a property approach ought to be favoured because of the dearth of protections offered by other branches of law, and to this end offer an analysis that looks at how encompassing human biological materials within the ambit of a property system might work. We argue that using a property analysis to deal with removed biomaterials allows us to draw on the same rules we

[4] M Quigley, 'Property in Human Biomaterials: Separating Persons and Things?' (2012) 32 *Oxford Journal of Legal Studies* 659, 661. For some relevant cases, see *R v Herbert* (1961) 25 JCL 163; *R v Welsh* (1974) RTR 478; *R v Rothery* [1976] RTR 550; (1976) 63 Cr App R 231; *R v Kelly and Lindsay* [1998] 3 All ER 741; *Doodeward v Spence* (1908) 6 CLR 406; *AB and others v Leeds Teaching Hospital NHS Trust* EWHC 644; *Moore v Regents of the University of California* 51 Cal 3d 120; *Greenberg v Miami Children's Hospital Research Institute* 264 F Sup2d 1064 (SD Fla, 2003); *Washington University v William J Catalona* 490 F 3d 667; *Jonathan Yearworth and Others v North Bristol NHS Trust* [2009] EWCA Civ 37; and *Jocelyn Edwards; Re the estate of the late Mark Edwards* [2011] NSWSC 478.

[5] On the breadth of these uses, and the various parties with interests in human bodily materials, see I Goold, 'Why Does it Matter How We Regulate the Use of Human Body Parts?' (2014) 40 *Journal of Medical Ethics* 3.

[6] One of us has outlined the range of possible approaches elsewhere: I Goold, 'Property or Not Property? The Spectrum of Approaches to Regulating the Use of Human Bodily Material' (2013) 21 *Journal of Law and Medicine* 299.

have already developed to manage relationships over a range of other things. This is helpful in relation to remedies, but has the wider benefit of providing a framework for clarifying and regulating the interests people have in relation to bodily materials. Such an approach need not be inflexible. Just as the rules of property law governing land, chattels and other objects differ in some regards, so too could we adapt property when applying it to human biological materials, retaining those characteristics that are useful or effective, and altering those that are problematic. We argue that on balance, such an approach would be preferable to a *sui generis* approach to biomaterials as it avoids the difficulties of creating a new scheme,[7] while opening up already well-developed legal avenues that address conflicts over the control of corporeal objects.

Human Biomaterials: On Uses, Value and Property

Prior to the medical advancements of the twentieth century, the deceased human body had two main values for those left behind. It was the remaining symbol of the person who had died – and hence was treated with care and respect as part of the rituals surrounding death – and it was highly valued for dissection as part of the study and teaching of anatomy. The case law from before the turn of the nineteenth century largely reflects this in the resistance to treating the body as property expressed in those early cases. However, the scientific breakthroughs of the twentieth century saw a fundamental shift in the value ascribed to human biological materials, which became vital for medical research and also as a source of intimate personal information. This shift brought with it a demand, and consequently a market, for such materials. It also gave rise to complex situations in which many parties desire access to, or control of, human biological materials.[8] A brief sketch of this new value and the conflicts to which it gives rise demonstrates the need for an effective framework for regulating biomaterials.

The Medical Research Council notes that 'the use of human tissue is crucial to increase understanding of human disease and to help develop new and improved treatments'.[9] In its explanation of the value of human tissue for research, the Human Tissue Authority takes a similar line stating:

> Types of research involving human tissue include developing screening tests for different types of cancer, testing new treatments for conditions such as heart disease and diabetes, looking at how the immune system works to help understand how it combats

[7] Our views on this are supported by the compelling case put by Lyria Bennett Moses for rejecting a *sui generis* approach to regulating human biological materials: Bennett Moses, ch 12 in this volume.

[8] Many chapters in this volume touch on how the value of biological materials has changed, and the varied interests different parties have in that material. See, eg Nicol, Chalmers, McWhirter and Dickinson, ch 2; and Stewart, Lipworth, Aparacio, Fleming and Kerridge, ch 3.

[9] Medical Research Council, 'Ethics and Research Policy: Use of Human Tissue', available at www.mrc.ac.uk/Ourresearch/Ethicsresearchguidance/Useofhumantissue/index.htm.

> diseases and researching how stem cells could be used to treat conditions like Parkinson's disease and multiple sclerosis.[10]

One could, when reading such statements, be forgiven for thinking that the main utility of human biomaterials is in the treatment of high-profile diseases and disorders, or for the conduct of morally and socially laudable research. These materials are undoubtedly crucial to the medical research endeavour, and to pursuing treatments for a multitude of diseases. However, framing the situation in this manner belies the convoluted topography of the human biomaterial landscape. It also does not give a robust sense of the broad and diverse use(s) and value(s) of human biomaterials in the biotechnological era.

Uses of biomaterials include: blood and blood products for transfusions (for blood loss and the treatment of blood disorders), as well as being a source of adult stem cells; whole solid organs and tissues such as skin and bone for transplantation and research; gametes and embryos for use in *in vitro* fertilisation and research into a variety of diseases; and the whole body after life where the deceased body is donated to medical schools.[11] Biomaterials are also being used for research connected to large-scale biobanks, brainbanks, tissue engineering, and for the development of biohybrid (part artificial/synthetic, part biological) cells, tissues and organs. Many of the uses of cells, tissues, and other biomaterials within the research contexts mentioned are, however, not used for therapeutic purposes directly. They are used instead to shed light on normal biological or disease processes.[12] Thus there is a seemingly vast array of uses of biomaterials.[13] However, the story is complicated by the fact that the samples are enmeshed in an institutional system that is difficult to disentangle. Catherine Waldby and Robert Mitchell give a sense of the intricacies:

> With the exception of some organs, donated tissues are not simply transferred intact from one person to another, but rather diverted through laboratory processes where they may be fractionated, cloned, immortalized, and multiplied in various ways. Tissue sourced from one person may be distributed in altered forms along complex pathways to multiple recipients at different times and at different locations throughout the world . . . Tissue donation is thus transformed from an act of direct civic responsibility between fellow citizens into a complex network of donor-recipient relations heavily mediated by biotechnical processes and an institutional complex of tissue banks, pharmaceutical and research companies, and clinics.[14]

When considering this institutional complex within which the body and biomaterials are situated, we should bear in mind that it is not limited to publicly funded endeavours, but includes a flourishing private bio-sector in which materials are bought and sold. This is illustrated, perhaps most vividly, by considering cell lines

[10] Human Tissue Authority, 'Donating your tissue for research', available at: http://www.hta.gov.uk/bodyorganandtissuedonation/howtodonateyourtissueforresearch.cfm.

[11] Nuffield Council on Bioethics, *Human Bodies: Donation for Medicine and Research* (London, Nuffield Council on Bioethics, 2011) 35–42.

[12] ibid, 38.

[13] ibid, 34–50.

[14] C Waldby and R Mitchell, *Tissue Economies: Blood, Organs and Cell Lines in Late Capitalism* (New York, Duke University Press, 2006) 22.

and cell therapies. It has been estimated that the global cell therapy industry has passed the $1 billion mark in annual turnover.[15] In addition, there are a range of research-related support activities involved in the procurement, storage, processing, and distribution of human biomaterials. These tissue services may be carried out by not-for-profit organisations such as NHS Blood and Transplant,[16] but may also be done on a for-profit basis by private companies.[17] While it is difficult to assess the total commercial worth of human biomaterials (and related activities), the cumulative effect is a booming global industry that makes significant profits.

As one of us has noted elsewhere, there are also markets in biomaterials outside the research context, such as that for human hair extensions, and the sales of artistic works such as Mark Quinn's *Self*. Quinn's piece was created entirely from his own blood, and an iteration of *Self* was sold to the National Portrait Gallery for £300,000 in 2012.[18]

Developments, such as those outlined, have given rise to a new way of looking at our bodies, their parts and their products. So, too, has our capacity to derive intimate information about person from their tissue, via a range of tests including those that examine genetic material. As Kenyon Mason and Graeme Laurie note: 'It is no longer true, as it once seemed, that the human body is valueless.'[19] This prompts us to question the control we (ought to) have over our bodies and biomaterials, and how much control should be available to persons other than those from whom the material was obtained. When considering these issues, we should note that the profit-making dimension of the use of biomaterials in research, as well as these other markets, is particularly pertinent in the context of the Human Tissue Act 2004. This is so because, first, the Act exempts from its general provisions materials created outside of the human body[20] and, secondly, it exempts from the general prohibition on commercial dealings those biomaterials that have become 'property' through the application of 'human skill'.[21] Many of the uses of biomaterials and related developments undoubtedly only come to fruition because of the resources and work of researchers, their institutions, and industry investment. However, none of the activities under discussion would be possible without access to the original donated raw materials. The source of the materials,

[15] See C Mason, DA Brindley, EJ Culme-Seymour and NL Davie, 'Cell Therapy Industry: Billion Dollar Global Business with Unlimited Potential' (2011) 6 *Regenerative Medicine* 265, 266.

[16] See NHS Blood and Transplant, 'Human Tissue Products You Can Trust', available at: www.nhsbt.nhs.uk/tissueservices/index.asp.

[17] See, eg A Bersenev, 'Public Versus Private Cell Therapy and Stem Cell Companies' available at: stemcellassays.com/2013/07/public-private-cell-therapy-stem-cell-companies/. Bersenev notes that in the cell therapy and regenerative medicine fields alone 80 per cent of companies are private.

[18] A Akbar, 'National Portrait Gallery Acquires Marc Quinn's Bloody Head' (London, Independent, 10 September 2009), available at: www.independent.co.uk/arts-entertainment/art/news/national-portrait-gallery-acquires-marc-quinns-bloody-head-1785133.html. See further I Goold, 'Why Does it Matter How We Regulate the Use of Human Body Parts?' (2014) 40 *Journal of Medical Ethics* 3.

[19] JK Mason and G Laurie, 'Consent or Property? Dealing with the Body and its Parts in the Shadow of Bristol and Alder Hey' (2001) 64(5) *Modern Law Review* 710–29, 712.

[20] Human Tissue Act 2004, s 54(7).

[21] Human Tissue Act 2004, s 32(9)(c). Note that materials collected solely for research purposes are not covered by this section of the Act.

therefore, remains fundamental to both the public research endeavour and the global private biomaterials industry. This raises important questions about who should have initial control over biomaterials upon separation from the body, and with whom this control should subsequently rest. In considering these questions, we should also reflect on the appropriate means to protect this control. In addition, where unjustified infringements do occur we need to consider which legal remedies might be the most appropriate and effective.

We do not, in this chapter, argue for any particular stance on where such control should vest. Rather, we argue that in addressing questions of control, a property-based approach provides the most appropriate and effective means of protecting control of human biomaterials, in whomever we decide that control should rightly vest. As Simon Douglas has argued, property is directed at managing the control of scarce but valuable resources.[22] As we have shown, human biological materials are such a resource, because of their value for research and other uses, and therefore clarity over how and by whom they may be controlled is increasingly necessary. Conflict over control also arises when more than one party seeks access to materials to gain information via testing, or for reproductive purposes. It is not surprising that these are the areas of concern that have most troubled the courts in recent times.[23] Property, we argue, is the most appropriate legal fit for regulating control of biological materials as it is the legal system's already existing means of managing conflicts over control of tangible objects.

The rest of this chapter will demonstrate how the law of property could meet various challenges raised by the use of biomaterials. We start by illustrating how attempting to avoid a property analysis has led to the courts resorting to contorted reasoning. We take the example of the theft cases, and offer some comparison with the recent decisions on control of reproductive materials in which the deployment of a property analysis provided a much clearer, more effective approach. We then explore cases of donation and of damage or loss in relation to biomaterials, highlighting the problems that arise when the legal rights of each party interested in tissue are not clearly determined. We make the case that a property approach has significant advantages over other potential legal approaches to resolving this lack of clarity.

[22] Douglas, ch 7 in this volume.

[23] Examples include conflicts over reproductive materials (*Yearworth and others v North Bristol NHS Trust* Court of Appeal WLR; *Bazley v Wesley Monash IVF* Supreme Court of Queensland QSC; *Re the estate of the late Mark Edwards*), access for testing purposes (*Roche v Douglas as Administrator of the Estate of Edward Rowan (dec'd)* (2000) WASC 146) and control of valuable research collections (*Washington University v Catalona* F Supp 2d (2006)).

Property or Not Property? Challenging Cases and Creative Judicial Reasoning

The law of property manages the rights of persons in relation to things.[24] When those rights are violated, various legal mechanisms come into play to protect transgressions against these rights. A prime example is the law of theft, which is engaged when one person interferes with another's right to possession of an object. By definition, theft is the taking of another's property without authority or permission. For a range of reasons, some of which we explore below, early cases dealing with interferences with, and takings of, bodies established the fundamental rule that a body cannot (or could not) be property. From the early twentieth century onwards, a number of cases arose in which the ongoing prohibition on owning a body presented the Anglo-Australian courts with some difficult challenges. In this section, we tease out the foundations of the rule, and then demonstrate how the exclusion of bodies and their parts from the ambit of property compelled later courts to find judicially creative ways around this exclusion to enable successful prosecutions for theft. We argue that including biomaterials within the definition of property would have avoided such exercises in creativity. We compare these cases with later decisions in which the courts did resort to conceptualising biomaterials as property, concluding that the courts were right to do so because biomaterials are most effectively and appropriately regulated as items of property.

While definitive authority is difficult to trace, the common law previously adhered to the rule that there was no property in a corpse. It is sometimes stated that one of the earliest references to the rule was in *Haynes's Case*.[25] After digging up their bodies, William Haynes removed the shrouds (winding sheets) from four corpses, before re-burying them. It is reported that the judges determined that 'the property of the sheets remain in the owners . . . when the dead body was wrapped therewith; for the dead body is not capable of it'.[26] Yet, in light of the example given in the report of the case, it seems more likely that the ruling in the case was that the corpse was not capable of owning property.[27] It stated that: 'If apparel be put upon a body, this is a gift in the law, for the body hath capacity to

[24] For the sake of succinctness, in this chapter we use the term 'rights' broadly to encompass a variety of legal relations (claim-rights, liberties, powers etc). In so doing we are conscious of the position that only claim-rights generate correlative legal duties (see further on this taxonomy the classic work of Wesley Hohfeld, 'Some Fundamental Legal Conceptions as Applied in Judicial Reasoning' (1917) 26 *Yale Law Journal* 16). The purpose of the chapter, however, is not to flesh out the detail of the legal relations relevant to property, but to outline a general argument.

[25] *Haynes's Case* (1614) 12 Co Rep 113, 77 ER 1389.

[26] ibid.

[27] For this point see also WF Kuzenski, 'Property in Dead Bodies' (1924) 9(1) *Marquette Law Review* 17, 18; TMK Chattin, 'Property in Dead Bodies' (1968–69) 71 *West Virginia Law Review* 377–78; and Mason and Laurie, 'Consent or Property?', above n 19 at 710–29, 714.

take it; but a corpse being but a lump of earth hath no capacity.'[28] That this is the more accurate interpretation of the judgment is supported by the comments of Sir Edward Coke in his *Institutes of the Laws of England* where he recounts consulting with the judges on the case, saying 'for the dead body is not capable of any property, and the property of the sheets must be in some body'.[29] The defendant was convicted of petty larceny in respect of the winding sheets. Later in the *Institutes* Coke states that the 'buriall of the *Cadaver* (that is, *caro data vermibus* [flesh given to worms]) is *nullis in bonis* [no one's property]'.[30] The comment, however, was likely to have been made specifically to draw a contradistinction between the jurisdiction of ecclesiastical law and that of the common law. As such, while the interment of the cadaver 'belongs to Ecclesiastical cognizance', the burial chamber or grave itself can give rise to actions at common law ('action is given at common law . . . for defacing thereof').[31] Nonetheless, whatever the earliest origins of the no-property rule, neither *Haynes's Case* nor Coke's comments were concerned with misdemeanours or felonies directly in relation to the body (of parts thereof) itself. For these we need to look at later cases involving the disinterment of deceased bodies.

A cluster of cases from the late 1700s to the late 1800s all seem to have incorporated the supposed no-property rule, but, as we shall see, this necessitated the creation of a range of misdemeanours in order to protect the deceased body. Key decisions in this area are those that centre on the disinterment of corpses. One of the earliest of these was *R v Lynn* (1788),[32] which involved a resurrectionist who appropriated a recently buried body for the purpose of dissection. The argument was made, drawing on Coke, that Lynn's actions were not a matter for the criminal court since 'carrying away a dead body was not criminal'.[33] The court, however, asserted that such a practice ought to be stopped on the grounds of common decency, regardless of the fact that it was for dissection, and, as such, Lynn was convicted (although only fined rather than jailed on grounds of possible ignorance).[34] Although the report of *Lynn* is consistent with the interpretation of Coke as simply denoting jurisdictional boundaries between ecclesiastical and common law, there must also have been an implicit acceptance that the corpse

[28] *Haynes's Case* (1614) 12 Co Rep 113, (1614) 77 ER 1389.

[29] E Coke, *The Third Part of the Institutes of the Laws of England: Concerning High Treason, and other Pleas of the Crown, and Criminal Causes* (London, 1669) 110 (3 Co Inst 110). This is why the case arises in the context of the law abandonment, as it raises (some argue) the question of whether property can become ownerless (or, put another way, whether divesting abandonment is possible). See further, M Pawlowski, 'Property in Body Parts and Products of the Human Body' (2009) 30 *Liverpool Law Journal* 35.

[30] E Coke, *The Third Part of the Institutes of the Laws of England: Concerning High Treason, and other Pleas of the Crown, and Criminal Causes* (London, 1669) 110 (3 Co Inst 110) 203 (3 Co Inst 203).

[31] ibid, 110 (3 Co Inst 110).

[32] *R v Lynn* 2 T R 732, 394, 2 Term Rep 733.

[33] ibid. The report also says that: 'The crime imputed to the defendant is not made penal by any statute: the only Act of Parliament which has any relation to this subject . . . makes it felony to steal dead bodies for the purposes of witchcraft; but that clearly cannot affect the present question.'

[34] *R v Lynn*, above n 32.

could not be property. The no-property rule was made more explicit in the latter case of *R v Sharpe* (1857).[35] This was a case again regarding the disinterment of a body, but not on this occasion for dissection; rather Sharpe dug up the body of his mother with the intention of reburying it alongside the body of his recently deceased father. Erle J, on behalf of the court, said: 'Our law recognises no property in a corpse, and the protection of the grave at common law, as contradistinguished from ecclesiastical protection to consecrated ground, depends upon this form of indictment.'[36] The defendant was convicted of removing a body from a grave without lawful authority.[37] Kuzenski posited that the position of the courts in these early cases may have been influenced by Blackstone's interpretation of *Haynes's Case* and Coke's comments.[38] Blackstone writes that 'stealing the corpse itself, which has no owner, (though a matter of great indecency) is no felony unless some of the grave-clothes be stolen with it'.[39] Thus, while the no-property rule appears to have had unconvincing origins, it was, nonetheless, proving influential by the end of the nineteenth century; something which is somewhat peculiar since, as Roger Magnusson points out, the rule appears to be 'confined to *obiter dicta*'.[40] Despite this, the now accepted no-property rule as set out in both *Lynn* and *Sharpe* was cited favourably in subsequent cases. The latter decision was cited in *Williams v Williams* (1882)[41] (in reaching its decision that a person could not dispose of their body at will), while the former in *R v Price* (1884),[42] where Stephen J said 'the act done would have been a peculiarly indecent theft if it had not been for the technical reason that a dead body is not the subject of property'.[43] Around the time of this case and well into the nineteenth century, the appropriation of deceased bodies by resurrectionists was on the rise, prompted by the increasing need for anatomical specimens for dissection.[44] We say 'appropriation' to emphasise the central problem encountered when trying to prosecute in such cases; that is, without deeming the corpse property, a prosecution for theft could

[35] *R v Sharpe* 169 ER 959, Dears & Bell 161.

[36] ibid.

[37] ibid. In this case he could also have been convicted for breaking and entering. Again the defendant was merely fined rather than being given a custodial sentence, since the judges were of the opinion that his motives were good.

[38] WF Kuzenski, 'Property in Dead Bodies', above n 27, 17, 22.

[39] W Blackstone, *Commentaries on the Laws of England in Four Books*, vol 2 (Philadelphia, JB Lippincott Co, 1893) 1753, 236. Later, in vol 4, he also says 'But though the heir has a property in the monuments and escutcheons of his ancestors, yet he has none in their bodies or ashes; nor can he bring any civil action against such as indecently at least, if not impiously, violate and disturb their remains, when dead and buried. The parson, indeed, who has the freehold of the soil, may bring an action of trespass against such as dig and disturb it; and if anyone in taking up a dead body steals the shroud or other apparel, it will be felony; for the property thereof.' (429 – he cites both Coke's comments and *Hayne's Case* here).

[40] R Magnusson, 'Proprietary Rights in Human Tissue' in N Palmer and E McKendrick (eds), *Interests in Goods* (London, Lloyd's of London Press, 1993) 242.

[41] *Williams v Williams* All ER 840 (Ch).

[42] *R v Price* (1884) 12 QBD 247.

[43] ibid at 252.

[44] R Richardson, *Death, Dissection and the Destitute*, 2nd edn (Chicago, University of Chicago Press, 2000) 52–72.

not be brought.[45] Thus, the no-property rule foreclosed prosecution for other, more established, indictments available within the law. In *Lynn*, for example, if it were not for the no-property rule the accused could simply have been tried for larceny (theft). Indictment on the grounds of disinterment for the purposes of dissection would not have been needed. The other aspect of creating these offences to deal with issues of disinterment and exhumation is that they were *misdemeanours* and not felonies. As such, as we have already seen, they attracted only minor sentences such as fines. The effect of this, as noted by Ruth Richardson, was that 'from the point of view of judicial punishment, exhuming the dead was for a very long period a relatively safe occupation'.[46] Had the deceased body been considered property, then a range of more serious indictments would have been available to the judiciary in such cases.[47] The challenge posed by the no-property rule to the notion of theft and the resourceful measures required to overcome it is not confined to the older cases discussed so far, and is illustrated in more recent cases.

R v Kelly and Lindsay (1999)[48] was a case in which a sculptor (Kelly) and a Royal College of Surgeons technician (Lindsay) were convicted of the theft of numerous body parts from the college.[49] These parts, including heads, limbs, torsos and more, had been obtained by Lindsay at Kelly's behest and were subsequently discovered buried or hidden in several different locations.[50] As part of their defence the men claimed that they could not be convicted for theft since the body parts were not property.[51] The court, however, drawing on the 1908 Australian case *Doodeward v Spence*,[52] rejected this claim, saying that 'parts of a corpse are capable of being property within section 4 of the Theft Act 1968 if they have acquired different attributes by virtue of the application of skill, such as dissection or preservation techniques, for exhibition or teaching purposes'.[53] The work/skill exception was also accepted in the later case of *AB and others v Leeds Teaching Hospital NHS Trust* (2004)[54] where, following post-mortems of deceased children, their parents brought an action for wrongful interference with their bodies.[55] Here it was held that the hospital pathologists had applied work and skill to body parts, which therefore gave rise to rights of possession.[56] While the idea of the application of work and/or skill to body parts as transformative is questionable (by their Lordships' own admission in *Kelly*[57]), *there are consequences of holding that body*

[45] Mason and Laurie, above n 19 at 714.

[46] Richardson, *Death, Dissection and the Destitute*, above n 44 at 59.

[47] This, of course, assumes a political will on the part of the judiciary to hand down more serious sentences and it is not altogether clear that this was the case.

[48] *R v Kelly and Lindsay* [1999] QB 621 [*Kelly*].

[49] ibid at 623.

[50] ibid.

[51] ibid at 622.

[52] *Doodeward v Spence* (1908) 6 CLR 406.

[53] *R v Kelly and Lindsay*, above n 48 at 630.

[54] *AB and others v Leeds Teaching Hospital NHS Trust* (2004) EWHC 644 (QB).

[55] See also *Dobson and Another v North Tyneside Health Authority and another* [1996] 4 All ER 474.

[56] ibid at 156, 160.

[57] [1999] QB 621 at 630.

parts can never be property. As counsel for the appellant in *Doodeward* noted, doing so would 'render many of the most valuable collections in hospitals and museums liable to be carried away with impunity'.[58] In this respect the exception in these cases can be seen as legal manoeuvring which was necessary if the courts were not to be hamstrung by the 'no-property' rule.

This raises the question, however, of whether such legal manoeuvring is problematic. Creativity in judicial reasoning in the face of new challenges is both a hallmark and a strength of the common law system. It allows for development, and for flexibility in the face of novel situations and problems. Nevertheless, such creative reasoning must rest on coherent, defensible extrapolation from accepted principles, or philosophically sound reasoning. The 'exception' to the no-property rule created in *Doodeward* and applied in *Kelly* and *AB* could be criticised both for the absence of a sound basis, and for its divergence from generally accepted tenets of the law of property on the mechanisms for generating rights to new things (which will be elaborated later in this chapter). The exception was deployed to achieve what were seen as the just results in *Kelly*. It would have been patently absurd for Kelly and his accomplice to avoid prosecution for the theft of things that were clearly in the possession of the Royal College, and which they clearly took without permission. For them to escape conviction because the dissected parts were not property and hence could not be stolen would have been a textbook case of what is referred to in common parlance as 'getting off on a technicality'. In *Doodeward*, the court was concerned with the implications of not regarding the preserved foetus as property. Not doing so would have undermined legal protection for the possession of collections by institutions. This was also a concern in *Kelly*. Similarly, in *AB* it could be said that there was a desire to protect the possession of hospitals' holdings of excised tissue (although there were other factors are play, which we will not delve into here).

Although such aims might be laudable and sensible, we have concerns with the means used to achieve those goals. Our concern is twofold. First, such backwards reasoning is inherently problematic because it proceeds not from a basis of theory or principle, but from what has already been decided is the 'right' result. In the absence of theoretical grounding, incoherence can result. Such incoherence is evident in this area when *Kelly*, *Doodeward* and *AB* are compared to the decision in the *Dobson v North Tyneside Health Authority* (1996).[59] As part of the case, Lord Justice Peter Gibson had to determine whether brain tissue removed during post-mortem and subsequently fixed in paraffin wax could the subject of a claim in conversion. He accepted that the exception raised in *Doodeward* existed (although he rejected that case as the basis for it),[60] but held that brain tissue did not fall

[58] *Doodeward v Spence* (1908) 6 CLR 408.

[59] *Dobson v North Tyneside Health Authority*, above n 55.

[60] He reasoned that while the majority in that decision did allow the action in detinue to lie, this was due only to the distinction Barton J in *Doodeward* was prepared to make between a stillborn foetus and a corpse awaiting burial. However, he was prepared to accept that there was academic opinion to support the exception, citing *Clerk & Lindsell on Torts*, which stated that there is an exception to the general prohibition on property rights in corpses when a body has undergone 'a process or other application

within the exception and hence the plaintiffs could not show a right to possession sufficient to found their claim. Given that the exception requires lawful work and skill to be applied to alter the nature of tissue into something other than a corpse awaiting burial, such preservation should arguably have been captured by the exception. We need not argue the finer points about whether this preservation was sufficiently different from that in *Kelly*, but instead note that such divergence is the essence of what is problematic with the sort of legal manoeuvring seen in these cases. The creation of the exception was, we would argue, driven by a need to reflect actual practice regarding the possession of body parts, while simultaneously sustaining the no-property rule. That is, it was based in pragmatism. In the absence of a clear, coherent principled or theoretical basis for the exception, its application cannot be clearly determined. Further, the application or otherwise of the exception is vulnerable to expedience-based arguments which might, depending on the circumstances, arguably result in unfairness or incoherency.

This leads to our second concern, which is that all of this manoeuvring, and the consequent problems, would have been avoided in these cases had the courts simply determined that the materials in question were property (or at a minimum that people were able to hold a right to possession over them). Such an approach is, from one perspective, 'simple' because it avoids the complexities we have seen in the theft cases. These arise when we try to exclude corporeal things from the legal rules we have established precisely to manage the possession and control of things. It also avoids the application of a poorly defined and theoretically problematic 'exception'. In two more recent cases the courts have refused to resort to such legal manoeuvring. As such, they avoided the complexities that would otherwise have arisen from resisting the inclusion of biomaterials within the ambit of property. It is to these that we now turn.

The first of these is *Roche v Douglas as Administrator of the Estate of Edward Rowan (dec'd)* (2000). In that case, Susan Roche sought an order for access to stored tissue from a deceased man for the purposes of determining her paternity. Under Order 52 rule 3(1) of the Rules of the Supreme Court 1971 (WA) the court is permitted to take, observe and experiment with any property to determine a matter before it. The defendant argued that the tissue was not property and therefore could not be subject to such an order, requiring the court to consider the question of whether tissue can be property head on. Following an exhaustive examination of the authorities, Master Sanderson found that the samples could be considered property for the purposes of the order, which was granted, and the samples were acquired by the court for testing.[61]

Master Sanderson accepted the existence of both the no-property rule and the exception to it, but still concluded that in the absence of any binding authority to the contrary (as the main case law refers to parts taken from corpses and the

of human skill, such as stuffing or embalming'. This exception included cadavers used for research and parts and substances taken from living persons. See JF Clerk, *Clerk & Lindsell on Torts*, 17th edn (London, Sweet & Maxwell, 1995) 653 [13]–[50].

[61] *Roche v Douglas*, above n 23.

instant case concerned a sample taken from a living person who had later died), that it was proper to hold human tissue samples to be property. Significantly, he held that it defied reason not to regard tissue as property as it has a real physical presence.[62] Doing so also avoided the difficulties of denying what he regarded as the reality of the situation – that tissue is dealt with as property.[63] He pointed out that those cases that deny its property status were of some age and were decided before the discovery of DNA. Although Master Sanderson accepted the authority of Griffith CJ's judgment in *Doodeward*, he nonetheless did not state that the tissue sample in the case before him was property because of the exception to the common law rule, only that it was good sense for it to be so. We would argue that this kind of reasoning is a tacit, and sensible, acceptance of the realities of the use of biomaterials, and the need to bring them within the ambit of rules that fit many of these uses. The alternative of excluding biomaterials from the application of the Rules of the Supreme Court on the grounds that they were not property would be perversely against the rules' purpose. Deploying the exception in *Doodeward* would be the only other option, and one that we have shown is not to be preferred.

Much has been said about the case of *Yearworth v North Bristol NHS Trust*, and we return to 14 in more detail later in this chapter,[64] so we note only the salient aspects of the decision here. In that case, the claimants sought compensation for the psychological harm they had suffered after the negligent destruction of their stored semen. They had clearly suffered a recognised harm, and the defendants accepted that this had resulted from their negligence. However, the claimants faced difficulties in finding a means to bring their claim. In the absence of a contractual arrangement, the claimants had to pursue a claim in tort. Liability for the negligent causing of pure psychiatric injuries is, however, limited largely to situations in which the claimant has narrowly escaped injury, had observed a close relative suffer harm, feels guilt for harm suffered by another, or has suffered workplace stress.[65] As the destruction of the semen was not a personal injury, they were potentially left without a basis on which to claim. Had their semen been property, they could have invoked the decision in *Attia v British Gas* (1987), in which it was held that recovery of damages was possible for psychiatric injuries suffered as a result of witnessing one's property being damaged.[66] Immediately, the problem becomes apparent. Destruction of the semen was not a personal injury. On this, both courts agreed. However, if the semen was not property either, it fell outside the ambit of both usual means of claiming for such injuries. Given the real impact on the men when their semen was destroyed, and the admit-

[62] ibid.

[63] ibid, [14], [20], [22] and [23] per M Sanderson.

[64] *Yearworth and Others v North Bristol NHS Trust*, above n 4. For a summary of the decision, see Skene, ch 15 in this volume.

[65] See, variously, *Alcock v Chief Constable of South Yorkshire* [1992] 1 AC 310; *McLoughlin v O'Brian* [1983] 1 AC 410; *Hunter v British Coal Corporation* [1998] 2 All ER 97; *W v Essex* [2001] 2 AC 592, [2000] 2 All ER 237; and *Barber v Somerset County Council* [2004] UKHL 13.

[66] *Attia v British Gas* [1987] 3 All ER 455. Specifically, her home and its contents were burned.

ted negligence, to deny them a remedy on such a basis would have been an arguably unjust outcome. As it was, the Court of Appeal found that the semen could be property sufficient to support a claim in the law of *bailment* (and hence avoided the need to apply *Attia*). Damages were calculated based on the measure for claims of mental distress consequent on the breach of a contract, where the major object of that contract is to provide peace of mind, pleasure, relaxation or other non-pecuniary personal or family benefits.[67]

Again, in this case the Court of Appeal accepted the existence and authority of both the rule against property in a corpse, and the exception in *Doodeward*, but declined to apply these authorities to determine the matter before it. A better approach, it said, was to rest its conclusions on a 'broader basis'.[68] Therefore, it concluded that the men had ownership of their sperm because they created and ejaculated the sperm by their own bodies with the sole purpose of later using it for procreation. The circumscription of their rights by the Human Fertilisation and Embryology Act 1990 was not such that they lost ownership, only that their right to use it was subject to some restrictions.[69] While it has certainly been argued that a degree of legal manoeuvring is in evidence in the Court of Appeal's reasoning on this point, such manoeuvring was at least based on a degree of principle. The decision was also driven by the need to find a solution. Property offered the most effective and applicable solution because it availed the court of remedies already created to deal with conflicts over or possession of objects.

This section has begun to show that attempting to avoid a property analysis in relation to human biomaterials can cause legal difficulties. First, it can result in a lack of (appropriate and effective) remedies in respect of preventing transgressions. This would have been the case in *Kelly* had the court not been able to apply the exception developed in *Doodeward*. Secondly, the use of creative (and at times arguably dubious) legal reasoning is necessitated in order to facilitate any corrective or remedial action. Leaving the courts boxed into a position where they must resort to problematic or unprincipled reasoning to do justice is undesirable. Decisions directed at achieving a fair outcome in the instant case at the expense of adherence to principle makes for incoherence, and can establish conflicting, confused precedents, leaving future courts floundering.

It could be argued, as others have done in this collection, that deeming human biological materials property is not, however, the right response to the problems identified in this section.[70] We have made some responses to this argument in this section. We now turn to another area of concern and pick up on this challenge in wake of the conclusions we draw on the regulation of human biomaterials.

[67] See *Jarvis v Swan Tours* [1973] QB 233, and subsequently *Watts v Morrow* [1991] 4 All ER 937 (Bingham LJ); *Farley v Skinner* [2001] UKHL 49 (Lord Steyn); and *Johnson v Unisys* Limited [2001] UKHL 13 (Lord Millett).

[68] *Yearworth and Others v North Bristol NHS Trust*, above n 4, 38.

[69] ibid, 131 ff.

[70] See, variously, Skene, ch 15, Wall, ch 8 and Herring, ch 13 in this volume.

Regulating Human Biomaterials

Although there might be different views about what the regulation of the uses of biomaterials should aim to achieve, one of us has argued elsewhere that there is a reasonable amount of agreement on what people want out of such a regulatory system.[71] Most would concur that promoting medical and scientific research is an important goal, as is pursuing increased health for all members of society. With some exceptions, there is also broad consensus regarding the need to protect individual privacy and promote individual autonomy in pursuit of those goals.[72] A good regulatory system will balance these sometimes conflicting demands effectively. In achieving that balance, the regulatory framework governing human biomaterials needs to have some means of resolving disputes and regulating those who do not comply with the rules laid down. It also needs a means to provide redress if harm occurs when those materials are misused, be it to individuals, their families or researchers.

Currently, the legal system attempts to strike this balance via the Human Tissue Act 2004, which governs the use of biomaterials in England and Wales. The Act has a wide remit and governs the removal, storage, and subsequent use of tissues from the deceased, and the storage and use of these in relation to the living.[73] Under the 2004 Act, appropriate consent is required for a range of activities involving biomaterials, including anatomical examinations, research, public display, and transplantation.[74] Non-consensual use is an offence, except when it falls within one of the exemptions in the Act, such as ethically approved research using anonymised tissue.[75] Undertaking prohibited activities or breaching the provisions of the Act may attract a fine, a custodial sentence, or both.[76] The Human Tissue Authority is empowered by the Act to oversee certain activities and is responsible for the licensing of institutions that deal with relevant materials. It

[71] Goold, 'Property or Not Property? The Spectrum of Approaches to Regulating the Use of Human Bodily Material', above n 6.

[72] ibid.

[73] Removal of tissue from the living is governed by the common law. Gametes and embryos are governed by the Human Fertilisation and Embryology Act 1990 (as amended 2008). The provisions of the Act are the result of perceived failures in its predecessor (Human Tissue Act 1961). The deficiencies in the older Act are seen as central to the subsequent organ retention scandals. These led to the inquiries at Bristol Royal Infirmary and the Royal Liverpool Children's Hospital (Alder Hey) which were the impetus for legislative change. See 'Inquiry Into the Management of Care of Children Receiving Complex Heart Surgery at the Bristol Royal Infirmary: Interim Report' (May 2000); Department of Health, 'The Royal Liverpool Children's Inquiry Report No 0012-II 2000-01' (London, The Stationery Office, 2001); 'Learning from Bristol: The Report of the Public Inquiry Into Children's Heart Surgery at the Bristol Royal Infirmary 1984–1995 CM 5207(1)' (2001); and Department of Health, 'Human Bodies, Human Choices: The Law on Human Organs and Tissues in England and Wales' (2002).

[74] Human Tissue Act 2004, sch 1.

[75] Human Tissue Act 2004 s 1(7)–(9). Section 7 of the Act provides for situations in which the consent requirements may be dispensed with, and sch 4 outlines a range of uses (and circumstances of use) where consent is not required.

[76] Human Tissue Act ss 5, 25, 32, 33 and 45.

can revoke licences where the standards set are not met or the terms of the licence are breached.[77]

In our view, the Act has significant shortcomings, some of which are specific to the Act itself, and some are more generally problems associated with a legislative scheme of the kind adopted in the Act. Specific to the Act, it is notable that few remedies are available to the person whose biomaterials are misused or misappropriated beyond the initial consent stage. While non-consensual use *per se* is captured by the 2004 Act, it is silent on who has the right to possess samples, who can control their uses and to what extent, and what ought to happen downstream if transfers are undertaken (for example, to other institutions). There are also no clear protections for researchers whose research samples are damaged or taken, or for holders of biomaterials outside the research or certain therapeutic areas. These are serious omissions, which leave a significant lacuna in the current legal framework, and which we examine in more detail in the next section.

Those in favour of a legislative scheme or a free-floating consent-based approach might assert that this lacuna could be filled by redrafting the legislation. This might be possible, but as Lyria Bennett Moses has pointed out elsewhere in this collection, there are significant problems with *sui generis* regulatory frameworks tailored to specific areas.[78] One obvious problem is the challenge of successfully capturing all the possible areas of concern within the scheme, so that appropriate protections, sanctions, and remedies for each are provided. The range and complexity of ways in which one person may interfere with items over which another person has some interest can be seen in, for example, the case law on conversion and trespass to goods. The multitude of possible bailments that may arise are also indicative of the numerous instances of conflict over objects to which the law has had to develop responses. When we take into account the increasing value of tissue, the proliferation of contexts in which that value arises, and the variety of parties wanting control of biomaterials and the personal information it contains, it is apparent that the regulation of biomaterials will challenge even the breadth of the law of property. Given this, a *sui generis* scheme that sets out to capture this array of potential conflicts would struggle to provide for even the majority of eventualities via specific provisions. It would need to be so extensive to cover each effectively, that it is likely to be unwieldy and exceptionally complex. It is likely, then, that drafters would resort to more general principles akin to those found in the law of property, as indeed the courts already have. It is in part for this reason, and also from a pragmatic standpoint, that it makes sense to utilise the well-established legal framework that property law provides.

Mere expediency is not, however, a sufficient reason to adopt a ready-made area of law to cover human biomaterials. We should look for 'Ms Right', not 'Ms

[77] Human Tissue Act, sch 3. The Human Fertilisation and Embryology Act 1990 also establishes a number of offences and operates a similar licensing scheme. However, here we are focusing on non-gametic materials.

[78] Bennett Moses, ch 12 in this volume.

Right-Now'.[79] We argue that the appeal of a property approach goes beyond the availability of an existing framework, and contend that property is also the best conceptual fit for the regulation of human biomaterials. To illustrate why this is the case we examine two situations that are of contemporary relevance: the donation of biomaterials for research and instances of loss, damage or interference with biomaterials. In each, we outline the particular implications of the lacuna we describe above, and suggest why property is conceptually the best framework for managing such situations. We conclude this discussion of the applicability of property law by also briefly addressing concern about the *inappropriateness* of deeming biomaterials 'property', a concern we do not share.

Donation of Biomaterials

Consider the following hypothetical example. Anne undergoes a biopsy to determine whether a lump in her breast is cancerous. Initially, the biopsied tissue is held by the hospital pathology laboratory, where it is tested. She subsequently agrees to donate it to a research project being conducted by a research team attached to the hospital. This donation would fall under the remit of the Human Tissue Act 2004. In making *appropriate consent* its guiding principle, at first glance, the 2004 Act appears to protect the interests that individuals, like Anne, might have in their biomaterials. It seems to be satisfactory, since the research team would be guilty of an offence if they use the tissue in a manner to which she has not consented. However, such a model is necessarily limited by the legislative framework that grounds it, and in the case of the Human Tissue Act this is problematic. First, it provides no guidance on who has a right to possess the biopsied tissue, or on who can control its uses. The result of this is that there is no clear indication of who the law will view as having control of biomaterials, and hence whose interests will be upheld in a conflict, or protected and compensated in the face of harm to them. We can imagine a number of situations in which Anne or others might want to take control of the fate of the tissue.

Imagine Anne wants to regain control of her tissue. Perhaps she wants to move it to another research study. Perhaps she wants to gain access to it for further testing (to avoid another biopsy, or to use information from the lump at the time it was first biopsied. This might be for her own health, or for legal purposes.[80] Let us also imagine that the research team refuses to give up factual possession. Here the Act cannot guide us on how to proceed; it does not tell us who has a better claim to possession: Anne or the research team.

We can easily think of other instances in which Anne or others might want to regain control of the tissue. Think of the growing practice of women retaining the

[79] We are indebted to Jesse Wall for this particularly apt means of summing up the issue.

[80] The latter situation is not so very different from that which arose in *Dobson v North Tyneside Health Authority*, above n 55.

placenta post-birth to eat it (following 'placenta encapsulation')[81] or to bury it. It is not difficult to imagine a woman initially giving up possession of her placenta (including for a research study), and then subsequently wishing for its return. There need not be a desire to regain actual possession, but simply to control who possesses it and what is done with it. Consider umbilical cord blood (UCB), which can be donated for research and other purposes; we know that many people now wish to control UCB obtained from their own children for their own purposes. As the science continues to advance, such desires will only increase, and it is certainly conceivable that women or their relatives may want to control UCB. Other contexts include access for testing for legal purposes, as in the cases of *Dobson* and *Roche*, for reproduction, for health testing (by the individual or family members), for paternity testing, or for burial as in *AB* and other organ retention situations.

An effective model of regulation for human biomaterials needs to be able to answer the questions of who has the right to control those materials at any given time, and what he or she may do with them. This includes not only being able to provide the answer at the point of donation of biomaterials, but also being able to trace the chain of possession and to make provisions for the transfer of those materials down the line. Where this cannot be done, or where there is a lack of procedural and justificatory clarity, problems arise. As biomaterials are transferred, and more people and organisations come into possession of them, these problems are exacerbated. This is particularly the case where tissue is transferred to commercial entities. We have listed only a few situations here, but there are many more that might be raised as contexts in which a lack of clear guidance about who has the right to control tissue might be seriously problematic.

A real example that demonstrates some of the issues that may arise regarding the donation of biomaterials is the case of *University of Washington v Catalona*.[82] We have chosen this case from the US because instances of competing claims over the use and possession of biomaterials for the purposes of research have not yet been tested in the English courts. William Catalona was a researcher and surgeon who had been instrumental in establishing a biorepository of tissue samples donated for research purposes, particularly prostate cancer research. The biorepository was held at Washington University and contained consensually donated samples from thousands of men.[83] Donors were asked to sign a consent form, which usually referred to the contribution as a 'donation' and or a 'free and generous gift' to the research.[84] They were informed that they could have their samples withdrawn from research upon request, at which point the samples would be destroyed.[85] These donated biomaterials were used in research studies both at

[81] Independent Placenta Encapsulation Network, 'Placenta Encapsulation', available at: placentanetwork.com/placenta-encapsulation/.

[82] *Washington University v Catalona*, above n 23.

[83] ibid at 988.

[84] ibid.

[85] Under state and federal law, Washington University was not required to destroy samples when a research participant withdrew consent, although they could do so if they wished. They could also opt to merely store the samples, or anonymise them and continue to use them in research. See 29 CFR

Washington University and other institutions. When used elsewhere, the samples were transferred in accordance with a Materials Transfer Agreement (MTA). In 2003, Catalona moved to a new institution and he intended to take with him those samples donated by his research participants. Washington University resisted his plans, and Catalona consequently wrote to all research participants who had contributed to the biorepository (even those who had not participated in his research), asking them to sign the enclosed form to authorise the release of their samples to Catalona himself.[86] Washington University sought a declaratory judgment that it owned the samples, and that the participants were not permitted to direct that their samples be transferred to Catalona at his new institution.

Fundamentally, this case was about a conflict over *control* of biomaterials, a conflict that arose because it was not wholly clear who had the right to possess and control the samples in question. This lack of clarity arose because the question of who had these rights was not clearly determined at the point when they were transferred to the biorepository. When the donations were made, the focus was on obtaining consent to use for a purpose, and the ability to have them withdrawn from research. When something beyond these aspects of the consent was contemplated (removal to another institution by a member of the research team), there was no guide as to who had the right to make this determination. The consent framework within which the samples were donated could only answer the questions: 'May they be used in this research?' and 'Must they be withdrawn upon request?' However, this gives no guidance on whether, or what, remedies will be available beyond these questions.[87] Yet it would seem important to know who has the right to possession, if and when this will terminate, and what the donee's responsibilities are if the item is lost, stolen, damaged, or destroyed (by a third party). It tells us nothing about what the donor can do if the donee refuses to return it (if anything at all), nor their options if the donee uses the tissue for commercial purposes.

In *Catalona*, the court turned to a quasi-property solution, although the language in which it did so was somewhat confused, due to its reluctance to explicitly draw on this framework, even though it used the language of gifts. By examining the court's approach, we will see how the law of property has developed mechanisms for regulating gifts and donations that fit transfers of biomaterials well, and would be likely to be reflected in any legislative scheme. We will also draw out the problems with a consent-based approach in contrast to the possessory rights-based approach of property.

The court in this case characterised each donation of biomaterials to the repository as an *inter vivos* gift, stating that: 'The elements of an inter vivos gift are: 1) present intention of the donor to make a gift; 2) delivery of property by donor to

§1910.1030, §§260.200 RSMo, 260.203 RSMo, 10 CSR §80–7.101 as cited in *Washington University v Catalona*, ibid, 992–93.

[86] The letter was sent to some 60,000 participants, of whom around 6,000 signed and returned the form: *Washington University v Catalona*, ibid at 993.

[87] The result would have been the same under the Human Tissue Act.

donee; and 3) acceptance by donee whose ownership takes effect immediately and absolutely'.[88] The first part of this definition mirrors a consent-model; it is based on and reflects intentions, as does the third part. The second part demands an act that together with the intentions makes the gift. Taken superficially, it seems to do no more than a consent-model, but there is a key distinction that makes all the difference. It expresses what occurs as a result of the transfer: 'ownership takes effect'. This describes what the new possessor obtains beyond mere factual possession, and it clarifies what he or she may do far more than a consent-relationship as it draws on the whole range of implications of possession that are managed via property. To see the importance of this, we need to take a step back and see property in the round.

Recognising property rights in biomaterials is a means of explicitly allocating rights of use and control to those materials. There may be a range of legitimate answers to the question of who has (or ought to have) this control. We might say 'the state', or 'the individual from whom they came', or 'the researcher who is using them in a research project', or even 'anyone and everyone, no one is excluded from control or access'. There is a prevailing view in the academic literature,[89] which can also be seen in the case law,[90] that separation from the source represents a normative line which (once crossed) 'render[s] human tissue capable of being governed by property considerations'.[91] If we took this view, we could then, for example, conceptualise this separation as the creation of a new thing.[92] Usually, the first possessor of a new thing is deemed to be the owner, who then has the control and use rights that are part of ownership.[93] If we accept this, then it raises the question of who ought to be considered as the legitimate first possessor,[94] for example, the source of the tissue, the surgeon who removes it, or the hospital in which the surgeon works?[95] In the context of the 2004 Act and the general common law provisions in England and Wales, as we have already seen, there is an emphasis on consent. One function of this is to protect the autonomous decisions of those individuals with respect to their bodies, health, and lives

[88] *Washington University v Catalona*, above n 23 at 997.

[89] JE Penner, *The Idea of Property in Law* (Oxford, Oxford University Press, 1997) 111; JW Harris, *Property and Justice* (Oxford, Oxford University Press, 2001) 332; R Hardcastle, *Law and the Human Body: Property Rights, Ownership, and Control* (Oxford, Hart Publishing, 2009) 15; and M Radin, *Reinterpreting Property* (Chicago, University of Chicago Press, 1993) 41.

[90] *R v Bentham* [2005] UKHL 18, [2005] 1 WLR 1057.

[91] M Quigley, 'Property in Human Biomaterials: Separating Persons and Things?' (2012) 32 *Oxford Journal of Legal Studies* 659, 669.

[92] Goold would take this position. See, eg Harris' 'creation-without-wrong' criterion, Harris, *Property and Justice*, above n 89 at 360.

[93] See, further, S Douglas, *Liability for Wrongful Interferences with Chattels* (Oxford, Hart Publishing, 2011) chs 2, 3. However, in some contexts different rules apply, and rules appropriate to the regulation of human biomaterials could be put in place.

[94] It is important to note that we need not adopt the 'first possessor is the owner' position. Property is sufficiently adaptable that an alternative stance on who is first owner could be adopted if more appropriate for the regulation of biomaterials. The crucial point is that whatever rule is adopted, the property approach provides a means to determine who has initial control of separated materials in a given situation.

[95] On this see, eg Skene, ch 15 in this volume.

more generally. If we accept that such protections are the legitimate domain of the law, then ascribing initial ownership to the person from whom the materials were taken could aid in this respect.[96] Alternatively, we could reject the moment of separation as the creation of a new thing that demands determination of its lawful possessor.[97] We might instead argue that no new thing is created, but rather this separated part is owned by the person from whom it was taken on the basis (put very simply) that he or she was already self-owning, and hence is the owner of any parts of that self once they are separated. Whichever route we support, the strength of property is that having determined the first owner, or even merely who had a right to initial possession, a property framework can provide guidance on what occurs at the point of transfer.

From this point, we can then avail ourselves of the benefits of a property approach. Whether we are thinking of loaning, donating, or selling particular items, property law provides an established and largely workable set of rules for governing these situations. Property can do this more readily than a free-floating consent-based framework. This is so because it does not focus on consensual relationships (including contractual ones), but rather it is arranged around the idea of title, providing answers to the possession and control questions by determining who has the best title (or claim) to the item in question. The law of property delineates how our rights regarding possession and control can be asserted against others who might interfere with them, by non-consensual taking, using, or damaging, and so on. These rights may be subject to various constraints or come with particular duties attached (either on their part or mine). If I loan my property, I retain ownership. The person to whom I loan it gains a right to possession, but this may be subject to various duties. If I donate an item of property, my ownership passes from me to the donee who then becomes the new owner and vested with all the rights that attend such status. If I sell an item over which I have the requisite property rights, all of my rights regarding that object pass to the buyer.[98] This comes within the provisions of legislation, such as the Sale of Goods Act 1979. We can, thus, know who holds which rights before and after transfers, as well as how these rights relate to one another. In contrast to consent-based approaches, the law of property provides guidance on what occurs – legally – when a thing moves from the control or possession of one person to another.[99]

[96] We could take a different view on the first owner, and different consequences would flow which we have not the space to consider here. However, the point about clarity of transfer and subsequent control would stand.

[97] Quigley has argued elsewhere that separability as a normative criterion for the creation of property rights is philosophically problematic, even when conjoined with other criteria such as intention to create property or creation-without-wrong. See M Quigley, 'Property in Human Biomaterials – Separating Persons and Things?' (2012) *Oxford Journal of Legal Studies 1*.

[98] This is best conceptualised as the conjoining of property and contract. The right to sell is not analytically necessitated by property. See, eg Penner, above n 89, who describes the right to sell as a hybrid right.

[99] We do not mean to suggest here that consent is not relevant to property. It is entirely relevant to determining, for example, whether transfers of biomaterials would be legitimate. Instead, by 'consent-based' approaches we mean those that utilise consent, but exclude property considerations.

Crucially, that guidance is founded on hierarchy of title, and so property will always be able to tell us who has the best right in relation an object, even if that person is a finder or a thief. This is a core advantage of property over consent-based and legislative models – its structure avoids the lacunae these regimes are prone to where they have not provided for particular situations. This is also the reason why a scheme that tries to avoid such lacunae would tend towards a property approach.

It is interesting to note that those who oppose property in biomaterials tend to use, and actively advocate, the language of gifting. This can be seen in organ donation campaigns, which talk of giving the 'gift of life', as well as in the academic literature.[100] It is sometimes suggested that human biomaterials may appropriately be conceived as gifts, but not as property *per se*. Yet legally (and we would argue as a matter of logic) gifting involves the exercise of property rights. You must have the right to possess it to give someone else the right to then possess it. This is what you have legally given to the donee, and this is how property conceives of transfers. Further, as a matter of logic, if you are to give something away, your set of rights regarding how that thing is used and controlled must include the right to transfer. You do not, for example, have the requisite title in order to donate your colleague's car to the work charity auction. Likewise, if we are to make gifts of our biomaterials, this necessarily entails having proper title to those materials, along with the right to control that aspect of their use. At law, gifts are essentially the passing of ownership, that is, the passing of the residual rights held by the 'owner', and this approach accurately captures what occurs when biomaterials are donated; they pass from one person's possession (with consent) and are then possessed, used and control by the new possessor. Property law provides relatively clear and established principles that would apply in these situations. The common law position on gifts is that the intention to give must be clear and unequivocal.[101] In a situation where a chattel is transferred and no clear intention has been expressed, the common law presumes that it was not meant as a gift. Furthermore, the donor must intend to benefit the donee immediately – an intention to benefit her in the future will not be sufficient.[102] The donee must also be prepared to accept the gift (although the law presumes acceptance unless there is evidence to the contrary).

As noted above, these principles mirror part of the approach in *Catalona*, and with good reason. The court was attempting to clarify what had occurred when the samples were transferred. It reasoned that someone had initial control and that this was passed to another. While it was managed by the terms of the consent form, there was a need to fill in the gaps about what had occurred during transfer. Property had the capacity to fill these gaps, and this is one of the benefits to con-

[100] See O Ben-David, *Organ Donation and Transplantation: Body Organs as an Exchangeable Socio-Cultural Resource* (Westport, CT, Praeger, 2005) 29.

[101] RJ Smith, *Property Law* (Edinburgh, Pearson Education Ltd, 2001) 112–13; B McFarlane, *The Structure of Property Law* (Oxford, Hart Publishing, 2008) 165–68.

[102] *Re Ridgway* (1885) 15 QBD 447, 449 per Cave J.

ceiving of transfers of tissue in such a manner. It clarifies what has occurred when tissue has moved from one person to another. As such, the donations by the men in *Catalona* could be viewed as *unconditional* gifts. Indeed, the court took the view that neither the donors nor Dr Catalona retained any proprietary interests in the tissue samples, but instead ownership had passed to Washington University.[103] Thus, once donated, if conceived of as an unconditional gift, the donors could no longer direct what was done with the tissue. It is, however, hard to reconcile this with the fact that the donors still retained the power to withdraw the biomaterials from the research conducted at the biorepository. For this reason, the donations might instead have been better seen as *bailments*, wherein, if the possessor breached the terms of the bailment, the bailor could demand their return.

An alternative, and potentially better, approach in *Catalona* could have been to regard the transfer as a bailment. This would have allowed the donee (either Catalona or Washington University) to use the materials for the purposes to which consent has been given and be in keeping with the fact that the donor could withdraw their consent and, thus, demand the return (or destruction) of the samples. Bailment is premised on the fact that the donor (bailor) retains the right to possession, despite having transferred physical possession of the materials, and the right to use them, to the researchers.[104] Although different in its context and facts, such an approach would also be in keeping with the recent decision in *Jonathan Yearworth and others v North Bristol NHS Trust* (*Yearworth*).[105] We will return to this case below when we discuss situations involving damage or loss of biomaterials, but for now we simply note that once a determination of property is made it opens up numerous legal avenues, mechanisms, and protections, which remain closed otherwise.[106] Without allowing that biomaterials are property at the point of donation, we cannot utilise the law of gifts or that of bailment, both of which require there to be property. Whichever of these approaches we take, they provide a clear determination of how control of an item has been transferred and what this entails.

As Cameron Stewart and others explore in their chapter in this collection, the clarity that the law of gifts lends to donations is a strength of taking a property approach.[107] The same is true of the law of bailment and its capacity to determine what occurs when more than one party has interactions with an object. By contrast, consent-based schemes could not resolve the situation in *Catalona* unless much more detail about how such situations ought to be dealt with were already outlined in the consent. Had they done so, however, the more they outlined these rights, the more they would have had to mimic the language of property by outlining who held which rights of control, possession and the like. Only by resorting

[103] *Catalona* 490 F 3d 667, 673–77 [Court of Appeals].

[104] This can be a right to immediate possession, but this is not always the case.

[105] *Yearworth* above n 4.

[106] Douglas' chapter in this volume provides some more detailed exploration of this point: ch 7 in this volume.

[107] Stewart et al, ch 3 in this volume.

to more general principles can the lacunae be avoided, and hence in this context property is not simply Ms Right-Now, because it offers the most effective means of avoiding situations in which we cannot determine who has the right to decide what is done with biomaterials.

Such a clear determination has benefits beyond clarifying what the donor has transferred away; it also provides vital certainty about the rights of the new possessor, who gains the right to possession that may be defender against those who interfere with the biomaterials. Such rights will be important when those materials are vulnerable to being taken or damaged. In the following section we explore the legal response to damage to or loss of biomaterials and argue for the applicability of property law in this context as well.

Damage to or Loss of Biomaterials

As we discussed at the beginning of this chapter, there are many contexts in which biomaterials are in some sense 'scarce', or least in demand. They may be commercially valuable, or important for research but in short supply. It might be that one family member wants access to the tissue of another. They might be necessary for legal proceedings. There are good reasons, then, for the possessor to want that possession to be protected against people who divest them of it, or who damage those biomaterials. In this section, we argue that property provides the most effective and appropriate means of such protection. We consider first the regulation of damage, followed by a consideration of unwanted, non-damaging, interferences.

The recent *Yearworth* case[108] represents a significant, albeit still uncertain, development of the approach of the courts to the issue of property in biomaterials.[109] The case represents the first time that the English courts have been faced with a claim for damage to biomaterials held by a third party on behalf of their source. The claimants brought a case against Bristol Southmead NHS Trust for the loss of their sperm samples that were being stored at the fertility unit. The samples were irrevocably damaged when the storage unit, in which they were held, failed. Claims for personal injury and damage to property as a result of negligence were heard in both the County Court and the Court of Appeal. At the request of the Court of Appeal, further arguments in bailment were also put forward. Both claims were rejected at first instance. On appeal, the court accepted that the sperm samples could be property of which the men had ownership. Having accepted that the samples could be considered property for the claim at

[108] Above, n 4.

[109] For some analyses of the case see M Quigley, 'Property: The Future of Human Tissue?' (2009) 17 *Medical Law Review* 457; J Lee, 'The Fertile Imagination of the Common Law: *Yearworth v North Bristol NHS Trust*' (2009) 17 *Torts Law Journal* 130; SHE Harmon and GT Laurie, '*Yearworth v North Bristol NHS Trust*: Property, Principles, Precedents, and Paradigms' (2010) 69 *Cambridge Law Journal* 476–93; C Hawes, 'Property Interests in Body Parts: *Yearworth v North Bristol NHS Trust*' (2010) 73 *Medical Law Review* 119; and L Skene, 'Proprietary Interests in Human Bodily Material: *Yearworth*, Recent Australian Cases on Stored Semen and their Implications' (2012) 20 *Medical Law Review* 227.

hand, the court also allowed the claim in bailment.[110] As discussed earlier, without recourse to property, it is difficult to see under current law what remedy could have been given for the damage done to the samples. The court itself noted the significant complications that would arise from trying to apply personal injury to *separated* materials, including the logical problems of how to conceive this as a physical injury to the men. Let us, therefore, look at why property is apt for dealing with loss or damage to biomaterials.

The legal system's mechanism for protecting rights regarding things is largely the system of property. In this respect, excised human materials are tangible 'things'. Once a person's tissue is removed, we can conceive of it as a corporeal thing now physically distinct from the living body. It is a thing in its own right. Whatever other values biomaterials might have or represent,[111] they are demonstrably treated as things, by those who use them, and so fall easily within the ambit of (personal) property.[112] At its core, property is about use and control; about who has the right to possess these things and to determine (within constraints) what is done with them. Further, as we noted earlier, property is the law's mechanism for managing scarce resources that are in demand by more than one party. Such demand fosters instability of possession, when the person who wants the object tries to divest it from the person in possession. As Douglas comments:

> In the absence of legal regulation, those in possession of such things are always vulnerable to being dispossessed by a more powerful party. This is something that the law tries to avoid, and it does this by allocating property rights in such things to individuals, thus imposing a legal duty on others to refrain from interfering with goods that are in a person's possession.[113]

In each of the contexts noted at the beginning of this section, and in numerous other cases, biomaterials might be (in Douglas's words) 'things that someone (such as the claimant or a rival researcher) would be able to seize and take away from the defendants' which creates vulnerability. As he points out, the law generally 'tries to protect peaceful possession by allocating property rights in the thing to a *particular* person'.[114] In the absence of such a right, he argues (and we concur) 'there would be nothing to stop someone, such as a rival researcher, from taking the tissue samples from [someone] with complete impunity'.[115]

It is often argued that property is essentially exclusionary, but we must avoid

[110] Until the decision in *Yearworth*, there was debate as to whether a claim could be brought 'in bailment', rather than conversion, trespass to goods or other relevant tort action. However, the Court of Appeal in this case allowed a claim in bailment itself. The decision has been criticised on this basis. See further J Lee, 'The Fertile Imagination of the Common Law: *Yearworth v North Bristol*' (2009) 17 *Torts Law Journal* 130; C Hawes, 'Property Interests in Body Parts: *Yearworth v North Bristol NHS Trust*' (2010) 73 *Modern Law Review* 130.

[111] See 'Property or Not Property? Challenging Cases and Creative Judicial Reasoning' above, n 6.

[112] On the relevance or otherwise of 'thingness', see S Douglas, 'The Argument for Property Rights in Body Parts: Scarcity of Resources' (2014) 40 *Journal of Medical Ethics* 23.

[113] Douglas, ch 7 in this volume.

[114] ibid (emphasis added).

[115] ibid.

exaggerating the implications of this. This exclusionary aspect of possession is generally another way of saying that the person legitimately in possession is the person who may use the thing. In the case of biological materials, legitimate possession effectively gives the possessor (in most cases) the capacity to determine how it is used.[116] The full picture is, of course, more nuanced than this since, as *Yearworth* exemplifies, those in current possession of an item may not have a full set of entitlements regarding use if someone else can exert greater claims to the materials. Nevertheless, what this suggests is that loss of, and damage to, biomaterials could be usefully regulated via the torts governing wrongful interference with property; namely, negligent interference with property, conversion, and trespass to goods.[117] These torts provide remedies where a wrong is done to the interests of someone who rightfully possesses a thing. Using the mechanisms available in tort to protect interests in property does not in and of itself determine *whose* interests are most important, nor *who should have interests*. We can argue about who has these interests, what kind of interests they are, and which are the most important, but once we have resolved these questions, tort protections for interference with property interests are exactly the type of protection needed for biomaterials.

Where objects are damaged, conversion and other torts for wrongful interference provide for compensation, but importantly they also encompass unwanted dealings with biological materials that do not result in damage. Many of the situations noted above do not entail physical harm, or even financial loss, but they do involve unwanted interference with objects that the possessor might legitimately want to prevent. Researchers need to be sure that their samples are not vulnerable to dispossession as this would disrupt or ruin research. Individuals may want to prevent unwanted testing by others, or simply prevent use for purposes that they find offensive. Here, it is a desire for control that encapsulates all these situations – the prevention of interference, damaging or not. Both trespass to goods and conversion are actionable without proof of damage. They protect the right to possession itself. This aspect of property law reflects the fact that control is inherently important in relation to scarce or important objects. Property rights do not exist merely to provide a means for damage to be compensated; they protect wider interests in controlling objects that others would interfere with in ways that we legitimately wish they would not. We also need not ascribe rights over objects where this is not the case, and so we could exclude some biomaterials from the ambit of property if this seemed appropriate, avoiding the concerns some raise about 'absurd' results, wherein constant conversions occur when we touch discarded tissue such as hair or dandruff.

[116] Finders are a notable exception.

[117] These torts are collected under the auspices of the Torts (Interference with Goods) Act 1977, but the common law rules governing them largely remain intact, s 1.

To bring a successful claim for trespass to goods, a claimant must show that he or she had possession of the chattel.[118] The claimant must demonstrate that the defendant intentionally interfered with his or her right to possession. An accidental interference will not suffice (although there is some authority that a negligent interference will).[119] It is not necessary to show that the defendant took the goods, only that he or she interfered with the claimant's right to possession. Even a mere unauthorised touching or use of the goods will be enough to found an action, regardless of whether any damage has been done.[120] To bring a conversion claim, a similar interest must be demonstrated, but the defendant must in some way have intended to assert his own entitlement that would effectively deny that of the claimant. According to Lord Nicholls, for an act to amount to conversion, it must also be 'so extensive an encroachment on the rights of the owner as to exclude him from use and possession' of the goods.[121] Liability for conversion is strict, and for trespass it is arguably so, although there is debate but we need not delve into this in detail here. In both actions, all that is required is an intention to deal with the goods. It is generally irrelevant whether the defendant knew she was committing a trespass or a conversion, nor that the action occurred due to an honest mistake, only that she intended to do the action that interfered with the claimant's possession (although accidental interferences are arguably not trespasses).[122] For both actions, the act must be deliberate.[123] Both trespass to goods and conversion provide protection against and remedies for mere interference. In the context of human biological materials, such a remedial response could be appropriate because of the nature of the materials. It is the control of them that is important to some, for example, the parents in *AB v Leeds Teaching Hospital* (see above). Neither action would have required the parents to demonstrate actual loss, merely that they had the right to possess the materials and that this right was interfered

[118] In trust situations, a trustee may bring a claim against an alleged trespasser even though the chattel is in the possession of a beneficiary.

[119] N McBride and R Bagshaw, *Tort Law*, 4th edn (London, Pearson Longman, 2012) 500.

[120] See, eg *Penfolds Wines Pty Ltd v Elliot* (1946) 74 CLR 204 per Latham CJ.

[121] *Kuwait Airways Corpn v Iraqui Airways Co (Nos 4 & 5)* [2002] 2 AC 883, [39].

[122] See, eg *Wilson v Lombank Ltd* (1963) 1 All ER 740 in which the defendant was guilty of trespass when he removed a car he (wrongly) believed to be his from a garage. According to *Halsbury's Laws of England*: 'It may be that an action for trespass to goods also lies for purely negligent conduct causing injury to goods,' citing *Fowler v Lanning* [1959] 1 QB 426, [1959] 1 All ER 290; but *cf Letang v Cooper* [1965] 1 QB 232, [1964] 2 All ER 929, CA. It goes on to say: 'The Torts (Interference with Goods) Act 1977 s 11(1) . . . in providing that contributory negligence is no defence in proceedings founded on intentional trespass to goods, might be seen as impliedly recognising that an action may lie for non-intentional trespass to goods' (*Halsbury's Laws of England/Tort* (vol 45(2) (Reissue))/ 2. Specific Torts/ (5) Trespass and Associated Torts/(ii) Wrongs to Property/D. Wrongful Interference with Goods /(c) Trespass to Goods/(a) In general/660. Unintentional harm). Compare *Clerk & Lindsell*, which seem slightly less accepting, but nonetheless states: 'An accidental interference of a non-negligent nature is not a trespass', citing *National Coal Board v JE Evans & Co (Cardiff) Ltd* [1951] 2 KB 861), and further: 'It is sufficient that he intended to do the act complained of, or was negligent in producing an injury; he need not foresee the legal consequence of his interference' [paras 17–129].

[123] Examples as cited by McBride and Bagshaw: *Arthur v Anker* [1997] QB 564, *Vine v Waltham Forest LBC* [2000] 1 WLR 2383, and *Hartley v Moxham* (1842) 114 ER 675. See, further, N McBride and R Bagshaw, *Tort Law*, 4th edn (London, Pearson Longman, 2012) 355.

with. The same would be true of other situations in which an individual rightly had control of his or her biomaterials.

Where biomaterials have been damaged, both trespass and conversion also provide further remedies. If damage is less than the destruction of the goods, then the person in possession, or with a right to immediate possession, may bring a claim for trespass to goods. If it entails destruction, conversion offers the better claim. Individuals do not need to 'own' the relevant materials in order to bring either of these actions, they can be brought by others, such as trustees, bailees, and finders, as they require only that the claimant has a right to possession. In each case, if that person has a right to possession that is interfered with, then he or she will have a claim. This would facilitate resolutions where damage is done to materials held by one person for another, for example, laboratories for testing and samples held on trust or under a bailment for research purposes. Since a finder may also defend his possession, this would capture loss or damage to materials legitimately held by a researcher who has come into possession of biomaterials in the absence of a clear transfer, protecting the security of such samples when used in research.

In contrast to merely making unauthorised use an offence, wrongful interference actions provide remedies for interference with interests, whosoever they may belong to. Where interference causes no loss, then damages are likely to be nominal, but, since they are actionable without proof of damage, this allows the courts to be flexible. Conversely, where loss does occur, the claimant can obtain compensatory damages for the market value of the materials, as well as any losses flowing from the interference (subject to the remoteness test of reasonable foreseeability).[124]

An alternative route to compensatory damages could be for the donor to seek the return (or perhaps destruction) of the materials in question. In this respect, the courts would have discretion to order specific restitution of the materials if damages will not be an adequate remedy. For example, if the collection of materials in *Catalona* had been taken by someone, the University of Washington would potentially have preferred its return rather than monetary compensation. The availability of such a remedy may be more appropriate for some situations and might offer a better response to wrongful use than penalising the user or fining them. The discretion to award damages or return of goods enables the court to tailor its response to particular harms. Additionally, the remedies for wrongful interference have the flexibility to account for improvements made to materials by the defendant.[125] Even if the goods (in this case tissue samples) are returned, defendants may still be liable for damages to the value of the use they have obtained from the goods.[126]

[124] On compensation for interferences with goods, see Torts (Interference with Goods) Act 1977 s 3; S Douglas, *Liability for Wrongful Interferences with Chattels* (Oxford, Hart Publishing, 2011) ch 10; S Green and J Randall, *The Tort of Conversion* (Oxford, Hart Publishing, 2009) ch 7.

[125] ibid.

[126] This could be an effective approach if a case similar to *Moore* arises in the future. See Greasley, ch 6 in this volume for the facts of this case.

These remedies stand in contrast to those generally offered by legislative schemes, such as the Human Tissue Act, which provides only for offences. It does not provide redress for those who are actually harmed, or whose interests are affected. Such schemes could provide remedies, but these would arguably be similar to those offered by tort for interferences with property interests, such as compensatory damages. Again, as we have argued throughout this chapter, property already offers what is needed to augment legislative schemes.

On Objections to Characterising Human Biomaterials as Property

Despite the evident practical benefits of applying property principles to human biomaterials, concern is sometimes raised that doing so is inappropriate because it objectifies that which should not be objectified.[127] This concern is usually intertwined with concerns about the sale of biomaterial, with some, such as Thomas Murray, arguing that its unique qualities and the fact that it was once part of a morally valuable person should preclude it from being treated as something that can be bought and sold. In Murray's view

> [t]he body, in its significant manifestations, is not suitable for markets because our most important religions and secular traditions treat is as 'dignity-property' or 'sacra', as an integral part of the person who is the locus of moral concerns and moral worth. It should not be traded in markets because markets in body parts, like all markets, will be subject to inequities and abuses. But these inequities and abuses will have special significance in body markets, because it is the morally significant body (and health, and life) that is being traded off.[128]

Others, such as Margaret Radin, argue that the conceptualisation of personal attributes (including the human aspects of biomaterials) as 'mere' commodities that are wholly fungible can 'undermine personhood by engendering inferior understandings – conceptualisations – of what a person is'.[129] It may be true that the sale of biomaterials is problematic for these, and indeed other, reasons. But these are not arguments against a property approach. Property status does not entail saleability, and if these concerns are sufficiently worrying, we could prevent the sale of biomaterials while still deeming them property. There are many examples of objects that are property but which cannot be sold, or where the power to sell is restricted – prescription drugs and handguns are two obvious examples.

[127] For a full discussion of these concerns, see Herring, ch 13 and Greasley, ch 6 in this volume.

[128] TH Murray, 'On the Human Body as Property: The Meaning of Embodiment, Markets, and the Meaning of Strangers' (1987) 20 *Journal of Law Reform* 1055, 1088. See also C Heyer, '*Moore v Regents of the University of California*: The Right of Property in Human Tissue and Its Effect on Medical Research' 16 *Rutgers Computer and Technology Law Journal* 629, 653. James Harris argues that it is an affront to human dignity to commodify organs: see Harris above n 89, 352.

[129] MJ Radin, *Contested Commodities* (Cambridge, MA, Harvard University Press, 1996) 15. Radin's argument is substantially more nuanced and complex, but we lack space to consider it fully here.

Aside from commodification concerns, the objectification claim reduces to a concern about treating human biomaterials as an object that can transferred or used like another object. Again, this might be a valid concern, but if it is, it is not an argument against a property approach; it is an argument against using human biomaterials at all. As they are already widely possessed, transferred and used, this objection comes rather too late. The reality is that human biomaterials are things that are used and controlled. Property transfer rules, and devices such as trusts and leases are all directed at organising people's relationships with each other in respect of things. Applying property principles to human biomaterials does not alter how we treat them, but instead gives legal protection to what we already do. We already treat biomaterials in very much the same way as we do other objects that are property, and this extra-legal conception of such materials as something that can be so treated is indicative of how naturally and effectively they fit within the *legal* conception of property. Property provides clarity and certainty about who may do what with something – whether it be a house, a car, or some other object and this can include biomaterials.[130] If something is my property in some sense, I know that I have strong claims on others not to interfere with it.[131] As James Harris has noted, it is this strong exclusionary protection that makes the language of property attractive to some who wish to express the degree to which we should be supported in preventing others from touching our bodies and their parts.[132] It is for these very reasons that property is the preferable means of regulating biomaterials.

Concluding Remarks

Human tissue can be unique, it is often seen as special (symbolically and otherwise), and it is certainly valuable. It can be (but is not always) valuable to the person from whom it was obtained, and it is often valuable to others – researchers, recipients of treatments, medical practitioners, and the wider community. It almost invariably contains genetic information that might be revealing of private information about the source and her relatives. It may have religious significance, or emotional power. These are all reasons to provide those who are rightly in control of tissue, or who have a strong, legitimate interest in it, the best legal pro-

[130] What counts as a 'thing' in the relevant sense is one aspect of the property question, which has been subject to debate when applied to the human body and biomaterials. We note that there is dispute over whether property relates only to 'things', and further that the inclusion of ideas here takes an (contested) expansive approach to the notion of property. However, debate over whether *only* 'things' can be property is not relevant in the context of this chapter and so we do not pursue it here. On the relevance (or otherwise) of 'thingness' and the inclusion of non-corporeals, such as ideas, see the useful discussion in Douglas, ch 7 in this volume.

[131] Douglas has provided an excellent overview of this dimension of property law, see ch 7 in this volume.

[132] W Harris above n 89, 184–88.

tection of that control and those interests. Property, for the reasons we have given in this chapter, is a useful and effective legal device to achieve this. A particular strength of taking a property approach is that it gives us the capacity to determine who has the best claim to an item, and from this to establish who can retain possession of it, use it, transfer it and so on. However far an item travels, property enables us to track these determinations through a string of transfers, interferences and loans. It also brings certainty when objects are transferred, telling us who has the right to do what with it post-transfer. This feature of property provides a means to ensure that we can ordinarily answer whose interests are to be protected by *the law*. Added to this, property also provides a determination of how items can be dealt with even when the owner is not known, whether they have been lost, abandoned or left. It can tell us (in conjunction with the law of bailment) how to resolve a situation in which one person damages an item that is owned by another person, but of which he has possession for the purposes of doing something with it at the owner's request.

Conversely, when a property approach is eschewed, there is an absence of clarity. In any given situation, under the current system, it will not necessarily be clear who has a right to possess biological materials, how they may be transferred, what happens when they are transferred, nor what their rights are if a third party interferes with those materials. This is particularly problematic when they are transferred multiple times. The reason is that such a model does not clearly determine who holds which rights over biomaterials in any particular context, but instead merely prescribes what may or may not be done in some limited, defined situations. In failing to outline these rights, and resting the protective framework on a relationship of consent, the model fails to provide a means to determine who has rights when biomaterials are transferred. Furthermore, in stark contrast to the current consent-based legislative scheme, the law of tort, of trusts, and of restitution would provide a range of flexible, applicable means for a person to seek redress for damage to, or misuse of their biomaterials if these were admitted as property. This would be true, whether the rights interfered with rested with the individual from whom the materials were originally obtained, or a subsequent *lawful* possessor such as a researcher or hospital. We can choose a property approach that vests the rights as we wish (in accordance with reasons from policy and ethics).[133] It does not matter here where they vest; the strength of property is that once we have chosen this, we can then access the well-worked-out rules of property to determine whose claim to possession or ownership will trump in each of these situations.[134]

All this said, a property approach is not incompatible with the provisions of the Human Tissue Act 2004, and utilising property rules to govern the uses of

[133] Douglas, ch 7 in this volume.

[134] We recognise that there is an argument that property would have to be adapted so far to admit human biomaterials due to problematic consequences; however, in our view the case made in this chapter demonstrates that these consequences are not significant. It is beyond the scope of this chapter to address this concern further.

biomaterials would provide a useful adjunct to the legislation. Any legislative scheme can only pre-emptively consider the situations outlined in this chapter. If legislation were to be amended, or newly drafted, as Jonathan Herring suggests in this collection, it would be difficult to predict the challenges that developing biotechnology might herald in the future. This is, of course, a problem for any legislation that attempts to govern fast-moving areas. To address this, more developed legislation is likely to turn to providing broad principles, as well as more specific rules, to cover all possible situations that might arise. In doing so, we contend, such legislation would very likely end up looking a great deal like a property approach comprising principles governing possession, transfer and use. This is partly because of the nature of the challenges that arise when people come into conflict over the control of things, the very problem that property law is directed at resolving.

15

Raising Issues With a Property Law Approach

LOANE SKENE

Introduction

Property law principles are appealing in many respects as a mechanism for regulating the collection, storage and use of human bodily material. However, difficulties will inevitably arise if all separated human bodily material is regarded as property, or more specifically, as the property of, or subject to property rights in favour of, the originator (the person from whom the material was derived). This chapter will argue that applying the principles of property law will raise issues that are so numerous and diverse that one may question whether it is advisable to adopt a broad property law approach as the starting point in regulation. The rules required in 'exceptional' cases will soon outnumber those in which the 'general rule' applies. If there are to be many exceptions to the general rule, it may be better to have rules that deal specifically with each case,[1] without a prior conceptualisation of all bodily material as the property of the originator, subject to a large number of exceptions and limitations.

Those who advocate such a case-by-case approach commonly argue that rights in bodily material should be governed by statute;[2] and that approach certainly has advantages in achieving a clear and consistent outcome. However, professional codes of conduct, ethical guidelines and case law may also play a part in regulating the use of bodily material as new situations inevitably arise that do not fall within the legislation, or may be more flexibly regulated in other ways. Other principles may then be developed in tandem with the legislation. The main point for this chapter is that each new principle should promote and protect the rights and interests it is designed to protect, rather than apply un-nuanced to all separated bodily material.

To make this argument, I will draw attention to some of the issues that have received little judicial attention to date regarding what is commonly called a

[1] See Herring ch 13 this volume.
[2] ibid.

'property approach' and show that it will be difficult in practice for the law to hold that human bodily material is, or is not, property. It may be property for one purpose, such as the law of theft or consumer protection; but not for another, such as surgical or research uses of bodily material. For example, human urine is not generally regarded as property but if it has been taken for the purpose of forensic drug testing, it is property for the law of theft and can be 'stolen'. Similarly, if a person's spilt blood is wiped up with a tissue, it would not generally be regarded as property, but if the blood is collected for medical purposes and supplied to a hospital, it may be property for the purpose of consumer protection laws if it is contaminated.[3] A similar argument might be made regarding semen ejaculated in sexual intercourse or masturbation and semen stored for later use in reproductive treatment, the latter being regarded as property and the former not.

Some commentators may take a different view. Instead of saying, as I have done, that the same type of bodily material may be property in some circumstances but not in others, they may contend that substances such as urine, blood and semen should be regarded as property in all circumstances when removed from the body; but any property rights that the originator might have had are abandoned in most cases. I do not support this view for the reasons given later in this chapter. If these commentators question how a property right can arise when there was none before, there are many examples of cases in which that occurs in law. One of particular note in the current context is the case of human bodily material becoming property when 'work and skill' is undertaken on it (the '*Doodeward* principle' discussed later in this chapter), that might perhaps cover the 'blood products' case above (testing the blood to ensure it is clinically suitable for medical uses).[4] Similarly, there may be work and skill in preserving semen for later use. However, the same cannot be said for urine removed for forensic purposes. In that case, the designation of the urine as property seems purely pragmatic and if property rights are to be properly justified, the basis should be legislation, as argued later in this chapter.

A decision that human bodily material is or may become property, in whatever circumstances that occurs, clearly has important legal implications. But even if it is property, there are further issues to be considered, as the material may be subject to some of the rights (and obligations) in the 'bundle of rights',[5] but not oth-

[3] See cases discussed in L Skene, 'The Current Approach of the Courts' (2014) 40 *Journal of Medical Ethics 10, 13*; and cases listed in n 8 below.

[4] There are many other examples. Wild animals are not property (or not owned by anyone) but may become subject to property rights if they are captured or killed; and they lose the status of property (or become ownerless) if they 'attain their natural liberty': *Kearry v Pattinson* [1939] 1 All ER 65 at 69; *The Case of Swans* (1592) 77 ER 435 at 438, cited in the current context by Bennett Moses, ch 12 in this volume; L Bennett Moses and N Gollan, '"Thin" Property and Controversial Subject Matter: *Yanner v Eaton* [(1999) 201 CLR 351, a native title case] and Property Rights in Human Tissue and Embryos' (2013) 21 *Journal of Law and Medicine* 307–11.

[5] The 'bundle or rights' was described in AM Honoré, 'Ownership' in AG Guest (ed), *Oxford Essays in Jurisprudence* (Oxford, Clarendon Press, 1961) 107–47. An example of a person having some rights in 'the bundle' but not others is a bailee of stored semen, who has the right to possession of the semen but not the right to sell or destroy it (without the consent of the bailor/originator).

ers. A diverse scheme of regulation will ultimately be needed and it will require complex legislation to give it effect, supported by principles developed in the case law, professional codes and ethical guidelines.

The Perceived Advantages of a Property Law Approach

It is not necessary to discuss in detail the recent case law and commentary in which there have been increasing references to property law principles as a means of dealing with the collection, storage and use of human bodily material. Many authors deal with the issues in this book.[6] It is enough to recall that in 2009 the Court of Appeal for England and Wales accepted, on the basis of the law of bailment, that men who had deposited their semen for freezing and later use by them were entitled to be compensated when it was negligently destroyed (*Yearworth and others v North Bristol NHS Trust*[7]). Later, in two Australian cases, the widows of deceased men were also held to be entitled to possession of their stored semen for reproductive treatment.[8] In both of those cases, as in *Yearworth*, the judges discussed the application of principles of bailment, which in turn involved a finding that bodily material can be property and that people may sometimes have property rights in their own bodily material.

The decisions in those cases departed from earlier court rulings that human bodily material is not property,[9] and, even if it becomes property by 'work and skill' being undertaken on it,[10] or changing its 'attributes',[11] the originators do not have property rights in it, even if other people may acquire such rights.[12] The decision in *Yearworth* in particular has stimulated many articles examining the underlying legal principles in the case.[13] Judges have pointed out inconsistencies in the

[6] See articles listed below in n 13.

[7] *Yearworth and others v North Bristol NHS Trust* [2009] EWCA Civ 37, [2010] QB 1. This case is discussed in more detail by other authors in this volume.

[8] *Bazley v Wesley Monash IVF Pty Ltd* [2010] QSC 118; *Jocelyn Edwards; Re the estate of* [2011] NSWSC 478; see also *Re H, AE (No 2)* [2012] SASC 177; *Re Section 22 of the Human Tissue and Transplant Act 1982; ex parte C* [2013] WASC 3.

[9] *Williams v Williams* [1882] 20 Ch D 659; *R v Kelly* [1998] EWCA Crim 1578, [1999] QB 621, [1998] 3 All ER 741.

[10] *Doodeward v Spence* [1908] HCA 45; (1908) 6 CLR 406.

[11] *R v Kelly*, above n 9.

[12] *Doodeward*, above n 10.

[13] See, eg M Quigley, 'Property: The Future of Human Tissue?' (2009) 17 *Medical Law Review* 457–66; C Hawes, 'Property Interests in Body Parts: *Yearworth v North Bristol NHS Trust*' (2010) 73 *Modern Law Review* 130–40; S Green, 'The Subject Matter of Conversion' (2010) *Journal of Business Law* 218–42; SHE Harmon, '*Yearworth v North Bristol NHS Trust*: A Property Case of Uncertain Significance' (2010) *Medicine, Health Care and Philosophy* 343–50; GT Laurie, '*Yearworth v North Bristol NHS Trust*: Property, Principles, Precedents and Paradigms' (2010) 69 *Cambridge Law Journal* 476–93; J Wall, 'The Legal Status of Body Parts: A Framework' (2010) 31 *Oxford Journal of Legal Studies* 783–804; SD Pattinson, 'Directed Donation and Ownership of Human Organs' (2011) 31 *Legal Studies* 392–410: L Skene, 'Proprietary Interests in Human Bodily Material: *Yearworth*, Recent Australian Cases on Stored Semen and Their Implications' (2012) 20 *Medical Law Review* 227–45.

case law and law reform agencies have considered changes that might be made, including the Australian Law Reform Commission;[14] and the Nuffield Council.[15]

Those who advocate a property law approach to the categorisation of all human bodily material do so for a range of reasons. Some argue along the lines: 'If I do not own my body, who else could own it?'[16] Others focus more specifically on a range of perceived advantages if the law adopts a property approach in regulating human bodily material. There are two main arguments. First, property law enables a remedy to be provided where otherwise there would be none in a case where some remedy seems warranted (as for the men in *Yearworth*). Secondly, property law seems the best means of providing continuing rights over bodily material in the hands of subsequent holders, because it can confer rights *in rem*, over a thing; as well as rights *in personam*, against a person. The argument is therefore made that the general rule should be that separated bodily material is property, or should be treated as property;[17] that it may be subject to property rights in favour of the originator; that the originator has the power to transfer property rights to others; and that others may claim on behalf of the originator. These elements are discussed more fully later in the chapter.

Different Types of Property Rights

However, even those who advocate the adoption of a broad property law approach to separated bodily material acknowledge that originators may not be entitled to all property rights in their own material. As Imogen Goold has pointed out, 'few commentators have presented a case for according tissue the status of "property" in the sense that all or most of the rights generally associated with ownership should be exercisable in relation to it'.[18]

[14] Australian Law Reform Commission, *Essentially Yours: The Protection of Human Genetic Information in Australia* (Australian Law Reform Commission, 2003) 96.

[15] Nuffield Council on Bioethics, *Human Bodies: Donation for Medicine and Research* (London, Nuffield Council on Bioethics, 2011).

[16] See, eg JW Harris, *Property and Justice* (Oxford, Clarendon Press, 1996) 351: 'Every person ought to be regarded as the owner of any separated part of his body'; G Laurie, *Genetic Privacy, A Challenge to Medico-Legal Norms* (Cambridge, Cambridge University Press, 2002) 321: '[The] next milestone [in medical law] will be the legal recognition of self-ownership'.

[17] These proposals are made interchangeably but a law stating that bodily material is property per se may be different from one stating that bodily material is to be treated according to the principles of property law. In the first case, one might say that bodily material is obviously a 'thing' which must belong to someone and the law should recognise that (*cf* n 16 above and accompanying text). In the second case, it might be decided that the most expedient way to deal with issues surrounding bodily material is to use property law principles, regardless of whether or not it is initially anyone's property. The law would then state who has property rights in respect of the bodily material, without any previous assumptions. However, although the two arguments may be slightly different, this does not seem to affect the legal proposal to adopt a property approach in a significant way.

[18] I Goold, 'Property or Not Property? The Spectrum of Approaches to Regulating the Use of Human Bodily Material' (2013) 21 *Journal of Law and Medicine* 299.

The right that was recognised in *Yearworth* (and also the later Australian cases) was a right to *possession*. In *Yearworth*, this right arose from the arrangement between the parties that the men's semen would be stored by the defendant with 'the sole object . . . that, in certain events, it might later be used for their benefit',[19] that is, for use in reproductive treatment.[20] Although the Court of Appeal said that the men had '*ownership* of the sperm which they had ejaculated',[21] the term 'ownership' was used loosely. 'Ownership' might mean that the men had the best title or, according to the well-accepted meaning of ownership, 'all such rights as by law are capable of being exercised over that type of property against all persons including the right to possession of the property and any proceeds of its sale'.[22] This would be consistent with other rights the men presumably had in addition to the right to possession, such as the right to use their semen and to prohibit others from using it, and to have it destroyed.[23] However, the court did not state that directly and noted that it was eliding ownership with 'possessory title'; and the latter was the basis for its decision in favour of the men.

The court said that the men had 'ownership of [their sperm] for the purposes of their claims in *tort*'.[24] That is, they had a right to possession which would found a claim in bailment if the semen to which they were entitled for their later use was negligently destroyed. They would also presumably have the right to sue in conversion for the wrongful destruction of their 'property' (though that was not in issue in the case and was not considered by the court). A claim in conversion may be based on a right to possession (against anyone but the owner) as well as a right to full ownership (against anyone).[25]

The distinction between different types of property rights is obviously important for the coherence and development of the law relating to human bodily material, but it has often been overlooked in the cases. Courts have been willing to decide that bodily material is property in particular circumstances but they have generally not been required or willing to consider the implications of that finding in a wider context. Other questions have barely arisen, concerning the rights of the 'owner' of that 'property'; the rights of other people; and the nature, restrictions and prioritisation of the various rights. In examining those questions, I believe that one can see the potential legal absurdities in applying a property approach to all separated bodily material.

The various questions in a property law approach will be considered in turn.

[19] *Yearworth*, above n 7 at [45](f).

[20] This agreement could have constituted a contract which might have been directly enforceable without resort to property principles. However, as treatment was given under the NHS, there was no payment and hence no consideration to constitute a contract.

[21] *Yearworth*, above n 7 at [45](f) (emphasis added).

[22] *Concise Australian Legal Dictionary*, 4th edn (Chatswood, NSW, Lexis Nexis, 2011) 421, definition of 'ownership'.

[23] Some of these rights may be limited by the Human Fertilisation and Embryology Act 1990, as noted in the judgment (at [42](d), [44]), but the men nevertheless had these rights.

[24] *Yearworth*, above n 7 at [47] (emphasis added).

[25] See, eg *Kuwait Airways Corporation v Iraqi Airways Company and others* [2002] 2 AC 883 at [38]: 'a concomitant deprivation of use and possession'; RFV Heuston and RA Buckley, *Salmond and Heuston on the Law of Torts*, 21st edn (London, Sweet & Maxwell, 1996) 97–98.

Questions in a Property Law Approach

Can Human Bodily Material be Property?

The answer is clearly yes, as many judges have now said. Indeed, it is only in the very early cases that judges said that a *corpse* could not be owned. The issue of the ownership of 'bodily material' in a general sense had not arisen at that time. Executors had a right to possession of a corpse for the purpose of burial but they did not 'own' the corpse.[26] In other words, they had a limited property right, in that their right to possession of the corpse was limited to possession for the purpose of burial; they could not transfer it to someone else, as they could with a thing that they owned totally, such as an item of furniture. The right to possession for burial was enough to give them a property right that would override a claim by someone else to the corpse or part of it, though it is clear from more recent cases that a burial right does not need to rest on a property right.[27] Because human bodies were not property, grave-robbers could not be charged with theft of the corpse, though they might be charged with another offence involving desecration of the burial site or theft of the material in which the corpse was wrapped.

Later, however, it was convenient for judges to find that human bodily material was property. This occurred first, in cases where a person was alleged to have wrongfully appropriated bodily material and another person was trying to get it back;[28] or to get compensation for the loss of it;[29] or to have the person convicted of a criminal offence.[30] A civil action in bailment or conversion,[31] and a criminal prosecution for theft, would only succeed if the 'thing' taken was 'property'.[32] Later, courts had to consider the liability of people who provided 'defective' bodily material to patients for treatment. The supplier would be subject to strict liability under consumer protection legislation only if the bodily material was 'property'.[33] Other

[26] Nor did anyone else own the corpse: *Williams v Williams* [1882] 20 Ch D 659; *R v Kelly*, above n 9; *R v Fox* (1981) 2 QB 246.

[27] That is, a claim based on a right to 'ownership' or possession. See, eg cases heard by the European Court of Human Rights, holding that the right of burial of a relative falls within Art 8, right to respect for private and family life, such as *Elli Poluhas Dödsbo v Sweden* (2006) ECHR (Application no 61564/00).

[28] *Doodeward*, above n 10.

[29] *Yearworth*, above n 7.

[30] *R v Welsh* [1974] RTR 478 (urine); *R v Rothery* (blood) (1976) 63 Cr App R 231.

[31] Before *Yearworth* was decided, there was significant debate about whether an action in bailment (as opposed to an action in tort or contract where there had been a bailment) could be brought; and even after the court ruled in *Yearworth* that actions are possible in bailment, the matter has remained in dispute; see, eg C Hawes 'Property Interests in Body Parts: *Yearworth v North Bristol NHS Trust*' (2010) 73 *Modern Law Review* 130.

[32] If a person 'stole' blood or urine that had been taken for forensic testing, there would be no recourse against that person except for theft of 'property': *R v Welsh* [1974] RTR 478 (urine); *R v Rothery* (blood) (1976) Cr App R 231.

[33] *PQ v Australian Red Cross Society* [1992] 1 VR 19.

cases concerned rights over bodily material used in research. Courts were concerned to protect the interests of researchers who had used the material to develop a new cell line that was potentially of significant commercial benefit, as well benefiting the wider biotechnology industry. That meant that the cell line had to be regarded as property.[34] Faced with pragmatic issues such as these, it is no wonder that an Australian judicial officer considering whether stored bodily material was 'property' to which access should be granted for a forensic test, said that 'it defies reason to not regard tissue samples as property'.[35]

It is clear from these cases that the courts have been prepared to regard excised human bodily material as property in a number of cases extending over many years. However, the reasons for those rulings, whether express or implicit, have not been detailed or analysed and have often been made for pragmatic reasons.[36] Moreover, the courts were generally not required to decide the more contentious issue: even if the material was property, whose property was it? In particular, what rights, if any, did the originator have in relation to the excised material?

If Human Bodily Material can be Property, Whose Property is it, and How does a Property Right Arise?

The first of these questions has arisen in a number of cases as it underlies many disputes about bodily material. In legal proceedings concerning rights in relation to a particular thing (such as a right to possess, sell, exploit or destroy the thing), a person generally cannot mount a successful claim without proving that he or she has some type of property right, such as a right to ownership, or a right to possession of the thing. The source of such rights has been less considered. For example, a property right may arise from undertaking 'work and skill' or conferring 'different attributes' on a thing (as discussed below); it may be conferred by a contract; or it may arise in other ways, for example under a trust (but, even in those cases, it could be argued that the contract or trust confers a property right; the right does not arise independently of the contract or trust).

The 'work and skill' principle has been long accepted. According to the so-called '*Doodeward* exception' to the rule that there is no property in human bodily material, people can acquire property rights in *another person's* bodily material (and presumably also in their own bodily material[37]), by the 'lawful exercise of

[34] *Moore v Regents of the University of California* (1990) 793 P 2d 479. It also meant that the rights of the originator had to be limited to personal autonomy rights (a right to compensation for tissue being removed without the person's informed consent and for being misled about its use in research), as occurred in that case.

[35] *Roche v Douglas* [2000] WASC 146 (a case concerning access to stored tissue for a forensic test to determine paternity). This was an issue in the case because the applicant claimed a share of the deceased person's estate.

[36] See my review of these cases in L Skene, 'The Current Approach of the Courts' (2013) *Journal of Medical Ethics*, doi:10.1136/medethics-2012-100994.

[37] So the artist Marc Quinn would be legally regarded as the 'owner' of a frozen sculpture he has made from his own blood and 'sold' to someone else: see en.wikipedia.org/wiki/Marc_Quinn#.22Self.22_.28ongoing_project.29.

work and skill' on it, so that it acquires 'different attributes'.[38] The principle was criticised in *Yearworth* as 'not entirely logical'[39] and the Court of Appeal preferred to rest its conclusions on a broader basis',[40] but it did not reject the *Doodeward* principle, insofar as it stated that bodily material may become property by work and skill being undertaken on it.[41]

The Court of Appeal said that the men had 'ownership of the sperm which they ejaculated', 'for the purposes of their claims in negligence' based on the bailment of their semen to the defendants for their later use.[42] The defendants were negligent in failing to take reasonable care in preserving the semen and therefore liable to compensate the men.[43] However, there is a prior issue that the court did not consider. What was the basis for the men's initial 'property' in their semen? The court certainly looked at the rights the men had, which were taken away or restricted by the Human Fertilisation and Embryology Act 1990 and concluded that the men retained enough rights for them to be called 'owners' ([45](f)), even with the limits and derogations imposed. But where did those rights come from initially? They could not arise simply from the bailment. If the men had 'bailed' semen taken from *a third party* without consent for the men's later use, that 'bailment' could presumably not make the semen their 'property' so that they would be entitled to compensation if it was negligently destroyed; or to which they would be entitled to regain possession. They would need to have some type of prior legal entitlement to it, a property right that would found a bailment.

This aspect was not considered in the case; but Imogen Goold has discussed it in a recent article.[44] She notes that 'the High Court of Australia in *Doodeward* accepted that a right to possession could arise by the lawful application of work and skill' and that 'Chief Justice Griffiths noted *obiter* that this was only one example of how property rights might arise, but he did not elaborate further on how they might do so'.[45] With regard to *Yearworth*, she says, the Court of Appeal ruled that the men held, on the facts, 'enough rights . . . akin to those held over

[38] *Doodeward*, above n 10 at [14] per Griffiths CJ.

[39] This is perhaps an understatement. The court said at [45](d): '[W]e are not content to see the common law in this area founded upon the principle in *Doodeward*. . . Such ancestry does not commend it as a solid foundation. Moreover a distinction between the capacity to own body parts or products which have, and which have not, been subject to the exercise of work or skill is not entirely logical.' However, this falls short of directly rejecting the *Doodeward* principle, at least to the extent suggested here. See Wall, ch 8 in this volume.

[40] *Yearworth*, above n 7 at [45](e).

[41] Perhaps semen that had merely been ejaculated could not readily be regarded as having undergone work and skill, or having different attributes. Even if that was the case, the men did not undertake the work and skill so the defendant would have to be regarded as their agent in doing it, another complication of that approach. In Australia, however, *Doodeward* would still be binding, at least on lower courts, as a decision of the High Court of Australia binds lower courts.

[42] The men's right to have the semen returned to them later was not vital in establishing their right to compensation. The court said specifically that reservation of a right to have the property (the semen) returned is not inherent to either contractual or gratuitous bailment (at [48]).

[43] The court turned to contract law to determine the measure of damages – the 'mental distress' measure based on *Jarvis v Swans Tours Ltd* [1973] 1 QB 233; *Yearworth*, above n 7 at [57].

[44] Goold, 'Property or Not Property?' above n 18.

[45] ibid, citing *Doodeward v Spence* (1908) 6 CLR 406, 412–14, per Griffith CJ.

items of property [that] . . . they could support a claim based in a bailment arrangement'.[46] While the judgment can be read in that way, it does appear a circular argument. If the men held 'enough rights . . . akin to those held over items of property' then they held a property right, namely the right to possession, that would support a claim in bailment. No basis is stated for the holding of the rights akin to property.

In relation to this point, Dr Goold has suggested that the court could have decided that the men had a possessory right that would found a bailment simply on the basis of the rights the law already affords men generally in relation to their semen the right to use their semen, to destroy it, to give it away and so on.[47] This would be a neat solution to many of the issues that have been considered in this book. It would mean that people 'own' all material removed from their bodies, since they have the same rights in relation to that material that the men in *Yearworth* had in relation to their semen. But the court did not say that was the case, and for good reason. Such a principle may have profound and unintended consequences and cannot be accepted without the most careful analysis.

Kate Greasley has also commented from an epistemological perspective on Dr Goold's point. She says that there is an interesting point to be made in the analysis of such an argument:

> Can it be said that, if an object seems to meet the conditions for an object of property, it is acceptable or desirable to treat it (in the relevant respect) like one? That is surely the way that conceptual analysis works. We hold in mind the concept we are thinking about (in this case property), survey a new candidate and then ask if it seems to be that sort of a thing. If the only thing which could possibly make something property is the law's existing recognition of it as such, then there wouldn't be any conceivable way for a judge to argue that something previously unrecognised as property really is that.[48]

These ideas raise broader issues for analysis and discussion, which are beyond the scope of this chapter.

If There are Co-existing Property Rights in Human Bodily Material, How are they to be Construed and Prioritised?

When bodily material is removed from the body, there may be a series of co-existing rights in it. In *Yearworth*, for example, the men were entitled to possession of their semen on their request. Presumably, they were also entitled to require that their semen should be removed from storage, transferred to another person, or destroyed.[49] However, the defendant presumably also had certain rights, such

[46] Goold, above n 18.

[47] I Goold, comment on an earlier draft of this chapter, 20 August 2013.

[48] K Greasley, comment on an earlier draft of this chapter, 20 August 2013. All points in this paragraph are made by Greasley.

[49] Although the men in *Yearworth* were held to be entitled to possession, these rights do not necessarily follow from the right to possession as such. A finder has a right to possession but not to other property rights. An owner has these rights as the owner, but they do not flow from a right to possession.

as the right to hold the semen and prevent other parties gaining access to it; an 'insurable interest' that would entitle it to claim on its insurance policy if the semen was stolen or accidentally destroyed;[50] and a right to take action against a third party who wrongfully removed the semen. Those rights may be regarded as arising from its possession of the semen; from the plaintiffs' bailment of the semen; or in a case where consideration is provided for storage and return of the semen, under a contract. (In *Yearworth* there was no contract as the storage was undertaken without charge by the NHS.) A question therefore arises as to how the various rights, together with the rights of other people, are to be prioritised if a dispute arises concerning rights to possess, recover, use, donate, sell, or otherwise deal with the bodily material.

In *Yearworth*, the court did not need to decide on the facts before it whether the men had any rights in relation to their semen other than a right to possession. However, on different facts, it is conceivable that the court might have recognised other kinds of rights. For example, would the men have had a legal right to sell their semen during the storage period (aside from statutory constraints on the sale of gametes)? Could they donate it to a third party, such as a woman who may want to use it to achieve a pregnancy? And if the woman had provided consideration, could she enforce the arrangement, and on what basis? If the men had only a right to possession, it would seem that they could confer only the interest they had, their right to possession, and not a right to destroy the semen by using it in conception. But if they had exercised their right to possession and regained possession of the semen, they could then give it to someone else to use in conception, or destroy it. On what basis would their right to possession be converted at that point to more extensive property rights when the semen is again in their control? Does the semen then revert to the legal status of other separated bodily material under the current law, not being subject to any property interest in favour of the originator, or in those circumstances, in favour of anyone else? Alternatively, if one accepts Imogen Goold's proposal that people have property rights in their own bodily material simply because they can use, donate, sell or otherwise deal with it (subject to statutory constraints), does the person have the more extensive property rights all the time, that is, in addition to the right to possession that was in issue in *Yearworth*? If that were so, then the men would be able to exercise those rights even during the bailment, by giving instructions to the bailee, for example, to transfer the semen to someone else, or to dispose of it.

It is not difficult to imagine future situations in which questions such as these will arise and have to be determined by a court. The dilemma for the current discussion is whether the law to be applied would be clearer if there was a general principle that people 'own' or have more limited property rights in their sepa-

[50] At common law, a person must have an insurable interest in a thing in order to claim for its loss under an insurance policy: F Marks and A Balla, *Guidebook to Insurance Law in Australia*, 3rd edn (Sydney, CCH, 1998) 91–92, citing *Macaura v Northern Assurance Co Ltd* [1925] AC 619; *FAI Insurances Ltd v Custom Credit Corp Ltd* (1980) 29 ALR 505. Later developments in insurance law are beyond the scope of this chapter.

rated bodily material, or if rules are developed to meet each new situation, or type of situation.[51] A general principle that everyone has property rights in their bodily material would assist at the initial stage, for example, by determining who has the first right to possession. But, without more, the general principle would not determine the nature and priority of rights that arise later. Other rules will be needed to deal with subsequent claims by other people. Imagine, for example, what might happen if the originator donates his or her bodily material to another person; or enters a contract permitting its use; and the recipient converts it into something else (like a cell line); or destroys it; or passes it on to another person without authority.[52] What legal rules would be used to determine and prioritise the rights of the originator in relation to those people? In some cases, the rules might follow property law principles but they are unlikely to be appropriate in all cases, so that specific rules for each situation may be more effective than making exceptions to the general principle that people always have property rights in their bodily material.

Options for a 'Re-analysis' of the Law

If the law is to be revised in a systematic way, there are two legal options that might be considered in a 're-analysis' of the kind that was called for by the court in *Yearworth*.[53]

Option 1

The law could be that everyone has property, or a property interest, in bodily material removed from his or her body[54] (as Goold has argued)[55] and any information derived from it, and then state the circumstances in which this property interest would cease, become restricted, or transferred to someone else. For example, this could happen by:

[51] Others may say that the dilemma is more basic. Should something like semen be the property of anyone, in the same way that ordinary household objects are someone's property? However, property law focuses on *legal rights* in a thing rather than the *status of the thing* in question (is it property or not?). It therefore 'takes some of the sting from those concerned about preserving respect for human bodies and potential human life': Bennett Moses and Gollan, '"Thin" Property and Controversial Subject Matter' above n 4.

[52] See also the bullet points in the next part of this chapter headed 'Option 1'.

[53] *Yearworth*, above n 7 at [45](a).

[54] There seems no reason to distinguish between bodily material such as organs, bone marrow and skin, and products of the body, such as semen, faeces and urine, although Jonathan Herring makes a persuasive argument in ch 13 in this volume that some bodily material clearly has more potential value than others. On the other hand, even bodily material that seems to have no value may sometimes be in demand, such as faeces to repopulate the flora in a diseased gut: see AK Hawkins and KC O'Doherty, '"Who Owns Your Poop?": Insights Regarding the Intersection of Human Microbiome Research and the ELSI Aspects of Biobanking and Related Studies' (2011) 4 *BMC Medical Genomics* 72.

[55] Goold, above n 18.

- a sale or licence to another person to use the material for consideration (if that is not contrary to public policy)[56] or otherwise;
- gift, either outright or subject to conditions, to another person for medical treatment such as a blood transfusion or organ transplant, research or to develop a product such as a cell line;
- bailment, where the bodily material would later be returned for the person's own use in medical or reproductive treatment; or
- abandonment, either express or implied.[57]

Some people would welcome such a legal principle, saying that it would clarify ownership rights in later disputes about the collection, use and control of separated bodily material. It respects the autonomy of people to decide what will and will not be done with their bodily material. Giving people the right to formally donate or dispose of something that they 'own' enables the recipient to have a clear title that cannot later be challenged if the thing or a product made from it is in the hands of other people.[58] Imposing conditions on the property interest need not detract from its status as property. Indeed, that is not uncommon in property law. Town planning laws, for example, commonly restrict the ways that people can use houses and land that they own. Mortgagees can repossess the property if payments are not made and tenants have the right to live in the house under a rental agreement. That is all part of the 'bundle of rights' in the house and land.

However, there are many arguments against a general principle that everyone has property rights in bodily material removed from their body. Jonathan Herring's chapter in this book gives examples of absurd claims that might arise. For example, '[i]f all your body is property you are committing the offence of littering if you leave property in a public place', such as a hair dropped on the pavement or dandruff left at a restaurant.[59] I have made similar points myself about

[56] Current human tissue and embryo research legislation forbids the sale of human bodily material and there is a substantial literature arguing against the commodification of bodily material. An exception has been proposed for the donation of eggs but that could be construed as a payment for undergoing the egg donation process; the payment would be made for that, even if no viable eggs are produced: E Haimes et al, 'EPP Position Statement on the Provision and Procurement of Human Eggs for Stem Cell Research' (ISSCR Ethics and Public Policy Committee) (2013) 12(2) *Cell Stem Cell* 285–91, available at: www.cell.com/cell-stem-cell/fulltext/S1934-5909(13)00057-X?large_figure=true.

[57] *cf* Goold, ch 9 in this volume. She argues that it is almost impossible to abandon something in the sense that one person's ownership ceases and no-one else is the owner.

[58] It is commonly said that people must own a thing in order to make a gift but that is not true. I can give my time or my talents neither of which is a thing. Although these 'gifts' may be seen more as doing something rather than giving something, the 'gift' may be of considerable value if I am usually well paid for my time or talents.

[59] *cf* Herring, ch 13 in this volume. It is true, as Goold observed in a personal communication, that the legislation on littering could be amended so that leaving tissue is not littering. She cites s 87(4A)(a) of the Environmental Protection Act 1990: 'No offence is committed under subsection (1) above where the depositing of the litter is– (a) authorised by law', to indicate that there are exceptions to the offence. However, it is difficult to imagine drafting an exemption for leaving tissue in a public place, especially if littering is to include some types of tissue (such as toenail clippings, perhaps, especially if collected for several months), but not others (such as skin cells and perspiration). It may be better to adopt Greasley's view, expressed in another personal communication: 'No law or state could ever impose

absurd consequences if all discarded tissue is property.[60] For example, could beneficiaries under a will inherit not only the possessions of a deceased person, but also the deceased's stored bodily material, so that a bequest of 'all my property to my son' would entitle the son to the deceased's stored tissue on slides, severed limbs and 'surgical waste'?[61] The son could, of course, waive this right but the hospital would be legally obliged to consult him about the matter before disposing of the material. And, in other cases, would hospitals be free to dispose of body parts and bodily material without permission from the originator, as waste, or if the hospital is being sold, or closed? If one thinks that should be allowed and could be governed by principles similar to those that apply to rubbish left out for collection, what will happen if the originator later seeks access to the stored material for forensic reasons or medical testing?

An equally vexing issue is the possible liability of people who acquire bodily material without being aware that they are perhaps committing an offence because it is still the property of the originator.[62] In many cases, it will be difficult to know whether the originator's property interest has ceased. The circumstances in which there is a formal disposition will be the exception. In the great majority of cases, the person who has acquired the bodily material will assume that it has been abandoned. That may be difficult to prove if there is later a dispute, especially if the 'finder' has not made a reasonable effort to find the 'owner'. The very fact that an issue has arisen about abandonment of an interest is likely to lead the originator to claim the contrary. Will the person seeking to take or use the material have to check with the originator that it has really been abandoned, in order to rely on the principle of abandonment, for example as a defence to an action for conversion? Even if the material is 'found' in a place which may signify that the 'owner' has no further wish for it, such as a rubbish dump, the finder does not necessarily have a legal right to keep or use it.[63] The finder may have a right to possession against all but the original owner; or the owner of the rubbish dump may own it.[64]

It may be said, in such a case, that the thing taken (such as hair or skin cells) would be of small value and there would be no 'intent' that might found a criminal charge; the 'owner' is not known. However, it is not difficult to imagine cases

liability on anyone for leaving skin cells lying around – it would break one of the essential principles for effective law making: the possibility of obedience,' and leave the legislation alone.

[60] L Skene, 'Arguments Against People Legally "Owning" their Own Bodies, Body Parts and Tissue' (2002) 2 *Macquarie Law Journal* 165.

[61] By 'surgical waste' I mean soiled bandages, pathology samples and the like. These should be distinguished from body parts that may have special significance for the patient or relatives, such as the preserved brains of deceased children, placentas, miscarried foetal tissue etc, about which there may need to be discussion before disposal.

[62] The *mens rea* for such an offence (and the potential liability of 'finders') is beyond the scope of this chapter but an intention to take and retain a thing may be sufficient without proof that the alleged perpetrator knew who was the 'owner' of the thing. On the other hand, a reasonable belief that the thing had been abandoned may be a defence to a charge of theft or an action in conversion, especially if the person tried to find the owner.

[63] *cf* Goold, ch 9 in this volume.

[64] J Griffiths-Baker, 'Divesting Abandonment: An Unnecessary Concept?' (2007) 36(1) *Common Law World Review* 16–26.

where bodily material or information may have an economic value,[65] the identity of the originator is not known, and the material is used in the belief that such a use is legitimate. A dispute may then arise. If the originator has property rights, the 'finder' may have a right to possession against everyone except the owner, but not a right to use or profit from the use of the material. To protect the rights of the originator and the user, it may be better to have a rule that bodily material or information derived from it may not be used without consent (or, in research, a waiver from an ethics committee), rather than a general rule that the originator has property rights and even an inadvertent user may be culpable.

Thus, in this case, as in others, a broad property law approach is not needed to protect the interests of originators in their bodily material. As suggested in the next section, rights of control can be provided by other areas of the law, some of which are more effective than property law in protecting rights when a thing is in the hands of other people; or the person holding it has used it unlawfully, or proposes to do so. If needed, other offences or causes of action could be established by statute, such as the offence of non-consensual genetic testing,[66] or unlawful forensic testing of tissue,[67] to protect people's privacy interests in their own genetic information.

Moreover, there are strong health and communitarian arguments for the law not to recognise that originators have property rights in their separated bodily material.[68] If people authorise the use of their organs or tissue for transplant, they should not be held liable for the supply of a 'faulty product' if a problem arises.[69] Close blood relatives should be able to gain access to their relative's stored bodily material for their own genetic tests without the need for consent from the 'owner', who could refuse. At some point, hospitals should be free to dispose of bodies and body parts without permission, as waste, or if the hospital is being sold, or closed.

It may be said, of course, that property rights include different categories of rights (see option 2 below) and that some of the issues raised above could be avoided by limiting the originator's rights in particular circumstances. It may also be argued that some of the absurd claims that I have outlined above are so far-fetched and unlikely to arise in practice that they need not be considered in law-

[65] Like Mr Moore's spleen cells: see *Moore*, above n 34.

[66] M Otlowski, 'Establishing the Offence of Non-Consensual Genetic Testing in Australia: A Call for Action' (2013) 21 *Journal of Law and Medicine* 335–42.

[67] As Jeremy Gans has argued, police powers to extract and test bodily material of a suspect for the purpose of an investigation or to use in evidence are controlled by strict legislation to protect their civil rights. However, there is no such legislative protection if police collect bodily material that has been separated from the person concerned, whether by chance at the scene of the crime, or deliberately collected by police, eg on the butts of cigarettes that have been offered to the suspect during questioning: J Gans, 'Extra-bodily DNA Sampling by the Police' (2013) 21 *Journal of Law and Medicine* 364–69, citing *R v Phuc & Van* [2000] VSC 242, [16]. This 'regulatory gap' could be filled by 'legislation, which could apply also to genetic material collected by police under other powers, such as '"random" testing of intoxication or arrest for minor offences': ibid.

[68] This point is well made by Herring in ch 13 in this volume, discussing the interconnectedness of families and communities.

[69] Though organ and tissue donation could be excluded from the Consumer Protection Act 1987 and Sale of Goods Act 1979.

making. However, if it is decided that complex rules are necessary to limit property rights in certain cases, it may be better, as I have suggested, to have rules that deal specifically with those cases, without conceptualising all bodily material as property, subject to a large number of exceptions and limitations.

Option 2

The second option for regulation is a principle that people generally do not have property interests in their bodily material. Instead, their right to control the collection, storage and use of their bodily material could be provided by the law on:

- battery, which prevents the removal of bodily material without consent or other lawful authority;
- negligence, through the need for 'informed consent' before bodily material is removed from the body;[70]
- procedures for ethical oversight of research: the provision of organs and bodily material for transplant;
- privacy;[71]
- equity, through injunctions to prevent particular uses of bodily material and information;
- contract, including a condition subsequent restricting later use;[72] or
- intellectual property and the like.

There could be specific statutory provisions stating people's rights concerning particular bodily material and the uses that may be made of it, without any law stating that it is, or is not, property. Examples can easily be suggested. Research would continue to be governed by ethical guidelines and ethical review, rather than by legislation,[73] which has been the longstanding tradition in Australia,[74] the UK and many other countries, perhaps bolstered by notions such as 'custodianship';[75] or

[70] Though as Stewart et al observe, the use of the principle of informed consent in determining ownership interests seems 'an odd fit, given that it is a doctrine concerned with the provision of negligent advice concerning treatment': Cameron Stewart, Jennifer Fleming and Ian Kerridge, 'The Law of Gifts, Conditional Donation and Biobanking' (2013) 21 *Journal of Law and Medicine* 351–56.

[71] Privacy principles with regard to collection, storage, use, access to and release of information; Australian law does not currently include a tort of privacy.

[72] See Stewart, Aparicio, Lipworth and Kerridge, ch 5 in this volume. They suggest that third parties who acquire donated bone marrow could be prevented from later misusing it by a Material Transfer Agreement with a condition subsequent that applies after the legal title has passed to the third party.

[73] Though there is also specific legislation on the use of human tissue in research; reproductive technology and other matters.

[74] For example, National Health Medical Research Council, *National Statement on Ethical Conduct in Research Involving Humans* (Canberra, NHMRC, 1999) replaced by the *National Statement on Ethical Conduct in Human Research* (Canberra, Australian Government, 2007).

[75] This term is used in the NHMRC *National Statement*, above n 74. The Australian Bone Marrow Donor Registry 'sees itself as the custodian of a "biobank" consisting of donor and matched donor-patient samples', which involves a 'moral and ethical duty to ensure its data and/or samples are used responsibly and respectfully in accordance with its purpose for the public good; and research participants' interests are taken into account': L Aparicio et al, 'Biobanking of Blood and Bone Marrow: Emerging Challenges for Custodians of Public Resources' (2013) 21 *Journal of Law and Medicine* 343–50). As custodian, the bank maintains control over the samples. If it releases material to scientists to do

'participatory governance' in which 'researchers or participants . . . work collaboratively to find mutually beneficial solutions' rather than using a property law regime to govern their relationship.[76] As at present, the ethical guidelines would be supplemented by professional codes of conduct that apply in a research context as well as a clinical one. Such guidelines and codes can provide greater flexibility than legislation.

Where greater or more direct enforceability is needed, guidelines could be supplemented by legislation, for example, to prohibit the purchase or sale of human organs and tissue and human embryos, and to punish those who do not comply with the legislative provisions. Similarly, with the repatriation of indigenous remains, specific legislation requiring people who 'find' indigenous remains to return them to indigenous people is likely to be more effective than a principle that indigenous people, or a group of them, 'own' the remains of their ancestors and are therefore legally entitled to have them returned, or to exercise other rights of 'ownership' in relation to them. It is likely to be difficult and costly for indigenous people to prove such an entitlement, as is evident from the relatively few native title cases to have come before the courts.

Legislation could create specific offences relating to unlawful testing or use of separated bodily material. This would protect a person's rights when bodily material is in the hands of other people who plan to misuse it. It would concentrate on the aspect that is of most concern to people (the wrongful use), without creating legal absurdities by its application in circumstances in which it was clearly not intended to apply (which could happen if all bodily material is regarded as 'owned' by the originator). Most people are not concerned about others inadvertently 'acquiring' their bodily material. Indeed, that happens all the time as microorganisms are exchanged between people's bodies in the ordinary interactions of life.[77] What they are worried about is people *using* their bodily material, or information from it, in ways that they would not approve, especially if others do that to harm them or their families or groups, or to gain a profit for themselves or other people. The elements of potential harm that justifies legislation are thus threefold: (1) infringing a person's autonomy (their control over their bodily material and per-

research, they must either return the material to the bank or destroy it after the research: ibid. However, the bank is currently considering whether it may be possible to transfer custodianship to a 'properly governed "second party"' to undertake research: ibid. The Nuffield Council has referred to custodianship in the context of organ transplants. The tissue removed for transplant would be in the custodianship of the third party giving a right to possession and use for the purpose of the consent: Nuffield Council on Bioethics, *Human Bodies: Donation for Medicine and Research*, above n 15, [2.31], [7.21].

[76] RE McWhirter, D Nicol, D Chalmers and JL Dickinson, 'Body Ownership and Research' (2013) 21 *Journal of Law and Medicine* 323–29.

[77] J Herring and P-L Chau, 'Relational Bodies' (2013) 21 *Journal of Law and Medicine* 294–98. The authors argue that people's bodies are not 'independent and self-contained', but 'interdependent and "leaky". . . In biological terms bodies are constantly interacting with other bodies and other biological entities and the environment'. Therefore, it is biologically impossible to have a law giving a person a right to exclude all others from his or her bodily material because 'bodies cannot be understood as independent and controlled'. Further, they state: 'It seems most odd to believe that the law on property can capture our interests in both the piece of dandruff that falls from our head in a restaurant; to an organ removed for transplant; to the egg donated by a woman about to undergo chemotherapy.'

sonal information); (2) misuse of information or other disadvantage, discrimination by employers, insurance companies, government agencies and the like; and (3) the loss of financial benefits. The law will be most effective if it focuses on the aspect of concern rather than establishing principles of broad application which may have unexpected consequences.

This option could be accompanied by an ad hoc series of rules for different situations, regardless of property law. In the absence of evidence to the contrary, hair cut by a hairdresser is assumed to be abandoned; in medical treatment, the originator is not liable under consumer law if a donated organ is found to be infected; in medical research, informed consent must be obtained from the originator, but in limited circumstances where it is not possible or practicable to obtain consent, stored tissue may be used in research with the consent of an ethics committee; hospitals are entitled to hold bodily material for audit and to defend claims, and to insure stored tissue under their general policies; in wills and intestacy, tissue would be assumed to be abandoned in the absence of evidence to the contrary, and so on. Such provisions could deal effectively with some of the issues raised earlier but would need to be comprehensive to cover all the circumstances that arise.[78]

Conclusion

It can be seen from this discussion that a broad principle that all separated bodily material is property subject to property rights in favour of the originator will raise many problems in future and may sometimes lead to absurd results. It would be better to develop rules that govern the rights and interests of people in relation to their bodily material in particular circumstances. Some of these rules will need to have statutory authority but others may be in codes of conduct and ethical guidelines, to provide greater flexibility in their operation.

[78] The Human Tissue Act 2004 and the procedures of the Human Fertilisation and Embryology Authority in the UK illustrate the type of regulatory structure that could be adopted.

16

Conclusion

IMOGEN GOOLD, KATE GREASLEY, JONATHAN HERRING
and LOANE SKENE

In this concluding chapter we will not seek to summarise all the points made throughout the volume. Rather we bring out from these discussions some practical proposals for how the law might move forward. Three models for reform will be outlined:

- The law should recognise that human bodily material is subject to the laws of property that apply to other 'things'. The tissue could then be owned, sold, stolen, commercially exploited, given away, and so on and these dealings would be governed by the developed principles of property, tort, criminal and other areas of law relevant to property. We shall call this the 'property model'.
- Parliament should pass a statute governing the storage, use and control of bodily material, reflecting a balance between individual and communal interests in different contexts. We shall call this the 'statutory model'.
- The courts should develop an ad hoc approach to bodily material allowing the case law to grow organically. We shall call this the 'ad hoc model'.

These three models will be developed in more detail shortly.[1]

We will indicate the issues which all models need to address and those specific to each. The aim is not to fully flesh out any proposal, but to set out clearly the issues which will be raised with each model. Before undertaking that task, a few further comments on the academic debates will be useful.

The Property versus Non-property Debate

It will be obvious to any readers of this book that the contributors disagree, sometimes strongly, on the best route for reform, most notably over whether a property model is or is not desirable. These disagreements reflect the fierce academic

[1] See also the detailed discussion in I Goold, 'Why Does It Matter How We Regulate the Use of Human Body Parts?' (2014) 40 *Journal of Medical Ethics* 3.

debates on the issue. However, a careful reading of the chapters of this book might reveal more consensus than at first appears.

Supporters of a property model generally accept that some adaptions to the standard property law approach will be required to ensure that it works appropriately when applied to the human body. As Imogen Goold has pointed out, 'few commentators have presented a case for according tissue the status of "property" in the sense that all or most of the rights generally associated with ownership should be exercisable in relation to it'.[2] Some supporters of the property model will agree that in certain contexts the property interests may be trumped by societal interests. For example, the chapters in this book supportive of a property approach are generally keen to emphasise that adopting that approach does not necessarily commit one to allowing commercial dealings in organs.[3] Similarly, supporters of a statutory model accept that in some ways their model would itself reflect a property-based approach. They are likely to agree that there will be contexts in which the statute should protect the rights of exclusive protection and control, which are indicative of a property approach.[4] However, the statutory model will, in other contexts, emphasise the importance of communal interests. Thus, both camps recognise that the legal response will be a mixture of (in effect) property and non-property approaches; the real debate is more concerned with where the balance should lie.

It is true that in very broad terms those who support a more communitarian approach to bodily material are likely to be drawn to a statutory model as more likely to take account of the societal interests (such as the need for genetic information to be available to close blood relatives so that they know their own familial genetic risks; and to benefit the wider community in medical research), and those who seek to emphasise private interests (such as ensuring rights of control over bodily material) are more likely to be drawn to a property account. However, that contrast is a gross simplification. One could imagine a property law approach that promotes communitarian interests. Indeed, Donna Dickenson's chapter (Chapter 11), with its emphasis on the property of the commons, is one such example. Similarly, it would be possible to draft a statute giving even stronger protections to individual interests than a property approach would give (for example, by protecting the interests of the originator of biological material even after ownership has been transferred to another). In other words, one cannot learn much about someone's response to a particular scenario being pro-community rights or pro-individual rights simply from whether they support a property or non-property based approach.

It might, in light of the points just made, be asked if the debate over whether we should take a property model or a non-property approach is somewhat irrelevant. At best, it is a dispute about which legal framework is the most effective in pursu-

[2] I Goold, 'Property or not Property? The Spectrum of Approaches to Regulating the Use of Human Bodily Material' (2013) 21 *Journal of Law and Medicine* 299.

[3] See, eg Goold, ch 9 and Greasley, ch 6 in this volume.

[4] See, eg Herring, ch 13 and Skene, ch 15 in this volume.

ing certain objectives. At worst, it is a technical dispute over legal terminology which disguises more important questions about how to balance the competing interests in particular situations involving claims on human body parts. While that analysis is not completely without validity, it over-simplifies the issue.

First, there are those in this volume who claim that choosing a property model will skew the debate in a particular direction, by emphasising the importance of individualistic values attached to property and downplaying relational and communal interests.[5] In any balance between individual and communal interests the property approach (with its emphasis on individual control and exclusion) loads the scales in favour of the individual interests. Therefore, when it comes to a discussion on, for example, directed organ donation, whether or not one starts with a property model as a given will have an impact on the outcome of that debate.[6] Further, if the property approach was adopted and a case arose on which there was no precedent, the court's starting point would be the protection of an individual's rights of control and protection. Supporters of property rights might deny that the protection of rights of control and protection is inherently individualistic. Giving an individual power over their property enables them to enter into relations with others, including giving their bodily material to other people. One can only give what one has a legal power to give. It provides the protection of individual rights that are needed to safely enter communal and relational contexts. Thus seen, property rights are not necessarily anti-relational or anti-communal. This debate plays into a much wider debate about the nature of the self and legal rights, which cannot be discussed in detail here.[7] However, it is clear, that to at least some commentators, the selection of a property or non-property approach is not just a matter of selecting the appropriate legal tool but of buying into a broader set of values, which slants the argument in a particular way. Others believe that irrespective of law and the usefulness of proprietary law applied to the body, we *do* own our organs absolutely as a matter of principle, and that should be the starting point when thinking about something like directed organ donation.

Second, as Jesse Wall notes in his chapter (Chapter 8), the language used by legal regulation speaks not just to courtrooms, but will be understood and used by philosophers, healthcare professionals and members of the public. While, therefore, lawyers may be clear that legal terminology has a technical meaning, that nuance may not be understood by others. The debates, therefore, are not just technical arguments for lawyers; the terminology used can have a power of its own. Hence, critics of a property approach might fear that the language of property will commercialise and objectify people. However, as proponents of the property approach note, items that clearly do have deep symbolic value, such as

[5] For example, Herring, ch 13 in this volume.

[6] See, eg S Pattinson who bases his arguments in favour of directed organ donation explicitly on ownership: S Pattinson, 'Directed Donation and Ownership of Human Organs' (2011) 31 *Legal Studies* 392.

[7] For example, J Nedelsky, *Law's Relations* (Oxford, Oxford University Press, 2013).

homes, wedding rings and photographs can be treated as property without denying their deeper significance. However, whether the broader social attitudes will pick up on those nuances may be a matter for debate. Donna Dickenson's book *Body Shopping: Converting Body Parts to Profit* provides good examples of the concerns that may be raised if bodies are treated simply as commodities.[8] However, there is a danger that not acknowledging property rights and emphasising communal interests will be treated as a green light to researchers to indicate that as long as they are acting for the 'greater good' they need not be concerned about the rights of the individuals whose material they are using. There are, therefore, dangers for supporters of either approach, in how the terminology of property or societal interests in bodily material will be understood by the general public, researchers or medical professionals.

Third, the choice between the models involves some important practical, as well as theoretical, considerations. A key issue is the ease of reform. One of the strong appeals of the property model is that we have a system of legal rules and regulations developed by the common law over centuries, which can be readily applied to bodily ownership. The shift to adopting these rules for bodily material could be made either by a decision of the courts, or, perhaps more likely, a short statute. A broader statutory model, by contrast, would be a major academic and political undertaking. The Human Tissue Act 2004, for example, contains over 60 complex sections, with seven schedules, all backed up by nine lengthy Codes of Practice issued by the Human Tissue Authority. This gives some insight into the complexity and length of the task of producing a complete statutory regime governing all of human tissue. That said, in the English context many of the most contentious issues are already addressed by the Human Tissue Act 2004 and the Human Fertilisation and Embryology Act 1990 and 2008, meaning there is less to do than might be feared. Many other jurisdictions have existing regulation in these areas which could be drawn upon.

A further issue relates to gaps in the regulation. Inevitably issues will arise which raise novel points. Supporters of the property approach may claim that as property rules have been developed over many centuries, nearly all the complex issues likely to arise will have been dealt with. This has the benefit of ensuring that there are no, or not many, situations where the law is unknown. However, as Imogen Goold's chapter (Chapter 9) demonstrates, there is plenty of ambiguity surrounding a doctrine as central as the abandonment principle. Thus the certainty that may be argued in the property regime may be exaggerated. An objection made against the statutory model is that it will be unable to pre-empt all scenarios that might arise, giving rise to gaps in governance. Moreover, a statutory model might lack the flexibility to respond to rapidly developing technologies. Contrariwise, the Human Fertilisation and Embryology Act 1990 and the use of the Human Fertilisation Authority and regulations and guidance issued could provide an example of a statutory based structure that has worked reasonably well

[8] D Dickenson, *Body Shopping: Converting Body Parts to Profit* (London, Oneworld, 2009).

and has proved capable of responding to sensitive and fast-changing developments in biotechnology and society.

There is the broader issue of complexity. As Bennett Moses's chapter argues, there is a temptation to provide a *sui generis* set of laws for each kind of property, but this itself generates complexity and the consequent disadvantages that flow from that.[9] In particular, it would leave too many areas of the law uncertain, putting medical professionals, researchers and members of the public in a difficult position. We could, as she suggests, have a law relating to churns, but it makes more sense to have generally applicable rules for all property than to attempt to develop a unique set of legal rules for every kind of property. She identifies the costs of amending and interpreting multiple legal regimes and the dangers that special interest politics will distort *sui generis* legislation as among the dangers of *sui generis* legislation.

Against those concerns must be placed Loane Skene's argument in Chapter 15 that if property law is used, the 'exceptional' cases where the normal property laws do not apply will outnumber those where the general property rules do apply. If this is correct, the benefits of the certainty offered by property approach fall away and a *sui generis* approach gains appeal. Perhaps here we have identified a key question. If (in considering the issues mentioned below) we produce a result which typically matches that in the standard property model and only exceptionally requires a departure, then the arguments for the property model are strong. However, if in many cases we need to create a departure from the result the standard property model would create, the arguments for the *sui generis* approach seem stronger.

Next the three models will be outlined before exploring some of the issues which will need to be addressed, whichever model is used.

The Property Model

Supporters of the property model emphasise that property law provides owners with the power of control that enables them to exclude others and transfer property to another person. This puts people in charge of their biological material. Supporters will urge that these rights must be protected particularly now that biological material is increasingly of value and ensure that remedies can be found in the kind of cases where the courts have struggled in recent years to find a solution. These rights are all the more important given, as Dickenson highlights, the commercial powers that are keen to collect biological material and draw information from it.

A particular advantage of the property approach is that it gives rights to the thing itself (*in rem*), meaning that the owner has rights against the whole world. For example, if a hospital holds a sample of human material for a patient and that

[9] See Bennett Moses, ch 12 in this volume.

sample is taken by a third party, only a right *in rem* will provide a remedy against the third party. Broadly speaking, other legal claims based in contract or tort, for example, are *in personam* and only available against an individual who is linked to the claimant (for example, by a contract or duty of care).[10]

Objections and Potential Responses

The current law in England, Australia and many other jurisdictions does not recognise bodily material as property, except in certain limited circumstances.[11] Any decisive move towards adopting the property model is liable to come either from the courts or Parliament.

One possibility is that a court, no doubt a superior court, will be persuaded to accept as a common law development that all or any removed human biological materials can now be regarded as property. But is that likely? In *R (Nicklinson) v Ministry of Justice*[12] the Court of Appeal refused to develop the common law defence of necessity to permit euthanasia. One of the reasons for doing so is that it is inappropriate for the courts to develop the law in an area of moral and social controversy. As the Master of the Rolls and Elias LJ have written:

> Parliament as the conscience of the nation is the appropriate constitutional forum, not judges who might be influenced by their own particular moral perspectives; the judicial process which has to focus on the particular facts and circumstances before the court is not one which is suited to enabling the judges to deal competently with the range of conflicting considerations and procedural requirements which a proper regulation of the field may require; and there is a danger that any particular judicial decision, influenced perhaps by particular sympathy for an individual claimant, may have unforeseen consequences, creating an unfortunate precedent binding in other contexts.[13]

A similar approach may well be taken by a court before taking the radical step of declaring all bodily material to be capable of being property. The issue raises moral controversy and may well be thought to require a detailed consideration of the policy ramifications, of a kind inappropriate in a court of law. Furthermore, the court may well be worried about changing a law which may have unforeseen consequences, given the wide range of circumstances in which the regulation of bodily material can be relevant. All of this strongly suggests that it is highly unlikely that there will be a straightforward judicial declaration that all bodily material is property at common law. It is more plausible that the courts will, as they have been doing to date, deal with cases on an ad hoc basis, incrementally expanding the circumstances in which bodily material may be legal property.[14] It may then take decades at least for a complete acceptance that bodily material is property.

[10] The division is more complex than this. Torts, like conversion, relate to *in rem* over property.

[11] For example, where blood or urine has been taken for forensic purposes and is unlawfully removed to avoid testing and use in evidence, it may be regarded as property for the purpose of the law of theft.

[12] *R (Nicklinson) v Ministry of Justice* [2013] EWCA Crim 961.

[13] ibid, [61].

[14] For a helpful analysis of the development of the case law, see L Skene, 'The Current Approach of the Courts' (2014) 40 *Journal of Medical Ethics* 10.

There is, perhaps, reason to question that analysis. That is, to question the extent to which it is true that recognising bodily material is property would be a change in the law. As a number of commentators have pointed out, the precedent basis for the 'no property' rule is somewhat shaky.[15] In the recent *Yearworth v North Bristol NHS Trust* decision,[16] the court stated:

> The law, as we will see, has to some extent begun to be refined in relation both to a human corpse and to *parts of a human corpse*; but it has remained noticeably silent about *parts or products of a living human body*, probably because, until recently, medical science did not endow them with any value or other significance.

And:

> In this jurisdiction developments in medical science now require a re-analysis of the common law's treatment of and approach to the issue of ownership of parts or products of a living human body, whether for present purposes (namely, an action in negligence) or otherwise.[17]

These dicta indicate that a court may be persuaded that the common law is not settled and that in declaring human material to be property the court was not changing the law, but rather clarifying a common law position that had not been specifically declared.[18] One argument that might be utilised if such an approach is put before a court is that of Simon Douglas, in Chapter 7 who argues that 'things' are normally treated by the law as property and bodily material is a thing. It might, therefore, be claimed that the burden of proof, as it were, rests on those seeking to deny that bodily material is property.

The other way that a move to an acceptance of a property model could be achieved would be through a statute. This could be a relatively short statute, declaring that for the purposes of the law, bodily material is to be understood as property. The statute may wish to set out a definition of bodily material. The Human Tissue Act 2004 provides a definition which could be used.[19] Section 53(1) states: 'In this Act, "relevant material" means material, other than gametes, which consists of or includes human cells.'

The section goes on to exclude hair and nails from the definition, but there seems no reason for doing that for the purpose of a more general regulation. The section also states that embryos outside the human body are not property. That raises a host of controversial issues which we cannot discuss in detail here.[20]

[15] P Matthews, 'The Man of Property' (1995) 3 *Medical Law Review* 251.

[16] *Yearworth v North Bristol NHS Trust* [2009] EWCA Civ 37, [30].

[17] ibid at [45].

[18] See Goold and Quigely, ch 14 in this volume, for further discussion of this point.

[19] Although, see J *Herring* and P-L *Chau*, 'Interconnected, Inhabited and Insecure: Why Bodies Should Not be Property' (2014) 40 *Journal of Medical Ethics* 39 for a somewhat nitpicking criticism of that definition, arguing, for example, that much of the human body is made up of non-human creatures.

[20] See M Ford, 'Property Model of Pregnancy' (2005) 1 *International Journal of Law in Context* 261 for one perspective.

A further issue for supporters of the property model, and one which is often overlooked (although see Imogen Goold's chapter in this book) is when the human material becomes property. It does not seem feasible that the transfer from the originator to a medical authority itself transforms an item into property. Furthermore, the doctrine of abandonment only makes sense if the item is property already. So we are left with the view that either the human material becomes property on separation or even intact bodily material is property and belongs to the person whose body it is.[21] An alternative approach, in line with the current law, would be to say that bodily material become property when it is subject to work and skill, yet much debate still surrounds the question of what constitutes work or skill in this context. All of this shows that although proponents of the property model, quite rightly, emphasise its ease of implementation and its comprehensive coverage, there are still areas of uncertainty around property law that would require further analysis and thought.

The Detailed Statutory Model

Those who oppose a property-based approach may be drawn to a detailed statutory model. This is because the standard legal alternatives of relying solely on contract, tort or human rights, are unlikely to be adequate protection for all cases which arise. The cases of *A and B v Leeds Teaching Hospitals*[22] and *Yearworth*[23] demonstrate the inadequacies of simply relying on non-property common law remedies. The benefit of a statutory model over a property model is that it enables a tailor-made response to particular situations. Supporters would claim that although we might want rights of possession and use over particular body parts in particular situations, those situations are relatively rare. Loane Skene in Chapter 15 argues that much depends on the circumstances in which the legal status of bodily material is considered – she believes a man would have a different attitude towards semen ejaculated in a sexual act, and semen that is stored for later use in infertility treatment. Detailed legislation may therefore be needed to cover situations in which it is appropriate for bodily material to be regarded as property and those in which it is not, to achieve a more nuanced and finely honed regulatory structure than the property approach.

Objections and Potential Responses

As indicated above, a detailed statute of this type would necessarily be complex and lengthy, although that is part of its appeal for its supporters. The argument that a tailored response to a careful balancing of the interests is needed for each

[21] Some tricky issues might arise over the ownership of a foetus. Presumably, given the law generally on personhood, on birth the baby owns her own body, but before then the foetus is the property of the mother. See ibid.

[22] *A and B v Leeds Teaching Hospitals* [2004] EWHC 644 (QB).

[23] *Yearworth*, above n 16 at [37].

scenario justifies specific provisions. No doubt if a statute were to be introduced, extensive work would be required by the Law Commission, or other law reform bodies, to work through the range of scenarios which would need to be covered.

Two major objections to statutory reforms are that there will be 'gaps' where the drafters have not foreseen a particular scenario and that the law will be restricted by the wording of a statute in a way which means that it cannot respond to scientific developments. There are two ways that a statute might deal with these legitimate concerns.

First, as Loane Skene discusses in her chapter, statutory reform could be accompanied by other kinds of regulation, most notably, guidance issued by professional bodies and licensing mechanisms. As already mentioned, these have played a significant role in the operation of the Human Tissue Act and the Human Fertilisation and Embryology Act 1990, and no doubt would do the same under any over-arching statutory response. Indeed these offer a way for the law to respond quickly to rapid technological and social changes.

Second, the statute could open with some guiding principles. For example, the 1996 Family Law Act opens: 'The court and any person, in exercising functions under or in consequence of Parts II and III, shall have regard to the following general principles.'

It goes on to list some key principles, for example, 'that the institution of marriage is to be supported'. The benefit of this approach is that it offers the courts some guidance in dealing with cases which do not fit neatly within the statutory structure. It can, therefore, supply courts with tools to deal with 'gaps' in the legislation. It can also protect against the statute being applied in an unforeseen way. The Nuffield Council of Ethics proposes the following key principles in their report on the use of human material:

- Uses of human tissue which injure in that they destroy, damage or degrade are unacceptable because such uses show lack of respect for human beings and their bodies. However, when action that would otherwise count as injury is undertaken for therapy, it is legitimate.
- It is ethically acceptable to make use of human tissue for medical treatment, and for medical training, for fundamental and applied research and for other purposes that may contribute indirectly to medical treatment.
- These uses of human tissue are only ethically permissible when the tissue has been removed with the consent of those whose tissue is used or, where that is not possible, by procedures that give equivalent protection.
- There are strong arguments against the commercial acquisition and supply of human tissue for medical and scientific purposes, however acceptable those purposes may be in themselves.[24]

Principles of this kind would guide courts in deciding cases that come before them and promote consistency in decision-making and legal developments.

[24] Nuffield Council on Bioethics, *Human Tissue Ethical and Legal Issues* (Nuffield Council, 1995) 13.5.

The Ad Hoc Model

The third option is not to seek to find a unitary response through property law or through a statute, but to encourage the development of an ad hoc approach. In effect, that would allow the courts to continue to develop the law in response to individual cases, using established principles. As Skene mentions in Chapter 15, the law on battery, negligence, ethical regulation, privacy, equity and contract could be brought to bear, as could human rights principles. Supporters of this approach might point to *Yearworth* as a case where the courts were able to give a satisfactory decision in the case before them, using established principles.[25] This is, of course, the standard common law approach – to let courts decide a series of cases on their facts, allowing general principles to emerge. The benefit of this is that it provides courts the flexibility to respond to different scenarios and ensure the hands of the court are not tied too much by statutory provisions or established law on property, in responding to the novel cases they will inevitably face in the years to come.

Objections and Potential Responses

Opponents will argue that this leaves too much uncertainty in the current law. Those whose bodily material is misused should have a clear remedy, rather than having to trust that the courts will find an imaginative way to provide them with one. That point will particularly strike home with those who agree with Nwabueze that the current law is 'arbitrary, selective, and discriminatory'.[26] Of course, not everyone will be convinced that a bit of uncertainty is necessarily a bad thing in the law. Certainly it is not difficult to find areas of uncertain law in other contexts and that does not necessarily lead to disaster. The question perhaps is whether the subject of human bodily material is so sensitive and important that we prefer a clear law over one that has flexibility.

Questions For All Models

Whichever model is adopted there are three primary issues which need to be addressed. It is around these issues that legal disputes have so far arisen and are likely to arise in the future:

- The acquisition of the material: in what circumstances is it lawful for someone to take possession of human material?
- The use of material: to what use can a person put human material which they have acquired lawfully?

[25] Although, of course, the reasoning is much disputed.
[26] Nwabueze, ch 10 in this volume.

– The profits and products of human material: who is entitled to the profits and products of human material?

Of course, the answers to these questions may vary depending on the kind of human material we are talking about and the circumstances of the removal and/or acquisition of the material.

The Acquisition of Material

A property analysis would be likely to hold as follows. The bodily material is initially owned by the person whose body generated the material (or the person whose body it is). Ownership can be transferred either through a transfer of ownership (for example, by gift or sale) or through abandonment. Transfer will require consent by the owner to the transfer of ownership. In the case of abandonment, there must a clear intention to disclaim an interest in the property (see further the chapter by Imogen Goold in Chapter 9). The transfer may restrict the use the recipient can put it to (that is likely to be by means of a trust or contract) and/or keep the originator with some proprietor interest (for example, if there is a trust or bailment).

The benefit of this approach is as follows. It makes it clear that people own their biological material and gives them strong claims to the use and control of it. It establishes a clear principle that no-one can take or use another person's biological material without their consent (or clear evidence of an intention to abandon). However, this approach raises a number of issues.

The Burdens of Ownership

Do we want to be owners of all bodily material? In this book Jonathan Herring and Loane Skene have raised concerns about the potential burdens of owning bodily material. Ownership brings with it responsibilities of ensuring it does not cause litter and of ensuring appropriate disposal or containment. We therefore have the concerns over being responsible for littering through the dropped hair or being consulted over and/or charged for dealing with waste products in a hospital.[27] More broadly, there is a concern that very rarely do we want the property rights attached to the bodily materials we produce. One powerful response to this is that concerns raised are hypothetical and that if we look at the cases that come (or are likely to come) before the courts, these are the kind of cases where a person does want control over their bodily material. Another response is that the law on abandonment can deal with many of the situations where a person has unwanted bodily material, although as Goold's chapter shows, the law on abandonment will need some development to do this effectively. However, critics will say that

[27] See Skene, ch 15 and Herring, ch 13 in this volume.

regarding all bodily material as property will put an impossible burden on hospitals, carers and others who handle bodily material, who are at risk of acting unlawfully unless they are sure they have the consent of the owner to use the material or to dispose of it. A statutory offence could limit property-type claims to the type of cases where they will be wanted (for example, where a hospital holds a patient's material for their later use). As Skene suggests, 'it may be better to have a rule that bodily material or information derived from it may not be used without consent (or, in research, a waiver from an ethics committee), rather than a general rule that the originator has proprietary rights and even an inadvertent user may be culpable'. However, we are then back to the problem of 'gaps' if the statute tried to list the specific situations in which a generator of bodily material had rights in that material. Would we inevitably miss out situation where people might need such a right?

Communal Interests

A second issue is the extent to which a person can be deprived of their removed biological material without their consent. Under a traditional property approach their rights are absolute, save perhaps if necessary to protect themselves, another person or even property from serious harm.[28]

Some supporters of a property regime may be willing to allow communal interests to restrict individual property rights in some contexts. At the most extreme a communal version of property could be adopted, as Donna Dickenson does in her chapter. That is such a different version of property from that commonly understood by the courts that it is hard to see it being developed within a common law development, but it could be used to underpin a statutory regime.

The standard property regime is designed to protect individuals' interests from invasion from others or claims based on the social good. Although there is scope for an individual's property to be taken from them, for example, through compulsory purchase, that normally requires an extremely strong justification based on the social good. A better analogy may be the taxation system. In the same way that a person might be expected to pay through their taxes to provide for the general good, they may be expected to pay through bodily material to some extent.

If such a model was adopted it would be necessary to set out some of the communal interests which might be referred to. These include:

- audit;
- artistic creations;
- education in medicine and allied disciplines;
- organ donation;
- public health;

[28] For example, under UK law it is a defence to the crime of criminal damage that one is acting reasonably to protect other property (Criminal Damage Act 1971, s 5).

- public information creations (such as the use of a picture of a person's body or organ for use in a public health campaign);
- research; and
- third parties.

The Human Tissue Act 2004 allows the interests of education and audit, for example, to trump the requirement of consent for use.[29]

Addressing the balance between individuals and societal interest is not easy. A standard form of analysis might require us to balance the interests of the individual and the interests of society in the use of the material. The difficulty of that analysis is that, carried out in an individual case, it will hard to show, except in the case of organ donation, that the public good in the use of this sample trumps the individual's property rights. A particular piece of human material is unlikely to be useful for audit or other reasons and certainly not sufficient to justify interference in property interests. Similarly, the interests that a particular individual has in how their material is to be used will vary greatly from person to person and is not readily reduced to some kind of numerical value.

There is also a difficulty in attempting to assess the communal importance of some of the activities listed. Views will differ on the extent to which artistic creations involving bodies enhance the public good. Do public information programmes using bodily material contribute very much to the discussion? The response to *Bodies: The Exhibition30* and similar shows demonstrate this argument.

If there was to be some statutory intervention in this area justifying the interference in people's property interests the regulation would be likely to focus on the kinds of public good which would justify interfering in the property interests and the ethical safeguards that should be imposed over the use of that material. It might also be possible to distinguish between an interference in property interests which is without consent and one that is against the expressed wishes of the individual. We might have some kind of, in effect, presumed consent or scope for opting out of any system. In chapter two of this volume Dianne Nicol, Don Chalmers, Rebekah McWhirter and Joanne Dickinson provide a very valuable discussion of how research in bodily material could be regulated in the light of claims to human bodily material, taking account of such factors.

Commercialisation and Property

A normal power associated with ownership is that one can sell the item. It should not be assumed that by describing bodily material as property one is wedded to the idea of allowing a full market in bodily material. There are three main reasons

[29] K Liddell, 'Beyond Bristol and Alder Hey: The Future Regulation of Human Tissue' (2005) 13 *Medical Law Review* 170.

[30] http://www.bodiestheexhibition.com/

which might be used by those concerned with commercialisation. These have been explored by Kate Greasley in Chapter 6, and elsewhere.[31] First, there are those who are concerned about exploitation if commercialisation is permitted. Second, there are those who find dignity-based objections to commercialisation compelling. Third, there are those concerned about the broader social consequences of treating the body as property.[32] The response to these concerns could take the following forms:

- Procedural steps may be put in place regulating the sale or transfer of bodily material, including, for example, a time for contemplation, counselling, and the like. Substantive limitations might include a minimum or maximum price or restriction on the uses that may be made of it. There may be restrictions on what kind of human bodily material can be sold. It might exclude non-regenerative material or material of a particular symbolic kind.
- There may be restrictions on who can purchase the material. For example, it may be that only state health systems can purchase organs or institutions committed to acceptable ethical practices.[33]
- There could be a complete ban on commercial dealings.[34]

Apart from a blunt total ban it is hard to see any of the other restrictions coming about other than through a statutory regime of some kind. The issues surrounding commercialisation are discussed further in the chapter by Kate Greasley in this volume.

These concerns go beyond simply the buying and selling of bodily parts. As Donna Dickenson argues in her chapter, 'elsewhere in biomedicine, particularly in the rapid establishment of private property-holding in genetic biobanks and the increased publicity surrounding personalised medicine based on individual genetic profiles, an individualised and privatised model is coming to predominate, even in publicly funded banks'. This takes us back to the downplaying of communal interests mentioned in the previous section.[35]

Use

The absolute owner of property under the common law is entitled to do what he wishes with property, subject to specific limitations imposed on such use by statute[36] and the general law, such as the criminal law. They are free to transfer the

[31] K Greasley, 'A Legal Market in Organs: The Problem of Exploitation' (2014) 40 *Journal of Medical Ethics* 51.

[32] Dickenson, *Body Shopping: Converting Body Parts to Profit*, above n 8.

[33] Greasley, 'A Legal Market in Organs' n 30.

[34] For example, Human Tissue Act 2004, s 32. For further discussion, see C Erin and J Harris, 'An Ethical Market in Human Organs' (2003) 23 *Journal of Medical Ethics* 137.

[35] D Dickenson, *Me Medicine vs. We Medicine: Reclaiming Biotechnology for the Common Good* (New York, Columbia University Press, 2013).

[36] For example, powers of compulsory acquisition.

property to others, to destroy it or do what they please. As already mentioned, the circumstances of acquisition may limit the use to which a piece of property may be put. The owner at law may hold the property on trust and then be restricted by the terms of the trust as to how she deals with the property. The owner may be restricted by the terms of a contract with the originator in what she does with the property. A government body may seize the property for infection control or other public purposes. A number of issues are raised here.

Originator's Rights

When ownership of bodily material passes to another, should the originator retain any kind of interest in the property? As already mentioned, unless the originator of the material used a trust or contract, those acquiring the property will become absolute owners. Realistically, it is highly unlikely that a person, unless particularly well versed in the law, will utilise a trust or contract, when handing over or abandoning their biological material. As Dickenson demonstrates in her chapter many people are handing over biological material to corporations with little idea of the potential significance of the material they are supplying and the use to which it will be put. Indeed, in Chapter 15, Loane Skene argues that it is the misuse of material which is of greater concern to people, rather than simply the acquisition or right of possession of it. She argues that a statute addressing unlawful testing or use of material would be more effective than the use of property rights in protecting people from that wrong. We may, alternatively (or in addition), want to require those holding the biological material of others to inform the originator of the use to which their material is being put, perhaps with the opportunity to object. Of course, such a statute could be created in addition to, or as an alternative to, granting property rights. However, before proceeding with that, we need more thought about what should happen if someone has used biological material in a way not foreseen by the provider. Loane Skene mentions three wrongs that may be committed:

- infringing a person's autonomy (their control over their bodily material and personal information);
- misuse of information or other disadvantage, discrimination by employers, insurance companies, government agencies and the like; and
- the loss of financial benefits.

This still leaves the difficult question of what amounts to consent in these circumstances and how detailed the information needs to be. Some of the difficulties with this are discussed in Chapter 5 on biobanking by Cameron Stewart, Lorena Aparicio, Wendy Lipworth and Ian Kerridge.

An alternative approach is to rely on biobanked and genetic information being regarded as a part of the communal good, along the lines outlined in Donna Dickenson's chapter. The use of charitable trusts may provide another approach, as outlined in Stewart et al's chapter. The benefit of both of these approaches is that consent is not the touchstone of regulation. As already mentioned, consent may be an insufficient bulwark against misuse, because of the general lack of understanding and indeed, the inability of anyone to know now what use may be made of bodily material in the future. A consent requirement means that people are asked to agree to what is unknown and often unknowable.

There may be other claims that an originator may wish to raise, apart from control over use. For example, someone may seek access to material for medical tests, or, more likely, their relative might do so. Many people believe that close blood relatives should be entitled to gain access to tissue or information they need for their own healthcare, even if the originator of that material does not consent. If a property model were adopted, it would be necessary to consider how such claims should be met, if at all.

Dignity Concerns

As mentioned earlier, the standard property approach allows the owner of property to do what they wish, subject to some limitations. However, it might be argued that in the case of human material there is a case for restricting what can be done with or to human body parts in the name of human dignity. Quite a few of these concerns may be dealt with by the current law. For example, the offence of causing harassment, alarm or distress in a public place is likely to prevent disturbing activities with human material in public. The offence of outraging public decency was used to prosecute a man who made earrings out of human foetuses.[37] The law is not without its gaps, however. Jonathan Herring has raised, as an example of where there are gaps in the law, reports of a case where the corpse of a Muslim woman was wrapped in bacon in an apparently racist incident, but the perpetrator could not be prosecuted for an offence. Charles Foster's ashtray made out of human ears would likewise fall outside the law, unless perhaps paraded in public.[38] There are also issues relating to over-criminalisation and it may be that the disgust at the ear ashtray, however unpleasant, is insufficiently serious to require legal intervention.

A trickier issue may be what has been described in this book as the 'me-ness' in an item.[39] Imagine, for example, a woman who donates a miscarried foetus to a charity, which works to investigate the causes of miscarriage. The charity decides to photograph the foetus and use it in publicity. Or a person donates material to a biobank, only to discover that it has been used in research of which she strongly disapproves. Under a traditional property analysis we might say that she has made a gift of her property and, had she wanted to restrict how it could be used, she should have made a contract restricting the use. It would need to be considered

[37] *R v Gibson* [1991] 1 All ER 439.

[38] C Foster, 'Dignity and the Use of Body Parts' (2014) 40 *Journal of Medical Ethics* 44.

[39] Referred to in Herring, ch 13 in this volume.

whether this was satisfactory. An analysis of that issue would require an identification of what the problem is.

The first issue is essentially a matter of lack of information. Is the real problem here that a person may donate their material without realising the use it will be put to? In such a case the answer may be to require a full disclosure of information when bodily material is transferred in certain circumstances. This is common in contract law, for example, where before certain financial products can be purchased, detailed information must be provided. This is clearly applicable in the biobank scenario. We could require a complete disclosure of all of the uses to which the material will be put. Critics will complain that disclosure alone will not be adequate to ensure protection of the donor's interests. It is unlikely that a donor to a biobank will comprehend the vast amount of information which will be provided or its potential significance. Furthermore, the biobank might understandably be unable to predict the uses to which the material will be put.

The second issue is an argument that the strength of the 'me-ness' claim is so strong that even if there is consent there should be restrictions on what can be done with the property. An analogy might be drawn with those jurisdictions which recognise artists' moral rights over their creations.[40] These rights limit the power of the owner of an artwork to destroy or treat in a degrading way a work of art, without at least obtaining the consent of the artist. We could develop a similar regime for bodily products. Even where bodily material is transferred, there could be a lingering interest in the originator. However, unlike artworks, it is hard to think of circumstances in which the originator may wish for the return of the product. It is more likely they will wish the material to be buried or interred.

It might be argued that a property approach can fail to capture the nature of the wrong when bodily material is misused. In the words of Nicky Priaulx, 'negligence illustrates a continued preference for physical bodily harm in determinations of actionability'.[41] She regards the decision in *Yearworth* as predominantly result-driven: while the damage suffered by the claimants is not readily classified as physical injury, 'to suggest that these individuals are *not* harmed, or that their suffering is less than that which would be sustained by virtue of a physical bodily injury seems absurd'.[42]

Profits and Products

Generally under English law the owner of an item of property is entitled to the profits and products of that property so unless there are restrictions imposed by trusts or contracts, the owner will be entitled to keep the proceeds. There are,

[40] H Hansmann and M Santilli, 'Authors' and Artists' Moral Rights: A Comparative Legal and Economic Analysis' (1997) 26 *Journal of Legal Studies* 95.

[41] N Priaulx, 'Humanising Negligence: Damaged Bodies, Biographical Lives and the Limits of Law' (2012) 33 *Adelaide Law Review* 177, 178.

[42] ibid, 188.

therefore, concerns that corporations receiving donated human material can then use it to make massive profits. These issues are discussed in several chapters in this book. It is, however, the natural consequence of a property approach and, in recent developments, the principles of intellectual property law have been used increasingly to support claims by those who have undertaken work and skill in research on bodily material and genetic information.

If it is considered that greater protection is necessary for people whose bodily material is used by other people without their consent, it is possible, as Quigley and Goold suggest in Chapter 14, that the tort of wrongful interference with goods or restitution could be used in some cases. However, this is not going to be sufficient to deal with the concerns of Dickenson and others that a communal resource is used to make large profits for institutions, based on a rather dubious consent.

The difficulty is that cases involving profits made from biological material will vary greatly. There can be no one-size-fits-all solution. The remedy in such a case may depend on the following factors:

- The extent to which an individual piece of material is linked to the profit making creation will vary from case to case. Cases such as Moore, where it is possible to identify the particular individual whose material led to the profitable creation are likely to be rare. More common will be cases where the valuable product relies on a large collection of bodily material;
- The amount of work performed by the scientists will vary. Clearly the greater the effort required to extract the profitable product, the greater the justification of the profit substantially falling to the scientists; and
- The importance and nature of the product.

Possible solutions include requiring companies or researchers who have used biological material to create profit generating items to share some of their profits with the originators, either as a collective group or the identified individuals. An alternative would be to require them to share those profits for the greater good, through payment to government or some kind of equivalent to the National Lottery Fund to spend on worthy projects.

Conclusion

It need hardly be said that there are no easy answers here. Indeed as should be clear from the discussion, the debate over whether or not there should be a property or non-property approach is only the tip of the iceberg of the debates that are necessary to formulate an effective law on bodily ownership.

In part, these issues are complex because they reflect some profound issues of the nature of the self and the structuring of society. Lurking barely beneath the surface of some of the issues raised in this chapter and throughout this book are arguments about the balance of power between the citizen, the government and commercial interests; and our relationships with our bodies. It is not surprising that consensus cannot be found.

This chapter has sought to bring out some of the key issues which will need to be addressed as the law moves forward. No doubt that law will need to balance the protection of rights and control offered by the property approach; the upholding of social and relational interests promoted by some supporting the detailed statutory approach; and the flexibility offered by the ad hoc approach. No one way ahead is without difficulty and quite clearly the answers do not all point one way.

INDEX

NB: Cases, legislation and institutes referenced all refer to the UK unless otherwise indicated.

abandonment, 125–55, 275, 284, 288
  'absurd consequences', 145
  academic interpretation, 141
  Australia, 136–37
  body-as-property debate, 138–46
  common law, 126–29
  concept, 126
  divesting all rights, 139–40
  divesting ownership, 140–41
  English law, 129–36
  implied abandonment, 139–40, 142
  liability of subsequent users of biomaterials, 138
    ownership, 291–92
    transfer of ownership, 291
  property concept and, 147–48
  'tissue as property' model, 149–54
    original ownership, 148–49
    presumption of abandonment, 151–53
  transfer of ownership distinguished, 145, 291
  UK, 129–36
  US, 137
  use of biomaterials removed during surgery, 138–39
  see also ownership; property approach to regulation
advances in medical science, 9, 11
  biobanks, 26
  blood transfusions, 11
  ethical debate, 11–12
    disclosure, 12
    privacy, 12
  genomic sequencing, 9, 11, 26
  in vitro fertilisation, 11
  perception of biomaterials, 56
  privacy and, 20
  stem cell research, 3, 9
  transplants, 11
Anatomy Act 1832, 14
Australia, 1–4
  abandonment, 129, 136–37
  biobanking, 37
    UCB, 54–56
  charitable trusts, 61–62
  consent, 4, 37
  ethical governance, 18–19
  excised human tissue:
    no property rule, 203
  legislation, 3
    governing research, 277
  no property rule, 14, 203, 206, 237
  ownership, 136–37
  right to possession, 270
    semen, 265–66
  semen, 265–66
    'no property in a body' exception, 206
  'thin' conception of property, 209–10
  umbilical cord blood banking, 54–56
  'work and skill' exception, 74–75, 240, 269–70
  see also Doodeward v Spence
Australian Code for the Responsible Conduct of Research (AUS), 18
Australian Law Reform Commission, 266
autonomy of the person, 6–7, 12–13
  battery and, 165–66
  biobanking practice, 27
  common good and, 27
  individual autonomy and common good dichotomy, 27
    charitable trusts, 64–65
  law reform:
    clarification of ownership rights, 274
    justification, 278–79
  no property rule and, 13, 73–74
  privacy and, 12, 149, 245
  principle, 13–14, 18, 20
  property approach and, 73
  respect for:
    choice and control, 153, 162, 295
    informed consent, 58
  'tissue-as-property' model, 149

battery, 231
  autonomy, 165–66
  law reform, 277, 290
  right to bodily integrity, 165
  strict liability, 96
bailment, 4, 15, 270–71
  Catalona decision, 16
  contract law and, 48, 119
  donation of biomaterial and, 253
    donor retaining right of possession, 253–54, 267
  law reform, 274
  negligence law, 40
    damages in negligence, 164
  'rights' model of tort law, 45–46
  transfer of ownership, 291

bailment *cont.*
  within a property framework, 76, 205–06, 261
  Yearworth decision, 15, 40, 116, 227–28, 265, 270–72
Bermuda statement 1996:
  human genome, 178
biobanking, 3, 6, 25–26
  charitable trusts, 65
    advantages, 64–65
  concerns:
    consent, 27–28, 295
    use of research findings, 28
  control, 28
  gifts law and, 25–26, 35–38
  informed consent, 25, 27–28, 35–36, 59
    individual autonomy and common good dichotomy, 27
  moral issues, 28
  networks, 29–31
    advantages, 29–30
    concerns, 30–31
  privacy, 28
  purpose, 26–27
  religious issues, 28
  stewardship and custodianship, 57–58, 64, 65
  storage of biomaterials, 17
  umbilical cord blood banking, 54–56
    charitable trusts, 63–64
  see also custodianship; gifts law; stewardship
biomaterials, 6–7
  abandonment, 125–55
    Australia, 136–37
    common law, 126–29
    concept, 126
    UK, 129–36
    US, 137
  damage or loss of biomaterials, 254–59
  donation of biomaterials, 247–54
  excised human tissue, 202–07
  liability of subsequent users of biomaterials, 138
  'ownership', 91–92
  property approach, 2–5, 89, 232–33
    case law, 237–44
    excised human tissue, 202–07
    inappropriateness, 259–60
  property rights, 108
    definition, 90–91
    exigibility, 90–91
    personal rights distinguished, 90
    recognition, 92–94
    self-ownership, 94–96
    separated biomaterials, 97–98
  recognition of property rights, 92–94
  regulation, 245–47
    damage or loss of biomaterials, 254–59
    donation of biomaterials, 247–54
  right to use, 104–08
    right to exclude, 104
  self-ownership, 94–96
  separated biomaterials, 97–98
    separation with intention to use, 15
  statute regime, 215–29
  uses, 234–36
    biomaterials removed during surgery, 138–39
  value, 233–34
  vulnerability to dispossessions, 99–101
  see also abandonment; property approach to regulation
biomedical research, 3, 5–7, 9–10, 22–23, 293, 296, 298
  advances, 9, 11
  biomaterials held under a bailment, 258
  donation of biomaterials, 247–54
  ethical governance, 17–22
  gift law, 35–26
  historical context, 11–13
  informed consent, 27–28, 59
  law reform, 274, 277–78, 279
  legal governance, 17–22
  moral issues, 28
  privacy issues, 28
  private rights and public interest dichotomy, 64, 217–23, 276–77, 281–85
  property rights hindering, 103
  religious issues, 28
  reporting findings, 28
  status of biomaterials, 15–17
  stem cell research, 3, 9
  umbilical cord blood banks, 55–56, 64
  value of biomaterials, 233–36
  see also biobanking; 'corporate commons'
body parts, *see* biomaterials
breach of fiduciary duty, 15, 160, 194
breach of privacy, 12–13, 21

cadavers, 157, 174–75
  remedies for unauthorised interference, 158–60
    battery, 165–66
    breach of fiduciary duty, 160
    causation, 162
    compensation, 161
    contractual claims, 168–70
    damages in negligence, 164
    human rights, 166–67
    intentional tort action, 164–65
    negligence, 160–63
    privacy, 166–67
    proprietary claims, 170–74
    unjust enrichment, 167–68
    US, 163
  unauthorised interference:
    remedies, 158–60

cell lines, 5, 10, 195, 234–35
  biobanking:
    gifts law, 35
  commercial benefit, 269
  equity rights, 78–82
  HeLa cell line, 12–13, 21–22
  Moore case, 15, 78–82, 101–02, 162
  privacy, 12–13
cell technologies, *see* advances in medical science
charitable trusts law, 65, 189–90
  advantages, 64–65
  Crown and, 62
  cy près schemes, 63
  express trusts distinguished, 60
  New Zealand, 61
  origins, 60
  private rights and public interest dichotomy, 64
  purposes, 60–61
    statutory tests, 61
  requirements, 60
  stewardship and custodianship, 57–58, 64, 65
  trustees, 60
  umbilical cord blood, 63–64
choses in action, 31, 35, 37, 93
  see also gifts law
commercialisation, *see* commodification
commodification, 6, 21, 67–72, 86–87
  commercial transfer of bodily material, 82–86
    coercion through poverty, 83
    'desperate exchanges' and consent, 82–83
  commercial use of the body, 82–86, 186
  control and possession of gametes, 75–77
  domino theory, 71, 72, 85–86
  equity rights:
    cell lines, 78–82
    converted bodily material, 78–82
    removed cells converted to profit, 79–80, 81–82
  inflicting harm by means of objectification, 70–72
  market-inalienable items, 70
  no property rule, 186
  organ sales and sperm sales distinguished, 84–85
  surrogacy, 85–86
  'work and skill' exception, 74–75
  see also objectification
common good, 222
  individual rights and, 22, 27
  see also corporate commons; custodianship; stewardship
compensation, 38, 40–41, 43, 47, 85–86, 121
  contractual claims, 169
  negligence, 160–61, 270
  organ retention, 226
  proprietary claims, 173, 186, 268
  psychological harm, 4
  wrongful interference, 256, 258–59
  see also commodification
conditional gifts model, 37–38
  informed consent model distinguished, 35–37
consent, 4, 6, 201–02, 250–51
  informed consent, 27–28
    conditional gifts model distinguished, 35–38
    donation, 58
    negligence, 58–59
  lack of informed consent, 15, 21
  participatory governance, 20–21
contingent rights, 110–11
  rights and rights-holder, 110–11, 116
  separability, 117
contract law,
  biobanking, 59
  claims in negligence distinguished, 46–47
  damages:
    psychological harm, 47
  NHS:
    no contractual relationship, 39–40
  unauthorised interference with cadavers, 168–70
control, *see* right of control
conversion, 10, 13, 15–16
  abandonment law and, 130–37, 138, 147, 150, 154
  damage or loss of biomaterials, 256–58
  defences, 101–02
  equity rights, 78–81
  liability, 257
  ownership, and 105, 127–28, 173
  property law, 105, 112–13, 170–71, 173, 194, 203
  separate biomaterials, 97
  wrongful interference, 116, 147, 256–57
cord blood, *see* umbilical cord blood
'corporate commons', 177–79, 194–95
  case study, 179–84
  public commons, 184–94
    no property rule, 185–86
corpses, *see* cadavers
custodianship, 277
  biobanking and, 53–54, 65
    duties, 57–58
  concept, 57–60
  informed consent, 58
  law reform, 277–78
  umbilical cord blood, 53–54
cy près schemes, 63, 65

damages, 118–19
  contract law, 168–69
  duty of care, 42–43
  law of churns, 200
  negligence, 76, 164
    duty of care 160–61

damages *cont.*
foreseeability, 119
psychiatric harm, 119, 243–44
property law, 119
tort law, 119–20, 122–23
see also compensation
dead bodies, *see* cadavers
Declaration of Helsinki, 18
Department of Health and Human Services (US), 58
dignity, 57, 80, 212, 217–18, 223
commodification and, 294
concerns, 296–97
Doodeward v Spence (AUS), 1, 14, 150
'no property in a body rule', 203, 240–41, 243–44
ownership, 269, 270
right to possess, 270
'work and skill' exception, 14, 74–75, 264, 269–70
duty of care, 39, 41–44, 119
duty of non-interference distinguished, 115–16
negligence, 160–61
voluntary assumption of responsibility, 51

embryos, see human embryos
equity rights, 37–38
cell lines, 78–82
charitable trusts, 61–62
commodification:
cell lines, 78–82
converted bodily material, 78–82
removed cells converted to profit, 79–80, 81–82
conditional gifts and, 34–35
converted biomaterials, 78–82
conversion, 78–81
gifts, 32, 34–35
ethical governance, 5, 8, 11–12, 17–22, 141, 181, 265, 277–78
Australia, 18–19
commodification, 186
Nuremberg Code, 17–18
property law, 211
UK, 19, 184, 245, 289
US, 17–18
European Convention on Human Rights, 166
European Group on Ethics in Science and New Technologies, 19
excised human tissue, 197–200, 214, 255, 269
Australia, 203
inalienable property rights, 211–13
no property rule, 185, 202–03, 213
ownership, 205
US, 203–04
see also biomaterials
exclusionary rights, 110, 111–12
basis, 112–13
claims 'actionable *per se*', 113
content of the duty, 115–16
duty of non-interference, 115–16
content of the right, 113–15
enforceability of rights-holders' rights, 112–13
interactive rights distinguished, 112, 114–15
legal relationship:
rights-holder and duty-bearer, 111–12
no property rule, 113
property rights, 111–16
structural features:
basis of the right, 112–13
content of the duty, 115–16
content of the right, 113–15

'fairness, justice and reasonableness':
duty of care, 42
'floodgates' argument, 40, 42–44
foreseeability, 45, 49
duty of care, 42–43
negligence, 119
psychiatric harm, 119
remoteness test, 258

gametes:
control and possession of gametes, 75–77
destruction:
loss of property, 40
personal injury, 40
psychological harm, 40
negligent loss or destruction, 4
case law, 243–44
'no property in a body' exception, 14–15, 205–06
sales, 84–85
genetic technologies, *see* advances in medical science
gifts:
absolute gifts, 33
choses in action, 31
conditional gifts, 32–33
conditions precedent, 32–33
conditions precedent and conditions subsequent distinguished, 32
conditions subsequent, 33–34
determinable interests, 33–34
goods and, 34–35
definition, 31
donation, 252–54
equity, 32, 34–35
goods, 31
see also gifts law
gifts law, 16–17, 25–26
biobanking and, 35–38
conveying gifts, 31–32
donation of biomaterials, 16
flexibility, 36

Greenberg v Miami Children's Hospital (US), 16, 163, 193–94
no property rule, 113
unjust enrichment, 168

Haematopoietic stem cell transplantation (HSCT):
umbilical cord blood, 53–54, 55–56
Haynes's Case, 13–14, 237–39
Hecht v Superior Court (Kane) (US), 14–15, 120
control and possession of gametes, 75–77
Hedley Byrne rule, 43–45
Honoré, AM:
ownership, 172
human biological material, *see* biomaterials
human embryos, 204–06
see also in vitro embryos
Human Fertilisation and Embryology Act 1990, 121–22, 228, 244, 270, 284, 289
storage and use of gametes, 76
human genome, 28
association studies, 26, 181–82
common heritage, as, 183, 185
property, 177–79
sequencing, 9, 11, 26
Human Tissue Act 1961, 3
Human Tissue Act 2004, 1, 121, 245, 284
commercial dealings in human organs, 82
consent, 250–51
presumption of abandonment, 145
property law versus, 261–62
shortcomings, 246
unauthorised interference with cadavers, 159
vulnerability to dispossessions, 103
'work and skill' exception, 5
Human Tissue Authority, 245
Codes of Practice, 284
licensing of institutions, 245–46

identity, 5, 217, 219, 221, 224
in vitro embryos:
Australia, 203
inalienable property rights, 211–13
no property rule, 202–03
US, 203–04
individual autonomy and common good dichotomy, 22, 27
charitable trusts, 64–65
individual rights:
common good and, 22
informed consent, *see* consent

joint patenting, 191–92

law reform, 273–79, 281, 298–99
acquisition of materials, 291
ad hoc model, 290
objections, 290
commercialisation, 293–94, 297–98
commodification, 297–98
communal interests, 292–93
custodianship, 277
detailed statutory model, 288
objections, 288–89
dignity, 296–97
ethical guidelines and review, 277
justification:
infringement of autonomy, 278–79
loss of financial benefit, 279
misuse of information, 279
privacy, 279
liability of those acquiring biomaterials, 275
originators' rights, 295–96
ownership, 291–92
property model, 285–86
objections, 286–88
public interest arguments, 276, 281–85
right to control, 277
use, 294–95
legislation, 1
legislative frameworks, 6–7
consent, 4
limitations to current framework:
breach of contract, 4
damages, 4
reforming the law, 273–79
liability of those acquiring biomaterials, 275
public interest arguments, 276
right to control, 277
statute regime, 215–217, 229
application, 226–28
benefits, 228
objections, 228–29
organ retention, 226–27
private rights and public interest dichotomy, 64, 217–23
recognition of value of different parts of the body, 223–25
Yearworth decision and, 227–28
legitimating transfers argument, 142, 144–45
liability rules, 120–21

Moore v Regents of University of California (US), 9–10, 105, 113, 170–72, 194
abandonment, 141–42
breach of fiduciary duty, 15
conversion, 15–16, 102, 171, 203
equity rights, 78–82
pre-existing basis of property rights, 113
lack of informed consent, 15, 20, 22, 163
negligence, 160–63
autonomy, 162–63
causation, 162
no property rule, 171–72, 203

Moore v Regents of University of California cont.
post-donation status of human tissue, 9
separation, 101–03
unjust enrichment, 167–68

National Bioethics Advisory Commission, 19
National Cancer Institute (US), 58
National Commission for the Protection of Human Subjects of Biomedical and Behavioral Research (US), 18
National Health Service, 39
no contractual relationship, 39–40
National Institutes of Health (US), 13, 58
National Research Act 1974 (US), 18
National Statement on Ethical Conduct in Human Research, Values and Ethics: Guidelines for Ethical Conduct in Aboriginal and Torres Strait Islander Health Research (AUS), 18–19
negligence, 107, 160–63
autonomy, 162–63
bailment, 40
causation, 162
claims in contract distinguished, 46–47
damages, 76, 164
foreseeability, 119
psychiatric harm, 119, 243–44
destruction of semen, 4, 107
duty of care, 160–61
Caparo test, 42, 43
foreseeability, 45, 49, 119
informed consent, 58–59
psychological harm and, 40, 119
remedies, 40, 160–63
contractual claims, 168–70
damages in negligence, 164
torts law, 44–45, 48–50
rights' model, 41, 44–46
unauthorised interference with cadavers, 160–63
causation, 162–63
damages, 164
duty of care, 161
US approach, 163
no property rule, 3, 13–14, 73–74, 97, 194, 237, 287
case law, 237–40
exceptions:
case law, 14–17
'work and skill' exception, 203, 269
excised human tissue, 202–03
interpretation, 178
sperm donation, 14–15
unauthorised interference with cadavers, 170
vulnerability to dispossessions, 103
Nuffield Council, 19, 266, 289
abandonment, 138–40, 142, 147–48
consent model, 139
right of control over removed biomaterials, 139
Nuremberg Code, 17–18

objectification, 67–68, 86–87, 259–60, 283
commercial use of the body, 82–86
commodification and, 68–72
equity rights, 78–82
human body as legal property, 72–74
control and possession of gametes, 75–77
'work and skill' exception, 74–75
inflicting harm by means of objectification, 70–72
removed cells converted to profit, 79–80, 81–82
'work and skill' exception, 74–75
Office of Biorepositories and Biospecimen Research (US), 58
organ sale, 83–85
see also commodification
organ-retention enquiries, 1, 21, 49, 227
ownership, 2, 13–16, 56, 91–92, 110, 171–74, 193–94, 267
abandonment, 130
Australia, 136–37
biobanks, 64, 183–84, 189
biomaterials, 268–73
'bundle of rights' approach, 92, 104, 106, 171, 173, 185, 264, 274
commodification and 'full rights of ownership', 197–98
common property and, 178, 183
damage or loss of biomaterials, 244, 254
donation of biomaterials, 249–53
gifts law, 31, 33
'incidences of ownership', 110, 111, 172
no property rule, 269
original ownership, 148–49
possession distinguished, 267
relative title, 100
relatives claiming ownership, 225
removed cells, 78
right to exclude, 91–92, 104–05
right to use, 104–08
self-ownership, 94–96
separated biomaterials, 97–98
transferring ownership, 73
abandonment distinguished, 145, 291
'work and skill' exception, 3, 269–70
see also abandonment; commodification

participatory governance, 20–21, 223, 277–78
personal injury, 4, 254–55
damage to sperm, 40, 41–42, 243
personal injury v psychological harm, 243–44
tort law:
loss model, 42–44
rights model, 44–46

privacy laws, 12, 201–02
biobanking, 28
cadavers:
remedies for unauthorised interference, 166–67
ethical research, 12–13
European Convention on Human Rights (ECHR), 166
legal obligations, 21
contractual obligations of researchers, 20
disclosure of personal information, 20
equitable duty of confidentiality, 19–20
US, 166–67
private rights and public interest dichotomy, 64, 217–23, 276–77, 281–85
property approach to regulation, 22–23, 201, 231–33, 260–61
abandonment, 147–48
body as property, 138–46
advantages, 265–66
biobanking:
rights *in rem*, 59–60
biomaterials, 2–5, 101–04, 245–60
exigibility, 90–91
personal rights distinguished, 90
recognition, 92–94
self-ownership, 94–96
separated biomaterials, 97–98
vulnerability to dispossessions, 99–101
body as property, 72–86
abandonment, 138–46
commercial transfer of bodily material, 82–86
commercial use of the body, 82–86
commodification and objectification, 70–72
concerns, 5
control and possession of gametes, 75–77
domino theory, 71, 72
equity rights, 78–82
no property rule, 237–40
partial property approach, 3
work and skill exception, 3, 74–75, 269–70
case law, 237–44
negligent loss or destruction of semen, 243–44
no property rule, 237–40
personal injury v psychological harm, 243–44
'work and skill' exception, 240–43
concerns, 263–65
'property', 207
commercial alienability, 208, 210
excised human tissue, 211–13
in vitro embryos, 211–13
recognition of inalienable property rights, 210–11
'thin' conception of property, 209–10
remedial framework, 157–75
rights, 186–87, 266–67
ownership, 267
possession, 267
trespassory rules, 100, 112, 174
unauthorised interference with cadavers, 170–74
value of the human body, 233–36
see also ownership
property law:
boundaries, 109, 123–24
concerns, 121–23
right to privacy, 123
contingent rights, 110–11
rights and rights-holder, 110–11, 116
separability, 117
entitlements, 111
exclusionary rights, 110, 111–12
basis, 112–13
content of the duty, 115–16
content of the right, 113–15
inappropriateness, 259–60
damage or loss of biomaterials, 254–59
donation of biomaterials, 247–54
interests, 109
conceptual, 110–11
functional, 110
structural, 110
legal relationships:
contingent rights, 110–11
dependent rights, 111
exclusionary rights, 110
interactive rights, 110
rights-holder and duty-bearer, 110
rights and rights-holder, 110–11
ownership, 111
Honoré, AM, 172
regulating excised biomaterials and embryos outside the human body, 197–98
structural features:
basis of the right, 112–13
content of the duty, 115–16
content of the right, 113–15
remedies, 118–20
transferability, 120–21
proximity, 163
duty of care, 42–43, 49
psychological harm, 4, 8, 15
American Diagnostic and Statistical Manual of Mental Disorders, 119
compensation, 4, 243
foreseeability, 119
International Statistical Classification of Mental and Behavioral Disorders, 119
loss suffered, 118–19
negligence and, 40, 48, 119, 243
personal injury v psychological harm, 243–44
recovery of damages, 49, 243
psychological harm *cont.*

remedies, 118–19
resulting from injury to another, 42–43
public trusts, *see* charitable trusts

R v Kelly, 14, 74–75
regulation of biomaterials, 1–8
law of consent, 2
legal perspective, 7–8
remedies, 8
medical research, 5
property approach, 2–5
remedies:
contract law, 40, 46–48
damages, 40
negligence law, 40
property law:
damages, 118
foreseeability, 119
interference with goods, 118
psychiatric harm, 118–19
wrongful interaction or transaction, 118
tort law, 40, 48–51
unauthorised interference with cadavers, 158–60
battery, 165–66
breach of fiduciary duty, 160
causation, 162
compensation, 161
contractual claims, 168–70
damages in negligence, 164
human rights, 166–67
intentional tort action, 164–65
negligence, 160–63
privacy, 166–67
proprietary claims, 170–74
unjust enrichment, 167–68
US, 163
restitution, 258, 298
unauthorised interference with cadavers, 167–68
unjust enrichment, 167
right of control, 139, 172
donation of biomaterials, 247–50
reforming the law, 277
rights, *see* private rights and public interest dichotomy
rights of possession, 85, 87, 114, 202, 211, 240, 288
see also bailment

semen, *see* gametes
separation of biomaterials, 15
separation with intention to use, 15
see also biomaterials; excised human tissues
sperm, *see* gametes
status of human tissue:
post-donation status, 9
separation, 15
Statute of Charitable Uses 1601, 60
Statute of Frauds 1677, 31, 32
statutory regulation, 215–217, 229
application, 226–28
benefits, 228
objections, 228–29
organ retention, 226–27
private rights and public interest dichotomy, 64, 217–23
recognition of value of different parts of the body, 223–25
Yearworth decision and, 227–28
stem cell research, 3, 9
see also advances in medical science; biomedical research
stewardship, 53–54
concept, 57
umbilical cord blood, 53–54
storage of biomaterials:
consent, 20–21
negligent loss or destruction:
sperm, 4, 15
non-disclosure of intended use for research, 15
see also biobanks
sui generis approach to regulation, 197–200, 206–07, 246, 285
disadvantages, 214, 246
excised human tissue, 204–06, 213–14
in vitro embryos, 204–06, 213–14
liability in bailment, 46
property approach distinguished, 214
surrogacy, 72
commercial use of the body, 85–86

tort law:
absence of contract law and, 39
battery, 165–66
duty of care, 42–44
fairness, justice and reasonableness, 42
foreseeability, 42, 43
proximity, 42, 43
liability:
'loss' model, 41, 42–44
'rights' model, 41, 44–46
'loss' model, 41
Aliakmon ratio, 42
Caparo decision, 42
duty of care, 42–44
voluntary assumption of responsibility, 43–44
negligence, 48–50
primary rights:
contract rights, 45
property rights, 45
right to bodily integrity, 45
right to freedom, 45
right to life, 45

psychological harm, 48–49
'rights' model, 41, 44–46
bailment, 45–46
contractual rights, 45–46
negligence, 44–45
personal injury, 45
primary rights, 44–45
secondary victims, 49
unauthorised interference with cadavers, 160–65
voluntary assumption of responsibility, 43–44
transferability of property rights, 120–21
trespass to goods, 112, 130, 246
damage or loss of biomaterials, 256–58
ownership, 91–92
trespassory rules, 100, 112, 174

UK law:
abandonment, 129–36
charitable trusts, 61
courts:
partial property approach, 3
ethical governance, 19
umbilical cord blood
advantages, 54–55
biobanking, 53–54
donation, 248
charitable trusts, 63–64
advantages, 64–65
storage, 3
testing, 3
UNESCO Declaration 1997:
property in the human genome, 177–78
United States law:
abandonment, 137
cadavers:
remedies for unauthorised interference, 163
tort law, 165
ethical governance, 17–18
excised human tissue, 203–04
human embryos, 204
privacy laws, 166–67
semen, 205
unjust enrichment:
unauthorised interference with cadavers, 167–68
Venner (US), 150, 155
abandonment, 137, 140, 142–43, 204
voluntary assumption of responsibility, 43–44

Washington University v Catalona (US), 16, 203
conditional gifts, 36–37, 249–50, 253–54
finality of gifts doctrine, 183, 189
possession:
use of biomaterials distinguished, 248–49
right of control, 248–49
separated biomaterials:
ownership, 97–98
use of biomaterials:
possession distinguished, 248–49
vulnerability to dispossessions, 103–04
widows, 4, 1202, 169, 218, 265
'work and skill exception', 3, 14, 5, 203, 264–65, 269–70
case law, 240–43
commodification and objectification, 74–75
Human Tissue Act 2004, 5
objectification, 74–75
proprietary status of biomaterials, 74–75
wrongful interference, 138, 240, 256
damage or loss of biomaterials, 258
remedies, 258–59
unauthorised interference with cadavers, 167–68

Yearworth and others v North Bristol NHS Trust, 1, 4, 254–59, 265–66
absence of contract, 39–40
co-existing property rights, 271–73
compensation, 40–41
control and possession of gametes, 75–77
damages, 40
loss of property, 40
negligence, 107
ownership, 75–77, 270
personal injury, 40
psychological harm, 15, 40
recognition of property rights, 115
right to possess, 271
tort law:
'loss' model, 42–44
'rights' model, 44–46

Lightning Source UK Ltd.
Milton Keynes UK
UKOW05f0252211016

285816UK00005B/91/P

9 781509 909896